Keys to Success

How to Achieve Your Goals

THIRD EDITION

Carol Carter

Joyce Bishop

Sarah Lyman Kravits

Prentice
Hall

Upper Saddle River, New Jersey 07458

Library of Congress Cataloging-in-Publication Data

Carter, Carol.
    Keys to success : how to achieve your goals / Carol Carter, Joyce Bishop, Sarah Lyman
Kravits.—3rd ed.
        p.   cm.
    Includes bibliographical references (p.) and index.
    ISBN 0-13-012883-X
    1. College student orientation—United States—Handbooks, manuals, etc.   2. Study
skills—Handbooks, manuals, etc.   3. College students—United States—Life skills guides
    I. Bishop, Joyce (Joyce L.), 1950-   II. Kravits, Sarah Lyman.   III. Title.

LB2343.32 .C37 2001
378.1'98—dc21

                                                                            00-025991

Publishing Unit President: Gary June
Acquisitions Editor: Sande Johnson
Assistant Editor: Michelle Williams
Production Editor: Holcomb Hathaway
Director of Manufacturing and Production: Bruce Johnson
Managing Editor: Mary Carnis
Manufacturing Manager: Ed O'Dougherty
Art Director: Marianne Frasco
Marketing Manager: Jeff McIlroy
Marketing Assistant: Barbara Rosenberg
Senior Manager for New Media: Frank Mortimer, Jr.
Manager of Media Production: Amy Peltier
New Media Project Manager: Stephen Hartner
Media Editor: Kateri Drexler
Cover Design: Maria Guglielmo
Composition: Aerocraft Charter Art Service
Printing and Binding: The Banta Company

Prentice-Hall International (UK) Limited, *London*
Prentice-Hall of Australia Pty. Limited, *Sydney*
Prentice-Hall Canada Inc., *Toronto*
Prentice-Hall Hispanoamericana, S.A., *Mexico*
Prentice-Hall of India Private Limited, *New Delhi*
Prentice-Hall of Japan, Inc., *Tokyo*
Pearson Education Singapore Pte. Ltd.
Editora Prentice-Hall do Brasil, Ltda., *Rio de Janeiro*

Photo Credits. Page 2, Laima Druskis, Pearson Education/PH College; p. 12, Doug Menuez, PhotoDisc, Inc.; p. 17, David Weintraub, Photo Researchers, Inc.; p. 26, Doug Menuez, PhotoDisc, Inc.; p. 28, Bob Daemmrich, Stock Boston; p. 34, Amy Etra, PhotoEdit; p. 50, Sarah Lyman Kravits; p. 54, Robert Brenner, PhotoEdit; p. 64, Larry H. Mangino, The Image Works; p. 82, Paul W. Liebhardt; p. 86, Will Hart; p. 102, Tomi, PhotoDisc, Inc.; p. 120, Elliot Smith; p. 133, Billy E. Barnes, PhotoEdit; p. 148, Beryl Goldberg; p. 158, PhotoDisc, Inc.; p. 165, PhotoDisc, Inc.; p. 178, Steve Dunwell, The Image Bank; p. 192, David M. Grossman, Photo Researchers, Inc.; p. 201, Steve Dunwell; p. 207, Michal Heron, Pearson Education/PH College; p. 228, Doug Menuez, PhotoDisc, Inc.; p. 233, Michael Newman, PhotoEdit; p. 251, Stephen Collins, Photo Researchers, Inc.; p. 270, Tom Herde, *The Boston Globe*; p. 280, Jeff Greenberg, Index Stock Imagery, Inc.; p. 290, Michael Newman, PhotoEdit; p. 306, Felicia Martinez, PhotoEdit; p. 312, Rick Singer, Pearson Education/PH College; p. 321, Mary Kate Denny, PhotoEdit; p. 344, Richard Woolf, PhotoDisc, Inc; p. 357, Collins, Monkmeyer Press; p. 367, Frank Siteman, Stock Boston; p. 382, Mark Richards, PhotoEdit; p. 390, Myrleen Ferguson, PhotoEdit; p. 396, Gary Conner, PhotoEdit.

Prentice Hall

10 9 8 7 6 5 4 3 2 1
ISBN 0-13-018557-4

Contents

PART I DEFINING YOURSELF AND YOUR GOALS   1

1

Becoming a Lifelong Learner   3
Opening Doors

WHO IS PURSUING AN EDUCATION TODAY?   4
The Diverse Student Body   4

HOW DOES EDUCATION PROMOTE SUCCESS?   6

HOW CAN YOU STRIVE FOR SUCCESS?   9
Get Motivated   9
Make a Commitment   9
Show Initiative   10
Be Responsible   11
Face Your Fears   12

HOW CAN YOU BUILD YOUR SELF-ESTEEM?   13
Think Positively   13
Take Action   14

WHAT IS YOUR ROLE IN A DIVERSE WORLD?   15
Diversity Is Real Life   15
Ethnocentrism   16
Diversity and Teamwork   16

WHY IS IT IMPORTANT TO EMBRACE CHANGE?   17
Change Shapes the World   17

WINDOWS ON THE WORLD   18
Be an Agent of Change   19

BUILDING SKILLS   20–25

2

Resources   27
Making the Most of Your Environment

WHAT RESOURCES ARE AVAILABLE AT YOUR SCHOOL?   28
People   28
Administrative Offices   32

Student Services   33
Organizations   33
Literature   34

WHAT SHOULD YOU KNOW ABOUT TECHNOLOGY?   35
Technology Strategies   35
Computer Use   37

WINDOWS ON THE WORLD   39

WHY IS ACADEMIC INTEGRITY IMPORTANT?   40
Following the Standards   40
Your School's Code   41
The Effects of Academic Integrity   41

BUILDING SKILLS   43–49

3

Goal Setting and Time Management   51
Mapping Your Course

WHAT DEFINES YOUR VALUES?   52
Sources of Values   52
Choosing and Evaluating Values   52
How Values Relate to Goals   53

HOW DO YOU SET AND ACHIEVE GOALS?   53
Identifying Your Personal Mission   53
Placing Goals in Time   54
Linking Goals with Values   56
Different Kinds of Goals   57

WHAT ARE YOUR PRIORITIES?   59

HOW CAN YOU MANAGE YOUR TIME?   60
Building a Schedule   61
Taking Responsibility for How You Spend Your Time   64
Being Flexible   66

WINDOWS ON THE WORLD   67

WHY IS PROCRASTINATION A PROBLEM?   68
Antiprocrastination Strategies   68
Other Time Traps to Avoid   69

BUILDING SKILLS   71–81

4

Self-Awareness 83

Knowing Who You Are and How You Learn

IS THERE ONE BEST WAY TO LEARN? 84

WHAT ARE THE BENEFITS OF KNOWING YOUR LEARNING STYLE? 84
Study Benefits 84
Classroom Benefits 85
Career Benefits 86

HOW CAN YOU DISCOVER YOUR LEARNING STYLE? 87
Multiple Intelligences Theory 87
Personality Spectrum 87
Using the Assessments 88
Perspective on Learning Style 89

WINDOWS ON THE WORLD 96

HOW DO YOU EXPLORE WHO YOU ARE? 97
Self-Perception 97
Interests 98
Habits 99

HOW CAN YOU START THINKING ABOUT CHOOSING A MAJOR? 100
Exploring Potential Majors 101
Planning Your Curriculum 101
Linking Majors to Career Areas 102
Changing Majors 103
Following Your Heart 103

BUILDING SKILLS 105–111

PART I FURTHER EXPLORATION 112–118
🌐 Web Activity 112
Reading Room One: Why the Walls Are Quickly Tumbling Down 113
Reading Room Two: Emotional Intelligence 115
Crossword Review 118

PART II DEVELOPING YOUR LEARNING SKILLS 119

5

Critical and Creative Thinking 121

Tapping the Power of Your Mind

WHAT IS CRITICAL THINKING? 122
Defining Critical Thinking 122
The Path of Critical Thinking 123
The Value of Critical Thinking 124
Learning How Your Mind Works 125
How Mind Actions Build Thinking Processes 128

HOW DOES CRITICAL THINKING HELP YOU SOLVE PROBLEMS AND MAKE DECISIONS? 128
Problem Solving 129
Decision Making 132

HOW DO YOU CONSTRUCT AND EVALUATE ARGUMENTS? 133
Constructing an Argument 134
Evaluating an Argument 135

HOW DO YOU THINK LOGICALLY? 136
Distinguishing Fact from Opinion 136
Identifying and Evaluating Assumptions 138

WHY SHOULD YOU EXPLORE PERSPECTIVES? 139
Evaluating Perspective 139
The Value of Seeing Other Perspectives 140

WHY PLAN STRATEGICALLY? 142
Strategy and Critical Thinking 142
Benefits of Strategic Planning 143

HOW CAN YOU DEVELOP YOUR CREATIVITY? 143
Characteristics of Creative People 144
Enhancing Your Creativity 145
Brainstorming Toward a Creative Answer 145
Creativity and Critical Thinking 146

WHAT IS MEDIA LITERACY? 146

WINDOWS ON THE WORLD 147

BUILDING SKILLS 150–157

6

Reading, Studying, and Using the Library   159

Maximizing Written Resources

WHAT ARE SOME CHALLENGES OF READING?   160
Working Through Difficult Texts   160
Managing Distractions   161
Building Comprehension and Speed   162
Expanding Your Vocabulary   163

WHY DEFINE YOUR PURPOSE FOR READING?   165
Purpose Determines Reading Strategy   165
Purpose Determines Pace   166

HOW CAN SQ3R HELP YOU OWN WHAT YOU READ?   166
Survey   167
Question   167
Read   168
Recite   169
Review   169

HOW CAN YOU RESPOND CRITICALLY TO WHAT YOU READ?   171
Use SQ3R to "Taste" Reading Material   171
Ask Questions Based on the Mind Actions   171
Engage Critical-Thinking Processes   171
Be Media Literate   174
Seek Understanding   174

HOW AND WHY SHOULD YOU STUDY WITH OTHERS?   175
Strategies for Study Group Success   175
Benefits of Working with Others   176

HOW CAN YOU MAKE THE MOST OF THE LIBRARY?   176
Start with a Road Map   176

WINDOWS ON THE WORLD   177
Learn How to Conduct an Information Search   178
Conduct Research Using a Search Strategy   180
Use Critical Thinking to Evaluate Every Source   183

BUILDING SKILLS   185–191

7

Note Taking and Writing   193

Harnessing the Power of Words and Ideas

HOW CAN YOU MAKE THE MOST OF NOTE TAKING?   194
Recording Information in Class   194

WHAT NOTE-TAKING SYSTEM SHOULD YOU USE?   197
Taking Notes in Outline Form   197
Using the Cornell Note-Taking System   198
Creating a Think Link   200
Other Visual Note-Taking Strategies   201

HOW CAN YOU WRITE FASTER WHEN TAKING NOTES?   201

WHY DOES GOOD WRITING MATTER?   202

WHAT ARE THE ELEMENTS OF EFFECTIVE WRITING?   203
Writing Purpose   203
Knowing Your Audience   204

WHAT IS THE WRITING PROCESS?   204
Planning   205
Drafting   209
Revising   213

WINDOWS ON THE WORLD   214
Editing   217

BUILDING SKILLS   220–227

8

Listening, Memory, and Test Taking   229

Taking In, Retaining, and Demonstrating Knowledge

HOW CAN YOU BECOME A BETTER LISTENER?   230
Know the Stages of Listening   231
Manage Listening Challenges   231
Become an Active Listener   233

HOW DOES MEMORY WORK?   234

HOW CAN YOU IMPROVE YOUR MEMORY?   235
Use Memory Improvement Strategies   235

Make the Most of Last-Minute Studying   238
Use Mnemonic Devices   238

HOW CAN TAPE RECORDERS HELP YOU LISTEN, REMEMBER, AND STUDY?   240

WHAT TYPES OF PREPARATION CAN IMPROVE TEST PERFORMANCE?   241
Identify Test Type and Material Covered   241
Use Specific Study Strategies   242
Prepare Physically   242
Work Through Test Anxiety   243

WINDOWS ON THE WORLD   *247*

WHAT STRATEGIES CAN HELP YOU SUCCEED ON TESTS?   248
Write Down Key Facts   248
Begin with an Overview of the Exam   248
Know the Ground Rules   249
Use Critical Thinking to Avoid Errors   249
Master Different Types of Test Questions   250
Use Specific Techniques for Math Problems   254

HOW CAN YOU LEARN FROM TEST MISTAKES?   255

BUILDING SKILLS   256–261

PART II FURTHER EXPLORATION   262–267

Web Activity   262

Reading Room One: The Fifth Discipline   263

Reading Room Two: Strong Writing Skills Essential for Success   265

Crossword Review   267

PART III   CREATING SUCCESS   269

9

Relating to Others   271

Appreciating Your Diverse World

WHY IS IT IMPORTANT TO UNDERSTAND AND ACCEPT OTHERS?   272
Diversity in Your World   272
The Positive Effects of Diversity   273

HOW CAN YOU THINK CRITICALLY ABOUT DIVERSITY?   274
Prejudice   275

Stereotyping   277
Fear of Differences   278
Accepting and Dealing with Differences   280

HOW CAN YOU EXPRESS YOURSELF EFFECTIVELY?   281
Adjusting to Communication Styles   281
The Power of Body Language   284
Addressing Communication Issues   285
Speaking/Oral Presentations   288

HOW DO YOUR PERSONAL RELATIONSHIPS DEFINE YOU?   290
Relationship Strategies   290

HOW CAN YOU HANDLE CONFLICT AND CRITICISM?   291
Conflict Strategies   291
Dealing with Criticism and Feedback   292

WINDOWS ON THE WORLD   *293*

WHAT ROLE DO YOU PLAY IN GROUPS?   295
Being an Effective Participant   295
Being an Effective Leader   296
Considering Cultural Differences   297

BUILDING SKILLS   299–305

10

Personal Wellness   307

Taking Care of Yourself

HOW CAN YOU MAINTAIN A HEALTHY BODY?   308
Eating Right   308
Exercising   310
Getting Enough Sleep   311
Taking Advantage of Medical Care   312

HOW DO YOU NURTURE A HEALTHY MIND?   315
Stress   315
Emotional Disorders   318

HOW ARE ALCOHOL, TOBACCO, AND DRUGS USED AND ABUSED?   321
Alcohol   321
Tobacco   322
Drugs   324
Identifying and Overcoming Addiction   324
Substance Abuse Affects Others   327

WHAT SHOULD YOU CONSIDER WHEN MAKING SEXUAL DECISIONS?   327
Sex and Critical Thinking   327

WINDOWS ON THE WORLD   *328*
  Birth Control   329
  Sexually Transmitted Diseases   331
  Sexual Harassment and Abuse   333
BUILDING SKILLS   **337–343**

11

Managing Career and Money   345

Reality Resources

HOW CAN YOU PLAN YOUR CAREER?   346
  Define a Career Path   346
  Map Out Your Strategy   350
  Expect Change   350
  Seek Mentors   352
  Know What Employers Want   352

HOW CAN YOU JUGGLE WORK AND SCHOOL?   354
  Effects of Working While in School   355
  Establishing Your Needs   356
  Sources of Job Information   356
  Making a Strategic Job Search Plan   358

WHAT SHOULD YOU KNOW ABOUT FINANCIAL AID?   360
  Student Loans   361
  Grants and Scholarships   362

HOW CAN STRATEGIC PLANNING HELP YOU MANAGE MONEY?   363
  Sacrifice in the Short Term to Create
    Long-Term Gain   363
  Put Your Money to Work   365
  Develop a Financial Philosophy   366

HOW CAN YOU CREATE A BUDGET THAT WORKS?   367
  The Art of Budgeting   367
  A Sample Budget   368
  Savings Strategies   369

WINDOWS ON THE WORLD   *370*

WHAT SHOULD YOU KNOW ABOUT BANKING AND CREDIT CARDS?   371
  Bank Accounts   371
  Credit Cards   371
  Managing Debt   373
BUILDING SKILLS   **375–381**

12

Moving Ahead   383

Building a Flexible Future

HOW CAN YOU BE FLEXIBLE IN THE FACE OF CHANGE?   384
  Maintain Flexibility   384
  Adjust Your Goals   386
  Be Open to Unpredictability   387

WHAT WILL HELP YOU HANDLE SUCCESS AND FAILURE?   387
  Dealing with Failure   388
  Dealing with Success   390
  Redefining Failure and Success:
    Learning Disabilities   391

WHY GIVE BACK TO THE COMMUNITY AND THE WORLD?   392
  Your Imprint on the World   392
  Valuing Your Environment   393

WHY IS COLLEGE JUST THE BEGINNING OF LIFELONG LEARNING?   394

WINDOWS ON THE WORLD   *395*

HOW CAN YOU LIVE YOUR MISSION?   397
  Live With Integrity   397
  Create Personal Change   398
  Learn from Role Models   399
  Broaden Your Perspective   399
  Aim for Your Personal Best   399

BUILDING SKILLS   **401–404**

PART III FURTHER EXPLORATION   **405–410**

🌐 **Web Activity**   **405**

Reading Room One: Keeping Hate Out of the Workplace   406

Reading Room Two: How the Navy Changed My Life   408

Crossword Review   **410**

Appendix

The Campbell Interest and
Skill Survey   **411**

Endnotes   *419*
Bibliography   *422*
Index   *426*

About the Authors

Carol Carter is Vice President and Director of Student Programs and Faculty Development at Prentice Hall. She has written *Majoring in the Rest of Your Life: Career Secrets for College Students* and *Majoring in High School.* She has also co-authored *The Career Tool Kit, Keys to Career Success, Keys to Study Skills, Keys to Thinking and Learning,* and *Keys to Effective Learning.* She has taught welfare to work classes, team taught in the La Familia Scholars Program at Community College of Denver, and  has conducted numerous workshops for students and faculty around the country. She is the host of the Keys to Lifelong Learning Telecourse, a twenty-six episode telecourse to help students at a distance prepare for college, career, and life success. In addition to working with students of all ages, Carol thrives on foreign travel and culture; she has been fortunate enough to have been a guest in forty foreign countries.

Joyce Bishop holds a Ph.D. and license in clinical psychology and has taught for more than twenty years, receiving a number of honors, including Teacher of the Year. For the past four years she has been voted "favorite teacher" by  the student body and Honor Society at Golden West College, Huntington Beach, CA, where she has taught since 1986 and is a tenured professor. She is currently working with a federal grant to establish Learning Communities and Workplace Learning in her district. A keynote speaker at national conferences, she is developing an extensive online faculty development program in the areas of multiple intelligences, cooperative learning, authentic assessment, and curriculum development for hybrid classes. She also co-authored *Keys to Effective Learning, Keys to Thinking and Learning,* and *Keys to Study Skills.* Joyce is the lead academic of the *Keys to Lifelong Learning Telecourse,* distributed by Dallas Telelearning.

Sarah Lyman Kravits is a student of life with a passion for learning. In her drive to help others discover their love for learning—and their essential selves—she has spent the last six years writing, researching, talking to students, and talking to teachers in pursuit of the best possible textbooks on student success. She has co-authored *The Career Tool Kit, Keys to Success, Keys to Effective Learning, Keys to Thinking and Learning,* and *Keys to Study Skills.* She originally hooked into the world of student success as  Program Director for LifeSkills, Inc., a nonprofit organization that aims to further the career and personal development of high school students. Even earlier, being a Jefferson Scholar at the University of Virginia helped to bring her love of learning to new levels. She encourages readers to make the most of this time in school—it is an incredible gift.

Welcome *to your Annotated Instructor's Edition*

HOW TO USE YOUR AIE

This is a special version of the text designed for teachers only. It includes running annotations in the margins (in blue type) to help you effectively explore the text with your students. The annotations provide teaching suggestions and new perspectives and information that will help enhance your presentation.

There are eight types of annotations, each with a specific focus:

- **Be a Team.** Ideas for using teamwork in the classroom, these tips help prepare students for teams at work.
- **Career Connection.** These annotations relate text material to the world of careers and career exploration.
- **Critical Thinking.** Here you'll find critical thinking questions that are linked to the text.
- **Learning Styles Tip.** These annotations alert you to alternate approaches for helping students with different learning styles.
- **Real World Link.** Here are a variety of ideas relating text material to the world outside of college.
- **Springboard.** These tips are intended to stimulate classroom discussion.
- **Teaching Tip.** These are helpful teaching suggestions tied to text material.
- **Teaching Tolerance.** These annotations raise awareness of individual differences and tolerance of diversity.

The hundreds of annotations in *Keys To Success* will enrich your teaching experience by putting new ideas and examples at your fingertips.

What You'll Find in These Opening Pages

In the following pages (x through xxxi), you will find a comprehensive description of the many materials available to you and your students when you adopt *Keys to Success* for classroom use. These pages will help you make full and best use of this innovative package.

How Is this AIE Different from Your Instructor's Manual?

This Annotated Instructor's Edition is the student version of *Keys* with marginal notes and suggestions for teachers. On the other hand, the Instructor's Manual (IM) contains chapter by chapter teaching and lecture suggestions. The IM is designed to help you integrate media and technology into the classroom. Each chapter of the IM includes exercises for each type of multiple intelligence so that faculty can easily help each type of learner in every classroom session.

Each chapter is designed to allow students to process, integrate, and internalize the chapter materials. The end-of-chapter exercises take students one step closer to becoming life-long learners by encouraging them to incorporate these strategies into their personal and professional lives.

Critical Thinking

These exercises are designed to help students analyze and apply what they have learned in the chapter so they can become more effective in making connections among seemingly unrelated things—a foundation of good thinking.

Critical Thinking
Applying Learning to Your Life

Identify Yourself

Where do you fit in today's student population? Describe your particular circumstances, opinions, and needs in a short paragraph. Here are some questions to inspire thought:

- How do you describe yourself—your culture, ethnicity, gender, age, lifestyle?
- How long are you planning to spend in college?
- What do you want out of your college experience?

Collaborative Learning

These exercises are designed to help students think through problems and issues together in groups. When students see how much there is to learn from others, they enhance their own thought process and prepare themselves for the world of work, where most things are accomplished through teamwork.

Teamwork
Combining Forces

Who Can Help You? Every school is unique and offers its own particular range of opportunities. Investigate your school. Use the resource table as a guide, and explore your student handbook. Make a check mark by the resources which you think will be most helpful to you.

_____ Advisors and counselors	_____ Adult education center
_____ Library/media center	_____ Support groups/hotlines
_____ Instructors	_____ Career/job placement office

Writing

These exercises are designed to strengthen students' abilities to write, think, and express their ideas about what they have read. Good writing promotes good thinking. The more that students apply the discipline of writing, the stronger they become overall.

Writing
Discovery Through Journaling

To record your thoughts, use a separate journal or the lined page at the end of the chapter.

Your Diverse World. Describe one particular person with whom you interact, a person who is different from you in some way. What have you learned from your relationship with this person? What is positive about spending time with him or her? What is negative? What is positive and negative about spending time with people who seem very similar to you?

Strategic Thinking/Portfolio Development

These exercises are designed to help students learn to look long term by realizing the impact of their actions and decisions in the short term. We encourage students to keep a file or a portfolio on themselves, so they can chart the progress of their accomplishments throughout college. At the end of their college experience, they will have something concrete to show prospective employers about the quality of the work of which they are capable, highlighting their part-time jobs, academic achievements, and extracurricular activities.

Career Portfolio
Charting Your Course

Educational Contract. This is the first item in your personal portfolio. Find a sturdy folder or notebook in which to keep each portfolio item you add as you read the chapters of this book. By the end of this course, you will have collected concrete evidence of your abilities and qualifications for success in the real world. Your portfolio will come in handy during your tenure as a student. You can also look back at it when you apply for jobs, because much of what you generate will give you practical help with the application, interview, and hiring processes in the workplace. In addition, your portfolio will help remind you of how much progress you've made and how far you've come.

Explore the Career Connection

Charts and graphs throughout the third edition depict real data and other types of information that students can, and should, use to inform their short-term and long-term goals.

Why invest in a college education?

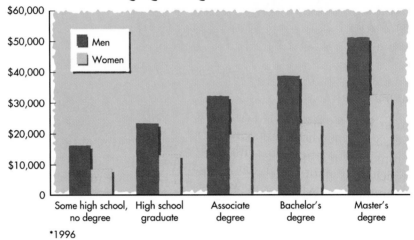

Median annual income of persons with income 25 years old and over, by highest degree attained and sex.*

$60,000

$50,000 ■ Men □ Women

$40,000

$30,000

$20,000

$10,000

0

Some high school, no degree | High school graduate | Associate degree | Bachelor's degree | Master's degree

*1996

Why is diversity awareness such an important issue in the 21st century?

Population distribution of the U.S., 2050 (projected), by percentage

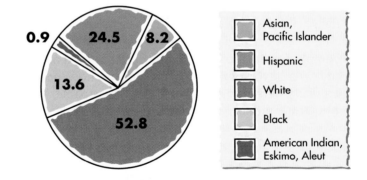

0.9   24.5   8.2

13.6

52.8

■ Asian, Pacific Islander
■ Hispanic
■ White
□ Black
■ American Indian, Eskimo, Aleut

How does my perspective compare with that of my peers?

WINDOWS ON THE WORLD
Real Life Student Issues

How do I make the most of college?

Matt Millard, University of Wyoming, undeclared major

I decided to attend college so I could have a job doing what I really like instead of just
~~~

Todd Montalvo, University of Alaska, Anchorage, Education major—junior year

I think it's very important to do what you love. That will really help your goal of lifelong learning. Even though having money to support yourself and your family is important, it's more

Each chapter ends with a conceptual summary featuring a word and concept from a language other than English.

In Chinese writing, this character has two meanings: One is "chaos"; the other is "opportunity." The character communicates the belief that every challenging, chaotic, demanding situation in life also presents an opportunity. By responding to challenges in a positive and active way, you can discover the opportunity that lies within the chaos.

Let this concept reassure you as you begin college. You may feel that you are going through a time of chaos and change. Remember that no matter how difficult the obstacles, you have the ability to persevere. You can create opportunities for yourself to learn, grow, and improve.

A world map is featured on the back end-papers of the new edition, to help students visualize the world around them.

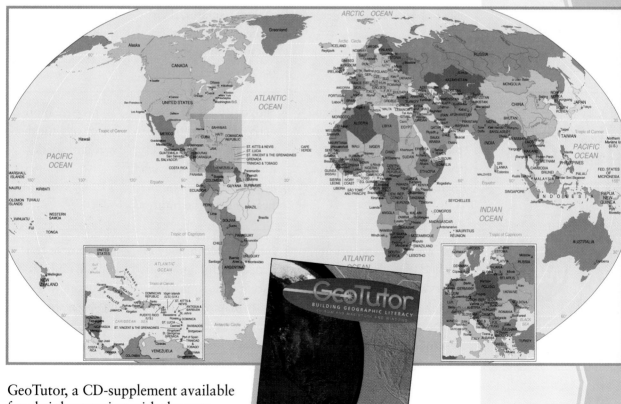

GeoTutor, a CD-supplement available for shrinkwrapping with the text, promotes geographic literacy in an active, engaging format.

OPTIONAL INTEGRATION OF TECHNOLOGY AND EMPLOYMENT SKILLS

ICON	CONCEPT	GOAL	BENEFIT
e-mail	This icon implies that the topic covered in the accompanying text warrants discussion amongst your peers and friends. E-mail facilitates communication and should be used to enhance breaking down of barriers, not creating them.	Suggest the importance of communication by reaching out to others.	To help students overcome fear of isolation.
COMPANION WEBSITE	This icon notes that there is an online study guide for students to review material.	To review and explore the concepts presented in the text.	To test comprehension and broaden search fields.
chat	This icon suggests that the accompanying text raises issues that students might want to further explore in class or with their professor.	The goal is to facilitate the flow of information and communication between students, their classmates, their professors, and other possible campus resources.	To show students the benefit of group interaction and the initiative needed to be a life-long learner.
Performance counts!	This icon is used to remind students that the responsibility for the outcome of their education is largely their own.	Set goals and be pro-active in generating a plan to achieve those goals. Realize that each action today has ramifications for the future.	To prepare more effectively for the world of work.
WEB	The Web icon appears at the end of each part and offers an Internet exploration activity that helps tie the chapter concepts together for the student.	Integrate technology in a meaningful and motivating way, simultaneously helping students summarize the parts of the text.	To promote conceptual abilities by linking what has been studied to other areas of work and life.

Intelligent Essay Grader

Keys to Success now has an essay assessor that grades essay answers instantaneously. This is available on the Companion Web Site; test it out at:

http://www.knowledge-technologies.com/PH

How does this work? For example, after reading a short passage from the *Keys to Success* text, students will be asked to write the answer for the following question:

How might a college education help you? Describe in detail three ways in which a college education can contribute to long-term life success. Please answer the question in 250–350 words.

INTELLIGENT ESSAY GRADER

Feedback on your essay

The IEA feedback is intended to help you learn the concepts presented in this book.

The IEA feedback can be tailored for different needs, e.g. student self-tests or instructor assessments. In this demonstration for *Keys to Success* we have provided a look at a variety of feedback for different assessment purposes.

The reading on which this question is based is on pages 8-11 of *Keys to Success* 3rd Ed.

- Word Count Requirements
- IEA Overall Feedback
- Comparison with Author's Essay
- Componential Scoring for Topic Coverage

Click on the Topic References to go directly to the textbook section. To answer this question, you did not necessarily have to cover all the topics in the text. This feedback tells you which topics you touched on in your essay and gives you the option of reviewing the text.

- Essay Content Coverage Score

  ★ Very Good! Your essay appears to cover a good bit of the relevant information.
  ★ Good! This essay is good but still needs some work
    This topic may require much more work.

Plagiarism Check

Judging by the sentences in the submitted essay, it appears that this is an original document.

Essay Validation Measures

None of the validity measures detected anything inappropriate with this essay.

Internal Coherence Measures

None of the coherence measures detected anything inappropriate with this essay.

Grammar and Readability Measures

None of the grammar and readability measures detected anything inappropriate with this essay.

By clicking on any of the specific areas located on the top bar menu, students can get information on the topic, which comes up automatically. They may also click on Goal Setting, Article, or Quiz to access additional features.

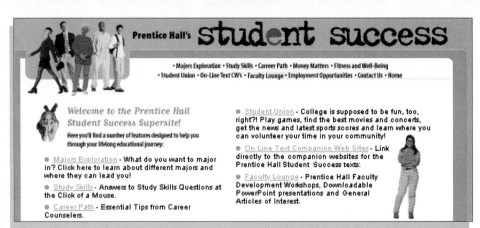

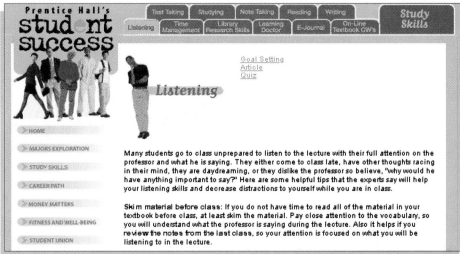

A brief look at the areas within the other categories:

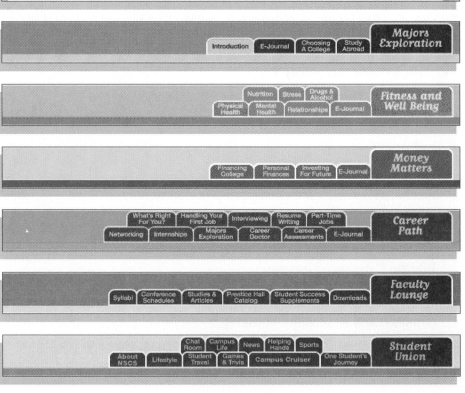

Integration of Technology

Keys to Success, Third Edition, offers a truly integrated technology solution, a text-specific Companion Website, and options to take the course completely online.

UPDATED!

Carter LIVE! http://www.prenhall.com/carter_sg

Link each chapter of *Keys to Success* to the rich resources found on the Internet! Whether you will test your student's knowledge through chapter-specific self-grading quizzes or have your students explore issues, these easy-to-use resources provide a fun and dynamic environment to learning.

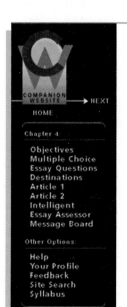

All companion web-sites have instant scoring multiple choice quizzes and essay questions, which can be sent via email to the professor. They have links to related sites and many have additional articles.

Student Organizer CD-ROM $5

- The ultimate organizational tool
- Designed exclusively for students by Centaur Academic Media
- Includes scheduler, timeline, major/minor planner, address book, personal finance planner, internet site, grade calculator, and tutorial

Prentice Hall Self Assessment Library $5

- Easy to use
- Provides instant feedback on more than 5 assessments
- Helps students learn more about themselves and how they relate to others
- The three categories: "What about me," "Working with others," and "Life in organizations" will provide students with insights they will need to be successful in the business world.

Simon & Schuster Handbook for Writers with Miriam-Webster's Collegiate Dictionary and Thesaurus $27

- Comprehensive multimedia handbook for writers
- While working in most popular word processing software, this CD will enable students to seamlessly access grammar tips, punctuation, guidelines for writing reports, advice on the writing process, as well as other dictionary and thesaurus resources.

Career Opportunity Locator $5

This employment opportunity database contains data from several prominent statistical resources that will enable students to make career decisions based on their own preferences for interest areas, geography, income expectations, and educational or training requirements.

These CD-ROMs, individually valued at over $40, are available for the prices listed above when shrink-wrapped with Keys to Success.

Success Online

CARTER / BISHOP / LYMAN KRAVITS

Prentice Hall's new online student success course offers you all the advantages of a custom-built program without all the hassle. Student Success Online supports and augments *Keys to Success* (Carter, Bishop, Lyman-Kravits). The Student Success Online course offers a complete array of features designed to assist you in helping your students achieve their personal, academic, and career goals—to use just as presented, or to be customized to fit your specific course syllabus.

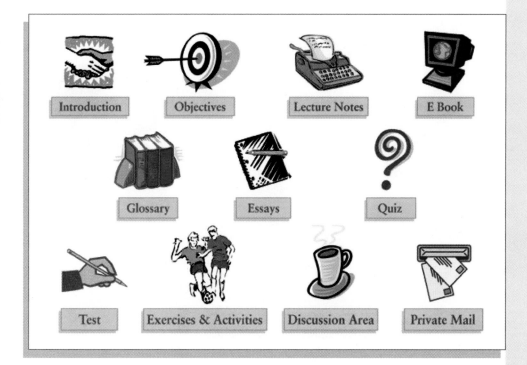

The entire *Keys to Success* text is available online!

To see a demo of this course visit:

http://webct.prenhall.com

Click Courses

Click Student Orientation

and Demo for Student Success Online

Announcing THE FIRST TELECOURSE IN STUDENT SUCCESS

Featuring

Keys to Success

How to achieve your goals

Carol Carter · Joyce Bishop · Sarah Lyman Kravits

Workbook

Text

Video

Companion Web Exercises

Essay Assessor

Prentice Hall's student success

· Majors Exploration · Study Skills · Carreer Path · Money Matters · Fitness and Well-Being ·
· Student Union · On-Line Text CW's · Faculty Lounge · Employment Opportunities · Contact Us · Home

Welcome to the Prentice Hall Student Success Supersite

Here you'll find a number of features designed to help you through your lifelong educational journey:

● Majors Exploration - What do you want to major in? Click here to learn about different majors and where they can lead you!
● Study Skills - Answers to Study Skills Questions at the Click of a Mouse.
● Career Path - Essential Tips from Career Counselers.
● Money Matters - Get rich quick! Or at least learn to manage your money while financing your college education. Essential tips from Finanoial Counselors.
● Fitness and Well-Being - To get in shape start by clicking here! Learn more about good nutrition, good mental health and how to manage stress and relationships.

● Student Union - College is supposed to be fun, too, right?! Play games, find the best movies and concerts, get the news and latest sports scores and learn where you can volunteer your time in your community!
● On Line Text Companion Web Sites - Link directly to the companion websites for the Prentice Hall Student Success texts.
● Faculty Lounge - Prentice Hall Faculty Development Workshops, Downloadable PowerPoint presentations and General Articles of Interest.
● Employment Opportunities - Have you considered a career in publishing? Find out more about the positions available in Prentice Hall.

Student Success SuperSite

Available from *Dallas Telelearning*

xx

DALLAS Telelearning

To receive a preview tape and/or more information, see our website at http://telelearning.dcccd.edu or send email to tlearn@dcccd.edu or phone 972-669-6666

Episodes

FULL VERSION OF TELECOURSE

1. EDUCATION TODAY: GETTING STARTED
2. LEARNING STYLES: USING YOUR STRENGTHS
3. SELF-AWARENESS: KNOWING WHO YOU ARE AND WHAT YOU WANT
4. GOALS AND VALUES: MAPPING YOUR COURSE
5. TIME MANAGEMENT: FILLING IT ALL IN
6. CRITICAL THINKING: TAPPING THE POWER OF YOUR MIND
7. CLARITY AND CREATIVITY: THE BUILDING BLOCKS OF UNDERSTANDING
8. READING: YOUR KEYS TO KNOWLEDGE
9. READING BETWEEN THE LINES: CRITICAL READING
10. DO YOU HEAR WHAT I HEAR?: HONING LISTENING SKILLS
11. THE MEMORY CHIP: REMEMBERING INFORMATION
12. NOTE-TAKING: THE SKILL OF GETTING IT DOWN
13. CONDUCTING RESEARCH: LEARNING FROM OTHERS
14. EFFECTIVE WRITING: COMMUNICATING YOUR MESSAGE
15. THE WRITING PROCESS: STEPS TO SUCCESSFUL WRITING
16. TEST TAKING: SHOWING WHAT YOU KNOW
17. THE ART OF TEST-TAKING: MASTERING ANY TEST
18. RELATING TO OTHERS: APPRECIATING YOUR DIVERSE WORLD
19. GETTING ALONG: RESPECTING OTHERS
20. SKILLS FOR THE 21ST CENTURY: TECHNOLOGY
21. SKILLS FOR THE 21ST CENTURY: MATH
22. SKILLS FOR THE 21ST CENTURY: SCIENCE
23. BODY AND MIND: PERSONAL WELLNESS
24. MANAGING YOUR FUTURE: REALITY RESOURCES
25. MONEY MATTERS: STARTING OUT RIGHT
26. MANAGING CHANGE: LIFELONG JOURNEY

BRIEF VERSION

1. EDUCATION TODAY
2. SELF-AWARENESS
3. GOAL SETTING AND TIME MANAGEMENT
4. CRITICAL AND CREATIVE THINKING
5. READING EFFECTIVELY
6. WRITING EFFECTIVELY
7. LISTENING AND MEMORY
8. NOTE-TAKING AND RESEARCH
9. EFFECTIVE TEST-TAKING
10. APPRECIATING YOUR DIVERSE WORLD
11. PERSONAL WELLNESS
12. MONEY MATTERS
13. MANAGING CAREER AND CHANGE

*Published by Prentice Hall, a division of Pearson Education, and distributed by Dallas Telelearning, LeCroy Center for Educational Telecommunications, 9596 Walnut St., Dallas, TX 75243.

Videos can be purchased separately from Prentice Hall for $100 each.

Annotated Instructor's Edition*

New to the 3/e, the AIE was developed to assist instructors in the classroom. The AIE includes 8 different types of marginal annotations, intended to help enrich discussion:

Teaching Tolerance	Springboard (for discussion)
Career Connection	Critical Thinking
Real World Link	Teaching Tips
Learning Styles Tip	Be a Team

Instructor's Manual*

Contains an abundance of useful materials to assist you in teaching student orientation or student success courses. Organized according to the objectives and lessons of each chapter, the IM includes transparency masters, Test Item File questions, pre- and post-class evaluations, lecture guides, and excerpts from specialists on a variety of topics including multiple intelligences, learning communities, and the Web.

Overhead Transparencies*

Full color acetates that relate directly to the course lecture material and help focus students on key objectives. Included with the 3rd edition are additional acetates pertaining to the brain, psychology of adjustment, leadership, diversity in the business world, and more.

Power Point also available.

Student Key Advice Video*

Brief segments showcasing motivational tips and advice by first-year through fourth-year college students and professionals in a variety of areas.

Faculty Development Training Video*

This library of teaching tips on student success and career development provides information on how to teach multiple intelligences, critical thinking, and school-to-work transition tips.

Free to qualifying adopters

Prentice Hall SuperSite— Faculty Lounge*

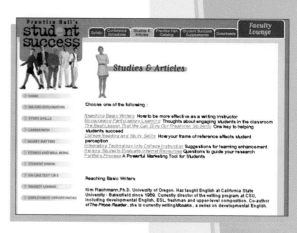

www.prenhall.com/success

Redesigned web site to offer a variety of resources for faculty under the faculty lounge area, including sample syllabi, conference schedules, and relevant articles.

Faculty Development Symposia/ School In-Service Programs

Prentice Hall sponsors a variety of faculty workshops on campuses and in specific cities throughout the year. Workshop topics focus on techniques and tools that will impact effective teaching and learning. Ask your local Prentice Hall representative for details for qualification.

Responding to Hate in School*

This supplement for teachers, produced by the Southern Poverty Law Center, provides a number of in-class activities and homework assignments to turn the tide of hate and prejudice to tolerance and open-mindedness among students.

Prentice Hall Reference Library in Student Success

This Reference Library features interviews with nationally known experts such as Dr. Lynn Troyka of the CUNY system; Dr. Tony Morris, University of Michigan; Dr. Bruce Bursten, The Ohio State University; Dr. Joyce Bishop, Golden West College; Dr. Kim Flachmann, CSU Bakersfield; Dr. Robb Sherfield, Community College of Southern Nevada; and Dr. Tom Cronin, President, Whitman College.

Video Segments, 30 minutes each

1. LEARNING STYLES AND SELF-AWARENESS
2. GOAL SETTING AND TIME MANAGEMENT
3. CRITICAL AND CREATIVE THINKING
4. READING EFFECTIVELY
5. LISTENING AND MEMORY
6. NOTE TAKING AND RESEARCH
7. WRITING EFFECTIVELY
8. EFFECTIVE TEST TAKING
9. RELATING TO OTHERS
10. SKILLS FOR THE 21ST CENTURY-TECHNOLOGY
11. SKILLS FOR THE 21ST CENTURY-MATH AND SCIENCE
12. PERSONAL WELLNESS
13. MANAGING MONEY AND CAREER

Policy: Each semester that professors order a new or shrinkwrapped Prentice Hall student success text, they are eligible for one of the above videos, valued at $100 each. Fax a copy of your bookstore order form, along with a letter stating your name, school, phone, email address, and how many students you have in the fall. Send to: Barbara Rosenberg, fax: 201-236-7788 or email Barb at Barbara_Rosenberg@prenhall.com. Limit: One video per school per semester.

*Free to qualifying adopters

ABC News Video Library*

This unique video library contains brief (5–20 minutes long) segments from award-winning ABC News programs, such as *20/20* and *World News Tonight*. This innovative resource provides a connection between student success and the real world.

SUBJECT	PROGRAM
Technology revolution	World News Tonight
Social promotion in public schools	World News Tonight
Violence against women	World News Tonight
Gang turned against violence, teaching values	Nightline
Beyond angry; pathologically angry children	20/20
HIV+ man infects women on purpose	Nightline
Availability of hate propaganda on the Internet	Nightline
Sexual harassment	Nightline
TV perpetuating stereotypes to young children	Nightline
An inner-city boy goes to Ivy League school; culture clash	Nightline
Children of Kosovo; psychological effects of war on children	World News Tonight
Video game violence and kids	World News Tonight
Community service; volunteerism	Nightline
Vaccines and clinical studies	Nightline
Gap in knowledge between investing in stocks and knowledge about them	World News Tonight
How to improve American students' math scores	ABC Primetime Live
Caring for the elderly or disabled relative at home	World News Tonight
Fraternity hazing leads to death	20/20

*Free to qualifying adopters

The Student Planner

Newly revised, this tool includes daily and monthly planner through the year 2002, an address book, course and class planners, grade calculators, and other organizing materials. This planner is designed to help students organize and manage their time more effectively.

Available free when packaged with a text.

Student Reflection Journal

Through this vehicle, students are encouraged to track their progress, share their insights, thoughts, and concerns.

Available free when packaged with a text.

Themes of the Times

These are abbreviated editions of the *Times* showcasing articles throughout any academic year that highlight issues pertaining to student success and career development.

Free when using the book.

NCS Career Testing Program

The Enhanced Version of the Career Assessment Inventory. This text compares occupational interests and personality preferences with individuals in hundreds of careers. Students complete the test, mail it, and receive the test results within seven to ten days.

Available at a discount when packaged with the text.

Ten Ways to Fight Hate*

This supplement, produced by the Southern Poverty Law Center, helps students to proactively deal with hate and prejudice within themselves and others.

*Free to qualifying adopters

Seven Habits of Highly Effective People

Audiocassette, by Stephen Covey

Audiotape program teaches listeners how to achieve success in both business and personal relationships. This approach broadens their way of thinking and leads to greater opportunities and effective problem solving.

Available at a discount when packaged with the text. (0-13-098377-2)

Learning and Study Strategies Inventory (LASSI)

To succeed in college students need effective cognitive and learning strategies, meaningful goals, self-generated motivation, and a systematic approach to studying. LASSI is a reliable and valid self-report measure of ten scales assessing students' preparation in these areas:

- Attitude
- Motivation
- Time Management
- Anxiety
- Concentration

- Information Processing
- Selecting Main Ideas
- Study Aids
- Self Testing
- Test Strategies

The LASSI:

- gives normed diagnostic information about a student's strengths and weaknesses in their college preparedness.
- can improve student retention by providing a basis for group or individual interventions.
- promotes student responsibility for their performance.

It is recommended to use one LASSI at beginning of the course and one at the end for optimal results.

PEEK: Perceptions, Expectations, Emotions, and Knowledge about College

"College is a whole 'nother world!" This quote from a student captures the problems many students find when they make the transition into college. There are many differences between high school and college and research has shown that students' expectations and perceptions of these changes can be a major factor in determining their success at negotiating the college environment.

The PEEK is a brief 30-item self-report measure that assesses students' expectations in three different clusters: their personal, academic, and social environment. The results can be compared to the responses of large groups of students from a single institution or an institution-specific key to help students identify areas where they may have incorrect or inappropriate expectations. This information can be used to help students develop a realistic perception of their college environment.

WORKING: Assessing Skills, Habits, and Style

This instrument measures nine key behaviors that directly affect how—and how well—a person performs on the job. These behaviors are sometimes referred to as SCANS competencies, work ethic, soft skills, or life skills. They include:

- Sense of responsibility
- Teamwork
- Persistence
- Sense of quality
- Interest in life-long learning
- Ability to adapt to change
- Ability to solve problems
- Information processing
- Systematic thinking

Inventory of Classroom Style and Skills (INCLASS)

INCLASS is a self-assessment instrument designed to help students, teachers, advisors, and counselors explore the underlying behaviors that influence a student's success in the classroom. It is diagnostic and prescriptive, and can be used to develop instructional and other interventions for students likely to have behavior patterns that might interfere with learning. It examines a student's proficiency in several competencies that directly relate to how that student approaches studying, homework, test-taking, class projects, attendance, time management, and class participation. Areas assessed include:

- Interest in life-long learning
- Commitment to quality
- Responsibility for work
- Persistence
- Working in teams
- Solving problems

Technology and Internet Assessment (TIA)

The TIA is available only on the web. It is designed to determine strengths and weaknesses related to a basic understanding of computer, Internet, and information technology skills. The TIA focuses on eight areas that present barriers for individuals seeking employment and for those striving to succeed in academic or workplace environments:

- Use of technology
- Specific computer skills
- Acquisition of technical knowledge
- Basic Internet knowledge
- Internet information skills
- Impact of technology
- Adapting to technological change
- Ethics in technology

Immediately upon completion of the TIA a two-page report is displayed listing the scores for each scale along with suggestions for improving each area. Administrators of the TIA can view previously administered results as well as the status of their institution's account at any time via the Web.

Shrinkwrapped with any Prentice Hall textbook, these self-scoring assessments are available only from your Prentice Hall representative for a nominal fee to the student. If you are not sure who your local representative is, please call Barbara Rosenberg at 201-236-7952 or e-mail barbara_rosenberg@prenhall.com. Each assessment takes approximately 20–30 minutes to complete.

User's manuals, technical assistance, and historical information about any of these assessments are available directly from H&H Publishing at 800-366-4079.

This interest and skill inventory, included as an appendix in the *Keys* text, is designed by one of the nation's leading authorities on career exploration and decision-making, David Campbell. Students can take the survey and mail in their results for a full, comprehensive analysis of those fields for which they would be best suited.

Part 1—Interests

The major purpose of this section is to assess your interests to determine the areas of work where you would be most likely to find satisfying activities.

Following are lists of occupations, school subjects, and varied work activities. Indicate how much you like each item by using the following scale:

L = STRONGLY LIKE
L = LIKE
l = slightly like
d = slightly dislike
D = DISLIKE
D = STRONGLY DISLIKE

Circle the letter corresponding to your answer. Don't worry about how good you would be at the activity, or whether you would be successful—just whether or not you would enjoy doing it. Don't think about how much money you might make, or how much status or prestige would be involved. Base your answer solely on how much you would like it.

Work quickly. Your first impression is generally most useful. You may wish to look up from your paper every now and then and take a short break. This will help you stay fresh and alert.

1. An actor or actress, performing on the stage, TV, or in movies   L L l d D D

2. An architect, designing new homes and buildings   L L l d D D

3. An artist, creating works of art   L L l d D D

4. An author, writing stories and novels   L L l d D D

5. A baker, making breads and pastries   L L l d D D

6. A building superintendent, managing a maintenance staff   L L l d D D

7. A bulldozer operator, helping to build a new road   L L l d D D

8. A bush pilot, flying a small plane in remote regions   L L l d D D

9. A cabinetmaker, building fine furniture   L L l d D D

For students who need career direction!

The First Step to Reduce Your Dropout Rate

Ask your entering students to complete the College Student Inventory™. Have their responses scored and analyzed. Then take action to make a difference.

Early Information for Early Interventions

You administer the College Student Inventory during the first weeks of your student success class. With the results in hand, you can establish meaningful rapport on first contact and advise students about relevant support services.

Complete Data on Student Concerns that May Lead to Attrition

Many campuses rely on poor academic performance as a trigger for early interventions. The Retention Management System goes a critical step further. It identifies the leading academic *and affective* indicators that lead to attrition. The result? You can intervene *earlier* to get students started right.

Time-Saving Direction, Priority Ranked

Advisors using the Retention Management System say it saves them hours of time discerning each student's needs. By revealing key student concerns and placing them in rank order, the system reduces the usual time required to build relationships and to get students started right. In addition, the resulting summary report helps student services offices to prioritize their use of staffing, money, and space.

SAMPLE ITEMS   NOT AT ALL TRUE   ① ② ③ ④ ⑤ ⑥ ⑦   COMPLETELY TRUE

I have some serious misgivings about my decision to come to college.

When faced with a tough decision, I like to open my imagination to many possible solutions.

I feel very comfortable with the changes in lifestyle that my going to college will require.

I often wonder if a college education is worth all the time, money, and effort that I'm being asked to spend on it.

I often take the initiative in solving my own problems.

Your drop-out prone students often start out looking just like your other students. Items like those above will help you get *beyond* the veneer.

For more information, visit www.noellevitz.com

For a customized presentation, mix and match from the following topics and add your own topics that you would like to see covered at the bottom. We will customize a day based on your needs as a staff.

Rate the following topics on a scale of 1–5, 1 being the highest interest, 5 being the least.

_____ MOTIVATING AT-RISK STUDENTS
Connecting college to future life goals

_____ SETTING GOALS AND EXPECTATIONS FOR STUDENTS
Gauging and evaluating student success

_____ DEVELOPING A POSITIVE TEACHER STUDENT RELATIONSHIP
How to have authority and still be personable and approachable

_____ CLIMBING OUT OF THE BOX
Using different teaching techniques to enliven the classroom experience

_____ DEALING WITH DIVERSE POPULATIONS
How to encourage students from all ages, stages, and backgrounds

_____ TEACHING RESPONSIBILITY, ETHICS, VALUES, AND CITIZENSHIP
Creating tomorrow's leaders and doers

_____ COLLABORATIVE LEARNING AND CRITICAL THINKING
Connecting both strategies for students in class

_____ USING POPULAR CULTURE TO TEACH STUDENT SUCCESS
Helping students understand themselves and the issues of their world through music, movies, magazines, and media

_____ MULTIPLE INTELLIGENCES
Based on Howard Gardner's research, this workshop emphasizes several assessments to help students understand their learning strengths and weaknesses

_____ WHAT EMPLOYERS OVERLOOK IN THE PEOPLE THEY HIRE
Using education and personal abilities to prepare for success out of college

_____ OTHER

_____ OTHER

*For adoptions of 1,000 copies or more, professors can select either a faculty development workshop or a student-oriented workshop to be given during the summer.

SEMINAR TOPICS FOR STUDENTS

Self-Awareness, Motivation, and Esteem

Discovering Who You Are and Feeling Good About Yourself. This session will explore how to maintain positive self-esteem and motivation through one's personal, academic, and career life.

Effective Relationships

This session will emphasize how to establish and maintain good relationships personally and academically while accomplishing academic goals through listening, conflict resolution, and group work.

Managing Yourself

Taking Care of Yourself Spiritually, Physically, and Mentally. This workshop deals with balancing the stresses of life while keeping goals achievable and in focus.

Choice Management Instead of Time Management

Establishing Priorities While Achieving Academic Goals. This workshop focuses on devising time for self, school, family, and other activities.

Critical Thinking Applied to Self, School, and Career

This session explores different ways of applying thinking skills to improve one's quality of life.

The Returning Student

There Is No Such Thing as "I Can't." This session helps returning students recognize their full value.

Learning to Be Accountable

How Your Actions Create Outcomes. This workshop helps students learn to keep their word and follow through on all agreements.

What Employers Look for In the People They Hire

This session helps students prepare early for career success.

*For adoptions of 1,000 copies or more, professors can select either a faculty development workshop or a student-oriented workshop to be given during the summer.

Part 1

Who Am I and Where Do I Go From Here?

 CHAPTER 1 Becoming a Lifelong Learner: Opening Doors

 CHAPTER 2 Resources: Making the Most of Your Environment

 CHAPTER 3 Goal Setting and Time Management: Mapping Your Course

CHAPTER 4 Self-Awareness: Knowing Who You Are and How You Learn

C H O O S E

Becoming a Lifelong Learner

Opening Doors

In this chapter, you will explore answers to the following questions:

- Who is pursuing an education today?
- How does education promote success?
- How can you strive for success?
- How can you build your self-esteem?
- What is your role in a diverse world?
- Why is it important to embrace change?

Welcome—or welcome back—to your education. You are embarking on a new millennium, both as an individual and as a member of the world community. In giving yourself the chance to learn and grow through education, you have the power to create a better world for yourself and others. *Keys to Success* will help you face the challenge by giving you keys—ideas, strategies, and skills—that can lead to success in college, career, and personal life.

This chapter will give you an overview of today's educational world and discuss the connection between education and success. You will explore specific success strategies that will help you maximize your educational experience. Finally, you will read about how building your self-esteem, focusing on teamwork, and embracing change can help you achieve your goals and make a difference in your life.

Teaching Tip

The following Web sites link to chapter content:

- National Center for Education Statistics - www.ed.gov/stats.html
- National Trio Clearinghouse - www.trioprograms.org
- Association on Higher Education and Disability: Links and Resources - www.ahead.org/links.htm

WHO IS PURSUING AN EDUCATION TODAY?

In various forms, learning took place in the ancient civilizations of Rome, Greece, Byzantium, and Islam. Learning institutions became formalized as universities, similar to those of present day, in medieval Europe as early as the 11th century. In the early life of the university, students and scholars were men, mostly white, seeking religious and intellectual pursuits. Since that time, higher education in all its forms has evolved into centers for cultural and social inspiration, intellectual growth, and scientific advancement.

Because of federal support and a universal understanding that a formal education should be the right of all people regardless of race, creed, color, age, or gender, institutions of higher education have become more diverse. See Figure 1.1 for the variety of schools available today.

Today's college students are more diverse than at any time in history. Although many students still enter college directly after high school, the old standard of finishing a four-year college education at the age of 22 no longer applies. Some students take longer than four years to finish. Some students complete part of their education, or go right into the workforce, and return to school later in life.

Teaching Tip
Higher education first became accessible to the masses when the G.I. Bill of Rights was passed after World War II. More than 4 million returning veterans received an allowance to attend college or get on-the-job training.

FIGURE 1.1 Types of Schools and Their Offerings

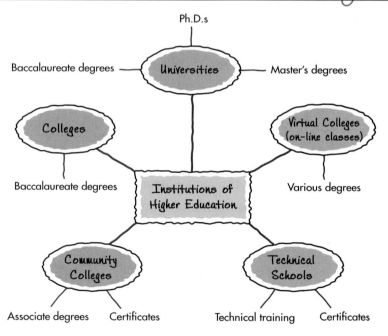

Critical Thinking
How does a diverse student body affect the nature of higher education? How does access to college change the nature of our society and our democracy? Why is educational opportunity increasingly important in the 21st century?

The Diverse Student Body

The following observations, based on statistics from the National Center for Education Statistics, indicate how the student population has changed since the 1980s:

- Students are older and many have family responsibilities.
- Students are more diverse in all ways: age, gender, ethnicity.

- Students are following less traditional educational paths. For example, more students attend 2-year colleges, more students attend school part-time, and more students work while attending school.

Not so long ago, if you were female, African-American, or physically challenged, for example, you had limited opportunity to attend college. Even 20 years ago, you might have given up on an education if you couldn't afford a four-year college or had to work during the day. Now, however, the needs of an increasingly diverse student body have molded a new educational experience. Whether you have limited finances, an unusual work schedule, a particular background, or any other special situation or need, you are likely to find a program that's right for you. Figures 1.2, 1.3, and 1.4 paint a picture of today's student population.

Be a Team
Ask students to think about people they know who carry heavy responsibilities while attending college and to define the traits that enable them to get everything done. Students should then find a partner and share their observations.

Students are Older and Have Varied Responsibilities   **FIGURE 1.2**

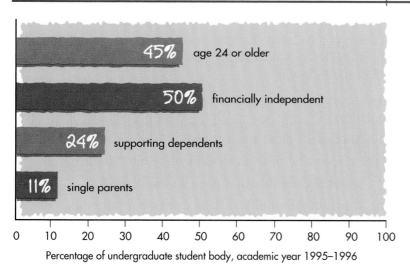

Percentage of undergraduate student body, academic year 1995–1996

Source: U. S. Department of Education, National Center for Education Statistics, *Digest of Education Statistics 1998,* NCES 1999-036, by Thomas D. Snyder. Washington, D.C.: U.S. Government Printing Office, 1999, pp. 235, 332; and U. S. Department of Education, National Center for Education Statistics, *Profile of Undergraduates in U. S. Postsecondary Education Institutions: 1995–96,* NCES 98-084, by Laura J. Horn, Jennifer Berktold, and MPR Associates, Inc. Washington, D. C.: U. S. Government Printing Office, 1998, p. 77.

Students Are More Diverse   **FIGURE 1.3**

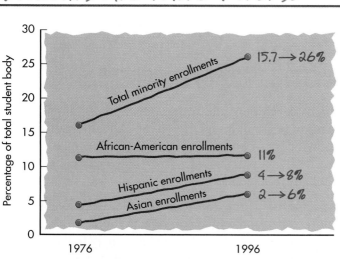

Source: U. S. Department of Education, National Center for Education Statistics, *Digest of Education Statistics 1998,* NCES 1999-036, by Thomas D. Snyder. Washington, D.C.: U.S. Government Printing Office, 1999, pp. 187–88.

FIGURE 1.4   *Students Are Following Less Traditional Educational Paths*

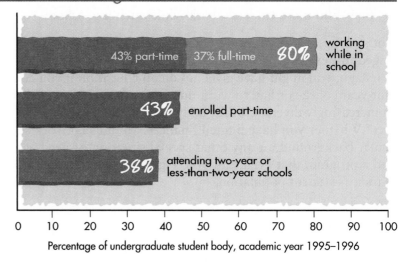

Source: U. S. Department of Education, National Center for Education Statistics, *Digest of Education Statistics 1998*, NCES 1999-036, by Thomas D. Snyder. Washington, D.C.: U.S. Government Printing Office, 1999, pp. 196–197; and U. S. Department of Education, National Center for Education Statistics, *Profile of Undergraduates in U. S. Postsecondary Education Institutions: 1995–96*, NCES 98-084, by Laura J. Horn, Jennifer Berktold, and MPR Associates, Inc. Washington, D. C.: U. S. Government Printing Office, 1998, p. 5.

No one can force you to learn. You are responsible for seeking out educational opportunities. Every student's life has unique challenges. You may face one or more of the following:

- adjusting to the cultural and communication differences in the diverse student population
- returning to school as an older student and feeling out of place
  - handling the responsibilities and stresses of being a single parent
    - having a physical disability that presents challenges
      - having a learning disability such as dyslexia or attention deficit disorder (ADD)
      - being responsible for an elderly or sick parent
      - balancing a school schedule with part-time or even full-time work
      - handling the enormous financial commitment college requires

Your school can help you work through these and other challenges if you actively seek out solutions and help from available support systems around you (see Chapter 2 for information on resources). Consider how working hard on your education can help you build the life you envision.

e-mail

What are your reasons for going to college? What are your personal challenges? Write to a friend to share your thoughts so that you can establish a mutual support system for your first year of college.

HOW DOES EDUCATION PROMOTE SUCCESS?

Education—the process of developing and training the mind—should be far more than the accumulation of credit hours. If you take advantage of all education has to offer, you will develop the skills and talents you need to succeed in your career and life.

How can education help you succeed?

Education gives you tools for lifelong learning. You learn facts while you are in school, but more importantly, you learn how to think. Although some of the facts and figures you learn today may not apply to the world of tomorrow, your ability to think will be useful always, in everything you do.

Critical Thinking
Ask students for their thoughts on the link between education and flexibility. How will higher education help them respond to career, societal, and personal change?

Education improves your employability and earning potential. Although education isn't an automatic guarantee of a high-level, well-paying job, it greatly increases the probability (see Figure 1.5 and Figure 1.6 for details). Having a college degree makes an impression on potential employers and makes you eligible for higher-salaried positions than applicants without a degree.

Career Connection
In our technologically based job market, students should expect to continue learning throughout their careers.

Education and Income
FIGURE 1.5

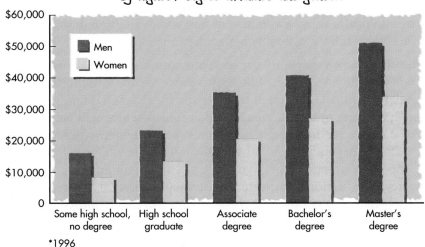

Median annual income of persons with income 25 years old and over, by highest degree attained and gender.*

*1996

Source: U.S. Department of Commerce, Bureau of the Census, *Current Population Reports,* Series P-60, "Money Income of Households, Families, and Persons in the United States: 1996."

Education and Employment
FIGURE 1.6

Unemployment rates of persons 25 years old and over, by highest degree attained.*

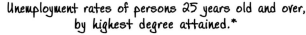
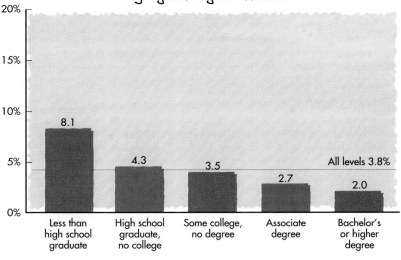

*1997

Source: U.S. Department of Labor, Bureau of Labor Statistics, Office of Employment and Unemployment Statistics, *Current Population Survey,* 1997.

Education expands your self-concept. As you rise to the challenges of education, you will discover that your capacity for knowledge and personal growth is greater than you imagined. As your abilities grow, so does your ability to learn and do more in class, on the job, and in your community.

Education enlarges your career possibilities. Education expands your career choices and gives you the know-how to choose your career goals. Through your courses you may learn about more potential careers and goals than you ever imagined. Through your education in general you gain the skills to achieve the goals you choose. For example, while taking a writing class, you may learn about journalism careers, which may lead you to take a class in journalistic writing and reporting. Later, you may decide to work on a newspaper and to make journalism your career. In this case, an awareness of the path available, combined with an ability to follow it, could change the course of your life.

Education improves your literacy. Your course work raises your competency in the three types of literacy—prose (reading and working with standard English), document (completing forms), and quantitative (understanding numbers, charts, and graphs)—which will help you fulfill the requirements of higher-level jobs. Because literacy will increase or decrease depending on how often you use your skills, education and on-the-job training will help you to reach and maintain high levels of literacy. The National Institute for Literacy reports: "Literacy is a range of tools that help people help themselves—and their children. It is not an end in itself, but a means to a better quality of life."[1] See Figure 1.7 for statistics on literacy.

FIGURE 1.7   Statistics on Literacy

In its 1991 National Literacy Act, Congress defined literacy as:

"An individual's ability to read, write, and speak in English, and compute and solve problems at levels of proficiency necessary to function on the job and in society, to achieve one's goals and develop one's knowledge and potential."

■ More than 20 percent of adults read at or below a fifth-grade level—far below the level needed to earn a living wage. The National Adult Literacy Survey found that over 40 million Americans age 16 and older have significant literacy needs.

■ American businesses are estimated to lose over $60 billion in productivity each year due to employees' lack of basic skills.

■ About 20 percent of America's workers have low basic skills, and 75 percent of unemployed adults have reading or writing difficulties.

■ The number of companies reporting skilled worker shortages more than doubled between 1995 and 1998, from 27 percent to over 47 percent.

Source: The National Institute for Literacy, "Fast Facts on Literacy" and "Fact Sheet for Workplace Literacy." www.nifl.gov/newworld/workforce.htm and www.nifl.gov/newworld/fastfact.htm.

Education broadens your worldview. As it introduces you to new ways of learning, doing, being, and thinking, education increases your understanding of diversity and your appreciation of areas that affect and enrich human lives, such as music, art, literature, science, politics, and economics.

Education affects both community involvement and personal health. Education prepares you to become involved in your community by helping you understand political, economic, and social conditions and how they affect each individual's life. Education also increases health knowledge, motivating you to practice healthy habits and to make informed decisions about your health.

Education is what you make of it. A dedicated, goal-oriented learner will benefit more than a student who doesn't try. The following discussion presents some important strategies that will help you maximize your educational opportunities.

Teaching Tip
The link between education and health is complex, as witnessed by the number of college students who smoke and binge drink. Discuss how peer pressure and feelings of immortality counteract the positive impact of education.

HOW CAN YOU STRIVE FOR SUCCESS?

Success is a process in motion, not a fixed mark. A successful person is one who is consistently learning, growing, and working toward goals. When people perceive success as an end point to a process instead of the process itself, they often wonder why they feel unsatisfied when they get there. If you don't continually grow and add new goals, you may feel dissatisfied, empty, aimless, or "stuck."

College provides an opportunity for you to investigate and reinvent yourself, to redefine your goals and work hard to achieve them. Tom Bradley, son of a Texas sharecropper, became the first African-American mayor of Los Angeles in 1973 and served five successive terms. More than 30 years after Ruth Bader Ginsberg was rejected as a Supreme Court clerk because Justice Felix Frankfurter didn't hire women, she became a Supreme Court justice herself. If you put your energies to the task, you can create the personal future you envision.

Striving for success takes effort. It requires motivation, commitment, initiative, responsibility, and a willingness to face your fears. In combination, these strategies will help you gather and retain knowledge as well as create new knowledge.

Springboard
Discuss why motivational problems are often difficult to analyze. For example, while a senior may believe that money problems are behind his inability to concentrate, on a deeper level, he may fear the changes he faces after graduation.

Get Motivated

Motivation is the energy that fuels your drive to achieve, and a motivator is anything that moves you forward. There are at least as many motivators as there are people, and what motivates any given person can change from situation to situation. For example, some potential motivators for attending school could be learning a marketable skill, supporting a family, or improving oneself.

It's human to lose your motivation from time to time. For reasons ranging from a stressful life change to simply a period of low energy, sometimes you might not feel like accomplishing anything. How can you build motivation or renew lost motivation?

■ Spend time reflecting on why your goal is meaningful to you. Remind yourself about what you wanted and why that goal is still important.

Motivation
A force that moves a person to action; often inspired by an idea, a fact, an event, or a goal.

- Make a decision to take one step toward your goal. Sometimes feeling overwhelmed by a goal immobilizes you. Don't worry about tomorrow. Focus on the step you can take today.

- After you take the first step, reward yourself for a job well done. Rewards can be material (a new CD) or they can be internal (a walk outside, time with a friend, an entry in your journal).

- Examine and deal with your obstacles. What's getting in your way? Maybe your health or finances are troubling you. Decide to examine and remove your obstacles. For example, see a doctor about your bad back or cut up your credit cards to avoid getting deeper into debt.

- Begin or begin again. If you can just get yourself started, you'll feel better as you continue to work toward your goals. Newton's first law of motion, a law of physics, is that things in motion tend to stay in motion and things at rest tend to stay at rest. *Be a thing in motion.*

For example, to pass an early morning writing class that you've already failed once, you decide to implement two strategies. First, you promise yourself that you will go to every class and turn in your work on time. Second, you make a commitment to write daily in a journal. Your motivation: Passing this course is necessary to continue your education, and the writing skills you learn will help you get a good job when you graduate. Moreover, you promise yourself a reward if you get at least a B– in the course.

> "A journey of a thousand miles must begin with a single step."
>
> Lao-tzu

Make a Commitment

How do you focus the energy of motivation? Make a **commitment.** Commitment means that you do what you say you will do. When you honor a commitment, you prove to yourself and others that your intentions can be trusted.

The tasks and rewards of commitment apply to academic goals, professional relationships, your working life, career goals, and self-improvement. Commitment often stretches over a period of time. You may commit to graduating in three years, to working on your marriage, or to recycling more often. Not only have you made a promise, but also you hold yourself to that promise for as long as necessary to reach your goal.

Commitment requires that you focus your energy on something specific. A decision to "change my life" or "make a million dollars" might intimidate you into staying motionless on the couch. Instead, break any goal into manageable pieces, naming the steps you will use to achieve it.

How do you go about making and keeping a commitment?

- State your commitment concretely. Set clear tasks. Be specific: "I'm going to turn in the weekly essay assignments on time."

- Get started and note your progress. The long road of a commitment can tire you out. Assessing your improvement along the way can keep you going.

- Renew your commitment regularly. How many times has your commitment to change faded away in a few weeks—or even a few days? You're not a failure if you lose steam; it's normal. Recharge by reflecting on the positive effects of your commitment and what you have already achieved.

Commitment

(1) A pledge or promise to do something, or (2) dedication to a long-term course of action.

Real World Link

Under coach Lou Holtz, the University of Notre Dame football team committed to five goals at the start of every season. Among these were winning the national championship and graduating all the team's seniors. These specific commitments helped the team achieve greatness.

- Keep track of each commitment. Find ways to remind yourself of your commitments. Keep a list of them in your date book, on your refrigerator, or on your computer. If they involve events or projects that take place on specific dates, note them on a calendar. Talk about your commitments with friends and family. Sometimes, just having someone supporting you and your goals helps you remain on track.

E-mail your professor or your on-line study group and clearly state your goals for the course. Enlist your professor's and your peers' support in helping you reach your goals.

For example, you might make this commitment: "I will write in my journal every night before going to sleep." You make journal entries for two weeks and then evaluate what positive effects this daily practice has had on your writing ability. If you were to skip your journal entries for a week, you could renew your commitment by reminding yourself how keeping a journal has improved your writing ability and relieved stress. You might boost your commitment by telling a partner or housemate to check on you.

Making and keeping your commitments help you to keep a steady focus on your most important goals. It gives you a sense of accomplishment as you experience gradual growth and progress.

Show Initiative

When you show **initiative,** you push yourself to take that first difficult step. Initiative jump-starts your journey and helps to renew motivation to strive for your goals. It enables you to respond continually to changes that occur.

Initiative means that you take the first step on your own instead of waiting for people, rules, requirements, or circumstances to drag you along. You show initiative when you go to a counselor for help with a personal problem, talk to a friend about something he or she said that upset you, raise your hand to speak in class, come up with a better way to do a job at work, take a political stand by voting, or start doing 50 abdominal crunches every morning.

Initiative requires you to keep on top of your goals and to listen to your instincts. You may discover that you want to do more than what is expected, which can be positive both at school and in the workplace.

Be Responsible

Being responsible is all about living up to your obligations, both those that are imposed on you and those that you impose on yourself. Through action, you prove that you are responsible, or "response-able," able to respond. When something needs to be done, a responsible person does the work—as efficiently as possible and to the best of his or her ability.

Responsibility can take enormous effort. Throughout your life you will have moments when you just don't want to respond. In those moments, you need to weigh the positive and negative effects and decide what to do. However, being responsible has definite benefits. For one, you make a crucial impression on others, earning the trust and respect of your instructors, supervisors, relatives, and friends. People who trust you may give you increasing power and opportunities for growth, because you have shown you are capable of making the best of both. Trust builds relationships, which in turn feed

---

Initiative

The power to begin or to follow through energetically with a plan or task; determination.

Be a Team

Ask students to think about a recent situation in which they lacked the initiative to reach a goal and to share the problem with a partner. Partners should look for common obstacles and suggest ways to increase determination.

Springboard

Ask students if responsible people are likely to be responsible in every area of their life or only in areas they consider important. Discuss whether responsibility is a character trait that defines one's entire personality or if it is situation specific.

Responsibility

The quality of being reliable, trustworthy, and accountable for one's actions.

progress and success. Even more important is the self-respect that emerges when you prove that you can live up to your promises.

When you complete class assignments on time, you demonstrate responsibility. When you correct errors, you demonstrate a commitment to doing well. An instructor who observes these behaviors is more likely to trust and respect you. You don't have to take on the world to show how responsible you can be. Responsibility is revealed in basic everyday actions; for example, attending class, fulfilling requirements, turning in work on time, being a good friend or parent, and being true to your word.

A government professor looks for a response to a question.

Face Your Fears

Everyone experiences fear. New experiences are often frightening and exciting at the same time. The changes involved in pursuing an education can inspire fear. You may wonder if you can handle the work, if you will get along with your instructors, or if you have chosen the right school or program. You may worry that family and friends may expect too much or may stand in your way. You may also have fears about the future: Will your education prepare you to find a job that you like and that pays well?

Making responsible choices will help you manage fear. It's hard to earn and manage money so you can pay your bills and save for the future, or perhaps care for children or an aging relative, and still find time for rest and relaxation. You should congratulate yourself on choosing to increase your abilities through education. Although some people give in to fear because they feel safer with the familiar—even if it doesn't make them happy—you are working to increase your opportunities.

Education presents challenges that demand a willingness to push your limits and face your fears. The following steps will help you face your fears with courage. Throughout your life you will find yourself taking these steps again and again.

Teaching Tip
Students who never face their fears may engage in self-defeating behaviors, which prevent them from reaching their goals. Among the worst self-defeating behaviors is procrastination.

1. **Acknowledge fears.** The act of naming your fear will begin to lessen its hold on you. Be specific. Knowing that you fear a course may not inspire you to action, whereas focusing in on a fear of an instructor or assignment gives you something to work on.

2. **Examine fears.** Sometimes one fear hides a larger one. If you fear a test, determine whether you fear the test itself or the fact that if you pass it, you will have to take a tougher class next semester. If you fear the test, take steps to prepare for it. If you fear the next class, you might talk with your instructor about it.

3. **Develop a plan of attack.** Evaluate what will help you overcome your fear. For example, if you are uneasy about your writing style, develop a realistic picture of your abilities by consulting your instructor, talking to friends in the class, or reading a variety of work by other writers.

4. **Move ahead with your plans.** Courage is the key to moving ahead. You may find that the drive to overcome fear forces you to work harder, or you may also discover that your fear is so great that you must delay or change your plans. Take the steps you decide will help you most.

As you work through your fears, talk about them with people you trust. Often the ideas other people have about gaining control can help you with your own fears. Everyone has fears, and when people share strategies, everyone benefits.

When you acknowledge and evaluate your fears, it can provide valuable clues as to what blocks your success. Facing your fears and taking action promote healthy self-esteem.

HOW CAN YOU BUILD YOUR SELF-ESTEEM?

Self-esteem is part of what propels every successful person. Often, if people believe strongly enough in their value and capabilities, this belief can help lead them toward their goals. Belief, though, is only half the game. The other half is action and effort that helps you feel that you have *earned* your self-esteem. Rick Pitino, a highly successful basketball coach, discusses the necessity of earning self-esteem in his book *Success Is a Choice*: "Self-esteem is directly linked to deserving success. If you have established a great work ethic and have begun the discipline that is inherent with that, you will automatically begin to feel better about yourself. It's all interrelated. You must deserve victory to feel good about yourself."[2]

Building self-esteem, therefore, involves both thinking positively and taking action. Together, they will help you generate the belief in yourself that will help you achieve your goals.

> **Self-esteem**
> A strong and deeply felt belief that as a person, you have value in the world.

Think Positively

Attitudes influence your choices and affect how you perceive and relate to others. On the one hand, a positive attitude can open your mind to learning experiences and inspire you to take action. On the other hand, a negative attitude can hinder learning and stifle initiative. For example, say you are enrolled in a required course unrelated to your major. If you feel that the course is a waste of time, you probably won't work hard or learn much. If, however, you keep an open mind, you might discover that the course teaches you something valuable, introduces you to a friend or instructor who influences your life, or shows you new career possibilities.

One of the ways in which you can create a positive attitude is through **positive self-talk.** When you hear negative thoughts in your mind ("I'm not very smart" or "I'm not good enough"), replace them with positive ones ("It won't be easy, but I'm smart enough to figure it out" or "I have a lot to offer"). You would probably never criticize a good friend in the same way that you sometimes criticize yourself. The following hints will help you put positive self-talk into action:

> **Learning Styles Tip**
> Students with weak language and logic skills often have a hard time in school. Encourage them to recognize their other strengths (see Chapter 4). Self-confidence will come when they experience success by learning about things in other ways.

> **Positive self-talk**
> Supportive and positive thoughts and ideas that a person communicates to himself or herself.

Stop negative talk in its tracks and change it to positive talk. If you catch yourself thinking, "I can never write a decent paper," stop and say to yourself, "I can do better than that and next time I will." Then think about some specific steps you can take to improve your writing.

Pay yourself a compliment. Be specific: "I have really improved my spelling and proofreading." Some people use calendars with daily affirmations. These are great reminders of positive self-talk.

Replace words of obligation—which rob you of power—with words of personal intent.

I should	*becomes*	I choose to
I have to	*becomes*	I want to
I'll try	*becomes*	I will

Words of intent give you power and control because they imply a personal decision to act. When you say, "I have to be in class by 9:00," you're saying that someone else has power over you and has handed you a required obligation. When you say, "I want to be in class by 9:00 because I don't want to miss anything I need to learn," you're saying that the choice is yours.

Note your successes. Even when you don't think you are at your best, congratulate yourself on any positive steps. Whether you do well on a paper, get to class on time all week, or have fewer mistakes on this week's paper than last week's, each success helps you believe in yourself. Try keeping a list of your successes in a notebook, and review them when you begin to doubt yourself.

It can be very difficult to think positively. If you have a deep-rooted feeling of unworthiness, you may want to see a counselor. Many people have benefited from skilled professional advice.

Take Action

Although thinking positively sets the tone for success, it cannot get you there by itself. You need to take action. Without action, positive thoughts can become empty statements or even lies.

Consider, for example, a student in a freshman composition class. This student thinks every possible positive thought: "I am a great student. I know how to write well. I can get a B in this class. I will succeed in school." And so on. She even writes her thoughts down on notes and posts them where she can see them. Then, during the semester, she misses about one-third of the class meetings, turns in some of her papers late, and completely misses a couple of assignments. She doesn't make use of opportunities to work with her study partner. At the end of the course, when she barely passes the class, she wonders how things went so wrong when she had such a positive attitude.

This student did not succeed because she did not earn her belief in herself through action and effort. You cannot maintain belief unless you give yourself something to believe *in*. By the end of a semester like this, positive thoughts look like lies. "If I can get a B, why did I get a D? If I am such a great student, why did I barely make it through this course?" Eventually, with nothing to support them, the positive thoughts disappear, and with neither positive thoughts nor action, a student will have a hard time achieving any level of success. Following are some ways to get yourself moving:

Career Connection
Positive language helps managers motivate employees. Instead of saying, "You had better not make a mistake," a manager will get better results by saying, "You're the right person for this account. I know you'll do well."

"They are able because they think they are able."

Virgil

Make action plans. Be specific about how you plan to take action for any given situation. Figure out exactly what you will do so that "I am a great student" is backed up by specific actions to ensure success.

Build your own code of discipline. Develop a general plan to follow, based on what actions are important to your success. Perhaps your top priorities are personal relationships and achievement in school. Construct each day's individual goals and actions so that they help you achieve your larger objectives.

Just do it. It takes a lot of energy to do what you have said you will do. Don't spend energy worrying about how hard it will be, when and how you should do it, what will happen if you do it or don't, and so on. Once you decide on your action, use your energy to just do it. Only then can you reap the benefit.

Acknowledge every step. Even the smallest action is worth your attention because every action reinforces a positive thought and builds self-esteem. First you believe that you are a great student, then you work hard in class, then you do well on a test, then you believe more emphatically that you are a great student, then you complete a successful group project, then you feel even better about yourself, and so on.

The process of building and maintaining self-esteem isn't easy for anyone. It involves many successes and disappointments. Only by having a true sense of self-esteem, though, can you have the initiative to achieve what you dream. Remember that you are in control of your self-esteem, because you alone are ultimately responsible for your thoughts and actions. Make the choice to both believe in yourself and take action that anchors and inspires that belief.

Self-esteem is a large part of what enables you to relate to others comfortably and successfully. With a strong sense of self-worth, you will be able to develop productive relationships with the diverse people that are an increasing part of your world.

WHAT IS YOUR ROLE IN A DIVERSE WORLD?

Diversity is the mosaic of differences that envelops your communities, your nation, and the world. In addition to racial and ethnic groups, diversity occurs in traditions, religions, family backgrounds, sexual preferences, abilities, economic levels, ages, habits, lifestyles, careers, artistic expressions, modes of dress, foods, health conditions, perspectives, opinions, experiences, and more. Diversity touches each of you in a very personal way.

Diversity Is Real Life

You encounter diversity every day through images and information—in newspapers and magazines, on television, and on the radio—that tell you about how different people think and live. People tend to focus on diversity they can see, such as skin color or eye shape, but there are other less visible forms of diversity. Your fellow student may have a different religion or a hidden disability, for example, or your coworker may have a different sexual orientation. Society is made up of people who transcend labels and have limitless worth.

Learning Styles Tip
Students with a strong interpersonal intelligence may be drawn to the challenge of living in a diverse world. They gladly accept the challenge because it gives them the opportunity to broaden their interpersonal network.

Teaching Tip
Rejecting ethnocentrism does not mean discrediting one's own background or heritage, but rather recognizing the equal value of other groups.

As people become more aware of other ways of living, they may be more sensitive to differences. The knowledge of differences can be a benefit. Unfortunately, it can also be used to spread harmful opinions. The problem is not in the differences but in the way in which people view and treat these differences.

Ethnocentrism

Ethnocentrism
The condition of thinking that one's particular ethnic group is superior to others.

When groups of people believe that their way of thinking is the only way, or a better way than anyone else's, they are practicing **ethnocentrism.** It's important to be proud of your identity, but it's another thing to think that your group is superior to all other groups.

A group can be organized around any sort of uniqueness—the same skin color, accent, country of origin, ideas, interests, religion, traditions, and much more. The problem arises when celebrating your own uniqueness conflicts with someone else's, and no effort is made to learn about or respect the beliefs or practices of others. If you find yourself thinking in terms of "right way, wrong way" instead of "different but legitimate," you may be guilty of ethnocentrism. Ethnocentrism has many negative effects. It can prevent effective communication, as you will see in more detail in Chapter 9. It can limit you by denying you exposure to people and ideas from which you could learn. Finally, it can hinder your ability to work with others, which can cause problems for you at school and on the job.

e-mail

E-mail one of your closest friends and tell them about a people, religion, or culture that you would like to learn more about. Ask them if they would conduct a similar investigation in the spirit of promoting tolerance and openmindedness.

Diversity and Teamwork

Think of the path of your accomplishments, and you will find that rarely do you achieve anything using your own efforts alone. Your success at school and at work depends on your ability to cooperate in a team setting—to communicate, share tasks, and develop a common vision.

- You deal with the challenges of day-to-day life in a *family/community* team, with the help of parents, siblings, relatives, and friends.
- You achieve work goals in a *work* team, with supervisors, coworkers, and/or consultants.
- You learn, complete projects, and pass courses as part of an *educational* team, with instructors, fellow students, tutors, administrators, and advisors.

Career Connection
The members of successful work teams often take time to get to know one another before a project begins. They may assess each other's language skills (important in a multinational team) and members' willingness to express opinions in front of other group members.

Teams gain strength from the diversity of their members. In fact, diversity is an asset in a team. Consider a five-person basketball team made up of a center, a power forward, a small forward, a shooting guard, and a point guard. Each person has a different role and a different style of play, but only by combining their abilities can the players achieve success. The more diverse the team members, the greater the chance that new ideas and solutions to problems will emerge. As a member of any team, use the following three strategies to maximize team success:

- Open your mind and accept that different team members have valuable roles and that no one person can do everything alone.
- Welcome the new information and ideas that others offer.

■ Evaluate any idea based on how it improves a situation instead of focusing on the person who had the idea. Successful teams use what works, no matter who came up with the suggestion.

Throughout this book you will find references to a diverse mixture of people in different life circumstances because diversity is a theme that touches every part of your life. Note especially the "Windows on the World" feature in every chapter, which highlights people from different backgrounds who are making the effort to learn about themselves and their world. Chapter 9 will go into more detail about communicating across lines of difference and addressing the problems that arise when people have trouble accepting each other's differences.

Students meet with an academic counselor at Stanford University

The focus on diversity is one side effect of the enormous changes going on today. Constant change is one of the few givens of modern life.

WHY IS IT IMPORTANT TO EMBRACE CHANGE?

At this point it may seem like enough of a job to get to class on time with the right books in hand. Right from the start, however, it is crucial to know that change lies in the future. You will experience change ranging from day-to-day surprises such as a schedule change or a car problem all the way to global changes such as weather patterns and world economic shifts.

Change will often throw you for a loop with little or no warning. You cannot stop change from happening, but you can embrace change through awareness and by making active, conscious choices about how to handle the changes that come your way. Embrace change so that you can benefit and grow from it rather than being trampled by it.

Change Shapes the World

As Russian-born author Isaac Asimov said, "It is change, continuing change, inevitable change, that is the dominant factor in society today. No sensible decision can be made any longer without taking into account not only the world as it is, but the world as it will be."[3] Two significant causes of change on a global level are technology and the economy.

Technological Growth

Today's technology has spurred change. Advances in technology happen daily: Computer companies update programs, new models of cars and machines appear, and scientists discover new possibilities in medicine and other areas. People make changes in the workplace, school, and home to keep up with the new systems and products that technology constantly offers. People and cultures are linked around the world through the Internet and World Wide Web.

The dominance of the media, brought on by technological growth, has increased the likelihood of change. A few hundred years ago, no television or

Springboard
In the last decade, the United States has moved from a manufacturing/ service economy to an information/ knowledge economy. Ask students what they think this means for their future.

WINDOWS ON THE WORLD
Real Life Student Issues

How can I decide on a major?

Hector Perez, University of Idaho, Moscow, Idaho, Major Undeclared

My older brothers and sisters, and most of my friends, seemed to know what they wanted to do right out of high school. That's not the case with me. When I first came to college, I wanted to go into physical therapy and be an athletic trainer, but I don't know if there's a future in that. I've also considered teaching, but many teachers I know work other jobs to make ends meet. I want to work only one job so that I have time to do other activities that I like.

One problem is that I have few things I really enjoy. One thing that does "click" with me is martial arts. I have been taking karate and jujitsu classes for 15 years and hold a black belt. I belong to a martial arts club on campus and work part-time as an instructor. I really like teaching, and I've thought about one day opening my own dojo, but it would be hard to make a living. History also interests me, especially Mexican history. My grandfather was a colonel in the Mexican Revolution. He died before I was born. I am planning to take a Spanish class next year because I'd like to visit my relatives in Mexico and to travel to other Latin countries.

It seems like every day one of my brothers has a new idea for a major for me. Sometimes I tell people I'm thinking about it just to get them off my back. Lately, I've been thinking that I'll just major in business or liberal arts because those can be applied to just about any field. Can you offer a few suggestions for how I can decide on a major that's right for me?

Theresa Ammirati, Dean of Freshmen, Connecticut College

I had a similar problem when I was in college, and I see students now who are wondering what to major in—either because, as with me, there are too many areas that interest them, or because, as with you, there isn't anything that both interests them and seems to lead to a job they want. Right now I think you're confusing a major with a job, or, worse, with your life's work.

First, don't think of your major as leading you irrevocably to a career for life. Most people change careers three or four times. I've seen students who majored in history become librarians or researchers. I know a person who majored in philosophy and is now a park manager in Nepal. Your major may lead you directly to a career, or more likely, it will teach you skills you can apply to many careers. A major in Mexican history, for example, will provide you with skills that employers value, such as organizational skills (think about managing historical data for a paper), writing skills, problem-solving skills, critical thinking skills, and global awareness.

Think about what you like and don't like to do and how this relates to particular academic disciplines. Do you like to think about causes and effects, relationships between and among events and people, and different cultures? History, sociology, and anthropology are areas that might appeal to you. Your extracurricular activities can complement your academic life. Although you can't major in martial arts, for example, your involvement helps to develop your collaboration and leadership skills, both important in the current job market.

The key is to think about the kinds of activities that appeal to you and then see how these play out in different fields. Try to satisfy as many parts of yourself as you can through your major and worry less about the job you will have than the kinds of skills you are developing.

magazines or Internet existed to show people what was happening elsewhere in the world. Now, the media constantly presents people with new ways of doing things. When people can see the possibilities around them, they are more likely to want to discover new horizons.

Economic Instability

The unpredictable economy is another powerful agent of change. Businesses have had to cut costs to survive, which affects many jobs and careers. Some businesses have replaced workers with computers. Some businesses have had to downsize and have laid off people to save money. Some businesses have merged with others, and due to duplicate jobs people were let go. The changing economy has also had an effect on personal finances. Many people face money problems at home that force them to make changes in how much they work, when they pursue an education, and how they live.

Be an Agent of Change

Once you are aware of how change shapes your world, you can respond to it with conscious choices. Being an agent of change means being aware of change, adjusting to what it brings, and sometimes even causing change yourself. Every choice now will affect what happens down the road—and, conversely, you can trace what happens to you back to actions taken (or not taken) in the past. The people you meet will affect courses you take—the courses you take will affect the career you will choose—how you feel about your career will affect your personal life—and so on. Starting now, be in charge of your choices.

> "He has not learned the lesson of life who does not every day surmount a fear."
>
> Ralph Waldo Emerson

For example, say that your school is planning to cancel a number of sections of a course that you need, which would result in your not being able to take the course in time for graduation. You could be a victim of change—you could take the class another time, graduate later, and suffer other consequences, such as putting off full-time employment. On the other hand, you can be an agent of change by speaking to your academic advisor about using another class to fulfill this requirement, gathering students who need the class and petitioning the school to keep those sections open, or finding an internship that will substitute for the class. In this way you could make the most of change.

Seek continual change and improvement in your education. Take to heart this quote from a student in Mississippi: "Without an education in the year 2000, we the people will be in serious trouble. Because now everything is moving forward fast and without an education you will be moving nowhere."[4] Let your ability to make change happen keep you on the move.

In Chinese writing, this character has two meanings: One is "chaos"; the other is "opportunity." The character communicates the belief that every challenging, chaotic, and demanding situation in life also presents an opportunity. By responding to challenges in a positive and active way, you can discover the opportunity that lies within the chaos.

Let this concept reassure you as you begin college. You may feel that you are going through a time of chaos and change. Remember that no matter how difficult the obstacles, you have the ability to persevere. You can create opportunities for yourself to learn, grow, and improve.

Name   Date

BUILDING SKILLS FOR COLLEGE, CAREER, AND LIFE SUCCESS

Critical Thinking
Applying Learning to Life

Identify Yourself

Where do you fit in today's student population? Make a brief "sketch" of yourself in words—describe your particular circumstances, opinions, and needs in a short paragraph. Here are some questions to inspire thought:

- How do you describe yourself—your culture, ethnicity, gender, age, lifestyle?
- How long are you planning to be in college?
- How would you describe your family?
- What is your work situation, if you work?
- What is your current living situation?
- What do you expect out of your college experience?
- What qualities make you special?

Activate Your Self-Esteem

Use the two aspects of building your self-esteem to move yourself toward an important school-related goal for this semester. Make your goal as specific as possible, for example, "I want to find a job that allows me to work at night and still have time to study for my day classes."

Your goal:

Think Positive. What positive thoughts about yourself and your abilities will help you achieve your goal? List them here:

_____

_____

_____

_____

_____

Take Action. Be specific about the actions you will take to back up your positive thoughts and achieve your goal. List them here:

_____

_____

_____

_____

_____

The last step is up to you: Just do it.

Facing Your Fears[5]

One valuable solution to any fear is to let go of the need to be perfect (which often prevents people from doing anything at all) and do something. The easiest way to do this is to break the task into manageable units and do one step at a time. First, think of an activity you have been postponing because of fear (fear of success, of failure, of the task, of perfectionism). Describe it here.

_____

Now list four small activities that would get you closer to working through that fear. If you don't want to start a major project, for example, you could read a book on the subject, brainstorm what you already know about it, or just write one page about it.

1. _____

2. _____

3. _____

4. _____

Commit yourself to one small step that you will take within the next two days. State it here.

_____

List the time you will begin the activity and how much time you will spend doing it.

What reward will you give yourself for having taken that step?

After taking the step, describe how it felt.

Affirm that you have taken that first step and are on the way to success by signing your name here and writing the date. Use the success strategies from the text to make sure you continue on the road toward conquering your fear.

Signature _____   Date_____

Teamwork
Combining Forces

Motivators Gather in a group of three to five students. Each person should take out a blank sheet of paper and write at the top what he or she thinks is his or her biggest motivation problem, that is, the situation or thing that most often kills that person's motivation. Don't include names on the pages. When everyone is done, each person should pass his or her page to the person to the left. On the page you receive, you should list one idea you have about fighting the particular motivation problem that is at the top of the page. Again, when everyone is done, pass the pages to the left. Continue until your page comes back to you.

Then, discuss the ideas together. Offer thoughts about which ideas might work better than others. Add other ideas to the list if you think of them. You may want to type up everyone's lists together so that each group member has a copy. You may also want to share your ideas with the class if you have time.

Writing
Discovery Through Journaling

To record your thoughts, use a separate journal or the lined pages at the end of the chapter.

Your Diverse World Describe a person who is different from you in some way with whom you interact. What have you learned from your relationship with this person? What is positive about spending time with him or her? What is negative? What is positive or negative about spending time with people who seem very similar to you?

Career Portfolio
Charting Your Course

Setting Career Goals Whether you have a current career, have held a few different jobs, or have not yet entered the workplace, college is an ideal time to take stock of your career goals. Even if you won't enter the workplace for a few years, now is not too early to consider what you might like to do after you have finished school. The earlier in your college education that you consider your career goals, the more you can take advantage of how college can help prepare you for work, in both job-specific and general ways.

Take some time to think about your working life. Spend a half-hour or so brainstorming everything that you wish you could be, do, have, or experience in your career. Either list your wishes on a blank piece of paper, draw them, depict them using cutouts from magazines, or combine these ideas—whatever you like best.

Here are some wish categories for you to consider, each with a few examples:

Career areas	Teaching elementary school Computer engineering Health-related career
Benefits	Day care Health insurance
Travel	Public transportation commute Opportunities to work on the road
Finances	Primary household income Secondary supplementary income
Family and relationships	Work days so I can spend evenings with family Work nights so I can be a parent during the day
Experiences	Work with people A job that involves travel Work with technology High-energy workplace Work solo from my home
Schedule	Full-time Part-time Flextime

> Performance counts!
>
> Once you begin to interview for your job after college, or a new job if you're changing careers, you will need to have a portfolio of information showing the quality of how you think and your ability to perform over time. These exercises are designed to help you create that portfolio.

Now look at your list. You probably have a wide variety of details. To discover how your wishes relate to one another, group them in order of priority. Take three pieces of paper and label them Priority 1, Priority 2, and Priority 3. Write each wish on the piece of paper where it fits, with Priority 1 being the most important, Priority 2 the second most important, and Priority 3 the third.

Look at your priority lists. What do they tell you about what is most important to you? What wishes are you ready to work toward right now? Circle three high-priority wishes that you want to achieve with your entry into a new career.

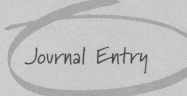

Journal Entry

Name _____   Date _____

Journal Entry

Name _____ Date _____

CONTACT

Resources
Making the Most of Your Environment

In this chapter, you will explore answers to the following questions:
- What resources are available at your school?
- What should you know about technology?
- Why is academic integrity important?

When you enroll as a student, you are joining a community. As part of that community, you have a wide range of organizations, people, and other resources that can help you navigate your educational experience. This chapter's discussion of resources and technology will give you an overview of what is available to you. A community, though, is not just a one-way street. You also have obligations to that community. Maintaining academic integrity is one way that you can fulfill your role as a community member.

Teaching Tip
The most helpful Web site for this chapter is operated by your school. Give students the site's Internet address and ask them to explore what it offers.

WHAT RESOURCES ARE AVAILABLE AT YOUR SCHOOL?

Resources help you make the most of your education. As a student, you are investing money and time. Whether you complete your studies over the course of 6 months or 60 years, resources can help you get where you want to go. It is up to you to track down the resources that you need. As ready as your school is to help you, people may not always reach out to you directly. Be vocal in requesting services and diligent in finding resources.

On pages 30–31 you will find Table 2.1, which is a general summary of resources, most or all of which can be found at your school. Most schools offer a student orientation, near the time you begin your first semester, that will explain resources and other important information. If none is offered, you can orient yourself. Helpful resources include people, administrative offices, student services, organizations, and literature (course catalogs and student handbooks).

People

Your school has an array of people who can help you make the most of your educational experience: instructors, teaching assistants, administrative personnel, and advisors and counselors. They are there to help you. Take the opportunity to get to know them and to let them get to know you. Together you can explore ways in which they can help you achieve your goals.

Instructors

Instructors are more than just sources of information during scheduled class time. They can clarify course material or homework and advise you on course selection in their departments. An instructor who knows you well may even introduce you to prospective employers or give you an excellent job reference. Although this book uses the term "instructor" for simplicity's sake, instructors have official titles that show their rank. From lowest to highest, these include lecturer, instructor, assistant professor, associate professor, and full professor (often just called professor).

Instructors have many responsibilities outside of teaching. They work to stay on the cutting edge of their fields and are often expected to publish articles and books. They prepare lectures and class plans and read stacks of student work. Sometimes they are students themselves. You can gain access to your instructors, however, while still respecting the demands on their time. Most instructors keep office hours and will tell you the office location and times they are available. You are responsible for seeking out your instructor during office hours. If your schedule makes this impossible, let your instructor know and perhaps you can schedule another time to meet. If your school has an electronic mail (e-mail) system that allows you to send messages by computer, you may be able to communicate with your instructor using e-mail.

Resources

People, organizations, or services that supply help and support for different aspects of college life.

Real World Link

At many schools, e-mail is changing the way students and instructors communicate. E-mail allows instructors to distribute course requirements, homework, and comments on papers and lab work. It enables students to raise questions about homework and to clarify material covered in the text or class. The give and take between instructors and students is not dependent on office hours.

An instructor and student confer on a paper at an Austin, Texas community college.

Teaching Assistants

Teaching assistants are people who help an instructor with a course. You may or may not have teaching assistants in your courses. Often they are studying to be instructors themselves. Sometimes they teach the small discussion or lab sections that accompany a large group lecture. They can be a great resource for help and advice, and they are often available if your instructor is too swamped to talk to you.

Administrators

Members of your school's *administrative staff* have the responsibility to deliver to you—the student consumer—a first-rate product. That product is the sum total of your education, comprising facilities, instructors, materials, and courses. Figure 2.1 shows a basic illustration of a college's administrative hierarchy. Smaller units of organization—schools and departments—also have their own administrative structure. Each school or division normally has its own dean, and each department has a *chair* or *chairperson*—one instructor named as head of that department. Your catalog or handbook should describe your school's particular chain of command.

E-mail your professor or teaching assistant about something from class that needs further clarification. Have a chat about the issue so that you can make sure you understand it. Remember, you are paying for your education, so take as much initiative as you can with your teaching assistants and professors.

Administrative Structure   FIGURE 2.1

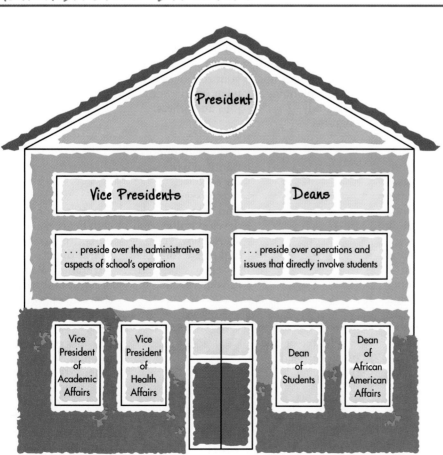

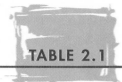

TABLE 2.1 How Resources Can Help You

RESOURCE	ACADEMIC ASSISTANCE	FINANCIAL ASSISTANCE	JOB/CAREER ASSISTANCE	PERSONAL ASSISTANCE
Instructors	Choosing classes, clarifying course material, helping with assignments, dealing with study issues		Can tell you about their fields, may be a source of networking contacts	During office hours, are available to talk to you
Administrators	Academic problems, educational focus, problems with school services		Can be a source of valuable contacts	Can help you sort through personal problems with instructors or other school employees
Academic Advisors	Choosing, changing, or dropping courses; getting over academic hurdles; selecting/changing a major		Can advise you on what job opportunities may go along with your major or academic focus	
Personal Counselors	Can help when personal problems get in the way of academic success	Services may be free or offered on a "sliding scale," depending on what you can afford		Help with all kinds of personal problems
Financial Aid Office		Information and counseling on loans, grants, scholarships, financial planning, work-study programs	Information on job opportunities within your school environment (work-study jobs and others)	
Academic Centers	Help with what the center specializes in (reading, writing, math)		Perhaps an opportunity to work at the center	
Organizations and Clubs	If an academic club, can broaden your knowledge or experience in an area of study; can help you balance school with other enriching activities		Can help you develop skills, build knowledge, and make new contacts that may serve you in your working life	Depending on the club focus, can be an outlet for stress, a source of personal inspiration, a source of important friendships, an opportunity to help others
Wellness/Fitness Center(s)		Usually free or low cost to enrolled students		Provides opportunity to build fitness and reduce stress; may have weight room, track, aerobic or dance classes, martial arts, team sports, exercise machines, etc.

How Resources Can Help You (continued)

TABLE 2.1

RESOURCE	ACADEMIC ASSISTANCE	FINANCIAL ASSISTANCE	JOB/CAREER ASSISTANCE	PERSONAL ASSISTANCE
Bulletin Boards	List academic events, class information, changes and additions to schedules, office hours, academic club meetings	List financial aid seminars, job opportunities, scholarship opportunities	List career forums, job sign-ups, and employment opportunities; offer a place for you to post a message if you are marketing a service	List support group meetings
Housing and Transportation Office		Can help find the most financially beneficial travel or housing plan		Can help commuters with parking, bus or train service, and permits; can help with finding on- or off-campus housing
Career Planning and Placement Office		Can help add to your income through job opportunities	Job listings, help with résumés and interviews, possible interview appointments, factual information about the workplace (job trends, salaries, etc.)	
Tutors	One-on-one help with academic subjects; assistance with specific assignments		If you decide to become a tutor, a chance to find out if teaching and working with people is for you	
Student Health Office		May provide low-cost or no-cost health care to enrolled students; may offer reduced-cost prescription plan		Wellness care (regular examinations), illness care, hospital and specialist referrals, and prescriptions
Adult Education Center	Academic help tailored to the returning adult student	May have specific financial aid advice	May have job listings or other help with coordinating work and classes	May offer child-care assistance and opportunities to get to know other returning adult students
Support Groups and Hotlines	If school-related, they offer a chance to hear how others have both stumbled and succeeded in school—and a chance to share your story			Personal help with whatever the hotline or support group specializes in; a chance to talk to someone whose job is to listen
School Publications	Academic news and course changes	News about financial aid opportunities or work-study programs	Job listings, information about the workplace and the job market	Articles and announcements about topics that may help you

Although students don't often have regular interaction with administrators, it is the business of administrative personnel to know how the school is serving you. If you have an issue that you haven't been able to resolve on your own, such as a conflict with an instructor, an inability to get into a class you need, or a school regulation that causes a problem for you, schedule a meeting with your dean or department chair. As a bonus, if you develop a positive relationship with an administrator, he or she may offer valuable support down the line.

Advisors and Counselors

Advisors and counselors can help with both the educational and personal sides of being a student. They provide information, advice, a listening ear, referrals, and other sources of help. Generally, students are assigned academic advisors with whom they meet at least once a semester. Your academic advisor will help you find out about classes, choose a schedule, and explore and select a **major.** Visit your academic advisor more than once a semester if you have questions or want to make scheduling changes.

Personal counselors, although not usually assigned, are available through student services or student health. Don't hesitate to seek a counselor's help if you have something on your mind. Life crises can wreak havoc on your schoolwork. If you put some effort into working through personal problems, you will be more able to do your work well and hand it in on time. Occasionally, an illness or family difficulty may interfere enough with your schoolwork to call for special provisions for the completion of your classes. Most colleges are very willing to assist you during challenging times.

Administrative Offices

As a student, you will be dealing with administrative offices that are part of your college, including the registrar's office, the bursar's office, and the financial aid office.

The registrar's office manages student registration and transcripts. When you register for courses, employees in the registrar's office try to make sure that you receive the courses you requested. They also send you your grades at the end of the semester. When you have a problem with course registration or need a copy of your transcript (comprehensive record of your college courses and grades), visit the registrar's office for help.

The bursar's office (cashier) manages the university's monetary transactions. The head of this office is called the *bursar.* The bursar's office issues bills for tuition and/or room and board and manages the collection of payments from students and financial aid sources. Employees of the bursar's office should be able to help you if you have questions about your bill or need to make any payments.

The financial aid office manages how students seek and implement sources of financial aid. The three main sources of financial aid are student loans (usually issued by the government, based on varying criteria, and requiring

Major
A subject of academic study chosen as a field of specialization, requiring specific coursework.

Learning Styles Tip
A personal counselor may be able to help students handle learning styles issues. A knowledgeable counselor will recommend strategies for dealing with instructors' varied teaching styles and for maximizing study time.

Career Connection
The registrar's office also issues official transcripts to prospective employers.

repayment), grants (also issued by the government, based on financial need, not requiring repayment), and scholarships (awarded to students who show talent or ability in the area specified by the scholarship, financed by government or private organizations, schools, or individuals). Because most sources of financial aid don't seek out recipients, you need to consult the financial aid office to find out how you can finance your education. You will read more about financial aid in Chapter 11.

> "I have always thought that one man of tolerable abilities may work great changes,
>
> and accomplish great affairs among mankind, if he first forms a good plan."
>
> Benjamin Franklin

Student Services

Your school has a variety of *services* aimed at helping students. Basic services offered by almost every school include academic advising and personal counseling, student health/wellness, career planning and placement, tutoring, and fitness/physical education. Depending on your school, you may also find other services: housing and transportation, adult education services (for adults returning to school), disabled student services, academic centers (writing center, math center, etc., for help with these specific subjects), various support groups, and school publications that help keep you informed.

Often a school will have special services for specific populations. For example, if you attend a school where most students commute, a transportation office will help students locate bus schedules and routes, find parking and sign up for permits, or track down car pools. Similarly, at a school where many students are parents, a child-care center may provide day care during class time and also refer students to off-campus babysitters. You will find additional details about school services in Table 2.1. They can help you earn the maximum benefit from your educational experience.

Teaching Tip
The career planning and placement office also helps undergraduates find summer jobs, internships, and part-time work. It may also connect students to alumni who work in careers about which students want to learn more.

Organizations

No matter what your needs or interests, your school probably has an *organization* that will satisfy them. Some organizations are sponsored by the school (academic clubs); some are independent but have a branch at the school (government ROTC programs); and some are student-run organizations (Latino Student Association). Some organizations focus on courses of study (Nursing Club); some are primarily social (fraternities and sororities); some are artistic (Chamber Orchestra); and some are geared toward a hobby or activity (Runner's Club). Some you join to help others (Big Brothers or Big Sisters); and some offer help to you (Overeaters Anonymous).

When you consider adding a new activity to your life, weigh its positive effects against the negative ones. Positive effects could be new friends, enjoyable activities, help, a break from schoolwork, stress relief, improved academic performance, increased teamwork and leadership skills, aid to others, and experiences that broaden your horizons. On the negative side there may be a heavy time commitment, dues, inconvenient locations or meeting times, or too much responsibility. Explore any club carefully to see if it makes sense for you. As you make your decision, consider this: Studies have shown that students who join organizations tend to persist in their educational goals more than those who don't branch out.[1]

e-mail

E-mail several friends who are attending college and ask them about the organizations they belong to, or would like to belong to. What are the pros and cons? How did they decide what organizations to devote time to?

To find out about organizations at your school, consult your student handbook, ask friends and instructors, or check the activities office if your school has one. During registration, different organizations may set up tables and offer information to interested students. Some organizations seek you out, based on your achievements. When you explore any organization, ask what is expected in terms of time, responsibility, and any necessary financial commitment. Talk to students who are currently involved. Perhaps give the group a test run to see if you like it.

If you try out an organization, make a decision that you will stay in it only for the right reasons. Don't be afraid of being labeled a "dropout"; if something becomes more than you can handle, bow out gracefully. In the best of all possible worlds, your involvement in organizations will enrich your life, expand your network of acquaintances, boost your time-management skills, and help you achieve goals.

An Army recruiter talks to a student at a job fair.

Literature

Two publications can help you find your way through course offerings, department and resource offices, and the campus layout—the college catalog and the student handbook. Most schools provide these materials as a standard part of their enrollment information.

FIGURE 2.2 *College Catalog Page*

Source: Baltimore City Community College 1998–2000 Catalog (BCCC, Division of Planning and Advancement, 1996), 158.

Course Descriptions

ENG 106: Creative Writing (Poetry) (3 credits)

45 lecture hours
Fall
Prerequisite: ENG 101

This course provides practice and constructive criticism in the composition of poetry through class discussion and presentation, individual conferences, and class review of student manuscripts. Readings and analyses of contemporary poets are included.

ENG 107: Creative Writing (Fiction) (3 credits)

45 lecture hours
Spring
Prerequisite: ENG 101

Practice and instruction in the writing of fiction, emphasizing the short story are offered. Class discussions provide analysis, criticism, and helpful information on the writing and marketing of fiction manuscripts.

ENG 112: Medical Writing (3 credits)

45 lecture hours
Fall, Spring - day, eve
Prerequisite: ENG 101

The principles and processes us tion of selected materials typica ical settings are presented. Th the composition of specific clear, straightforward langu priate to modern medic

ENG 113: Busin

45 lecture hour
Fall, Spring -
Prerequisit

The
tion
ne

course emphasizes the composition of sp nical reports in clear, straightfoward la formats appropiate to modern techr standards.

ENG 175: Writing for Teach

45 lecture hours
Offered by contract for Bo
System teachers

Teachers and ot
with a thorough
the kinds of
the job. Stu
exercises
ing and
activi
inp
r

The *college catalog* is your school's academic directory. It lists every department and course available at the school. Each course name will generally have two parts, for example, EN101 or CHEM205. The first part is one or more letters indicating the department and subject matter, and the second part is a number indicating the course level (lower numbers for introductory courses and higher numbers for more advanced ones). The catalog groups courses according to subject matter and lists them from the lowest level courses to the most advanced, indicating the number of credits earned for each class. See Figure 2.2 for a segment of an actual college catalog from Baltimore City Community College. A course book released prior to each semester will indicate details such as the instructor, the days the course meets, the time of day, the location (building and room), and the maximum number of students who can take the course.

Your college catalog contains a wealth of other information. It may give general school policies such as admissions requirements, the registration process, and withdrawal procedures. It may list the departments to show the range of subjects you may study. It may outline instructional programs, detailing core requirements as well as requirements for various majors, degrees, and certificates. It may also list administrative personnel as well as faculty and staff for each department. The college catalog is an important resource in planning your academic career. When you have a question, consult the catalog before you look elsewhere.

Your *student handbook* looks beyond specific courses to the big picture, helping you to navigate student life. In it you will find some or all of the following, and maybe more: information on available housing (for on-campus residents) and on parking and driving (for commuters); overviews of the support offices for students, such as academic advising, counseling, career planning and placement, student health, financial aid, and individual centers for academic subject areas; descriptions of special interest clubs; and details about library and computer services. It may also list hours, locations, phone numbers, and addresses for offices, clubs, and organizations.

Real World Link
An increasing number of colleges are putting valuable information for students on the college's Web site. Encourage students to spend time on their own computer or at the school's computer lab looking at the site to discover what it contains and how it can help them.

Your student handbook will also describe important policies such as how to add or drop a class, what the grading system means, campus rules, drug and alcohol policies, what kinds of records your school keeps, safety tips, and more. Keep your student handbook where you can find it easily, in your study area at home or someplace safe at school. It can save you a lot of trouble when you need to find information about a resource or service.

WHAT SHOULD YOU KNOW ABOUT TECHNOLOGY?

As the world continues to become more technologically complicated, computers have taken on an increasingly important role. In almost every job, basic computer knowledge is a necessity. The use of computers in composing letters, desktop publishing, maintaining databases, keeping spreadsheets, working on the Internet, communicating by **e-mail,** and numerous other tasks will make computer literacy a requirement in the job market.

E-mail
Electronic mail sent from computer to computer through systems that provide the electronic connection.

More immediately, computers play a role in your current student life. Computers regulate your class schedule and keep a record of your tuition payments. Computer centers on campus provide an opportunity for students to type papers, work on assignments, take tests, log lab results, and send e-mail to instructors and fellow students. You may even have your own personal computer on which you do schoolwork and manage your personal schedule or finances. See Figure 2.3 for some statistics on information technology on campus.

Technology Strategies

Explore the ways in which you can make the most of the technology available to you.

Know what you want. People have different technology needs and wants. Some want to know the inner workings of how computers operate and look forward to a career in programming or computer systems. Others only want to use technology as a tool to achieve a goal, for example, to write articles, to make financial calculations, or to design graphics.

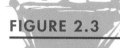

FIGURE 2.3 *College Technology Statistics*

Classes using the Internet

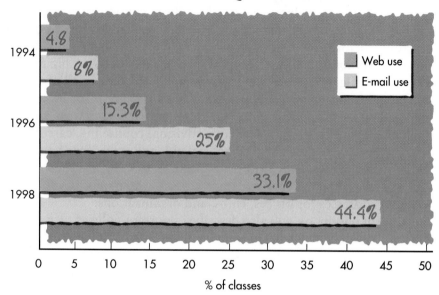

Source: The 1998 National Survey of Information Technology in Higher Education.

Colleges requiring students to take computer classes or fulfill a competency requirement

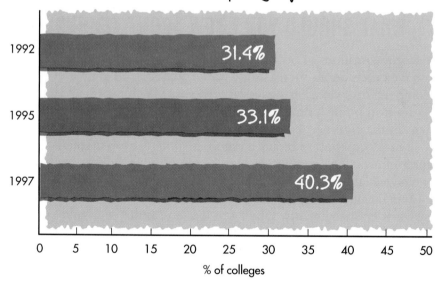

Source: The 1997 National Survey of Information Technology in Higher Education.

Get training. Once you know what you need, give yourself a chance to learn. If you want to focus on programming, look into courses that will earn you a degree in that area. If you will use a computer for other goals, look for software training programs, school-sponsored short courses, or computer learning centers. A typing course can be extremely useful.

Investigate your school's systems. Each school has its own particular systems. Find out what computers are available, when and where you can use them, what software they have, when and how to print your work, and any other policies of your school's computer rooms.

Save, back up, and back up some more. First, save your work onto hard drive or disk every few minutes—you never know when a power outage might mean that you lose everything you did in the last hour. Second, always back up (copy) your work in a location other than the computer's hard drive, such as on a 3.5-inch diskette or a Zip disk. You can never be too safe.

Computer Use

The basics in computer use fall into four general categories: word processing, databases and spreadsheets, the Internet, and e-mail. You will probably encounter most of these uses, if not all, in your college career and beyond.

Word Processing

The ability to use a computer to write papers, assignments, letters, and so on is now a requirement at most institutes of higher learning. Many businesses also require the use of these skills. Most word-processing software programs share basic features, although each has its own quirks. Two of the most commonly used are Microsoft Word and WordPerfect. Besides composing documents, features such as spell check and revision markings (showing you where you have made changes in a document) can be extremely useful.

Databases and Spreadsheets

The ability to organize and store large volumes of information and data has always been important in many businesses. The easiest way to do this is through the use of computer software for managing a **database** or **spreadsheet.** Again, there are many software programs specifically designed to handle, organize, and analyze large volumes of information. Some of the more common programs are Lotus 1-2-3, Symphony, Microsoft Excel, and Quicken. Knowing how to use one or more of these may help you get a good job—and even manage your personal finances.

The Internet

The Internet is a worldwide computer network that connects businesses, universities, governments, and people by transmitting information over phone and other data-transfer lines. Much of the information on the Internet is displayed on "Web pages" or "Web sites," individual locations in cyberspace developed by companies, organizations, or individuals. Together, these sites are referred to as the World Wide Web. The Internet links you to information from around the world. You can now do extensive research on any topic as well as buy, sell, and market products on the Internet. The following information will help you to make the most of your time on line.

Search directories and search engines. Usually, you will use one of these two systems to locate information or Web sites. A *search directory* is an index of Web sites that allows you to search for topics using keywords. By contrast, a *search engine* searches for keywords through the entire Internet—news-

Learning Styles Tip
Word processing programs automatically format letters and other documents, create outlines and headings, incorporate graphics, among other features. Easy access to graphics helps students with visual-spatial intelligence present material in a "comfortable" way.

Database
A collection of data organized by computer so that you can quickly organize, store, and retrieve it.

Spreadsheet
A ledger layout, usually found in an accounting program, that allows the user to list and calculate numerical data.

groups, Web sites, and other resources—instead of just Web sites. When searching, you might want to start with a search directory before moving to a search engine, since search directory results may be more manageable (search engines can produce a huge number of "hits"—occurrences of your keyword). Try search directories Yahoo or Galaxy, and search engines AltaVista or HotBot.

On-line "addresses." Just as people have mailing addresses, people and information on-line have "addresses" as well. These are strings of text and numerals called URLs (Universal Resource Locators). You can type in a URL to access a specific site. On any given Web site you might also find a *hyperlink*—a URL that appears underlined and in a highlighted color—that you can click on to go directly to the location it lists. Some locations will have files that you can download over the Internet, for free or for a fee, depending on the file.

Connecting with others. Through chat rooms and newsgroups, people can interact with each other on line. *Chat rooms* are Internet locations where people can type messages to each other in real time—messages appear immediately after they are typed and sent. Chat rooms are often set up to focus on a particular topic of interest. *Usenet,* the system of *newsgroups,* is a series of "bulletin boards" where users can type in messages and "post" them on the newsgroup. Then other users can read postings and respond to them. Like chat rooms, newsgroups focus on individual topics.

Getting help. If you need help learning about the Internet, don't hesitate to ask a librarian, fellow student, or tutor to show you the ropes. Some schools may have tutorials that can help you learn to navigate. Many Web sites will also have FAQs—"Frequently Asked Questions" pages—that may answer any questions you have about the information on, or the navigation of, that particular site.

Distance learning. The technology of the Internet has also helped to bring distance learning to the forefront. *Distance learning* refers to courses that happen without the teacher and students having to gather in the same location—interaction occurs through any combination of phone, Internet, e-mail, fax, videotape, audiotape, and teleconferencing. Distance learning is a great alternative for students who, for whatever reason, don't have the freedom or flexibility to attend classes at a remote location and/or on a particular schedule. Distance learning also affords students the freedom to attend class and complete assignments at their own pace and on their own time.

It's important for anyone involved in distance learning to be aware of their increased responsibility. When you take a distance learning course, no one tells you what to do and when to do it. You are responsible for setting your own time line for taking in information and completing assignments. Dr. Sally Johnstone, Director of the Western Cooperative for Educational Telecommunications at WICHE (Western Interstate Commission for Higher Education), says, "Distance learning . . . is for people who understand what they need and how they learn, and who recognize that no one's going to be sitting over their shoulder and demanding that they pay attention. They have to be self-motivated. They would rather be strategic, and work directly in the mode or in the environment they choose."

How can I connect to my university community?

Ruth Ham, Dallas Theological Seminary, Dallas, Texas, Christian Education Major

Before I came to Texas, I studied English in my native home of Bangkok, Thailand. Now, I am finding that the classes I took there, such as English poetry, were interesting but not very practical. The language barrier has made it difficult for me to get to know people.

I am ashamed of my English. If someone asks me a direct question, I will answer the best I can, but I don't seek out conversations with English-speaking students. I have found it very hard to make friends. Instead of seeing  people as people, I am always aware that they are different. If a student sits next to me in class and doesn't greet me, I feel hurt. I know I could also say hello, but it's very hard for me to take that first step. Sharing my ideas with other people is also very hard for me, so I usually stay quiet during class discussions.

One thing that has helped is joining the international students club. I've met other students who are also struggling to feel like they belong. We practice our English together. I've also found that my English has improved by writing my thoughts in a journal in English. It would be nice to find an American friend who has the time to help me with my English. One thing I notice here, though, is that people seem to always be in a hurry. I want to be more involved at school than just going to class. What else can I do to feel more a part of my school?

Hiromi Kodakehara, University of Nebraska, Omaha, Nebraska

I had to take English for six years in school in Japan, but I couldn't speak it well at all.

When I got to the United States, I was ashamed of my English. In my ESL (English as a Second Language) program in Omaha, not many Americans paid attention to me or to any international students. The only time I spoke English was when I was in class or when I was with my teachers.

One day, I realized: "I am Japanese, and of course I cannot speak English well. Why am I so worried about it? I can talk and act like I am an international student."  This helped me to think positively and start reaching out to people. Fortunately, my school has a program called Conversation Partners, established by American volunteers to help international students improve their English. My school also had a homestay program, where registered American families would take in international students for two weeks. These two programs helped me to improve my English and to make some good friends. My friends told me that they respected my learning a foreign language. They would say, "Your English is much better than my Japanese."

I am sure your school has international student advisors who can help you find an organization that helps international students. There probably are also nonprofit organizations in your city that want to help foreign students get used to American culture and people. Through their events and activities, you can make American friends, practice your English, and eventually feel more comfortable talking to Americans. There are, of course, some people who ignore international students, but there are also many Americans who want to be friends but don't know how. Remember that you don't have to speak perfect English. You can be proud of living in the United States, taking regular classes with American students, and keeping up with them.

E-mail

The ability to send electronic mail, or e-mail, is changing the way people communicate. Through e-mail, students and instructors exchange ideas and assignments, coworkers send questions and gather information, and friends and family keep in touch. E-mail is sent instantly at a touch of a button and is received almost immediately after being sent.

If your college has an e-mail system, you may be required to communicate with your instructor on e-mail, submit homework via e-mail, and even take exams via e-mail. You might also have e-mail at home or at your workplace. To learn about e-mail, many schools offer orientation sessions. Every student who has access to e-mail should spend time becoming proficient in electronic communication.

Following are three e-mail cautions:

Be careful of miscommunication. Body language (vocal tone, facial expression, body position) can account for over 75 percent of what you communicate in a face-to-face conversation. With e-mail, however, words communicate on their own. Therefore, you should be especially careful about how you word your communications. Choose words carefully, be diplomatic and pleasant, and try to think before you respond to an e-mail that upsets you. If you write back too quickly, it is easy to "flame" someone, that is, to write an angry, emotional, or accusatory e-mail. If you take your time responding, chances are your message will be more effective.

Teaching Tip
To write an effective e-mail: (1) get to the point in the first paragraph; (2) use short paragraphs; (3) use headings to divide long e-mails into digestible sections; (4) use numbered and bulleted lists; and (5) send separate e-mails for different messages.

Use effective writing techniques. Your e-mail messages tell a lot about you. To make the best impression—especially when communicating with an instructor or employer—use words carefully to express exactly what you want to say. Organize your thoughts and use proper spelling and grammar.

Rein in social e-mailing. Prioritize your e-mailing. Respond to the most important and time-sensitive requests first—especially school- or work-related ones—and save personal and conversational e-mail for when you have more time.

WHY IS ACADEMIC INTEGRITY IMPORTANT?

Integrity
Adherence to a code of moral values; incorruptibility, honesty.

Integrity is at the heart of your actions as a member of your academic community as well as of other communities such as your workplace and family. Having academic integrity means acting with integrity in all aspects of your academic life: classes, assignments, tests, papers, labs, projects, and relations with students and faculty.

Following the Standards

The fine points of the definition of academic integrity may vary from school to school, but the general principles usually include the following forbidden actions:

- Plagiarism (copying of the words, ideas, or structure of another person's work and claiming it as your own)

- Cheating on tests by referring to materials, or using devices, that are not authorized by the instructor (e.g., looking at a test that a friend has taken in a section of a course that meets a few hours before your own)

- Submitting work that you have already submitted elsewhere, such as in another class or at a previous school

- Getting help with a project on which you are supposed to be working alone

- Altering your academic record without authorization

- Misusing library materials (taking materials without checking them out, keeping materials late, removing materials that are not permitted to be removed, damaging materials)

- Ignoring copyright restrictions on computer software

- Providing unethical aid to another student by allowing your work to be copied, helping a student cheat on a test, aiding a student on an independent project, selling your work or tests

"The very spring and root of honesty and virtue lie in good education."

Plutarch

Pay special attention to this last item. Even if you are not the one cheating or copying, you will violate your academic integrity just as much if you aid another student in an activity that you know is not permitted.

Your School's Code

Explore your school's specific requirements. Your school's code of honor, or academic integrity policy, should be printed in your student handbook. Read it to be sure you know what is expected of you. As a student enrolled in your school, you have agreed to abide by that policy.

You have also agreed to suffer the consequences should you be discovered violating any of your school's academic integrity policies. Different schools have different methods of dealing with alleged violations. Most every school brings the student before a committee of instructors or perhaps a 'jury' of other students to determine whether the offense has actually taken place. What happens to a student found guilty varies from school to school. The University of Virginia, for example, expels any student found guilty of an honor code violation. North Carolina State University requires some students to participate in an academic integrity seminar. Other schools use suspension, grade reduction, or course failure, depending on the offense.

The Effects of Academic Integrity

Maintaining an image of academic integrity will certainly help you pass your classes and graduate. But the effects of living with integrity can be life altering and wide ranging, involving far more than a few good grades on tests and papers. Having academic integrity can positively affect the following:

Your behavior patterns. When you are used to doing what's right, you set a pattern that will follow you on the job and in your personal relationships. The more you condition yourself to play fair now, the more you will be able to do so later. Any work environment will value someone who follows the rules, cares about others, is honest, and is responsible.

Your knowledge level. Sure, if you cheat on a test you might pass the test—and the course. But what do you remember after you receive your final grades? The point of being in college is to learn information and skills that you will be able to use long after you graduate. Retaining knowledge leads to retaining jobs.

Your interaction with others. When you act with academic integrity, you show respect to others, such as instructors who assign tests and papers, fellow students who work hard to learn, and administrators who design the systems. In turn, you earn trust and respect from them, which may lead to companionship and opportunities. Also, you will condition yourself to behave with integrity on the job, allowing you to form fruitful interactions with coworkers, supervisors, and employees.

Your self-esteem. Remember that self-esteem is tied to action. The more you act in ways that you and others know are respectful and honorable, the better you will feel about yourself. The better you feel about yourself, the more you will be able to succeed.

Above all, you are responsible for your own integrity. You can choose actions that will build your confidence, your ability, your knowledge, your respectability, and your reputation, and you will stand or fall based on those choices. Make choices that will serve you well.

Atii

Inuktitut is the traditional language of the Inuit, formerly known as the Eskimo people, who live in central and eastern arctic Canada. The Inuit have at least 40 different words that describe different forms of snow and ice. Over the centuries, they have adapted their language and their lifestyle to suit the resources available to them. They make the most of their world, living successfully and contentedly in a climate that most others would find forbidding.

Atii is an Inuktitut word that means "let's go." Think of the Inuit when you consider the resources all around you in your student life. Take the initiative to name them, explore them, know them, and use them. The energy you put out to explore your world will be returned to you in benefits from your resources. *Atii!*

Name _____ Date _____

BUILDING SKILLS FOR COLLEGE, CAREER, AND LIFE SUCCESS

Critical Thinking
Applying Learning to Life

Broadening Your Horizons

Outside of an education in your chosen field, what do you want out of being in school? What else would you like to explore, learn, or develop? Brainstorm a list of five ideas here.

1. _____
2. _____
3. _____
4. _____
5. _____

Next to each of your ideas, write down one resource that you think will help you explore it.

Finally, write the steps you will take to explore the idea that seems most important to you so far.

_____
_____
_____
_____

Your Technology Needs

As a student, and perhaps even as an employee if you currently work, you need some level of technological knowledge. First, brainstorm a list of all the encounters you have with technology in a normal week.

_____
_____
_____
_____

Next, indicate your technology needs as you currently see them. Do you want to use technology as a tool, or are you interested in delving further into it as a career?

Finally, considering your needs and the technology available to you, write down what technology resources you plan to use at school and at work (e-mail, computer rooms, technology courses, etc.). Be specific—investigate what is available and when, and indicate how you plan to use the resources you name.

Teamwork
Combining Forces

Who Can Help You? Every school is unique and offers its own particular range of opportunities. Investigate your school. Use the resource table (Table 2.1, p. 30) as a guide, and explore your student handbook. Make a check mark by the resources that you think will be most helpful to you.

_____ Advisors and counselors	_____ Adult education center
_____ Library/media center	_____ Support groups/hotlines
_____ Instructors	_____ Career/job placement office
_____ Clubs/organizations	_____ Administration
_____ Bulletin boards	_____ Academic centers
_____ Student health center	_____ School publications
_____ Housing and transportation	_____ Tutoring
_____ Wellness/fitness centers	_____ Financial aid office

Gather in small groups; or if you have a small class, work as one large group together. Each member of each group should choose one or more different resources (make sure no two people within a group explore the same resource). Be sure all resources on the grid on pages 46–47 are accounted for. Then, each group member will investigate his or her resources and fill in the information on the grid, answering the questions listed across the top. The three blank spaces at the bottom are for you to use if you find resources not listed here.

After each person has completed his or her investigation, meet again to exchange information and fill in the information on the grid. You now have a resource guide that you can refer to at any time. Write here the three resources that you feel will benefit you the most and how you will use them.

1. _____
   _____
   _____
   _____

2. _____
   _____
   _____
   _____

3. _____
   _____
   _____
   _____

Writing
Discovery Through Journaling

To record your thoughts, use a separate journal or the lined page at the end of the chapter.

Academic Integrity For you, what are the most important principles of academic integrity? Do you feel that acting with academic integrity will help you or not? Discuss how you feel about your school's academic integrity policy (you can probably find it in your student handbook or course catalog).

Career Portfolio
Charting Your Course

Matching Career to Curriculum Your success in most career areas will depend in part on your academic preparation. Some careers, such as medicine, require very specific curriculum choices (e.g., you will have to take a number of biology and chemistry courses to be considered for medical school). Some careers require certain courses that teach basic competencies; for example, to be an accountant, you will have to take accounting and

RESOURCE	WHO PROVIDES IT?	WHERE CAN YOU FIND IT?	WHEN IS IT AVAILABLE?	HOW CAN IT HELP YOU?	HOW DO YOU ASK FOR IT?	PHONE # OR OTHER KEY DETAILS
Administrative help						
Instructor advice						
Academic advising						
Personal counseling						
Financial aid						
Academic centers						
Organizations and clubs						
Bulletin boards						
Housing and transportation						
Career planning and placement						

RESOURCE	WHO PROVIDES IT?	WHERE CAN YOU FIND IT?	WHEN IS IT AVAILABLE?	HOW CAN IT HELP YOU?	HOW DO YOU ASK FOR IT?	PHONE # OR OTHER KEY DETAILS
Tutoring						
Student health						
Adult education center						
Fitness/ Wellness center						
Support groups/ hotlines						
Services for students with disabilities						
English as a Second Language						

Performance counts!

Being strategic about your future is one of the best ways to ensure success. Knowing what is required at any given point—in school and in your career—will help you to achieve your personal best.

bookkeeping. Other career areas, such as many business careers, don't have specific requirements, but employers often look for certain curriculum choices that indicate the mastery of particular skills.

Choose three of the career areas in which you are interested. For each, investigate the curriculum choices that would benefit you or that are required by asking instructors, students on those career tracks, your career planning and placement office, people you know who are employed in these areas, and advisors. Create three lists here—one for each career area—of recommended courses. Write each career in the space at the top of its list. To set off the courses that are absolutely required from those that are simply recommended, mark them with a star.

CAREER AREAS		

COURSES		

Journal Entry

Name _____   Date _____

ASPIRE

ASPIRE

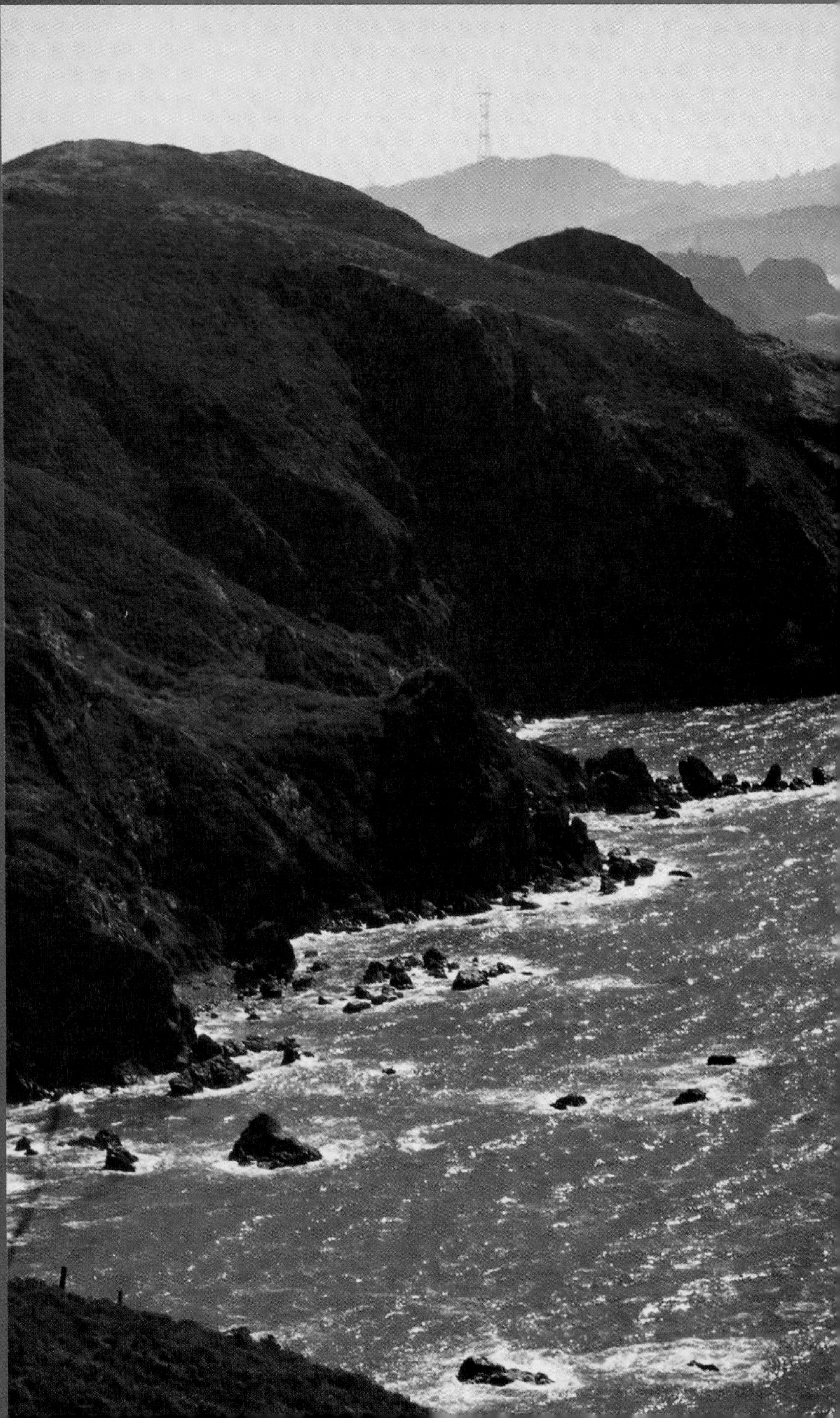

Goal Setting and Time Management

Mapping Your Course

In this chapter, you will explore answers to the following questions:

- What defines your values?
- How do you set and achieve goals?
- What are your priorities?
- How can you manage your time?
- Why is procrastination a problem?

People dream of what they want out of life, but dreams often seem too difficult or completely out of your reach. When you set goals, prioritize, and manage your time effectively, you can develop the kind of "big picture" vision that will help you achieve what you dream. This chapter explains how taking specific steps toward goals can help you turn your dreams into reality. The section on time management will discuss how to translate your goals into daily, weekly, monthly, and yearly steps. Finally, you will explore how procrastination can derail your dreams and how to avoid it.

WHAT DEFINES YOUR VALUES?

Your personal values, for example, family togetherness, a good education, caring for others, and worthwhile employment, are the beliefs that guide your choices. The total of all your values is your value system. You demonstrate your particular value system in the priorities you set, how you communicate with others, your family life, your educational and career choices, and even the material things with which you surround yourself.

Start exploring your values by looking at their sources.

Sources of Values

Values are choices. You are in control of choosing what you value. It may not always seem that way, however, because people often choose values based on what others seem to value. A value system is constructed over time, using information from many different sources, including the following:

- parents, guardians, or relatives
- friends and peers
- religious belief and study
- instructors, supervisors, mentors, and other authority figures
- books, magazines, television, the Internet, and other media
- workplace and school

A particular value may come from one or more sources. For example, a student may value education (primary source: parents), music (primary sources: media and friends), and spiritual life (primary sources: religious leader and grandparents). Another student may have abandoned many of the values that he or she grew up with and adopted the values of a trusted mentor. Still another may find that adopting certain values became important in order to succeed in a particular career area. Being influenced by the values of others is natural, although you should take care to follow what feels right to you.

Choosing and Evaluating Values

Examining the sources of your values can help you define those values, trace their origin, and question the reasons why you have adopted them. Value sources, however, aren't as important as the process of considering each value carefully to see if it makes sense to you. Your individual value system is unique. Your responsibility is to make value choices based on what feels right for you, for your life, and for those involved in your life.

You can be more sure of making choices that are right for you if you try to periodically question and evaluate your values. Ask yourself: Does this value feel right? What effects does it, or might it, have on my life? Am I choosing it to please someone else, or is it truly my choice? Values are a design for life, and you are the one who has to live the life you design.

Life change and new experiences may bring a change in values. From time to time, try to evaluate the effects that each value has on your life and see if a shift in values might suit your changing circumstances. For example, after

Sidebar

Values
Principles or qualities that one considers important, right, or good.

Be a Team
Have students list some of the values they've held for many years and values they've recently adopted. Then, with a partner, encourage them to explore why the old values have remained and why the new values are taking hold.

COMPANION WEBSITE

Teaching Tip
Sometimes it is hard to decide whether values reflect conscious, personal choices or the choices of those with the greatest influence in our lives. The values closest to our heart often reflect the influence of parents and are the most difficult to change.

growing up in a homogeneous town, a student who meets other students from unfamiliar backgrounds may come to value living in a diverse community. Your values will grow and develop as you do if you continue to think them through.

How Values Relate to Goals

Understanding your values will help you set goals because any **goal** can help you achieve what you value. If you value spending time with your family, a related goal may be living near your parents. A value of financial independence may generate goals, such as working part-time and keeping credit card debt low, that reflect this value. If you value helping others, you might make time for volunteer work.

Goals enable you to put values into practice. When you set and pursue goals that are based on values, you demonstrate and reinforce values by taking action. The strength of those values, in turn, reinforces your goals. You will experience a stronger drive to achieve if you build goals around what is most important to you.

Goal
An end toward which effort is directed; an aim or intention.

HOW DO YOU SET AND ACHIEVE GOALS?

A goal can be something as concrete as buying a health insurance plan or as abstract as working to control your temper. When you set goals and work to achieve them, you engage your intelligence, abilities, time, and energy in order to move ahead. From major life decisions to the tiniest day-to-day activities, setting goals will help you define how you want to live and what you want to achieve.

Paul Timm, an expert in self-management, believes that focus is a key ingredient in setting and achieving goals: "Focus adds power to our actions. If somebody threw a bucket of water on you, you'd get wet. . . . But if water was shot at you through a high-pressure nozzle, you might get injured. The only difference is focus."[1] Focus your goal-setting energy by defining a personal mission, placing your goals in long-term and short-term time frames, evaluating goals in terms of your values, and exploring different types of goals.

Learning Styles Tip
A journal is an indispensable goal-setting tool. It is especially valuable for intrapersonal and verbal-linguistic learners. Visual-spatial learners might depict their goals in pictures.

"Obstacles are what people see when they take their eyes off the goal."

New York subway bulletin board

Identifying Your Personal Mission

If you choose not to set goals or explore what you want out of life, you may look back on your past with a sense of emptiness. You may not know what you've done or why you did it. However, you can avoid that emptiness by periodically thinking about where you've been and where you want to be.

One helpful way to determine your general direction is to write a personal mission statement. Dr. Stephen Covey, author of *The Seven Habits of Highly Effective People*, defines a mission statement as a philosophy outlining what you want to be (character), what you want to do (contributions and achievements), and the principles by which you live. Dr. Covey compares the personal mission statement to the Constitution of the United States, a statement of principles that guides the country: "A personal mission statement based on correct principles becomes the same kind of standard for an individual," he says. "It becomes a personal constitution, the basis for making major, life-directing decisions, the basis for making daily decisions in the midst of the circumstances and emotions that affect our lives."[2]

Your personal mission isn't written in stone. It should change as you move from one phase of life to the next—from single person to spouse, from student to working citizen. Stay flexible and reevaluate your personal mission from time to time.

The following personal mission statement was written by Carol Carter, one of the authors of this text.

> My mission is to use my talents and abilities to help people of all ages, stages, backgrounds, and economic levels achieve their human potential through fully developing their minds and their talents. I also aim to balance work with people in my life, understanding that my family and friends are a priority above all else.

A company, like a person, needs to establish standards and principles that guide its many activities. Companies often have mission statements so that each member of the organization clearly understands what to strive for. If a company fails to identify its mission, thousands of well-intentioned employees might focus their energies in just as many different directions, creating chaos and low productivity.

Here is a mission statement from the company that publishes this text:

> To provide the most innovative resources—books, technology, programs—to help students of all ages and stages achieve their academic and professional goals inside the classroom and out.

You will have an opportunity to write your own personal mission statement at the end of this chapter. Thinking through your personal mission can help you begin to take charge of your life. It can put you in control instead of allowing circumstances and events to control you. If you frame your mission statement carefully so that it truly reflects your goals, it can be your guide in everything you do.

Competitors strive to complete the New York marathon.

Placing Goals in Time

Everyone has the same 24 hours in a day, but it often doesn't feel like enough. Have you ever had a busy day flash by so quickly that it seems you accomplished nothing? Have you ever felt that way about a longer period of time, like a month or even a year? Your commitments can overwhelm you unless you decide how to use time to plan your steps toward goal achievement.

If developing a personal mission statement establishes the big picture, placing your goals within particular time frames allows you to bring individual areas of that picture into the foreground. Planning your progress step-by-step will help you maintain your efforts over the extended time period often needed to accomplish a goal. There are two categories: long-term goals and short-term goals.

Setting Long-Term Goals

Establish first the goals that have the largest scope, the long-term goals that you aim to attain over a lengthy period of time, up to a few years or more. As a student, you know what long-term goals are all about. You have set yourself a goal to attend school and earn a degree or certificate. Becoming educated is an admirable goal that often takes years to reach.

Some long-term goals are lifelong, such as a goal to continually learn more about yourself and the world around you. Others have a more definite end, such as a goal to complete a course successfully. To determine your long-term goals, think about what you want out of your professional, educational, and personal life. Here is Carol Carter's long-term goal statement:

> *E-mail one of your oldest, most trusted friends and share your long-term goals with them. Ask them to keep these goals in mind and to provide continuous support for you through the years. Offer to do the same for them.*

> To accomplish my mission through writing books, giving seminars, and developing programs that create opportunities for students to learn and develop. To create a personal, professional, and family environment that allows me to manifest my abilities and duly tend to each of my responsibilities.

For example, you may establish long-term goals such as these:

- I will graduate from school and know that I have learned all that I could, whether my grade point average reflects this or not.

- I will use my current and future job experience to develop practical skills that will help me get a satisfying, well-paying job.

- I will build my leadership and teamwork skills by forming positive, productive relationships with classmates, instructors, and coworkers.

Career Connection
Point out that many companies require employees to set work goals for the coming year and base salary increases, in part, on goal achievement.

Long-term goals don't have to be lifelong goals. Think about your long-term goals for the coming year. Considering what you want to accomplish in a year's time will give you clarity, focus, and a sense of what needs to take place right away. When Carol thought about her long-term goals for the coming year, she came up with the following:

1. Develop programs to provide internships, scholarships, and other quality initiatives for students.

2. Write a book for students emphasizing an interactive, highly visual approach to learning.

3. Allow time in my personal life to eat well, run five days a week, and spend quality time with family and friends. Allow time daily for quiet reflection and spiritual devotion.

In the same way that Carol's goals are tailored to her personality and interests, your goals should reflect who you are. Personal missions and goals are as unique as each individual. Continuing the example above, you might adopt these goals for the coming year:

- I will look for a part-time job with a local newspaper or newsroom.

- I will learn to navigate the Internet and research topics on-line.

- I will join two clubs and make an effort to take a leadership role in one of them.

Setting Short-Term Goals

When you divide your long-term goals into smaller, manageable goals that you hope to accomplish within a relatively short time, you are setting short-term goals. Short-term goals narrow your focus, helping you to maintain your progress toward your long-term goals. Say you have set the three long-term goals you just read in the previous section. To stay on track toward those goals, you may want to accomplish these short-term goals in the next six months:

- I will make an effort to ask my coworkers for advice on how to get into the news business.
- I will use Yahoo.com and Askjeeves.com to conduct research.
- I will attend four of the monthly meetings of the journalism club.

These same goals can be broken down into even smaller parts, such as the following one-month goals:

- I will have lunch with my office mate at work so that I can talk with him about his work experience.
- I will learn to use the most effective language choices in my Internet searches.
- I will write an article for next month's journalism club newsletter.

Real World Link
Computer software, such as Microsoft Outlook, can help students plan short-term goals by automatically reminding them of deadlines.

In addition to monthly goals, you may have short-term goals that extend for a week, a day, or even a couple of hours in a given day. Take as an example the article you have planned to write for the next month's journalism club newsletter. Such short-term goals may include the following:

- Three weeks from now: Final draft ready. Submit it to the editor of the newsletter.
- Two weeks from now: Second draft ready. Give it to one more person to review.
- One week from now: First draft ready. Ask my writing instructor if he will review it.
- By the end of today: Freewrite about the subject of the article, and narrow down to a specific topic.

As you consider your long- and short-term goals, notice how all of your goals are linked to one another. As Figure 3.1 shows, your long-term goals establish a context for the short-term goals. In turn, your short-term goals make the long-term goals seem clearer and more reachable. The whole system works to keep you on track.

Linking Goals with Values

If you are not sure how to start formulating your mission statement, look to your values to guide you. Define your mission and goals based on what is important to you. For example, if you value physical fitness, your mission statement might emphasize your commitment to staying in shape throughout your life. Your long-term goal might be to run a marathon, while your short-term goals might involve your weekly exercise and eating plans.

Linking Goals Together

FIGURE 3.1

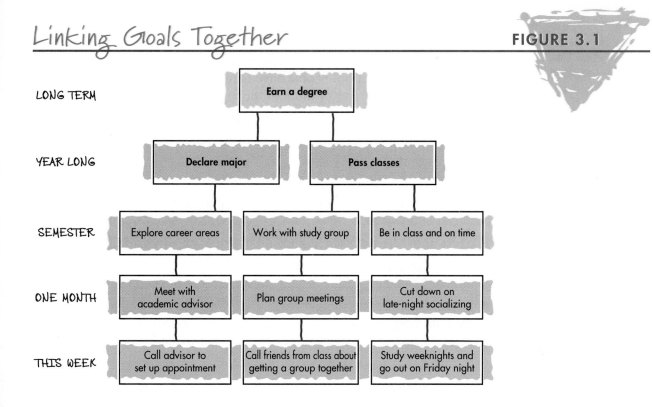

LONG TERM — Earn a degree

YEAR LONG — Declare major | Pass classes

SEMESTER — Explore career areas | Work with study group | Be in class and on time

ONE MONTH — Meet with academic advisor | Plan group meetings | Cut down on late-night socializing

THIS WEEK — Call advisor to set up appointment | Call friends from class about getting a group together | Study weeknights and go out on Friday night

Current and Personal Values Mean Appropriate Goals

When you use your values as a compass for your goals, make sure the compass is pointed in the direction of your real feelings. Watch out for the following two pitfalls:

Setting goals according to other people's values. Friends or family may encourage you to strive for what they think you should value. You may, of course, share their values. If you follow advice that you don't believe in, however, you may have a harder time sticking to your path. For example, someone who attends school primarily because a parent thought it was right may have less motivation than someone who made an independent decision to become a student. Staying in tune with your own values will help you make decisions that are right for you.

Setting goals that reflect values you held in the past. Life changes can alter your values. The best goals reflect what you believe today. For example, a person who has been through a near-fatal car accident may experience a dramatic increase in how he or she values time with friends and family and a decrease in how he or she values material possessions. Keep in touch with your life's changes so your goals can reflect who you are.

Different Kinds of Goals

People have many different goals, involving different parts of life and different values. Because school is currently a focus in your life, examine your educational goals.

Learning Styles Tip
Verbal learners may want to record their goals for different parts of their lives on tape and listen several times to be sure that their words reflect their feelings. Only then should they transfer their ideas to paper.

Identifying Educational Goals

First, to define a context for your school goals, explore why you have decided to pursue an education. People have many reasons for attending college. You may identify with one or more of the following:

- I want to earn a higher salary.
- I want to build marketable skills in a particular career area.
- My supervisor at work says that a degree will help me move ahead in my career.
- Most of my friends were going.
- I want to be a student and learn all that I can.
- It seems like the only option for me right now.
- I am recently divorced and need to find a way to earn money.

- Everybody in my family goes to college; it's expected.
- I don't feel ready to jump into the working world yet.
- I got a scholarship.
- My friend loves her job and encouraged me to take courses in the field.
- My parent (or a spouse or partner) pushed me to go to college.
- I need to increase my skills so I can provide for my kids.
- I don't really know.

All of these answers are legitimate, even the last one. Being honest with yourself is crucial if you want to discover who you are and what life paths make sense for you. Although it isn't easy to enroll in college, pay tuition, sign up for classes, and actually get yourself into the classroom, somehow your reasons have been compelling enough for you to have arrived at this point. Thinking about why you value your education will help you stick with it.

After considering why you are here, start thinking about your educational goals—what you want out of being here. Consider what is available to you, for example, classes, instructors, class schedule, and available degrees or certificates. Think about your commitment to academic excellence and whether honors and awards are important goals. If you have an idea of the career you want to pursue, consider the degree(s), certificate(s), or test(s) that may be required. Don't forget to ponder what you want out of your time in school in terms of learning, relationships, and personal growth.

Goals in Your Career and Personal Life

Establish your long- and short-term goals for your other two paths—career and personal life—as well as for your educational path. Remember that all your goals are interconnected. A school goal is often a step toward a career goal and can affect a personal goal.

Career. Think of your career goals in terms of both job and financial goals.

- **First, consider the job you want after you graduate**—requirements, duties, hours, coworkers, salary, transportation, and company size, style, and location. How much responsibility do you want? Do you want to become a manager, a supervisor, an independent contractor, or a business owner?

- **Then, consider financial goals.** How much money do you need to pay your bills, live comfortably, and save for the future? Do you need to borrow money for school or a major purchase such as a car? Do you need to reduce your bills? Compare your current financial picture to how you want to live, and set goals that will help you bridge the gap.

Personal Life. Consider personal goals in terms of self, family, and lifestyle.

- **First, look at yourself**—character, personality, health/fitness, and conduct. Do you want to gain confidence and knowledge? Get in shape? Change your social circle? Examine the difference between who you are and who you want to be.

- **Then, consider your family goals.** Do you want to stay single, be married, be a parent, or increase a family you've already started? Do you want to improve relations with a spouse or other family members? Do you want to live near relatives or far away?

- **Finally, consider your ideal lifestyle**—where you want to live, in what kind of space, and with whom. How do you want to participate in your community? What do you like to do in your leisure time? Consider goals that allow you to live the way you want to live.

Like learning a new physical task, setting and working toward goals takes a lot of practice and repeated efforts. As long as you do all that you can to achieve a goal, you haven't failed, even if you don't achieve it completely or in the time frame you had planned. Even one step in the right direction is an achievement. For example, if you wanted to raise your course grade to a B from a D, and you ended up with a C, you have still accomplished something important.

Achieving goals becomes easier when you are realistic about what is possible. Setting priorities will help you make that distinction.

Springboard
Discuss ways to make family a top priority, including drawing a clear line between work and family time and increasing family "talk time" for planning, analyzing, problem-solving, and listening.

WHAT ARE YOUR PRIORITIES?

When you set a priority, you identify what's important at any given moment. Prioritizing helps you focus on your most important goals, especially when the important ones are the most difficult. Human nature often leads people to tackle easy goals first and leave the tough ones for later. The risk is that you might never reach for goals that are crucial to your success.

To explore your priorities, think about your personal mission and look at your school, career, and personal goals. Do one or two of these paths take priority for you right now? In any path, which goals take priority? Which goals take priority over all others?

You are a unique individual, and your priorities are yours alone. What may be top priority to someone else may not mean that much to you, and vice versa. You can see this in Figure 3.2, which compares the priorities of two very different students. Each student's priorities are listed in order, with the first priority at the top and the lowest priority at the bottom.

First and foremost, your priorities should reflect your goals. In addition, they should reflect your relationships with others. For example, if you are a parent, your children's needs will probably be high on the priority list. You

Priority
An action or intention that takes precedence in time, attention, or position.

Career Connection
Technology is making it more difficult to separate career time from personal time. Students who value their personal and family lives must be willing to carve out time each day for these activities and stick with their priorities despite job demands.

FIGURE 3.2 *Two Students Compare Priorities*

K. COLE,
Returning Adult Student

1	Caring for my daughter
2	Working at my part-time job
3	Studying, classes, projects
4	Relationships and entertainment
5	Household tasks and chores
6	Personal time and wellness
7	Church and meditation

Education/classes

Work

Family

Friends/relationships

Personal time

Chores/household tasks

Extracurricular activities

School and community involvement

Spiritual life

M. CONNELL,
Traditional-Aged Freshman

1	Close friends
2	Classes and studying
3	School and community group responsibilities
4	Extracurricular events and entertainment
5	Personal time for exercise and relaxation
6	Chores, errands, groceries
7	Time spent with parents and sisters

Write one of your professors and ask what the greatest learning priorities are for the course you are taking. What does he or she consider to be the top three issues? Why?

may be in school so you can get a better job than you have now and give them a better life. If you are in a committed relationship, you may schedule your classes so that you and your partner are home together as often as possible. Even as you consider the needs of others, though, be true to your own goals and priorities so that you can make the most of who you are.

Setting priorities moves you closer to accomplishing specific goals. It also helps you begin planning to achieve your goals within specific time frames. Being able to achieve your goals is directly linked to effective time management.

HOW CAN YOU MANAGE YOUR TIME?

Time is one of your most valuable and precious resources. Everyone has the same 24 hours in a day, every day; your responsibility and potential for success lie in how you use yours. You cannot change how time passes, but you can spend it wisely. Efficient time management helps you achieve your goals in a steady, step-by-step process.

People have a variety of approaches to time management. Your learning style (see Chapter 4) can help you understand how you use time. For example, students with strong logical-mathematical intelligence and Thinker types tend to organize activities within a framework of time. Because they stay aware of how long it takes them to do something or travel somewhere, they are usually prompt. By contrast, Adventurer types and less logical learners with perhaps stronger visual or interpersonal intelligences may neglect details such as how much time they have to complete a task. They can often be late without meaning to be.

Time management, like physical fitness, is a lifelong pursuit. No one can plan a perfect schedule or build a terrific physique and then be "done." Throughout your life, your ability to manage your time will vary with your stress level, how busy you are, and other factors. Don't expect perfection—just do your best and keep working at it. Time management involves building a schedule, taking responsibility for how you spend your time, and being flexible.

Building a Schedule

Just as a road map helps you travel from place to place, a schedule is a time-and-activity map that helps you get from the beginning of the day (or week, or month) to the end as smoothly as possible. Schedules help you gain control of your life in two ways: They allocate segments of time for the fulfillment of your daily, weekly, monthly, and longer-term goals, and they serve as a concrete reminder of tasks, events, due dates, responsibilities, and deadlines.

Keep a Date Book

Gather the tools of the trade: a pen or pencil and a *date book* (sometimes called a planner). A date book is indispensable for keeping track of your time. Some of you have date books and may have used them for years. Others may have had no luck with them or have never tried. Even if you don't feel you would benefit from one, give it a try. Paul Timm says, "Most time management experts agree that rule number one in a thoughtful planning process is: Use some form of a planner where you can write things down."[3]

Critical Thinking
Ask students to look at Figure 3.3. Why are action verbs important in date-book writing? Ask students for examples of other verbs that make the point as they motivate action.

There are two major types of date books. The day-at-a-glance version devotes a page to each day. Although it gives you ample space to write the day's activities, it's harder to see what's ahead. The week-at-a-glance book gives you a view of the week's plans but has less room to write per day. If you write detailed daily plans, you might like the day-at-a-glance version. If you prefer to remind yourself of plans ahead of time, try the book that shows a week's schedule all at once. Some date books contain sections for monthly and yearly goals.

Another option is an electronic planner—a compact minicomputer that can hold a large amount of information. You can use it to schedule your days and weeks, make to-do lists, and create and store an address book. Electronic planners are powerful, convenient, and often fun. However, they certainly cost more than the paper version, and you can lose a lot of important data if something goes wrong with the computer inside. Evaluate your options and decide what works best for you.

Set Weekly and Daily Goals

The most ideal time management starts with the smallest tasks and builds to bigger ones. Setting short-term goals that tie in to your long-term goals lends the following benefits:

- increased meaning for your daily activities
- shaping your path toward the achievement of your long-term goals
- a sense of order and progress

For college students as well as working people, the week is often the easiest unit of time to consider at one shot. Weekly goal setting and planning allows you to keep track of day-to-day activities while giving you the larger perspective of what is coming up during the week. Take some time before each week starts to remind yourself of your long-term goals. Keeping long-term goals in mind will help you determine related short-term goals you can accomplish during the week to come.

Figure 3.3 shows parts of a daily schedule and a weekly schedule.

Learning Styles Tip
Students with visual-spatial intelligence may find it helpful to use a flowchart to track their progress on projects.

FIGURE 3.3 Daily and Weekly Schedule

Monday, March 20		2000
Time	Tasks	Priority
7:00 AM		
8:00	Up at 8am — finish homework	*
9:00		
10:00	Business Administration	
11:00	Renew driver's license @ DMV	*
12:00 PM		
1:00	Lunch	
2:00	Writing Seminar (peer editing today)	*
3:00	↓	
4:00	check on Ms. Schwartz's office hrs.	
5:00	5:30 work out	
6:00	↳6:30	
7:00	Dinner	
8:00	Read two chapters for Business Admin.	
9:00	↓	
10:00		
11:00		

Monday, March 20

8		Call: Mike Blair	1
9	BIO 212	Finanical Aid Office	2
10		EMS 262 *Paramedic	3
11	CHEM 203	role-play*	4
12			5
Evening	6pm yoga class		

Tuesday, March 21

8	Finish reading assignment!	Work @ library	1
9			2
10	ENG 112	(study for quiz)	3
11	↓		4
12			5
Evening		↓ until 7pm	

Wednesday, March 22

8		Meet w/advisor	1
9	BIO 212		2
10		EMS 262	3
11	CHEM 203 *Quiz		4
12		Pick up photos	5
Evening	6pm Aerobics		

Link Daily and Weekly Goals with Long-Term Goals

After you evaluate what you need to accomplish in the coming year, semester, month, week, and day to reach your long-term goals, use your schedule to record those steps. Write down the short-term goals that will enable you to stay on track. Here is how a student might map out two different goals over a year's time:

This year: Complete enough courses to graduate.

Improve my physical fitness.

This semester: Complete my accounting class with a B average or higher.

Lose 10 pounds and exercise regularly.

This month: Set up study group schedule to coincide with quizzes.

Begin walking and weight lifting.

This week: Meet with study group; go over material for Friday's quiz.

Go for a fitness walk three times; go to weight room twice.

Today: Go over Chapter 3 in accounting text.

Walk for 40 minutes.

Prioritize Goals

Prioritizing enables you to use your date book with maximum efficiency. On any given day, your goals will have varying degrees of importance. Record your goals first, and then label them according to their level of importance, using these categories: Priority 1, Priority 2, and Priority 3. Identify these categories by using any code that makes sense to you. Some people use numbers, as above. Some use letters (A, B, C). Some write activities in different colors according to priority level. Some use symbols (*, +, −).

Priority 1 activities are the most important things in your life. They may include attending class, picking up a child from day care, and paying bills.

Priority 2 activities are part of your routine. Examples include grocery shopping, working out, participating in a school organization, or cleaning. Priority 2 tasks are important but more flexible than Priority 1 tasks.

Priority 3 activities are those you would like to do but can reschedule without much sacrifice. Examples might be a trip to the mall, a visit to a friend, a social phone call, or a sports event. As much as you would like to accomplish them, you don't consider them urgent. Many people don't enter Priority 3 tasks in their date books until they are sure they have time to get them done.

Prioritizing your activities is essential for two reasons. First, some activities are more important than others, and effective time management requires that you focus most of your energy on Priority 1 items. Second, looking at all your priorities helps you plan when you can get things done. Often, it's not possible to get all your Priority 1 activities done early in the day, especially if they involve scheduled classes or meetings. Prioritizing helps you set Priority 1 items and then schedule Priority 2 and 3 items around them as they fit.

Springboard

Discuss with students the difference between a prioritized list of daily goals and a non-prioritized to-do list. Point out that a random to-do list may be filled with so many Priority 3 items that students may lose site of Priority 1 items linked to long-term goals.

"Even if you're on the right track, you'll get run over if you just sit there."

Will Rogers

Keep Track of Events

Your date book also enables you to schedule events. Think of events in terms of how they tie in with your long-term goals, just as you would your other tasks. For example, being aware of quiz dates, due dates for assignments, and meeting dates will aid your goals to achieve in school and become involved.

Note events in your date book so that you can stay aware of them ahead of time. Write them in daily, weekly, monthly, or even yearly sections, where a quick look will remind you that they are approaching. Writing them down will also help you see where they fit in the context of all your other activities. For example, if you have three big tests and a presentation all in one week, you'll want to take time in the weeks before to prepare for them.

Following are some kinds of events worth noting in your date book:

- due dates for papers, projects, presentations, and tests
- important meetings, medical appointments, or due dates for bill payments
- birthdays, anniversaries, social events, holidays, and other special occasions
- benchmarks for steps toward a goal, such as due dates for sections of a project or a deadline for losing 5 pounds on your way to 20

List Low-Priority Goals Separately

Priority 3 tasks can be hard to accomplish. As the least important tasks, they often get put off. One solution is to keep a list of Priority 3 tasks in a separate place in your date book. That way, when you have an unexpected pocket of free time, you can consult your list and see what you have time to accomplish—making a trip to the post office, returning a borrowed tape, giving some clothes to charity. Keep this list current by crossing off items as you accomplish them and writing in new items as soon as you think of them. Rewrite the list when it gets too messy.

Taking Responsibility for How You Spend Your Time

When you plan your activities with an eye toward achieving your most important goals, you are taking responsibility for how you live. The following strategies will help you stay in charge of your choices:

Plan your schedule each week. Before each week starts, note events, goals, and priorities. Decide where to fit activities like studying and Priority 3 items. For example, if you have a test on Thursday, you can plan study sessions on the preceding days. If you have more free time on Tuesday and Friday than on other days, you can plan workouts or Priority 3 activities at those times. Looking at the whole week will help you avoid being surprised by something you had forgotten was coming up.

A University of Madrid student checks her schedule.

A Sample Monthly Calendar

FIGURE 3.4

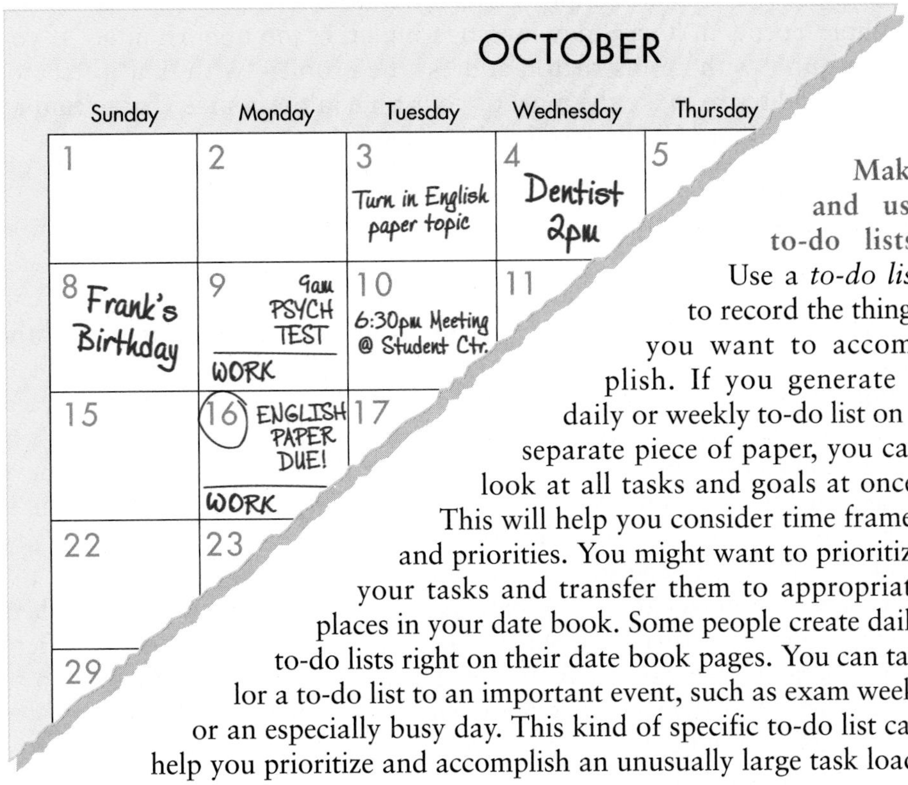

OCTOBER

Sunday	Monday	Tuesday	Wednesday	Thursday
1	2	3 Turn in English paper topic	4 Dentist 2pm	5
8 Frank's Birthday	9 9am PSYCH TEST WORK	10 6:30pm Meeting @ Student Ctr.	11	
15	(16) ENGLISH PAPER DUE! WORK	17		
22	23			
29				

Make and use to-do lists. Use a *to-do list* to record the things you want to accomplish. If you generate a daily or weekly to-do list on a separate piece of paper, you can look at all tasks and goals at once. This will help you consider time frames and priorities. You might want to prioritize your tasks and transfer them to appropriate places in your date book. Some people create daily to-do lists right on their date book pages. You can tailor a to-do list to an important event, such as exam week, or an especially busy day. This kind of specific to-do list can help you prioritize and accomplish an unusually large task load.

Make thinking about time a priority. Take a few minutes a day to plan. Although making a schedule takes time, it can mean hours of saved time later. Say you have two errands to run, both on the other side of town; not planning ahead could result in your driving across town twice in one day. Also, when you take time to write out your schedule, be sure to carry it with you and check it throughout the day. Find a date book size you like—there are books that fit into your briefcase, your bag, or even your pocket.

Post monthly and yearly calendars at home. Keeping a calendar on the wall will help you stay aware of important events. You can purchase one or draw it yourself, month by month, on plain paper. Use a yearly or a monthly version (Figure 3.4 shows part of a monthly calendar), and keep it where you can refer to it often. If you live with family or friends, make the calendar a group project so that you stay aware of each other's plans. Knowing each other's schedules can also help you avoid problems such as two people needing the car at the same time.

Schedule downtime. When you're wiped out from too much activity, you don't have the energy to accomplish as much. A little **downtime** will refresh you and improve your attitude. Even half an hour a day will help. Fill the time with whatever relaxes you—reading, watching television, chatting online, playing a game or sport, walking, writing, or just doing nothing. Make downtime a priority.

Shake off the judgments of others. A student who feels no one will hire him because of his weight may not search for jobs. A student who feels her

Career Connection

At work, create tomorrow's to-do list at the end of today. That way, all the open details will be fresh in your mind.

Downtime

Quiet time set aside for relaxation and low-key activity.

Judgments

Considered opinions, assessments, or evaluations.

instructor is prejudiced against her might not study for that instructor's course. Instead of letting judgments like these rob you of your control of your time, choose actions that improve your circumstances. If you lose a job, for example, spend an hour a day investigating other job opportunities. If you have trouble with an instructor, address the problem with that instructor directly and try to make the most of your time in the course. Try to find an active option that will allow you to be in control.

Being Flexible

No matter how well you plan your time, the changes that life brings can make you feel out of control. One minute you seem to be on track, and the next minute chaos hits—in forms as minor as a room change for a class or as major as a medical emergency. Coping with changes can cause stress. As your stress level rises, your sense of control dwindles.

Although you cannot always choose your circumstances, you may have some control over how you *handle* them. Dr. Covey says that language is important in trying to take action. Using language like "I have to" and "They made me" robs you of personal power. For example, saying that you "have to" go to school or move out of your parents' house can make you feel that others control your life. However, language like "I have decided to" and "I prefer" helps energize your power to choose. Then you can turn "I have to go to school" into "I prefer to go to school than to work in a dead-end job."

Use the following ideas to cope with changes large and small.

Day-to-Day Changes

Anytime, small changes can result in priority shifts that jumble your schedule. On Monday, a homework assignment due in a week might be Priority 2; then, if you haven't gotten to it by Saturday, it becomes Priority 1. Or perhaps a class may be canceled, and you will have extra time on your hands.

Think of change as part of life, and you will be able to more effectively solve the dilemmas that come up. For some changes that occur frequently, you can think through a backup plan ahead of time. For unexpected extra time on your hands, you could keep some work or reading with you. For others, the best you can do is to keep an open mind about possibilities and to remember to call on your resources in a pinch. Your problem-solving skills (see Chapter 5) will help you build your ability to adjust to whatever changes come your way.

"The right time is any time that one is still so lucky as to have. . . . Live!"

Henry James

Life Changes

Sometimes changes are more serious than a class schedule shift. Your car breaks down; your relationship falls apart; you fail a class; you or a close family member develops a medical problem; you get laid off at work. Such changes call for more extensive problem solving. They also require an ability to look at the big picture. While a class change affects your schedule for a day, a medical problem may affect your schedule for much longer.

When life hands you a major curve ball, first remember that you still have some choices about how to handle the situation. Then sit down and figure

How can I stay focused on my school goals?

Rosalia Chavez, University of Arizona, Tucson, Arizona, Public Administration Major

I married at 18 and didn't finish high school. My husband became a cocaine addict and grew very possessive of me. After our two sons were born, I decided to get my GED, but he didn't want me to. At this point I knew I had to start making opportunities for myself.

Shortly after I had begun to further my education, my husband overdosed on drugs. His death was very traumatic and difficult to deal with. I am now taking classes full-time at the University of Arizona, and I work part-time in the Chicano/Hispano Student Affairs Office. I don't feel I'm getting an education just for myself but for future generations of Hispanic women. There's a view in traditional Hispanic families that the women stay home and only the men provide. I would like to empower women by telling them my story and letting them know that they deserve to follow their dreams.

Even though I feel blessed, I have to make daily decisions about priorities, such as do I take this test or stay home with my sick child? Recently, I had to drop a class because my children were sick and I couldn't keep up. My son, who is 11, has ADHD (attention deficit hyperactivity disorder). He was on medication and under a doctor's care, but when I reapplied for state medical assistance I was denied. Now I can no longer afford his medicine. These situations hinder me as a student because I am so preoccupied. Can you offer suggestions about how I can keep focused on my school goals?

Norma Seledon, Director, Las Mujeres en Accion, Chicago, Illinois

Your story is not atypical. Your taking control of your life is, however, exemplary. Setting and sticking to your goals is not easy, particularly when you have cultural, societal, and even religious factors working against you. While women are often strong and tolerant, we sometimes don't give ourselves credit for our strengths. We need to surround ourselves with individuals and experiences that "feed our souls." Another essential is to maintain a balance. With many higher education programs designed for those without families, it is challenging to meet the demands of school and family. Your desire to learn and grow, not only for yourself but for your family and for the community at large, will fuel your efforts.

I recognize some of your challenges. In my last year of college I had a newborn, was pregnant, worked full-time, and attended school full-time. You must prioritize and pace yourself. It may help to speak to professors about your situation. My daughter was due at the middle of my last semester, and some professors were flexible with my assignments. It can't hurt to try.

As director of an organization whose primary focus is Latina leadership and working with survivors of domestic violence, it is difficult being a mother of two preteens and a preschooler. My son is also diagnosed with ADHD. I demand periodic meetings with a team of school officials so that we may approach my son's education from a team perspective.

With patience and perseverance, you will achieve your current goals and set more for yourself. Continue to develop a support system and to share your story. We must all continue to figure out how to distill the beauty and strength of our culture and traditions and discard those elements that hinder women's development. *Felicidades!*

them out, ideally with people who can help you think everything through. Explore all of your options before making a decision (again, the problem-solving and decision-making skills in Chapter 5 will serve you well here). Finally, make full use of your school resources. Your academic advisor, counselor, dean, financial aid advisor, and/or instructors may have ideas and assistance to offer you—but they can only help if you let them know what you need.

No matter how well you schedule your time, you will have moments when it's hard to stay in control. Knowing how to identify and avoid procrastination and other time traps will help you get back on track.

WHY IS PROCRASTINATION A PROBLEM?

Procrastination

The act of putting off a task until another time.

Procrastination occurs when you postpone tasks. People procrastinate for different reasons. Having trouble with goal setting is one reason. People may project goals too far into the future, set unrealistic goals that are too frustrating to reach, or have no goals at all. People also procrastinate because they don't believe in their ability to complete a task or don't believe in themselves in general. Procrastination is human, and not every instance of procrastination means trouble. If it is taken to the extreme, however, procrastination can develop into a habit that will cause problems at school, on the job, and at home.

Jane B. Burka and Lenora M. Yuen, authors of *Procrastination: Why You Do It and What To Do About It,* say that habitual procrastinators are often perfectionists who create problems by using their ability to achieve as the only measure of their self-worth: "The performance becomes the only measure of the person; nothing else is taken into account. An outstanding performance means an outstanding person; a mediocre performance means a mediocre person. . . . As long as you procrastinate, you never have to confront the real limits of your ability, whatever those limits are."[4] For the procrastinator, the fear of failure prevents taking the risk that could bring success.

Be a Team

Ask student teams to compile a list of reasons group members procrastinate and another list of what they do to motivate action. Ask team leaders to share solutions with the class.

Antiprocrastination Strategies

Following are some ways to fight your tendencies to procrastinate:

Weigh the benefits (to you and others) of completing the task versus the effects of procrastinating. What rewards lie ahead if you get it done? What will be the effects if you continue to put it off? Which situation has better effects? Chances are you will benefit more in the long term from facing the task head-on.

Set reasonable goals. Plan your goals carefully, allowing enough time to complete them. Unreasonable goals can be so intimidating that you do nothing at all. "Pay off the credit card bill next month" could throw you. However, "Pay off the credit card bill in 10 months" might inspire you to take action.

Break the task into smaller parts. Look at the task in terms of its parts. How can you approach it step-by-step? If you can concentrate on achieving one small goal at a time, the task may become less of a burden. In addition, setting concrete time limits for each task may help you feel more in control.

Get started whether or not you "feel like it." Going from doing nothing to doing something is often the hardest part of avoiding procrastination. The motivation techniques from Chapter 1 might help you take the first step. Once you start, you may find it easier to continue.

Ask for help with tasks and projects at school, work, and home. You don't always have to go it alone. For example, if you avoid a project because you dislike the employee with whom you have to work, talk to your supervisor about adjusting tasks or personnel. Once you identify what's holding you up, see who can help you face the task.

Don't expect perfection. No one is perfect. Most people learn by starting at the beginning and wading through plenty of mistakes and confusion. It's better to try your best than to do nothing at all.

Procrastination is natural, but it can cause you problems if you let it get the best of you. When it does happen, take some time to think about the causes. What is it about this situation that frightens you or puts you off? Answering that question can help you address what causes lie underneath the procrastination. These causes might indicate a deeper issue that you can address.

Other Time Traps to Avoid

Procrastination isn't the only way to spend your time in less-than-productive ways. Keep an eye out for these situations too.

Saying yes when you really don't have the time. Many people, in their efforts to please others, agree to help with tasks they can't easily fit into their schedules. Avoid being reliable at your own expense by learning to say no when you need to. First, think before you respond. Ask yourself what effects a new responsibility will have on your schedule. Be honest with yourself about whether you have the time to make the commitment. If it will cause you more trouble than it seems to be worth, say no graciously.

Studying at a bad time of day. Do you study at the time of day when you have the most energy? If not, you may be wasting time. When you are tired, you may need extra time to fully understand your material. If you study when you are most alert, you will be able to take in more information in less time.

Studying in a distracting location. Find an environment that helps you maximize study time. If you need to be alone to concentrate, for example, studying near family members or roommates might interfere with your focus. Conversely, people who require a busier environment to stay alert might need to choose a more active setting.

Not thinking ahead. Forgetting important things is a big time drain. One book left at home can cost you extra time going back and forth. One forgotten phone call can mean you have to do what you wanted to ask someone else to do. Five minutes of scheduling before your day starts can save you hours.

Not curbing your social time. You plan to make a quick telephone call, but the next thing you know you've been talking for an hour, losing sleep or

Springboard
If students commit to an activity, then realize that it takes too much time, what do they do? Discuss whether keeping a commitment to a low-priority activity is worth jeopardizing their goals.

study time. Don't cut out all socializing, but stay aware. If friends invite you for dinner and you don't have the time, consider joining them for coffee beforehand. Smart choices will have results that will boost your self-respect.

Not delegating. No one can take a test or read a chapter for you, but you can delegate some tasks to others. A friend could pick up postal stamps for you. Another day-care parent could pick up your child on a day when your time runs short. Check into those possibilities, and don't forget to return the favor.

Pushing yourself too far. You've probably experienced one of those study sessions during which, at a certain point, you realize that you haven't absorbed anything for the last hour. When you just can't seem to concentrate anymore, take a break—stretch, get a drink or a snack, go for a walk, take a nap. You're much better off using some of your time to revive yourself rather than trying in vain to focus.

Of course no one is going to be able to avoid all of these time traps all of the time. Do the best that you can. The first step is awareness of your particular tendencies. Once you know how you tend to procrastinate and waste time, you can take steps to change your habits. Time is your ally—make the most of the time that you have.

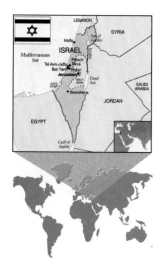

In Hebrew, the word above, pronounced "chai," means "life," representing all aspects of life—spiritual, emotional, family, educational, and career. Individual Hebrew characters have number values. Because the characters in the word *chai* add up to 18, the number 18 has come to be associated with good luck. The word *chai* is often worn as a good luck charm. As you plan your goals, think about your view of luck. Many people feel that a person can create his or her own luck by pursuing goals persistently and staying open to possibilities and opportunities.

Consider that your vision of life may largely determine how you live. You can prepare the way for luck by establishing a personal mission and forging ahead toward your goals. If you believe that the life you want awaits you, you will be able to recognize and make the most of luck when it comes around. *L'chaim*—to life, and good luck.

Name _____   Date _____

BUILDING SKILLS FOR COLLEGE, CAREER, AND LIFE SUCCESS

Critical Thinking
Applying Learning to Life

Your Values

Begin to explore your values by rating the following values on a scale from 1 to 4, 1 being least important to you, and 4 being most important. If you have values that you don't see in the chart, list them in the blank spaces and rate them.

VALUE	RATING	VALUE	RATING
Knowing yourself		Mental health	
Physical health		Fitness and exercise	
Spending time with your family		Close friendships	
Helping others		Education	
Being well-paid		Being employed	
Being liked by others		Free time/vacations	
Enjoying entertainment		Time to yourself	
Spiritual/religious life		Reading	
Keeping up with the news		Staying organized	
Being financially stable		Having an intimate relationship	
Creative/artistic pursuits		Self-improvement	
Lifelong learning		Facing your fears	

Considering your priorities, write your top five values here:

1. _____

2. _____

3. _____

4. _____

5. _____

Short-Term Scheduling

Take a close look at your schedule for the coming month, including events, important dates, and steps toward goals. On the calendar layout on the next page, fill in the name of the month and appropriate numbers for the days. Then record what you hope to accomplish, including the following:

- due dates for papers, projects, and presentations
- test dates
- important meetings, medical appointments, and due dates for bill payments
- birthdays, anniversaries, and other special occasions
- steps toward long-term goals

This kind of chart will help you see the monthly "big picture." To stay on target from day to day, check these dates against the entries in your date book and make sure that they are indicated there as well.

Discover How You Spend Your Time

In the chart below, estimate the total time you think you spend per week on each listed activity. Then add the hours. If your number is over 168 (the number of hours in a week), rethink your estimates and recalculate so that the total is equal to or below 168. Then subtract your total from 168. Whatever is left over is your estimate of hours that you spend in unscheduled activities.

ACTIVITY	ESTIMATED TIME SPENT
Class	
Work	
Studying	
Sleeping	
Eating	
Family time/child care	
Commuting/traveling	
Chores and personal business	
Friends and important relationships	
Telephone time	
Leisure/entertainment	
Spiritual life	
Total	

168

Minus total _____

Unscheduled time _____

Now spend a week recording exactly how you spend your time. The chart on pp. 74–75 has blocks showing half-hourly increments. As you go through the week, write in what you do each hour, indicating when you started and when you stopped. Don't forget activities that don't feel like "activities," such as sleeping, relaxing, and watching TV. Also, be honest—record your actual activities instead of how you *want* to spend your time or how you think you *should* have spent your time. There are no wrong answers.

After a week, go through the chart and look at how many hours you actually spent on the activities for which you estimated your hours

MONTH CHART

MONDAY		TUESDAY		WEDNESDAY		THURSDAY	
Time	Activity	Time	Activity	Time	Activity	Time	Activity
5:00 AM		5:00 AM		5:00 AM		5:00 AM	
5:30 AM		5:30 AM		5:30 AM		5:30 AM	
6:00 AM		6:00 AM		6:00 AM		6:00 AM	
6:30 AM		6:30 AM		6:30 AM		6:30 AM	
7:00 AM		7:00 AM		7:00 AM		7:00 AM	
7:30 AM		7:30 AM		7:30 AM		7:30 AM	
8:00 AM		8:00 AM		8:00 AM		8:00 AM	
8:30 AM		8:30 AM		8:30 AM		8:30 AM	
9:00 AM		9:00 AM		9:00 AM		9:00 AM	
9:30 AM		9:30 AM		9:30 AM		9:30 AM	
10:00 AM		10:00 AM		10:00 AM		10:00 AM	
10:30 AM		10:30 AM		10:30 AM		10:30 AM	
11:00 AM		11:00 AM		11:00 AM		11:00 AM	
11:30 AM		11:30 AM		11:30 AM		11:30 AM	
12:00 PM		12:00 PM		12:00 PM		12:00 PM	
12:30 PM		12:30 PM		12:30 PM		12:30 PM	
1:00 PM		1:00 PM		1:00 PM		1:00 PM	
1:30 PM		1:30 PM		1:30 PM		1:30 PM	
2:00 PM		2:00 PM		2:00 PM		2:00 PM	
2:30 PM		2:30 PM		2:30 PM		2:30 PM	
3:00 PM		3:00 PM		3:00 PM		3:00 PM	
3:30 PM		3:30 PM		3:30 PM		3:30 PM	
4:00 PM		4:00 PM		4:00 PM		4:00 PM	
4:30 PM		4:30 PM		4:30 PM		4:30 PM	
5:00 PM		5:00 PM		5:00 PM		5:00 PM	
5:30 PM		5:30 PM		5:30 PM		5:30 PM	
6:00 PM		6:00 PM		6:00 PM		6:00 PM	
6:30 PM		6:30 PM		6:30 PM		6:30 PM	
7:00 PM		7:00 PM		7:00 PM		7:00 PM	
7:30 PM		7:30 PM		7:30 PM		7:30 PM	
8:00 PM		8:00 PM		8:00 PM		8:00 PM	
8:30 PM		8:30 PM		8:30 PM		8:30 PM	
9:00 PM		9:00 PM		9:00 PM		9:00 PM	
9:30 PM		9:30 PM		9:30 PM		9:30 PM	
10:00 PM		10:00 PM		10:00 PM		10:00 PM	
10:30 PM		10:30 PM		10:30 PM		10:30 PM	
11:00 PM		11:00 PM		11:00 PM		11:00 PM	
11:30 PM		11:30 PM		11:30 PM		11:30 PM	

FRIDAY		SATURDAY		SUNDAY		NOTES
Time	Activity	Time	Activity	Time	Activity	for the week of _____
5:00 AM		5:00 AM		5:00 AM		
5:30 AM		5:30 AM		5:30 AM		
6:00 AM		6:00 AM		6:00 AM		
6:30 AM		6:30 AM		6:30 AM		
7:00 AM		7:00 AM		7:00 AM		
7:30 AM		7:30 AM		7:30 AM		
8:00 AM		8:00 AM		8:00 AM		
8:30 AM		8:30 AM		8:30 AM		
9:00 AM		9:00 AM		9:00 AM		
9:30 AM		9:30 AM		9:30 AM		
10:00 AM		10:00 AM		10:00 AM		
10:30 AM		10:30 AM		10:30 AM		
11:00 AM		11:00 AM		11:00 AM		
11:30 AM		11:30 AM		11:30 AM		
12:00 PM		12:00 PM		12:00 PM		
12:30 PM		12:30 PM		12:30 PM		
1:00 PM		1:00 PM		1:00 PM		
1:30 PM		1:30 PM		1:30 PM		
2:00 PM		2:00 PM		2:00 PM		
2:30 PM		2:30 PM		2:30 PM		
3:00 PM		3:00 PM		3:00 PM		
3:30 PM		3:30 PM		3:30 PM		
4:00 PM		4:00 PM		4:00 PM		
4:30 PM		4:30 PM		4:30 PM		
5:00 PM		5:00 PM		5:00 PM		
5:30 PM		5:30 PM		5:30 PM		
6:00 PM		6:00 PM		6:00 PM		
6:30 PM		6:30 PM		6:30 PM		
7:00 PM		7:00 PM		7:00 PM		
7:30 PM		7:30 PM		7:30 PM		
8:00 PM		8:00 PM		8:00 PM		
8:30 PM		8:30 PM		8:30 PM		
9:00 PM		9:00 PM		9:00 PM		
9:30 PM		9:30 PM		9:30 PM		
10:00 PM		10:00 PM		10:00 PM		
10:30 PM		10:30 PM		10:30 PM		
11:00 PM		11:00 PM		11:00 PM		
11:30 PM		11:30 PM		11:30 PM		

before. Tally the hours in the boxes in the following table using straight tally marks; round off to half hours and use a short tally mark for each half hour. In the third column, total the hours for each activity. Leave the "Ideal Time in Hours" column blank for now.

ACTIVITY	TIME TALLIED OVER ONE-WEEK PERIOD	TOTAL TIME IN HOURS	IDEAL TIME IN HOURS
Example: Class	‖‖ ‖‖ ‖‖ ⁝	16.5	
Class			
Work			
Studying			
Sleeping			
Eating			
Family time/child care			
Commuting/traveling			
Chores and personal business			
Friends and important relationships			
Telephone time			
Leisure/entertainment			
Spiritual life			

Add the totals in the third column to find your grand total. Compare your grand total to your estimated grand total; compare your actual activity hour totals to your estimated activity hour totals. What matches and what doesn't? Describe the most interesting similarities and differences.

What is the one biggest surprise about how you spend your time?

Name one change you would like to make in how you spend your time.

_____
_____
_____

Think about what kinds of changes might help you improve your ability to set and achieve goals. Ask yourself important questions about what you do daily, weekly, and monthly. On what activities do you think you should spend more or less time? Go back to the chart on p. 76 and fill in the "Ideal Time in Hours" column. Consider the difference between actual hours and ideal hours when you think about the changes you want to make in your life.

To-Do Lists

Make a to-do list for what you have to do tomorrow. Include all tasks—Priority 1, 2, and 3—and events.

Tomorrow's Date: _____

1. _____   7. _____
2. _____   8. _____
3. _____   9. _____
4. _____   10. _____
5. _____   11. _____
6. _____   12. _____

Use a coding system of your choice to indicate priority level of both tasks and events. Use this list to make your schedule for tomorrow in the date book, making a separate list for Priority 3 items. At the end of the day, evaluate this system—write below if the list made a difference, and if so, how. If you liked it, use this exercise as a guide for using to-do lists regularly.

_____
_____
_____

Your Procrastination Habits

Name one situation in which you habitually procrastinate.

_____
_____
_____

What are the effects of your procrastination? Discuss how procrastination may affect the quality of your work, motivation, productivity, ability to be on time, grades, or self-perception.

What you would like to do differently in this situation? How can you achieve what you want?

Teamwork
Combining Forces

Individual Priorities In a group of three or four people, brainstorm long-term goals and have one member of the group write them down. From that list, pick out 10 goals that everyone can relate to most. Each group member should then take five minutes alone to evaluate the relative importance of the 10 goals and rank them in the order that he or she prefers, using a 1 to 10 scale, with 1 being the highest priority and 10 the lowest.

Display the rankings of each group member side by side. How many different orders are there? Discuss why each person has a different set of priorities, and be open to different views. What factors in different people's lives have caused them to select particular rankings? If you have time, discuss how priorities have changed for each group member over the course of a year, perhaps by having each person re-rank the goals according to his or her needs a year ago.

Writing
Discovery Through Journaling

To record your thoughts, use a separate journal or the lined page at the end of the chapter.

Personal Mission Statement Using the personal mission statement examples in the chapter as a guide, consider what you want out of your life and create your own personal mission statement. You can write it in paragraph form, in a list of long-term goals, or in a visual format such as a think link (see Chapter 7 for information on think links). Take as much time as you need in order to be as complete as possible. Write a draft on a separate sheet of paper and take time to revise it before you write the final version here. If you have created a think link rather than a verbal statement, attach it separately.

Career Portfolio
Charting Your Course

Performance counts!

Career Goals and Priorities The most reasonable and reachable career goals are ones that are linked with your school and life goals. First, name a personal long-term career goal.

_____

_____

_____

_____

Goal setting and accountability are key assets in the business world. Developing these habits now in your personal life will put you in a stronger frame of mind in the future.

Then, imagine that you will begin working toward it. Indicate a series of smaller goals—from short-term to long-term—that you feel will help you achieve this goal. Write what you hope to accomplish in the next year, the next six months, the next month, the next week, and the next day.

TIME FRAME	CAREER GOAL
One Year	
Six Months	
One Month	
This Week	
Today	

Now, explore your job priorities. How do you want your job to benefit you?
Note your requirements in each of the following areas.

Duties and responsibilities _____

_____

_____

Salary and benefits _____

_____

_____

Hours (part-time vs. full-time) _____

_____

Job requirements (e.g., travel, location) _____

_____

_____

Industry or field _____

Flexibility _____

Affiliation with school or financial aid program _____

_____

_____

What kind of job, in the career area for which you listed your goals, might fit
all or most of your requirements? List two possibilities here.

1. _____

2. _____

Journal Entry

Name _____ Date _____

E X P L O R E

EXPLORE

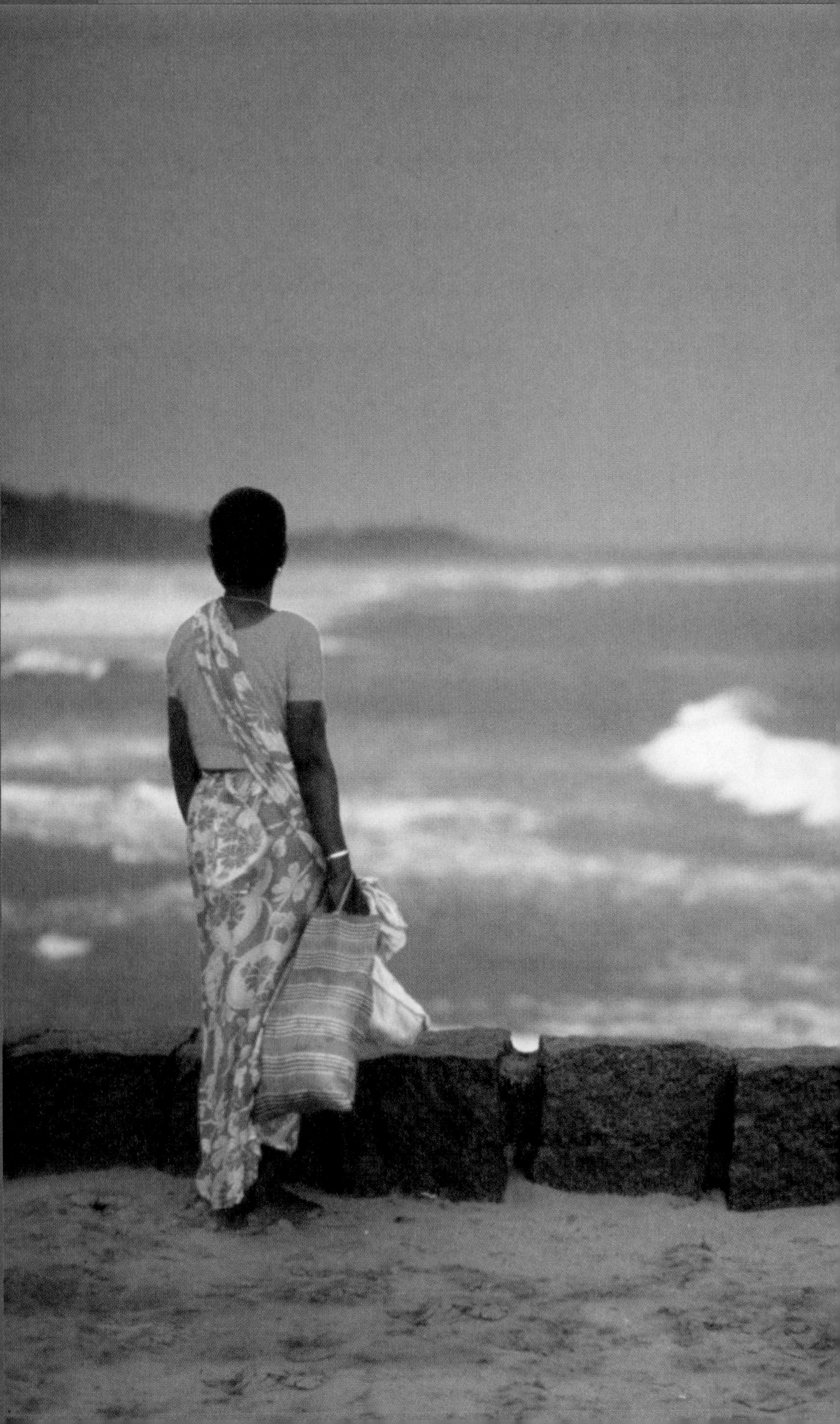

Self-Awareness 4

Knowing Who You Are and How You Learn

In this chapter, you will explore answers to the following questions:

- Is there one best way to learn?
- What are the benefits of knowing your learning style?
- How can you discover your learning style?
- How do you explore who you are?
- How can you start thinking about choosing a major?

The ability to learn is much more than a college skill. Being a learner for life means that you will be able to keep pace with rapidly changing workplace technology, stay aware of world developments and how they affect you, and continue to grow as a person. To learn effectively, you need to understand *how* you learn. This chapter will help by introducing you to two different personal assessments—one focusing on how you take in information, and one that helps you determine how you interact with others. You will then explore other important elements of self: your self-perception, interests, and habits. The more you know about your learning style, interests, and abilities, the better prepared you will be to choose a career that makes the most of who you are and what you can do.

Teaching Tip
See Dr. Howard Gardner's Web site (http://edweb.cnidr.org/edref.mi.gardner.html) for his explanation of multiple intelligences and their role in traditional education.

IS THERE ONE BEST WAY TO LEARN?

Your mind is the most powerful tool you will ever possess. You are accomplished at many skills and can process all kinds of information. However, when you have trouble accomplishing a particular task, you may become convinced that you can't learn how to do anything new. Not only is this perception incorrect, it can also damage your belief in yourself.

Every individual is highly developed in some abilities and underdeveloped in others. Many famously successful people were brilliant in one area but functioned poorly in other areas. Winston Churchill failed the sixth grade. Abraham Lincoln was demoted to a private in the Black Hawk war. Louis Pasteur was a poor student in chemistry. Walt Disney was fired from a job and told he had no good ideas. What some might interpret as a deficiency or disability may be simply a different method of learning. People have their own individual gifts—the key is to identify them.

> **Learning style**
>
> A particular way in which the mind receives and processes information.

There is no one "best" way to learn. Instead, there are many different learning styles, each suited to different situations. Each person's **learning style** is unique. Knowing how you learn is one of the first steps in discovering who you are. Before you explore your learning style, consider how the knowledge you will gain can help you.

WHAT ARE THE BENEFITS OF KNOWING YOUR LEARNING STYLE?

Although it takes some work and exploration, understanding your learning style can benefit you in many ways—in your studies, the classroom, and the workplace.

Study Benefits

Most students aim to maximize learning while minimizing frustration and time spent studying. If you know your strengths and limitations, you can use techniques that take advantage of your highly developed areas while helping you through your less developed ones. For example, say you perform better in smaller, discussion-based classes. When you have the opportunity, you might choose a course section that is smaller or that is taught by an instructor who prefers group discussion. You might also apply specific strategies to improve your retention in a large-group lecture situation.

> **Springboard**
>
> Discuss possible strategies for large lecture classes. Suggestions:
> (1) Students can take advantage of breakout sessions run by teaching assistants; (2) Students can schedule a study group immediately after class to discuss the ideas they just heard.

Following each of this chapter's two assessments, you will see information about study techniques that tend to complement the strengths and shortcomings of each intelligence or spectrum. Remember that you have abilities in all areas, even though some are dominant. Therefore, you may encounter useful suggestions under any of the headings. What's important is that you use what works. During this course, try a large number of new study techniques, eventually keeping those you find to be useful.

Classroom Benefits

Knowing your learning style can help you make the most of the teaching styles of your instructors. Your particular learning style may work well with the way some instructors teach and be a mismatch with other instructors. Remember that an instructor's teaching style often reflects his or her learning style. After perhaps two class meetings, you should be able to make a pretty good assessment of teaching styles (instructors may exhibit more than one). Once you understand the various teaching styles you encounter, plan to make adjustments that maximize your learning. See Figure 4.1 for some common teaching styles.

Assess how well your own styles match up with the various teaching styles. If your styles mesh well with an instructor's teaching styles, you're in luck. If not, you have a number of options.

Bring extra focus to your weaker areas. Although it's not easy, working on your weaker points will help you break new ground in your learning. For example, if you're a verbal person in a math- and logic-oriented class, increase your focus and concentration during class so that you get as much as you can from the presentation. Then spend extra study time on the material, make a point to ask others from your class to help you, and search for additional supplemental materials and exercises to reinforce your knowledge.

Ask your instructor for additional help. For example, a visual person might ask an instructor to recommend visuals that would help to illustrate the points made in class. If the class breaks into smaller groups, you might ask the instructor to divide those groups roughly according to learning style, so that students with similar strengths can help each other.

Teaching Tip
Think about how you engage different intelligences in your teaching style and what your style says about your dominant intelligence. Improvement suggestions: Attend a multiple intelligence workshop and/or team-teach with someone with complementary strengths.

Teaching Tip
Many schools give students the opportunity to drop courses without penalty early in the semester. Students who believe that a teacher's style is incompatible with their learning style should consider this option—but only as a last resort.

Learning Styles Tip
Visual learners can use computer graphics programs to convert blocks of text into colorful charts and tables that will make learning easier.

Teaching Styles

FIGURE 4.1

Lecture	Instructor speaks to the class for the entire period, little to no class interaction.
Group Discussion	Instructor presents material but encourages class discussion throughout.
Small Groups	Instructor presents material and then breaks class into small groups for discussion or project work.
Visual Focus	Instructor uses visual elements such as diagrams, photographs, drawings, transparencies.
Verbal Focus	Instructor relies primarily on words, either spoken or written on the board or overhead projector.
Logical Presentation	Instructor organizes material in a logical sequence, such as by time or importance.
Random Presentation	Instructor tackles topics in no particular order, jumps around a lot, or digresses.

"Convert" class material during study time. For example, an interpersonal learner takes a class with an instructor who presents big-picture information in lecture format. This student might organize study groups and, in those groups, focus on filling in the factual gaps using reading materials assigned for that class. Likewise, a visual student might rewrite notes in different colors to add a visual element—for example, assigning a different color to each main point or topic, or using one color for central ideas, another for supporting examples.

Instructors are as individual as students. Taking time to focus on their teaching styles, and on how to adjust, will help you learn more effectively and avoid frustration. Don't forget to take advantage of your instructor's office hours when you have a learning style issue that is causing you difficulty.

Career Benefits

Because different careers require differing abilities, there is no one "best" learning style. Develop self-knowledge through honest analysis and then accurately match what you do best with a career that makes the most of your strengths (in addition to this chapter's assessments, the Campbell Interest and Skill Survey in the appendix of this book can help). Specifically, how can knowing your learning style help you in your career?

You will perform more successfully. Your learning style is essentially your working style. If you know how you learn, you will be able to look for an environment that suits you best. You will perform at the top of your ability if you work at a job in which you feel competent and happy. Even when you are working at a job that isn't your ideal, knowing yourself can lead you to on-the-job choices that make your situation as agreeable as possible.

An instructor speaks in sign language.

You will be able to function well in teams. Teamwork is a primary feature of the modern workplace. The better your awareness of your abilities, the better you will be able to identify what tasks you will best be able to perform in a team situation. The better your awareness of personality traits—your own as well as those of others—the more skillful you will be at communicating with and relating to your coworkers.

You will be more able to target areas that need improvement. Awareness of your learning styles will help you pinpoint the areas that are more difficult for you. That has two advantages: One, you can begin to work on difficult areas, step by step. Two, when a task requires a skill that is tough for you, you can either take special care with it or suggest someone else whose style may be better suited to it.

Now that you know you have something to gain, look at some ways you can explore your particular learning style.

HOW CAN YOU DISCOVER YOUR LEARNING STYLE?

Many different types of assessments are available to promote self-discovery. Each type provides a different means of exploring strengths and weaknesses, abilities and limitations. This chapter contains one each of two particular types—learning style assessments and personality assessments.

Learning style assessments focus on the process by which you take in, retain, and use information. Students may use learning style assessment results to maximize study efficiency and to choose courses that suit their styles. *Personality assessments* indicate how you respond to both internal and external situations—in other words, how you react to thoughts and feelings as well as to people and events. Employers may give such assessments to employees and use the results to set up and evaluate teams.

The learning styles assessment in this chapter is called *Pathways to Learning* and is based on the Multiple Intelligences Theory, discussed below. It can help you determine how you best take in information as well as how you can improve areas in which you have more trouble learning. The second assessment tool, *Personality Spectrum,* is a personality assessment that helps you evaluate how you react to people and situations in your life. *Pathways to Learning* and the *Personality Spectrum* provide two different perspectives that together will give you a more complete picture of how you interact with everything you encounter—information, people, and your own inner thoughts.

Teaching Tolerance

Learning style assessments should never be used to fuel racial, ethnic, or cultural stereotypes that claim that group members are likely to have the same strengths and weaknesses just because of their group identity.

e-mail

E-mail or write friends and tell them about the multiple intelligences. Ask them which intelligence they think they might be dominant in. Take the *Pathways to Learning* inventory with them when you see them next.

Multiple Intelligences Theory

There is a saying, "It is not how smart you are, but how you are smart." In 1983, Howard Gardner, a Harvard University professor, changed the way people perceive intelligence and learning with his theory of *Multiple Intelligences.* Gardner believes there are at least eight distinct intelligences possessed by all people, and that every person has developed some intelligences more fully than others. Most people have at one time learned something quickly and comfortably. Most have also had the opposite experience: no matter how hard they try, something they want to learn just won't sink in. According to the Multiple Intelligences Theory, when you find a task or subject easy, you are probably using a more fully developed intelligence; when you have more trouble, you may be using a less developed intelligence.[1]

Table 4.1 offers brief descriptions of the focus of each of the intelligences. You will find information on related skills and study techniques on page 92. The *Pathways to Learning* assessment will help you determine the levels to which your intelligences are developed.

Intelligence

As defined by H. Gardner, an ability to solve problems or fashion products that are useful in a particular cultural setting or community.

Be a Team

Ask students to list games they enjoy, share this information with a group, and brainstorm what their choices say about their intelligence. For example, Scrabble lovers may be verbal-linguistic learners, chess fans logical-mathematical learners, and puzzle addicts spatial learners.

Personality Spectrum

One of the first instruments to measure psychological types, the Myers-Briggs Type Inventory (MBTI), was designed by Katharine Briggs and her daughter, Isabel Briggs Myers. Later, David Keirsey and Marilyn Bates combined the

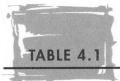

TABLE 4.1

Multiple Intelligences

Career Connection

Possible careers for each intelligence type:

journalist, speech writer, politician

computer scientist, engineer, medical researcher

athlete, gym teacher, chiropractor

film maker, interior decorator, artist

sales rep, teacher, career counselor

writer and other activities involving independent work

conductor, composer, ad agency jingle writer, choreographer

farmer, environmental activist, oceanographer

INTELLIGENCE	DESCRIPTION
Verbal-Linguistic	Ability to communicate through language (listening, reading, writing, speaking)
Logical-Mathematical	Ability to understand logical reasoning and problem solving (math, science, patterns, sequences)
Bodily-Kinesthetic	Ability to use the physical body skillfully and to take in knowledge through bodily sensation (coordination, working with hands)
Visual-Spatial	Ability to understand spatial relationships and to perceive and create images (visual art, graphic design, charts and maps)
Interpersonal	Ability to relate to others, noticing their moods, motivations, and feelings (social activity, cooperative learning, teamwork)
Intrapersonal	Ability to understand one's own behavior and feelings (self-awareness, independence, time spent alone)
Musical	Ability to comprehend and create meaningful sound (music, sensitivity to sound, understanding patterns)
Naturalistic	Ability to understand features of the environment (interest in nature, environmental balance, ecosystem, stress relief brought by natural environments)

sixteen Myers-Briggs types into four temperaments and developed an assessment based on those temperaments, called the Keirsey Sorter. These assessments are two of the most widely-used personality tests, both in psychology and in the business world.

The *Personality Spectrum* assessment in this chapter can help you better understand yourself and those around you. Based on the Myers-Briggs and Keirsey theories, it adapts and simplifies their material into four personality types—Thinker, Organizer, Giver, and Adventurer—and was developed by Joyce Bishop (1997). The *Personality Spectrum* will give you a personality perspective on how you can maximize your functioning at school and at work. Each personality type has its own abilities that improve work and school performance, suitable learning techniques, and ways of relating in interpersonal relationships. Page 94 will give you more details about each type.

Using the Assessments

The two assessments follow this section of text. After each assessment you will find a page that details the traits of each dimension and offers strategies to help you make the most of that dimension's tendencies.

Complete both assessments, trying to answer the questions objectively—in other words, mark the answers that best indicate who you are, not who you want to be. The more closely you can see yourself today, the more effectively you can set goals for where you want to go from here. Then, enter your scores on p. 95, where you will see a brain diagram on which to plot *Personality Spectrum* scores and boxes in which to enter your *Pathways to Learning* scores. This page is organized so that you can see your scores for both assessments at a glance, giving you an opportunity to examine how they relate to one another. Don't be concerned if some of your scores are low—that is true for most everyone. For *Pathways to Learning*, 21–24 indicates a high level of development in that particular type of intelligence, 15–20 a moderate level, and below 15 an underdeveloped intelligence. For the *Personality Spectrum*, 26–36 indicates a strong tendency in that dimension, 14–25 a moderate tendency, and below 14 a minimal tendency.

Knowing how you learn will help you improve your understanding of yourself—how you may function at school, in the workplace, and in your personal life. Keep in mind that these or any other assessments are intended not to label you but to be *indicators* of who you are. Your thinking skills—your ability to evaluate sources of information—will best enable you to see yourself as a whole, including both gifts and areas for growth. Your job is to verify and sift each piece of information and arrive at the most accurate portrait of yourself at this point in time.

> "To be what we are, and to become what we are capable of becoming, is the only end of life."
> Robert Louis Stevenson

Perspective on Learning Style

Both of the assessments in the chapter—and the survey in the appendix—provide you with self-knowledge that can help you manage yourself in school, at work, and at home in the most effective way possible. However, no one assessment can give you the final word on who you are and what you can and cannot do. It's human to want an easy answer—a one-page printout of the secret to your identity—but this kind of quick fix does not exist. You are a complex person who cannot be summed up by a test or evaluation.

Use Assessments for Reference

The most reasonable way to approach any assessment is as a reference point rather than as a label. There are no "right" answers, no "best" set of scores. Instead of boxing yourself into one or more categories, which limits you, approach any assessment as a tool with which you can expand your idea of yourself. Think of it as a new set of eyeglasses for a person with somewhat blurred vision. The glasses will not create new paths and possibilities for you, but they will help you see more clearly the paths and possibilities that already exist. They give you the power to explore, choose, and act with confidence.

You will continually learn, change, and grow throughout your life. Any evaluation is simply a snapshot, a look at who you are in a given moment. The answers can, and will, change as you change and as circumstances change. They provide an opportunity for you to identify a moment and learn from it by asking questions: Who am I right now? How does this compare to who I want to be?

Teaching Tolerance
While intelligences are not linked to group stereotypes, they may be influenced by cultural expectations. While a child with spatial intelligence may become an artist in one culture, a similar child may be encouraged to become a sea captain in another.

Use Assessments for Understanding

Understanding your tendencies will help you understand yourself. Avoid labeling yourself narrowly by using one intelligence or personality type, such as if you were to say, "I'm no good in math" or "I'm never a thinker." Anyone can learn math; however, some people learn math more efficiently through intelligences other than logical–mathematical. For example, a visual–spatial learner may want to draw diagrams of as much of a math problem as possible. Everyone is a thinker; however, some people tend to approach life situations more analytically than others.

Ask one of your professors or one of your TAs which type of intelligences they are dominant in. If they don't know, share the Pathways to Learning with them so you have a springboard for discussion.

People are a blend of all the intelligences and personality types, in proportions unique to them. Most often one or two intelligences or types are dominant. When material is very difficult or when you are feeling insecure about learning something new, use your most dominant areas. When something is easy for you, however, this is an opportunity for you to improve your less developed areas. All of your abilities will continue to develop throughout your lifetime.

In addition, you may change which abilities you emphasize, depending on the situation. For example, an organizer-dominant student might find it easy to take notes in outline style when the instructor lectures in an organized way. However, if another instructor jumps from topic to topic, the same student might choose to use a think link. The more you know yourself, the more you will be able to assess any situation and set appropriate goals.

Elsewhere in the text you will see how your personality types and intelligences influence other skills and life areas. As you read, try to examine how your tendencies affect you in different areas—study techniques, time management, personal wellness, communication, and so on. Knowing your style can help you improve how you function in every area of your life.

Avoid Overreacting to Challenges

Real World Link

Many corporations run workshops to help employees develop various intelligences. For example, employees at New York-based Chase Manhattan Bank attend workshops to improve interpersonal communication skills.

The assessments you complete reveal areas of challenge as well as ability. If you assume that your limitations are set in stone or let them dominate your self-image, you may deny yourself growth. Rather than dwelling on limitations (which often results in a negative self-image) or ignoring them (which often leads to unproductive choices), use what you know from the assessments to face your limitations and work to improve them.

In any area of challenge, look at where you are and set goals that will help you reach where you want to be. If a class is difficult, examine what improvements you need to make in order to succeed. If a work situation requires you to perform in an area that causes trouble for you, face your limitations head-on and ask for help. Exploring what you will gain from working on a limitation will help you gain the motivation you need to move ahead.

If you are interested in an additional method of self-discovery, please refer to the Campbell Interest and Skill Survey in the appendix. You might also find additional assessments and information through your school's career counselors.

Your learning style is one important part of self-knowledge. Following the assessments, you will explore other important factors that help to define you.

Developed by Joyce Bishop, Ph.D., and based upon Howard Gardner *(Frames of Mind: The Theory of Multiple Intelligences)*.

Directions: Rate each statement as follows:

Write the number of your response (1–4) on the line next to the statement and total each set of six questions.

1 rarely   *2* sometimes   *3* usually   *4* always

1. _____ I enjoy physical activities.
2. _____ I am uncomfortable sitting still.
3. _____ I prefer to learn through doing.
4. _____ When sitting I move my legs or hands.
5. _____ I enjoy working with my hands.
6. _____ I like to pace when I'm thinking or studying.
_____ **TOTAL for Bodily–Kinesthetic**

7. _____ I enjoy telling stories.
8. _____ I like to write.
9. _____ I like to read.
10. _____ I express myself clearly.
11. _____ I am good at negotiating.
12. _____ I like to discuss topics that interest me.
_____ **TOTAL for Verbal–Linguistic**

13. _____ I use maps easily.
14. _____ I draw pictures/diagrams when explaining ideas.
15. _____ I can assemble items easily from diagrams.
16. _____ I enjoy drawing or photography.
17. _____ I do not like to read long paragraphs.
18. _____ I prefer a drawn map over written directions.
_____ **TOTAL for Visual–Spatial**

19. _____ I like math in school.
20. _____ I like science.
21. _____ I problem-solve well.
22. _____ I question how things work.
23. _____ I enjoy planning or designing something new.
24. _____ I am able to fix things.
_____ **TOTAL for Logical–Mathematical**

25. _____ I listen to music.
26. _____ I move my fingers or feet when I hear music.
27. _____ I have good rhythm.
28. _____ I like to sing along with music.
29. _____ People have said I have musical talent.
30. _____ I like to express my ideas through music.
_____ **TOTAL for Musical**

31. _____ I need quiet time to think.
32. _____ I think about issues before I want to talk.
33. _____ I am interested in self-improvement.
34. _____ I understand my thoughts and feelings.
35. _____ I know what I want out of life.
36. _____ I prefer to work on projects alone.
_____ **TOTAL for Intrapersonal**

37. _____ I like doing a project with other people.
38. _____ People come to me to help settle conflicts.
39. _____ I like to spend time with friends.
40. _____ I am good at understanding people.
41. _____ I am good at making people feel comfortable.
42. _____ I enjoy helping others.
_____ **TOTAL for Interpersonal**

43. _____ I enjoy nature whenever possible.
44. _____ I think about having a career involving nature.
45. _____ I enjoy studying plants, animals, or oceans.
46. _____ I avoid being indoors except when I sleep.
47. _____ As a child I played with bugs and leaves.
48. _____ When I feel stressed I want to be out in nature.
_____ **TOTAL for Naturalistic**

Adapted by Joyce Bishop, Ph.D., from *Seven Pathways of Learning*, David Lazear, © 1994.

SKILLS	STUDY TECHNIQUES
Verbal–Linguistic ■ Analyzing own use of language ■ Remembering terms easily ■ Explaining, teaching, learning, using humor ■ Understanding syntax and meaning of words ■ Convincing someone to do something	**Verbal–Linguistic** ■ Read text and highlight no more than 10% ■ Rewrite notes ■ Outline chapters ■ Teach someone else ■ Recite information or write scripts/debates
Musical–Rhythmic ■ Sensing tonal qualities ■ Creating or enjoying melodies and rhythms ■ Being sensitive to sounds and rhythms ■ Using "schemas" to hear music ■ Understanding the structure of music	**Musical–Rhythmic** ■ Create rhythms out of words ■ Beat out rhythms with hand or stick ■ Play instrumental music/write raps ■ Put new material to songs you already know ■ Take music breaks
Logical–Mathematical ■ Recognizing abstract patterns ■ Reasoning inductively and deductively ■ Discerning relationships and connections ■ Performing complex calculations ■ Reasoning scientifically	**Logical–Mathematical** ■ Organize material logically ■ Explain material sequentially to someone ■ Develop systems and find patterns ■ Write outlines and develop charts and graphs ■ Analyze information
Visual–Spatial ■ Perceiving and forming objects accurately ■ Recognizing relationships between objects ■ Representing something graphically ■ Manipulating images ■ Finding one's way in space	**Visual–Spatial** ■ Develop graphic organizers for new material ■ Draw mind maps ■ Develop charts and graphs ■ Use color in notes to organize ■ Visualize material (method of loci)
Bodily–Kinesthetic ■ Connecting mind and body ■ Controlling movement ■ Improving body functions ■ Expanding body awareness to all senses ■ Coordinating body movement	**Bodily–Kinesthetic** ■ Move or rap while you learn; pace and recite ■ Use "method of loci" or manipulatives ■ Move fingers under words while reading ■ Create "living sculptures" ■ Act out scripts of material, design games
Intrapersonal ■ Evaluating own thinking ■ Being aware of and expressing feelings ■ Understanding self in relationship to others ■ Thinking and reasoning on higher levels	**Intrapersonal** ■ Reflect on personal meaning of information ■ Visualize information/keep a journal ■ Study in quiet settings ■ Imagine experiments
Interpersonal ■ Seeing things from others' perspectives ■ Cooperating within a group ■ Communicating verbally and nonverbally ■ Creating and maintaining relationships	**Interpersonal** ■ Study in a group ■ Discuss information ■ Use flash cards with others ■ Teach someone else
Naturalist ■ Deep understanding of nature ■ Appreciation of the delicate balance in nature	**Naturalist** ■ Connect with nature whenever possible ■ Form study groups of people with like interests

STEP 1.   Rank order all four responses to each question from most like you (4) to least like you (1). Place a 1, 2, 3, or 4 in each box next to the responses.

1. I like instructors who

   a. ☐ tell me exactly what is expected of me.

   b. ☐ make learning active and exciting.

   c. ☐ maintain a safe and supportive class-room.

   d. ☐ challenge me to think at higher levels.

2. I learn best when the material is

   a. ☐ well organized.

   b. ☐ something I can do hands-on.

   c. ☐ about understanding and improving the human condition.

   d. ☐ intellectually challenging.

3. A high priority in my life is to

   a. ☐ keep my commitments.

   b. ☐ experience as much of life as possible.

   c. ☐ make a difference in the lives of others.

   d. ☐ understand how things work.

4. Other people think of me as

   a. ☐ dependable and loyal.

   b. ☐ dynamic and creative.

   c. ☐ caring and honest.

   d. ☐ intelligent and inventive.

5. When I experience stress I would most likely

   a. ☐ do something to help me feel more in control of my life.

   b. ☐ do something physical and daring.

   c. ☐ talk with a friend.

   d. ☐ go off by myself and think about my situation.

6. I would probably not be close friends with someone who is

   a. ☐ irresponsible.

   b. ☐ unwilling to try new things.

   c. ☐ selfish and unkind to others.

   d. ☐ an illogical thinker.

7. My vacations could be described as

   a. ☐ traditional.

   b. ☐ adventuresome.

   c. ☐ pleasing to others.

   d. ☐ a new learning experience.

8. One word that best describes me is

   a. ☐ sensible.

   b. ☐ spontaneous.

   c. ☐ giving.

   d. ☐ analytical.

STEP 2.   Add up the total points for each letter.

TOTAL for a. ☐ Organizer

TOTAL for b. ☐ Adventurer

TOTAL for c. ☐ Giver

TOTAL for d. ☐ Thinker

STEP 3.   Plot these numbers on the brain diagram on page 95.

THINKER

Personal strengths—You enjoy solving problems and love to develop models and systems. You have an abstract and analytical way of thinking. You love to explore ideas. You dislike unfairness and wastefulness. You are global by nature, always seeking universal truth.

Work/school—You work best when assigned projects that require analytical thinking and problem solving. You are inspired by futuristic ideas and potentials. You need the freedom to go beyond the established rules. You feel appreciated when praised for your ingenuity. You dislike repetitive tasks.

Relationships—You thrive in relationships that recognize your need for independence and private time to think and read. Stress can come from the fear of appearing foolish. You want others to accept that you feel deeply even though you may not often express it.

Learning—You like quiet time to reflect on new information. Learning through problem solving and designing new ways of approaching issues is most interesting to you. You may find it effective to convert material you need to learn into logical charts and graphs.

ORGANIZER

Personal strengths—You value the traditions of family and support social structures. You never take responsibility lightly. You have a strong sense of history, culture, and dignity. You value order and predictability. You dislike disobedience or nonconformity. You value loyalty and obligation.

Work/school—You enjoy work that requires detailed planning and follow-through. You prefer to have tasks defined in clear and concrete terms. You need a well-structured, stable environment, free from abrupt changes. You feel appreciated when you are praised for neatness, organization, and efficiency. You like frequent feedback so you know you are on the right track.

Relationships—You do best in relationships that provide for your need of security, stability, and structure. You appreciate it when dates that are important to you are remembered by others.

Learning—You must have organization to the material and know the overall plan and what will be required of you. Depending on your most developed Multiple Intelligences, organizing the material could include any of the following: highlighting key terms in text, rewriting and organizing notes from class or text, making flash cards.

GIVER

Personal strengths—You value honesty and authenticity above all else. You enjoy close relationships with those you love and there is a strong spirituality in your nature. Making a difference in the world is important to you, and you enjoy cultivating potential in yourself and others. You are a person of peace. You are a natural romantic. You dislike hypocrisy and deception.

Work/school—You function best in a warm, harmonious working environment with the possibility of interacting with openness and honesty. You prefer to avoid conflict and hostility. You thrive when your creative approach to your work is appreciated and praised.

Relationships—You thrive in relationships that include warm, intimate talks. You feel closer to people when they express their feelings and are open and responsive. You think romance, touch, and appreciation are necessary for survival. You blossom when others express a loving commitment to you and you are able to contribute to the relationship.

Learning—You enjoy studying with others and also helping them learn. Study groups are very effective for you to remember difficult information.

ADVENTURER

Personal strengths—Your strength is skillfulness. You take pride in being highly skilled in a variety of fields. Adventure is your middle name. A hands-on approach to problem solving is important to you. You need variety, and waiting is like "emotional death." You live in the here and now. It is your impulsiveness that drives everything you do. You dislike rigidity and authority.

Work/school—You function best in a work environment that is action-packed with a hands-on approach. You appreciate the opportunity to be skillful and adventurous, and to use your natural ability as a negotiator. You like freedom on the job so you can perform in nontraditional ways and in your own style. Keeping a good sense of humor and avoiding boredom on the job is important to you. You feel appreciated when your performance and skills are acknowledged.

Relationships—You function best in relationships that recognize your need for freedom. You thrive on spontaneous playfulness and excitement.

Learning—You learn exciting and stimulating information easiest, so pick classes and instructors carefully. Study with fun people in a variety of ways and places. Keep on the move. Develop games and puzzles to help memorize terminology.

THINKER

Technical
Scientific
Mathematical
Dispassionate
Rational
Analytical
Logical
Problem Solving
Theoretical
Intellectual
Objective
Quantitative
Explicit
Realistic
Literal
Precise
Formal

Directions: Place a dot on the appropriate number line for each of your four scores, connect the dots, and color each polygon. Write your scores in the four shaded boxes.

GIVER

Interpersonal
Emotional
Caring
Sociable
Giving
Spiritual
Musical
Romantic
Feeling
Peacemaker
Trusting
Adaptable
Passionate
Harmonious
Idealistic
Talkative
Honest

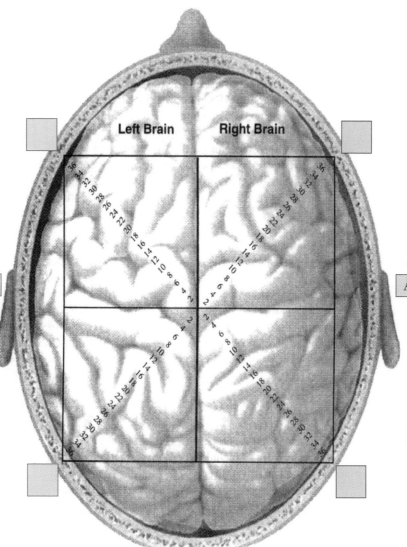

Left Brain   Right Brain

ORGANIZER

Tactical
Planning
Detailed
Practical
Confident
Predictable
Controlled
Dependable
Systematic
Sequential
Structured
Administrative
Procedural
Organized
Conservative
Safekeeping
Disciplined

ADVENTURER

Active
Visual
Risking
Original
Artistic
Spatial
Skillful
Impulsive
Metaphoric
Experimental
Divergent
Fast-paced
Simultaneous
Competitive
Imaginative
Open-minded
Adventuresome

Source: *Understanding Psychology*, 3/e, by Morris, © 1996. Adapted by permission of Prentice-Hall, Inc., Upper Saddle River, NJ.

Pathways to Learning

From page 91, write your 8 Multiple Intelligences in the boxes, according to your total scores.

Scores: 21–24 = Highly Developed	15–20 = Moderately Developed	below 15 = Underdeveloped

WINDOWS ON THE WORLD
Real Life Student Issues

How can I make the most of my learning style?

Anwar Smith, Taylor University, Upland, Indiana, Education major

Recently I took a multiple intelligences assessment. Some of it confirmed what I already knew, but some results were more surprising. I always knew I like to talk things out. I learn best through discussion. I also answered questions that showed I have a high degree of interpersonal intelligence, and I scored well in the verbal–linguistic category.

In addition to academics, I play football at Taylor and am managing to keep my GPA

up. I'm trying to get all I can out of my education. When I graduate I would like to go back to the inner-city of Chicago where I grew up and help young people achieve their goals. I am wondering how my learning style will affect what I want to do with my future. What do you think all this means in regard to my study and work habits?

Rev. Eric Gerard Pearman, M. Div., Ph.D. candidate at the University of Denver, Denver, Colorado

First of all, I want to commend you on your vision and your desire to return to the inner-city of Chicago and help young people. Your verbal and interpersonal intelligences are well-suited for one who feels the "call" to reach out and meet the needs of youth in Chicago's inner city. Your verbal–linguistic results indicate that you like to talk things out and that you learn best in group discussions. Should you ever find yourself in a classroom setting that doesn't permit much discussion, find a classmate that you can talk with about the things you are learning.

Communication is key to solving the problems that affect inner-city children. We need people like you who will talk *to* them rather than *at* them and who will show them that they can achieve success rather than falling victim to the negative influences around them. We need people who will help them to help themselves rather than depending on others to help them.

I mention this because God has brought me from a single-parent home in the Ida B. Wells housing project on Chicago's south side through street gang activity and into a doctoral program with the desire to reach out to the "least of these" in my old neighborhood. My mother demanded excellence and provided me with the values that helped me make good choices during difficult moments. Participating in gang-related activity, and seeing fellow peers killed during my adolescent years, made me realize that I needed to explore another path in life. Positive influences at

a church across the street reinforced values that my mother taught and helped me to see that because I lived in "projects" did not mean that the projects had to live in me.

You obviously have a strong work ethic and deep concern for people. These skills, along with your intelligences, might lead you to consider a seminary education. Seminary can give you an academic challenge and a chance to develop the skills needed for urban ministry. My 1990 Master of Divinity degree has given me opportunities from the teaching to the pastoral.

I challenge you to pursue a Ph.D. in the future, whether to teach, pastor, and/or work within some capacity of youth-related ministry. Furthering your education will help you provide young people with an understanding of and appreciation for educational achievement, and the benefits that result from such hard studying and determination.

HOW DO YOU EXPLORE WHO YOU ARE?

You are an absolutely unique individual. Although you may share individual characteristics with others, your combination of traits is one-of-a-kind. It could take a lifetime to learn everything there is to know about yourself because you are constantly changing. However, you can start by exploring these facets of yourself: self-perception, interests, and habits.

Self-Perception

Having an accurate self-perception isn't easy. It's important to see yourself in a broad capacity, not limited by the ideas that you or others may have of you. How you react to your assessment scores is an indicator of your self-perception. As mentioned earlier in the chapter, the most productive reaction involves seeing the scores as informational indicators, not as defining and undeniable labels.

Feeling inadequate from time to time is normal, but a constantly negative self-perception is likely to have destructive effects. Negative self-perception can be a self-fulfilling prophecy: First you believe that you are incapable of being or doing something, then you neglect to try, and finally you probably don't do or become what you had already decided was impossible. For example, say you think you can't pass a certain course. Since you feel you don't have a chance, you don't put as much effort into the work. Sure enough, at the end of the semester, you don't pass. Unfortunately, you may see your failure as proof of your incapability, instead of realizing that you didn't allow yourself to try. When this chain of events occurs in the workplace, people lose jobs. When it happens in personal life, people lose relationships.

Negative self-images may come from one or more different sources, some of which are shown in Figure 4.2. The following strategies might help you refine your self-image so that it reflects more of your true self.

- **Believe in yourself.** If you don't believe in yourself, others may have a harder time believing in you. Work to eliminate negative self-talk. Have faith in your areas of strength. When you set your goals, stick to them. Know that your mind and will are very powerful.

- **Talk to other people whom you trust.** People who know you well often have a more realistic perception of you than you do of yourself.

- **Take personal time.** Stress makes having perspective on your life more difficult. Take time out to clear your mind and think realistically about who you are and who you want to be.

- **Look at all of the evidence.** Mistakes and limitations can loom large in your mind. Consider what you do well and what you have accomplished as carefully as you consider your stumbles.

Building a positive self-perception is a lifelong challenge. If you maintain a bright but realistic vision of yourself, it will take you far along the road toward achieving your goals.

Self-perception
How one views oneself, one's opinion of oneself.

Teaching Tip
Ask students to list 10 personal characteristics that reflect how they see themselves. Encourage them to free write the list without censoring any characteristics. If the list is filled with more negative than positive traits, the student may have a negative self-image.

Be a Team
Longitudinal studies have shown that life experiences can change self-image. With this in mind, ask students to think about experiences that have changed them and the reasons for their formative power. Have them share and discuss their thoughts with a partner.

"The greatest discovery of any generation is that human beings can alter their lives by altering their attitudes of mind."
Albert Schweitzer

FIGURE 4.2 *Self-Image Sources*

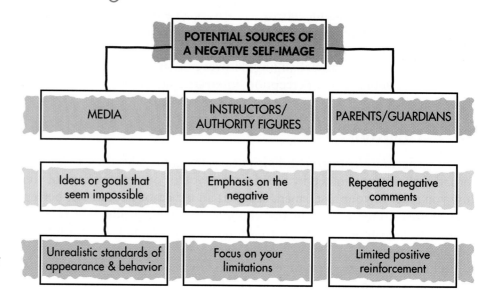

Teaching Tip
Help students understand the danger of aiming for perfection. Personal perfection is an unattainable goal that inevitably leads to failure. Encourage them, instead, to be the best that they can be.

Interests

Taking time now to explore your interests will help you later when you select a major and a career. Looking at your dominant intelligences and personality traits may give you clues about your interests. For example, a giver may be interested in service professions, an interpersonal learner may want to work with people, or a naturalistic learner might have nature as a primary interest.

Other ideas about your interests may come from asking yourself questions such as these:

■ What areas of study do I like?

■ What activities make me happy?

■ What careers seem interesting to me?

■ What kind of daily schedule do I like to keep (early riser or night owl)?

■ What type of home and work environment do I prefer?

Interests play an important role in the workplace. Many people, however, do not take their interests seriously when choosing a career. Some make salary or stability their first priority. Some take the first job that comes along. Some may not realize they can do better. Not considering what you are interested in may lead to an area of study or a job that leaves you unhappy, bored, or unfulfilled.

Career Connection
Learning styles assessments can help target a career field. For example, a well-organized, mathematical student might choose a career in banking while a giver with strong interpersonal skills might choose to work for a charitable foundation.

Choosing to consider your interests and happiness takes courage but brings benefits. Think about your life. You spend hours attending classes and studying outside of class. You will probably spend at least eight hours a day, five or more days a week, up to fifty or more weeks a year as a working contributor to the world. Although your studies and work won't always make you deliriously happy, it is possible to spend your school and work time in a manner that suits you.

Here are three positive effects of focusing on your interests:

You will have more energy. When you're doing something you like, time seems to pass quickly. Contrast this with how you feel about disagreeable activities. The difference in your energy level is immense. You will be able to get much more done in a subject or career area that you enjoy.

You will perform better. When you were in high school, you probably got your best grades in your favorite classes. That doesn't change as you get older. The more you like something, the harder you work at it—and the harder you work, the more you will improve.

You will have a positive attitude. A positive attitude creates a positive environment and might even make up for areas in which you lack ability or experience. This is especially important when working in a team. Because businesses currently emphasize teamwork to such a great extent, your ability to maintain a positive attitude might mean the difference between success and failure.

Attitude
A state of mind or feeling toward something.

For additional information about your interests, take the Campbell Interest and Skill Survey in the appendix and mail it to the address given. You will receive a report that shows your likely interests, indicated by your answers in the inventory.

Habits

A preference for a particular action that you do a certain way, and often on a regular basis or at certain times, is a *habit*. You might have a habit of showering in the morning, channel surfing with the TV remote control, talking for hours on the phone, or studying late at night. Habits can be linked to personality types and intelligences. A verbal learner might have a habit of reading the paper every morning, while a visual learner may prefer to get the news from TV. An adventurer may habitually go out of town on the weekend, while an organizer may spend weekends getting things in order at home. Your habits reveal a lot about you. Some habits you consider to be good habits, and some may be bad habits.

Bad habits earn that title because they can prevent you from reaching important goals. Some bad habits, such as chronic lateness, cause obvious problems. Other habits, such as renting movies three times a week, may not seem bad until you realize that you needed to spend those hours studying. People maintain bad habits because they offer immediate, enjoyable rewards, even if later effects are negative. For example, going out to eat frequently may drain your budget, but at first it seems easier than shopping for food, cooking, and washing dishes.

Good habits are those that have positive effects on your life. You often have to wait longer and work harder to see a reward for good habits, which makes them harder to maintain. If you cut out fattening foods, you won't lose weight in two days. If you reduce your nights out to gain study time, your grades won't improve in a week. When you strive to maintain good habits, trust that the rewards are somewhere down the road. Changing a habit can be a long process.

Take time to evaluate your habits. Look at the positive and negative effects of each, and decide which are helpful and which harmful to you. Here

are steps you can take to evaluate a habit and, if necessary, make a change (if the habit has more negative effects than positive ones). Be careful to change only one habit at a time—trying to reach perfection in everything all at once can overwhelm you.

> "To fall into a habit is to begin to cease to be."
> Miguel Unamuno

1. **Honestly admit your habit.** Admitting negative or destructive habits can be hard to do. You can't change a habit until you admit that it is a habit.

2. **Evaluate your habit.** What are the negative and positive effects? Are there more negatives than positives, or vice versa? Look at effects carefully, because at times the trouble may not seem to come directly from the habit. For example, spending every weekend working on the house may seem important, but you may be overdoing it and ignoring friends and family members.

3. **If necessary, decide to change.** You might realize what your bad habits are but not yet care about their effects on your life. Until you are convinced that you will receive a benefit, efforts to change will not get you far.

4. **Start today.** Don't put it off until after this week, after the family reunion, or after the semester. Each day lost is a day you haven't had the chance to benefit from a new lifestyle.

5. **Reward yourself appropriately for positive steps taken.** If you earn a good grade, avoid slacking off on your studies the following week. If you've lost weight, avoid celebrating in an ice-cream parlor. Choose a reward that will not encourage you to stray from your target.

6. **Keep it up. To have the best chance at changing a habit, be consistent for at least three weeks.** Your brain needs time to become accustomed to the new habit. If you go back to the old habit during that time, you may feel like you're starting all over again.

Finally, don't get too discouraged if the process seems difficult. Rarely does someone make the decision to change and do so without a setback or two. Being too hard on yourself might cause frustration that tempts you to give up and go back to the habit. Take it one step at a time and use what you know from Chapter 1 to spur your motivation when you lose steam.

All of the self knowledge you are building will be very important for your educational decisions. Take what you know into account when thinking about your choice of major.

HOW CAN YOU START THINKING ABOUT CHOOSING A MAJOR?

Many students come to college knowing what they want to study, but many do not. That's completely normal. College is a perfect time to begin exploring your different interests. In the process, you may discover talents and strengths you never realized you had. For example, taking an environmental class may teach you that you have a passion for finding solutions to pollution problems, or you may discover a talent for public speaking and decide to explore on-camera journalism.

Although some of your explorations may take you down paths that don't resonate with your personality and interests, each experience will help to clarify who you really are and what you want to do with your life. Thinking about choosing a **major** involves exploring potential majors, being open to changing majors, linking majors to career areas, and following your heart.

Exploring Potential Majors

The following steps will help you explore majors that interest you:

Consider your learning style. Many majors emphasize particular learning styles. For example, science and math curricula demand strength in analytical thinking, and education courses often involve extensive interpersonal interaction. Look at your stronger and weaker areas and see what majors are likely to make the most of what you do well. If you are drawn to a major that requires ability in one of your weaker areas, explore the major to see where you would need extra help and where your strengths would benefit you.

Take a variety of classes. Although you will generally have core requirements to fulfill, use your electives to branch out. Try to take at least one class in each area that sparks your interest.

Know your interests. The more you know about yourself, the more ability you will have to focus on areas that make the most of who you are and what you can do. Pay close attention to which areas inspire you to greater heights and which areas seem to deaden your initiative.

Work closely with your advisor. Begin discussing your major early on with your advisor, even if you don't intend to declare right away. For any given major, your advisor may be able to tell you about the coursework and career possibilities. Consider a double major (completing the requirements for two different majors) if your school offers that possibility.

Take advantage of other resources. Seek opinions from instructors, friends, and family members. Talk to students who have declared majors that interest you. Explore the course materials your college gives you in order to see what majors your college offers.

Develop your critical-thinking skills. Working toward any major will help you develop your most important skill—knowing how to use your mind. Critical thinking is the most crucial ingredient in any recipe for school and career success. More than anything, your future career and employer will depend on your ability to contribute to the workplace through clear, effective, and creative thinking.

Planning Your Curriculum

You won't necessarily want to plan out your entire college course load at the beginning of your first semester. However, you might find some advantages

Major
A subject of academic knowledge chosen as a field of specialization, requiring a specific course of study.

Real World Link
Work-study programs provide the kind of hands-on experiences that help students choose their major. Summer internships also help guide students to a specific major.

to thinking through your choices ahead of time. Planning ahead can help you feel more in control of your choices by giving you a clearer idea of where you are headed. It can also help you avoid pitfalls, such as not being able to secure a space in a course that you need to complete your major. When students wait until the last minute to register for the following semester, some courses they want have already been filled; as a result, they may have to take courses they would not necessarily have chosen.

Take advantage of the following ideas and strategies when working to plan your college curriculum.

Consult your college catalog. You will get the broadest idea of your possibilities by exploring everything your college offers. In addition, what is available to you may go beyond your college's doors. Check into "study abroad" programs (spending a semester or a year at an affiliated college in a different country) or opportunities to take courses at nearby schools that have arrangements with your school.

Look at the majors that interest you. Each major offered by your college has a list of required courses, which you will find on-line or in your catalog, or can get from an academic advisor. The list may also indicate a recommended order in which you should take the courses—certain courses your first year, others your second year, and so on. The list will help you determine whether you will like what you will be doing over the next few semesters if you choose a particular major.

Branch out. Even if you already have a pretty clear idea of your primary area of study, look into courses in other interesting areas that don't necessarily connect to your major. Enlarging the scope of your knowledge will help to improve your critical thinking, broaden your perspectives, and perhaps introduce you to career possibilities you had never even considered.

Get creative. Do you have a particular idea about what you want to major in but don't see it listed in your college catalog? Don't immediately assume it's impossible. Talk with your academic advisor. Some schools allow certain students to design their own majors, with help and approval from their advisors. In such a case, you and your advisor would come up with a unique list of courses on your own.

Students check the bulletin board for job and internship opportunities.

Linking Majors to Career Areas

The point of declaring and pursuing a major is to help you reach a significant level of knowledge in one subject, often in preparation for a particular career area. Before you discard a major as not practical enough, consider where it might be able to take you. Thinking through the possibilities may open doors that you never knew existed. Besides finding an exciting path, you may discover a path that is highly marketable and beneficial to humankind as well.

For each major there are many career options that aren't obvious right away. For example, a student working toward teaching certification doesn't have to teach public school. This student could develop curricula, act as a consultant for businesses, develop an on-line education service, teach overseas for the Peace Corps, or create a public television program. The sky's the limit.

Explore the educational requirements of any career area that interests you. Your choice of major may be more or less crucial depending on the career area. For example, pursuing a career in medicine almost always requires a major in some area of the biological sciences, whereas aspiring lawyers may have majored in anything from political science to philosophy. Many employers are more interested in your ability to think than in your specific knowledge; therefore they may not pay as much attention to your major as they do to your critical-thinking skills. Ask advisors or people in your areas of interest what educational background is necessary or helpful to someone pursuing a career in that area.

Changing Majors

Some people may change their minds several times before finding a major that fits. Although this may add to the time you spend in college, being happy with your decision is important. For example, an education major may begin student teaching only to discover that he really doesn't feel comfortable in front of students. Or, a student may declare English as a major only to realize that her passion is in religion.

If this happens to you, don't be discouraged. Changing a major is much like changing a job. Skills and experiences from one job will assist you in your next position, and some of the courses from your first major may apply— may transfer as credits—to your next major. Talk with your academic advisor about any desire to change majors.

Whatever you decide, realize that you do have the right to change your mind. Continual self-discovery is part of the journey. No matter how many detours you make, each interesting class you take along the way helps to point you toward a major that feels like home.

Following Your Heart

Friends or parents may have warned you against certain careers, encouraging you to stay with "safe" careers that seem socially acceptable or that pay well. Prestige and money may be important—but they usually are not viable replacements for deep personal satisfaction. If for you the path of the heart diverges from the safe path, the choice may be very challenging. Only you can decide which is the best for you. Remember that this is your life, and you are the one who has to live the choices you make. Make a choice that leads you toward the life you have dreamed of. Make a choice that makes the most of the real you.

Teaching Tip
Changing majors may prevent students from graduating on time, especially if the change occurs in the junior or senior year. Help students put the delay in the perspective of their entire lives. If they find the right career, spending extra time in college may be well worth it.

Be a Team
Ask students to write down their dream career. Then, with a partner, ask them to brainstorm different ways to turn the dream into reality. For example, if a music lover is unsure whether he wants to perform, he can choose a career in record production or in other music-related fields.

Sabiduría

In Spanish, the term *sabiduría* represents the two sides of learning: knowledge and wisdom. Knowledge—building what you know about how the world works—is the first part. Wisdom—deriving meaning and significance from knowledge and deciding how to use it—is the second. As you continually learn and experience new things, the *sabiduría* you build will help you make knowledgeable and wise choices about how to lead your life.

Think of this concept as you discover more about how you learn and receive knowledge in all aspects of your life—in school, work, and personal situations. As you learn how your unique mind works and how to use it, you can more confidently assert yourself. As you expand your ability to use your mind in different ways, you can create lifelong advantages for yourself.

BUILDING SKILLS FOR COLLEGE, CAREER, AND LIFE SUCCESS

Critical Thinking
Applying Learning to Life

How Do You Learn Best?

List your four strongest intelligences.

_____

_____

Describe a positive experience at work or school that you can attribute to
these strengths.

_____

_____

_____

_____

Name your four least-developed intelligences.

_____

_____

What challenge do you face that may be related to your least-developed
intelligences?

_____

_____

_____

_____

Making School More Enjoyable

Name a required class that you are not necessarily looking forward to taking this year. How does your learning style relate to how you feel? Name three study techniques from the chapter that may help you get the most out of the class and enjoy it more.

Your Habits

You have the power to change your habits. List here three habits that you want to change. Make brief notes about the effects of each habit and how those effects keep you from reaching your goals.

1.

2.

3.

Out of these three, put a star by the habit you want to change first. Write down a step you can take today toward overcoming that habit.

What helpful habit do you want to develop in its place? For example, if your problem habit were a failure to express yourself when you are angry, a replacement habit might be to talk calmly about situations that upset you as soon as they arise. If you have a habit of cramming for tests at the last minute, you could replace it with a regular study schedule that allows you to cover your material bit by bit over a longer period of time.

One way to help yourself abandon your old habit is to think about how your new habit will improve your life. List two benefits of your new habit.

1. _____

2. _____

Give yourself one month to complete your habit shift. Set a specific deadline. Keep track of your progress by indicating on a chart or calendar how well you did each day. If you avoided the old habit, write an X below the day. If you used the new one, write an N. Therefore, a day when you only avoided the old habit will have an X; a day when you did both will have both letters; a day when you did neither will be blank. You can use the chart below or mark your own calendar. Try pairing up with another student to check on each other's progress.

1	2	3	4	5	6	7	8	9	10	11	12	13	14	15	16
17	18	19	20	21	22	23	24	25	26	27	28	29	30	31	

Don't forget to reward yourself for your hard work. Write here what your reward will be when you feel you are on the road to a new and beneficial habit.

_____

_____

_____

Interests, Majors, and Careers

Start by listing activities and subjects you like.

1. _____

2. _____

3. _____

4. _____

5. _____

6. _____

Name three majors that might relate to your interests and help you achieve your career goals.

1. _____
2. _____
3. _____

For each major, name a corresponding career area you may want to explore.

1. _____
2. _____
3. _____

Keep these majors and career areas in mind as you gradually narrow your course choices in the time before you declare a major.

Teamwork
Combining Forces

Ideas About Personality Types Divide into groups according to the four types of the Personality Spectrum—Thinker-dominant students in one group, Organizer-dominant students in another, Giver-dominant students in a third, and Adventurer-dominant students in the fourth. If you have scored the same in more than one of these types, join whatever group is smaller. With your group, brainstorm four lists for your type: the strengths of this type, the struggles it brings, the things that cause particular stress for your type, and career ideas that tend to suit this type.

Strengths	Struggles
1.	1.
2.	2.
and so on	

Stressors	Careers
1.	1.
2.	2.
and so on	

If there is time, each group can present this information to the entire class to enable everyone to have a better understanding and acceptance of one another's intelligences. You might also brainstorm strategies for dealing with your intelligence's struggles and stressors, and present those ideas to the class as well.

Writing
Discovery Through Journaling

To record your thoughts, use a separate journal or the lined page at the end of the chapter.

Your Learning Style Discuss the insights you have gained through exploring your multiple intelligences. What strengths have come to your attention? What challenges have been clarified? Talk about your game plan for using your strengths and addressing your challenges both at school and in the real world.

Career Portfolio
Charting Your Course

Self-Portrait A self-portrait is an important step in your career exploration, because self-knowledge will allow you to make the best choices about what to study and what career to pursue. Use this exercise to synthesize everything you have been exploring about yourself into one comprehensive "self-portrait." You will design your portrait in "think-link" style, using words and visual shapes to describe your self-perception, learning style, attitudes, habits, preferences, and abilities.

A think link is a visual construction of related ideas, similar to a map or web, that represents your thought process. Ideas are written inside geometric shapes, often boxes or circles, and related ideas and facts are attached to those ideas by lines that connect the shapes. You will learn more about think links in the note-taking section in Chapter 7.

Use the style shown in the example in Figure 4.3, or create your own. For example, in this exercise you may want to create a "wheel" of ideas coming off your central shape, entitled "Me." Then, spreading out from each of those ideas (interests, learning style, etc.) you would draw lines connecting all of the thoughts that go along with that idea. Connected to "Interests," for example, might be "Singing," "Stock market," and "History." You don't have to use the wheel image. You might want to design a treelike think link or a line of boxes with connecting thoughts written below the boxes, or anything else you like. Let your design reflect who you are, just as the think link itself does.

Your vision of yourself reflects how much you think of yourself and your potential. Having a positive sense of your future is just as important as developing an idea of how you can do a job well, or of how you can run a company.

FIGURE 4.3 Sample Self-Portrait Think Link

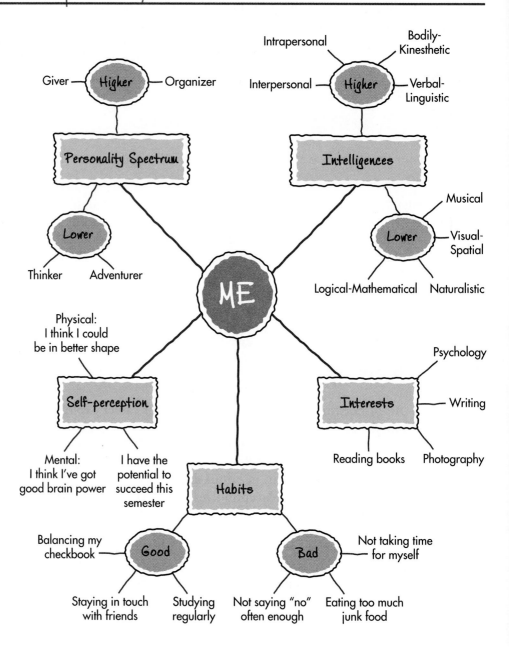

Journal Entry

Name _____   Date _____

Web Activity
Defining Yourself and Your Goals

Now that you are familiar with your own learning style, along with your strengths and weaknesses, use that information to help you to choose a major.

Using the Prentice Hall super-site, take a look at college majors. Go to www.prenhall.com/success and click on Majors Exploration. Choose two majors that are of interest to you and use the site to answer the following questions for each of the majors.

A. What is this major all about? Is it what you expected it to be?

B. What careers can you enter after graduating with this major?

C. What classes do students typically need to take in order to graduate with this major? Go to your school's Web site to see what the specific course requirements are for your school? What do you need to do in order to be accepted into this major?

D. How do your learning style and personality make you a good candidate for this major?

E. Now that you know all of this you can set some goals. Set short-term goals: What do you need to do this week, or this semester, in order to achieve your goal of entering this major? Set long-term goals: What do you need to accomplish next semester in order to enter and graduate with this major? What courses do you need to take? Is there a club or organization that you should join to make you a better candidate? More long-term goals include what you need to do throughout college and beyond. Will an internship help you with this major? How about participation in a study abroad program? You can learn more about study abroad programs through the Prentice Hall super-site at www.prenhall.com, and from your school's Web site. You may find information on internships on your college's Web site, or you can try to search the Internet in general. You should find internships that are available for college credit, and even those that pay! Finally, is graduate school attendance necessary? If so, what do you need during college in order to gain graduate admittance after graduation?

F. As you think about your major you may start to worry about all of the money that is involved. Using the Internet, find two scholarships or some grant money that is available to students that are interested in this field. Is this money eligible to undergraduate students? Is there additional money out there for graduate students?

One of the biggest challenges you'll face as a college student is deciding on a major—a field of study that will probably lead to a career after graduation. The good news is that there are more majors today than ever before, thanks to an interdisciplinary learning approach offered by many colleges and universities across the nation. As you will see in this Reading Room selection, an interdisciplinary major may give you the tools you need to succeed in the twenty-first century.

The multitalented have a clear advantage in an increasingly complex world, where biologists studying the brain must understand chemistry and physics to make real progress, and architects need to consider environmental issues in designing buildings. "No single field can solve the practical problems we now face as a society—things like AIDS, poverty, pollution," says Julie Thompson Klein, a professor of humanities in the interdisciplinary studies program at Wayne State University in Detroit. As a result, students today are less likely to pursue a major in pure history or biology, for example, and are more apt to study a mix of disciplines. The most recent edition of *Interdisciplinary Undergraduate Programs: A Directory* lists 410 options up from 235 a decade before.

Interdisciplinary learning is not new, of course: Path-breaking fields such as American and women's studies first emerged in the 1940s and 1960s, respectively. But they have gained stature and students in the past decade have encountered a flood of new interdisciplinary fields across all subject areas, particularly the sciences. Bioengineering, for example, borrows courses and professors from physics, chemistry, biology, and mathematics and prepares students to apply engineering principles to medical problems. A graduate might enter either medicine or engineering, specializing in rehabilitation, say, or the creation of medical devices. Cognitive science combines linguistics, computer science, and psychology, among other fields, for a wide-ranging view of how the mind works. The philosophy, politics, and economics major aims to produce thinkers who bring a moral and ethical framework to policy analysis.

Students majoring in leadership studies at the University of Richmond in Virginia take courses in history, ethics, and political science and then hear from prominent thinkers in the field. The six speakers in last year's "Leadership in a Democratic Society" forum included noted race scholar Cornel West and Nobel Peace Prize winner Oscar Arias, the former president of Costa Rica.

Good programs also give undergrads an opportunity to help create new knowledge through internships. Media studies majors at the University of Southern Maine in Portland are encouraged to do internships at local newspapers and TV stations and are required to take a "Community Involvement Practicum" that connects their course-work with a community issue. Last year, one group created a documentary-style fund-raising video for a local shelter for battered women.

Universities can't always keep up with student interest in an emerging field. Thus many schools allow highly motivated students to design their own interdisciplinary majors. The result is customized programs like "Third World Community Health," a combination of anthropology, nursing, and political science. Experienced faculty and students stress that plotting your own course of study requires tremendous energy and self-discipline—from the start of the application process until the delivery of the oft-required final research paper—and is appropriate only for those whose educational needs can't be met by any single department.

Students like Matt Witten, for example. The video-game junkie took advantage of the individualized major program (IMP) at Indiana University–Bloomington and, with the help of an adviser and the okay of a three-member faculty committee, created his own curriculum in computer animation and digital media. "I don't have to look at just one section of the course book anymore," says Witten. "Anything that looks interesting I have a chance of fitting into my major." This fall, among other courses, he's taking a computer science class on building Web programs and an independent study that involves reading nine books on Maya, a computer animation program. But while IMP is giving Witten a chance to turn his passion into an education, he does wonder how it will be perceived in the real world. "I mean, Indiana isn't exactly a school that's known for computer animators," he says.

You never know. The individualized major of today is often tomorrow's newest interdisciplinary department.

Source: Excerpted and adapted from Carolyn Kleiner, "Why the Walls Are Quickly Tumbling Down: Chances Are Good that the Major You Choose Will Draw From Several Disciplines." Copyright © August 30, 1999, *U.S. News & World Report.*

Think. Discuss. Talk amongst yourselves.

READING ROOM

Emotional Intelligence

SELECTION TWO

You'll learn a lot in college that will help you be successful in life, but it may surprise you that many of your most valuable learning experiences will have nothing to do with history, science, art, English literature, and other academic studies. They will center on your emotional intelligence—your ability to be at peace within yourself, to motivate yourself to accomplish your goals, to understand and relate to others, and more. As you will see in the following Reading Room selection, author Daniel Goleman considers emotional intelligence to be more important to life success than IQ.

Jason H., a sophomore and straight-A student at a Coral Springs, Florida, high school, was fixated on getting into medical school. Not just any medical school—he dreamt of Harvard. But David Pologruto, his physics teacher, had given Jason an 80 on a quiz. Believing that grade—a mere B—put his dream in jeopardy, Jason took a butcher knife to school and, in a confrontation with Pologruto in the physics lab, stabbed his teacher in the collarbone before being subdued in a struggle.

A judge found Jason innocent, temporarily insane during the incident—a panel of four psychologists and psychiatrists swore he was psychotic during the fight. Jason claimed he had been planning to commit suicide because of the test score, and had gone to Pologruto to tell him he was killing himself because of the bad grade. Pologruto told a different story: "I think he tried to completely do me in with the knife" because he was infuriated over the bad grade.

After transferring to a private school, Jason graduated two years later at the top of his class. A perfect grade in regular classes would have given him a straight-A, 4.0 average, but Jason had taken enough advanced courses to raise his grade-point average to 4.614—way beyond A+. Even as Jason graduated with highest honors, his old physics teacher, David Pologruto, complained that Jason had never apologized or even taken responsibility for the attack.

The question is, how could someone of such obvious intelligence do something so irrational—so downright dumb? The answer: Academic intelligence has little to do with emotional life. The brightest among us can founder on the shoals of unbridled passions and unruly impulses; people with high IQs can be stunningly poor pilots of their private lives.

115

One of psychology's open secrets is the relative inability of grades . . . to predict unerringly who will succeed in life. [In fact], there are widespread exceptions to the rule that IQ predicts success—many or more exceptions than cases that fit the rule. At best, IQ contributes about 20 percent to the factors that determine life success, which leaves 80 percent to other forces. As one observer notes, "The vast majority of one's ultimate niche in society is determined by non-IQ factors, ranging from social class to luck."

My concern is with a key set of these "other characteristics," emotional intelligence: abilities such as being able to motivate oneself and persist in the face of frustrations; to control impulse and delay gratification; to regulate one's moods and keep distress from swamping the ability to think; to empathize and to hope. No one can yet say exactly how much of the variability from person to person in life's course it accounts for. But data suggest it can be as powerful, and at times more powerful, than IQ.

If anyone sees the limits of the old ways of thinking about intelligence, it is Howard Gardner, a psychologist at the Harvard School of Education [Gardner defined the concept of multiple intelligences, which is discussed in Chapter 4 of this book] and Peter Salovey, a Yale psychologist who mapped in great detail the ways in which we can bring intelligence to our emotions. Gardner, [Salovey, and other psychologists] have taken a wider view of intelligence, trying to reinvent it in terms of what it takes to lead life successfully. And that line of enquiry leads back to an appreciation of just how crucial "personal" or emotional intelligence is.

[The result of their combined research] is a basic definition of the five domains of emotional intelligence:

1. **Knowing one's emotions.** Self-awareness—recognizing a feeling as it happens—is the keystone of emotional intelligence. The ability to monitor feelings from moment to moment is crucial to psychological insight and self-understanding. . . . People with greater certainty about their feelings are better pilots of their lives, having a surer sense of how they really feel about personal decisions from who to marry to what job to take.

2. **Managing emotions.** Handling feelings so they are appropriate is an ability that builds on self-awareness. [Included is] the capacity to soothe oneself, to shake off rampant anxiety, gloom, or irritability—and the consequences of failure. . . . People who are poor in this ability are constantly battling feelings of distress, while those who excel in it can bounce back far more quickly from life's setbacks and upsets.

3. **Motivating oneself.** Marshaling emotions in the service of a goal is essential for paying attention, for self-motivation and mastery, and for creativity. Emotional self-control—delaying gratification and stifling impulsiveness—underlies accomplishment of every sort. And being able to get into the "flow" state enables outstanding performance of all kinds. People who have this skill tend to be more highly productive and effective in whatever they undertake.

4. **Recognizing emotions in others.** Empathy, another ability that builds on emotional self-awareness, is the fundamental "people skill." People who are empathetic are more attuned to the subtle social signals that indicate what others need or want. This makes them better at callings such as the caring professions, teaching, sales, and management.

5. **Handling relationships.** The art of relationships is, in large part, skill in managing emotions in others. Included are the abilities that undergird popularity, leadership, and interpersonal effectiveness. People who excel in these skills do well at anything that relies on interacting smoothly with others.

Of course, people differ in their abilities in each of these domains. Some of us may be quite adept at handling, say, our own anxiety, but relatively inept at soothing someone else's upsets. The underlying basis for our level of ability is, no doubt, neural, but the brain is remarkably plastic, constantly learning. Lapses in emotional skills can be remedied: to a great extent each of these domains represents a body of habit and response that, with the right effort, can be improved on.

Source: From *Emotional Intelligence: Why It Can Matter More Than IQ,* by Daniel Goleman, pp. 33–34, 42–44. Copyright © 1995 by Daniel Goleman. Used by permission of Bantam Books, a division of Random House, Inc.

Think again . . . talk more!

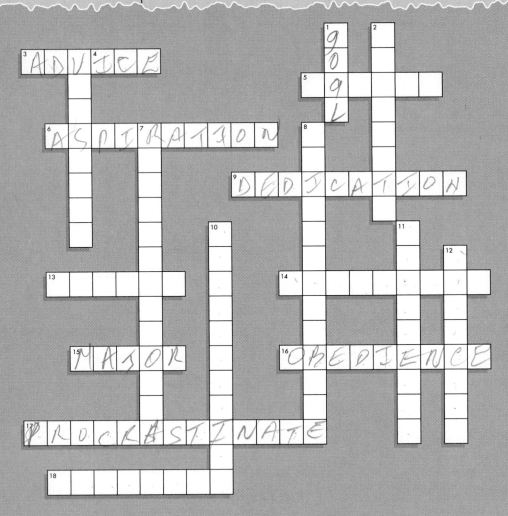

Across answers filled in:
- 3. ADVICE
- 1 (down). GOAL
- 5. (blank word filled)
- 6. ASPIRATION
- 9. DEDICATION
- 15. MAJOR
- 16. OBEDIENCE
- 17. PROCRASTINATE

ACROSS

3. People who can provide one-on-one help with academic subjects
5. Preferences for actions done a certain way, often on a regular basis or at particular times
6. A promise or pledge to do something in the future
9. Determination; the power to begin or to follow through with a plan or task
13. Principles, standards, or qualities considered important, right, or good
14. The variety that occurs in every aspect of humanity
15. A subject of academic study in which a student chooses to specialize
16. Adherence to a code of moral values; honesty
17. To put off an action or task until later
18. A time-and-activity map that allocates time for tasks and serves as a reminder

DOWN

1. An end toward which an effort is directed; an aim
2. Something that is rated high in importance
4. A method of putting daily tasks down on paper
7. A type of intelligence that focuses on an ability to relate to others and their feelings
8. The ability to solve problems or fashion products that are useful in a community
10. Reliable, trustworthy
11. People, organizations, or services that provide help and support
12. State of mind or feeling toward something

Part II

Developing Your Learning Skills

CHAPTER 5 Critical and Creative Thinking: Tapping the Power of Your Mind

CHAPTER 6 Reading, Studying, and Using the Library: Maximizing Written Resources

CHAPTER 7 Note Taking and Writing: Harnessing the Power of Words and Ideas

CHAPTER 8 Listening, Memory, and Test Taking: Taking In, Retaining, and Demonstrating Knowledge

KATALAVOX

KATALAVOX

SPEECH
RECOGNITION
CONTROL SYSTEM

KATALAVOX

SPEECH
RECOGNITION
CONTROL SYSTEM

Critical and Creative Thinking

Tapping the Power of Your Mind

In this chapter, you will explore answers to the following questions:

- What is critical thinking?
- How does critical thinking help you solve problems and make decisions?
- How do you construct and evaluate arguments?
- How do you think logically?
- Why should you explore perspectives?
- Why plan strategically?
- How can you develop your creativity?
- What is media literacy?

Your mind's powers can show in everything you do, from the smallest chores (comparing prices on cereals at the grocery store) to the most complex situations. (Martine Kempf, shown in the photograph, invented a voice-activated wheelchair.) Critical thinking and creative thinking enable your mind to process, store, and create with the facts and ideas it encounters. Understanding how your mind works is the first step toward critical thinking. When you have that understanding, you can perform the essential critical-thinking task: asking important questions about ideas, information, and media. This chapter will show you both the mind's basic actions and the thinking processes that incorporate them. You will explore how being an open-minded critical and creative thinker will promote your success in college, career, and life.

WHAT IS CRITICAL THINKING?

Although you might figure that the word *critical* implies something difficult and negative, critical thinking is "critical" mainly in the sense of one definition of *critical*: "indispensable" and "important." You think critically every day, though you may not realize it.

Defining Critical Thinking

The following is one way to define critical thinking:

> Critical thinking is thinking that *goes beyond the basic recall of information* but depends on the information recalled. It focuses on the *important*, or *critical, aspects* of the information. Critical thinking means *asking questions*. Critical thinking means that you *take in information, question it,* and then *use it* to create new ideas, solve problems, make decisions, construct arguments, make plans, and refine your view of the world.

One way to clarify a concept is to look at its opposite. Not thinking critically means not examining important aspects through questioning. A person who does not think critically tends to accept or reject information or ideas without examining them. Table 5.1 compares how a critical thinker and a non–critical thinker might respond to particular situations.

Think about responses you or others have had to different situations. Consider when you have seen critical thinking take place, and when you haven't, and what resulted from each way of responding. This will help you begin to see what kind of an effect critical thinking can have on the way you live.

TABLE 5.1 Not Thinking Critically vs. Thinking Critically

YOUR ROLE	SITUATION	NONQUESTIONING (UNCRITICAL) RESPONSE	QUESTIONING (CRITICAL) RESPONSE
Student	Instructor is lecturing on the causes of the Vietnam War.	You assume everything your instructor says is true.	You consider what the instructor says, write questions about issues you want to clarify, and discuss them with the instructor or classmates.
Spouse/Partner	Your partner feels he/she does not have enough quality time with you.	You think he/she is wrong and defend yourself.	You ask your partner why he/she thinks this is happening, and together you decide how the situation can be improved.
Employee	Your supervisor is angry with you about something that happened.	You avoid your supervisor or deny responsibility for the incident.	You determine what caused your supervisor to place the blame on you; you talk with your supervisor about what happened and why.

The Path of Critical Thinking

Look at Figure 5.1 to see a visual representation of critical thinking. The path involves taking in information, questioning information, and then using information.

Taking In Information

Although most of this chapter focuses on questioning and using information, the first step of the process is just as crucial. The information you receive is your raw material that you will examine and mold into something new. If you take in information accurately and without judgment, you will have the best material with which to work as you think. Once you have the clearest, most complete information possible, you can begin to examine its important aspects through questioning.

Questioning Information

A critical thinker asks many kinds of questions about a given piece of information, such as: *Where did it come from? What could explain it? In what ways is it true or false? How do I feel about it, and why? How is this information similar to or different from what I already know? Is it good or bad? What caused it, and what effects does it have?* Critical thinkers also try to transform information into something they can use. They ask whether information can help them solve a problem, make a decision, learn or create something new, or anticipate the future.

As an example of the questioning process, consider the following as your "information in": You encounter a number of situations—financial strain, parenting on your own, and being an older student—that seem to be getting in the way of your success at school. Whereas nonquestioning thinkers may assume defeat, critical thinkers will examine the situation with proactive questions such as these:

What exactly are my obstacles? Examples of my obstacles are a heavy work schedule, single parenting, being in debt, and returning to school after 10 years. *(recall)*

Are there other cases different from mine? I do have one friend who is going through problems worse than mine, and she's getting by. I also

Real World Link
Standard IQ tests do not predict how successful students will be in achieving their life goals. The ability to think in ways that lead to practical successes is linked to critical and creative thinking.

The Critical Thinking Path   **FIGURE 5.1**

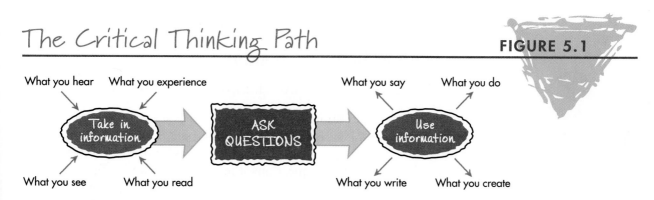

know another guy who doesn't have too much to deal with that I can tell, and he's struggling just like I am. *(difference)*

Who has problems similar to mine? Well, if I consider my obstacles specifically, my statement might mean that single parents and returning adult students will all have trouble in school. That is not necessarily true. People who have trouble in school may still become successful. *(similarity)*

What is an example of someone who has had success despite obstacles? What about Oseola McCarty, the cleaning woman who saved money all her life and raised $150,000 to create a scholarship at the University of Southern Mississippi? She didn't have what anyone would call advantages, such as a high-paying job or a college education. *(idea to example)*

What conclusion can I draw from my questions? From thinking about my friend and about Oseola McCarty, I conclude that people can successfully overcome their obstacles by working hard, focusing on their abilities, and concentrating on their goals. *(example to idea)*

Why am I worried about this? Maybe I am scared of returning to school. Maybe I am afraid to challenge myself. Whatever the cause, the effects are that I feel bad about myself and don't work to the best of my abilities, which can hurt me and others who depend on me. *(cause and effect)*

How do I evaluate the effects of my worries? I think they're harmful. When we say that obstacles equal difficulty, we can damage our desire to try to overcome them. When we say that successful people don't have obstacles, we might overlook that some very successful people have to deal with hidden disadvantages such as learning disabilities or abusive families. *(evaluation)*

Remember these types of questions. When you explore the seven mind actions later in the chapter, refer to these questions to see how they illustrate the different actions your mind performs.

Using Information

After taking in and examining information, critical thinkers try to transform it into something they can use. They use information to help them solve a problem, make a decision, learn or create something new, or anticipate what will happen in the future. This part of the critical thinking path is where you benefit from the hard work of asking questions. This is where inventions happen, new processes are born, theories are created, and information interacts with your own thoughts to create something new.

The Value of Critical Thinking

Critical thinking has many positive effects, or benefits, including the following:

You will increase your ability to perform thinking processes. Critical thinking is a learned skill, just like shooting a basketball or using a word-processing program. As with any other skill, the more you use it, the better you become. The more you ask questions, the better you think. The better you think, the more effective you will be in school, work, and life situations.

You will produce knowledge rather than just reproduce it. The interaction of newly learned information with what you already know creates new knowledge. Its usefulness can be judged by your ability to apply it. For instance, it won't mean much for students studying education to quote the stages of child development on an exam unless they can evaluate children's needs when they begin working as teachers.

You will be a valuable employee. You won't be a failure if you follow directions. However, you will be even more valuable if you ask strategic questions—ranging from "Is there a better way to deliver phone messages?" to "How can we increase business?"—that will improve productivity. Employees who think critically are more likely to make progress in their careers than those who simply do what they are told.

You will increase your problem-solving creativity. Creativity is essential in producing new and different questions to ask, possibilities to explore, and ideas to try. Being creative also improves your sense of humor and your attitude while you cope with problems.

Your mind has some basic moves, or actions, that it performs in order to understand relationships among ideas and concepts. Sometimes it uses one action by itself, but most often it uses two or more in combination. These actions are the blocks you will use to build the critical-thinking processes you will explore later in the chapter.

Learning How Your Mind Works

Identify your mind's actions using a system originally conceived by educators Frank Lyman, Arlene Mindus, and Charlene Lopez[1] and developed by numerous other instructors. Based on their studies of how students think, they named seven basic building blocks of thought. These actions are not new to you, although some of their names may be. They represent the ways in which you think all the time.

Through exploring these actions, you can go beyond just thinking and learn *how* you think. This will help you take charge of your own thinking. The more you know about how your mind works, the more control you will have over thinking processes such as problem solving and decision making.

Following are explanations of each of the mind actions, including examples. As you read, write your examples in the blank spaces. Icons representing each action will help you visualize and remember them.

Recall: *Facts, sequence, and description.* This is the simplest action. When you **recall** you name or describe facts, objects, or events, or put them into sequence. *Examples:*

■ You name the steps of a geometry proof, in order.
■ You remember your best friends' phone numbers.

Your example: Recall two important school-related events this month.

_____

_____

The icon: Capital R stands for recall or remembering.

e-mail

The next time you e-mail or talk to one of your close friends, ask as many questions as you can think of to find out what is happening in his or her life. Cultivate the habit of question-asking in all aspects of your life.

Career Connection
The technological revolution that is transforming the workplace is based on the willingness of entrepreneurs to discover what can be, rather than what is. Trailblazers, like Bill Gates and Steven Jobs, are devising new solutions no one had ever considered.

Learning Styles Tip
These symbols are especially helpful to visual-spatial learners.

Teaching Tip
Recall sets the foundation for critical thinking because it allows us to compare new information with what we already know to solve problems, make decisions, and construct arguments.

Similarity: *Analogy, likeness, comparison.* This action examines what is **similar** about one or more things. You might compare situations, ideas, people, stories, events, or objects. *Examples:*

- You compare notes with another student to see what facts and ideas you both consider important.
- You analyze the arguments you've had with your partner this month and then see how they all seem to be about the same problem.

Your example: Tell what is similar about two of your best friends.

The icon: The **Venn diagram** illustrates the idea of similarity. The two circles represent the things being compared, and the shaded area of intersection indicates that they have some degree or element of similarity.

Difference: *Distinction, contrast.* This action examines what is **different** about one or more situations, ideas, people, stories, events, or objects, contrasting them with one another. *Examples:*

- You see how two instructors differ—one divides the class into small groups for discussions; the other keeps desks in place and delivers lectures.
- You contrast a day when you combine work and school with a day when you attend class only.

Your example: Explain how your response to a course you like differs from your response to a course you don't like as much.

The icon: Here the Venn diagram is used again, to show difference. The nonintersecting parts of the circles are shaded, indicated that the focus is on what is not in common.

Cause and Effect: *Reasons, consequences, prediction.* Using this action, you look at what has **caused** a fact, situation, or event and/or what **effects,** or consequences, come from it. In other words, you examine what led up to something and/or what will follow because of it. *Examples:*

- Staying up late causes you to oversleep, which causes you to be late to class. This causes you to miss some material, which has the further effect of your having problems on the test.
- When you pay your phone and utility bills on time, you create effects such as a better credit rating, uninterrupted service, and a better relationship with your service providers.

Your example: Name what causes you to like your favorite class and the effects that class has on you.

The icon: The arrows, pointing toward one another in a circular pattern, show how a cause leads to an effect.

Example to Idea: *Generalization, classification, conceptualization.* From one or more **examples** (facts or events), you develop a general **idea** or ideas. Grouping facts or events into patterns may allow you to make a general statement about several of them at once. Classifying a fact or event helps you build knowledge. This mind action moves from the specific to the general. *Examples:*

- You have had trouble finding a baby-sitter. A classmate even brought her child to class once. Your brother drops his daughter at day care and doesn't like not seeing her all day. From these examples, you derive the idea that your school needs an on-campus day-care program.
- You see a movie, and you decide it is mostly about pride.

Teaching Tolerance
Prejudice is often based on example-to-idea thinking. Racists use this thinking when they condemn every member of a group because of the perceived behavior of a single group member.

Your example: Name activities you enjoy. Using them, derive an idea of a class you want to take.

The icon: The arrow and "Ex" pointing to a light bulb on their right indicate how an example or examples lead to the idea (the light bulb, lit up).

Idea to Example: *Categorization, substantiation, proof.* In a reverse of the previous action, you take an **idea** or ideas and think of **examples** (events or facts) that support or prove that idea. This mind action moves from the general to the specific. *Examples:*

- For a paper, you start with this thesis statement: "Computer knowledge is a must for the modern worker." To support that idea, you gather examples, such as the number of industries that use computers or the kinds of training employers are requiring.
- You talk to your advisor about changing your major, giving examples that support your idea, such as the facts that you have worked in the field you want to change to and you have fulfilled some of the requirements for that major already.

Your example: Name an admirable person. Give examples that show how that person is admirable.

The icon: In a reverse of the previous icon, this one starts with the light bulb and has an arrow pointing to "Ex." This indicates that you start with the idea and then move to the supporting examples.

Evaluation: *Value, judgment, rating.* Here you **judge** whether something is useful or not useful, important or unimportant, good or bad, or right or wrong by identifying and weighing its positive and negative effects (pros and cons). Be sure to consider the specific situation at hand (a cold drink might be good on the beach in August but not so good in the snowdrifts in January). With the facts you have gathered, you determine the value of something in terms of both predicted effects and your own needs. Cause-and-effect analysis always accompanies evaluation. *Examples:*

Springboard
Ask students how they feel about this mind action. Help them see the difference between judging the decisions of others and making judgments about things that are right and wrong for themselves.

■ For one semester, you schedule classes in the afternoons and spend nights working. You find that you tend to sleep late and lose your only study time. From this harmful effect, you evaluate that this schedule doesn't work for you. You decide to schedule earlier classes next time.

■ Someone offers you a chance to cheat on a test. You evaluate the potential effects if you are caught. You also evaluate the long-term effects of not actually learning the material and of doing something ethically wrong. You decide that it isn't right or worthwhile to cheat.

Your example: Evaluate your mode of transportation to school.

The icon: A set of scales out of balance indicates how you weigh positive and negative effects to arrive at an evaluation.

You may want to use a *mnemonic device*—a memory tool, as explained in Chapter 8—to remember the seven mind actions. You can make a sentence of words that each start with a mind action's first letter, such as "Really Smart Dogs Cook Eggs In Enchiladas."

How Mind Actions Build Thinking Processes

> "We do not live to think, but, on the contrary, we think in order that
>
> we may succeed in surviving."
>
> José Ortega y Gasset

The seven mind actions are the fundamental building blocks that indicate relationships among ideas and concepts. You will rarely use one at a time in a step-by-step process, as they are presented here. You will usually combine them, overlap them, and repeat them, using different actions for different situations. For example, when a test question asks you to explain prejudice, you might give *examples, different* from one another, that show your *idea* of prejudice (combining difference with example to idea).

When you combine mind actions in working toward a goal, you are performing a thinking process. Following are explorations of six of the most important critical-thinking processes: solving problems, making decisions, constructing and evaluating arguments, thinking logically, recognizing perspectives, and planning strategically. Each thinking process helps to direct your critical thinking toward the achievement of your goals. Figure 5.6, which appears later in the chapter, reminds you that the mind actions form the core of the thinking processes.

HOW DOES CRITICAL THINKING HELP YOU SOLVE PROBLEMS AND MAKE DECISIONS?

Problem solving and decision making are probably the two most crucial and common thinking processes. Each one requires various mind actions. They overlap somewhat because every problem that needs solving requires you to make a decision. However, not every decision requires that you solve a problem (for example, not many people would say that deciding what to order for lunch is a problem).

Although both of these processes have multiple steps, you will not always have to work through each step. As you become more comfortable with solving problems and making decisions, your mind will automatically click through the steps. Also, you will become more adept at evaluating which problems and decisions need serious consideration and which can be taken care of more quickly and simply.

Problem Solving

Life constantly presents problems to be solved, ranging from average daily problems (how to manage study time) to life-altering situations (how to design a child-custody plan during a divorce). Choosing a solution without thinking critically may have negative effects. If you use the steps of the following problem-solving process, however, you have the best chance of coming up with a favorable solution.

You can apply this problem-solving plan to any problem. Taking the following steps will maximize the number of possible solutions you generate and will allow you to explore each one as fully as possible.

Step 1. Identify the problem accurately. What are the facts? *Recall* the details of the situation. To define a problem correctly, focus on its causes rather than its effects. Consider the Chinese saying: "Give a man a fish, and he will eat for a day. Teach a man to fish, and he will eat for a lifetime." If you state the problem as "The man is hungry," giving him a fish seems like a good solution. Unfortunately, the problem returns—because hunger is an effect. Focusing on the cause brings a new definition: "The man does not know how to find food." Given that his lack of knowledge is the true cause, teaching him to fish will truly solve the problem.

Sample problem: A student is not understanding course material.

Step 2. Analyze the problem. Analyze, or break down into understandable pieces, what surrounds the problem. What *effects* of the situation concern you? What *causes* these effects? Are there hidden causes? Look at the causes and effects that surround the problem.

Sample problem: If some effects of not understanding include poor grades and lack of interest, some causes may include poor study habits, not listening in class, or lack of sleep.

Step 3. Brainstorm possible solutions. Brainstorming will help you to think of examples of how you solved similar problems, consider what is different about this problem, and come up with new possible solutions (see p. 145 for more about brainstorming). Remember that to get to the heart of a problem, you must base possible solutions on the most significant causes instead of putting a bandage on the effects.

Sample problem: Looking at his study habits, the student comes up with ideas like seeking help from his instructor or working with a study group.

Step 4. Explore each solution. Why might your solution work, or not? Might a solution work partially, or in a particular situation? *Evaluate* ahead of time the pros and cons (positive and negative effects) of each plan. Create a chain

Critical Thinking
Ask students if they think that a positive, can-do attitude is necessary to become a great problem solver. Can they think of instances in their own lives where their attitude contributed to their success—or failure?

Brainstorming
The spontaneous, rapid generation of ideas or solutions, undertaken by a group or an individual, often as part of a problem-solving process.

Teaching Tip
Encourage students to brainstorm many different solutions to each problem.

FIGURE 5.2   *Problem-Solving Plan*

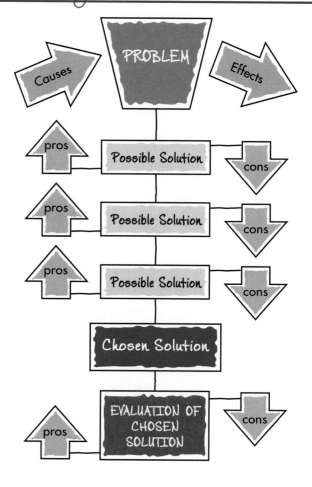

Learning Styles Tip
Encourage verbal-linguistic and interpersonal learners to debate with a partner the pluses and minuses of various solutions.

of causes and effects in your head, as far into the future as you can, to see where this solution might lead.

Sample problem: The student considers the effects of improved study habits, more sleep, tutoring, or dropping the class.

Step 5. Choose and execute the solution you decide is best. Decide how you will put your solution to work. Then, execute your solution.

Sample problem: The student decides on a combination of improved study habits and tutoring.

Step 6. Evaluate the solution that you acted upon, looking at its effects. What are the positive and negative *effects* of what you did? In terms of your needs, was it a useful solution or not? Could the solution use any adjustments to be more useful? Would you do the same again or not? In evaluating, you are collecting data.

Sample problem: Evaluating his choice, the student may decide that the effects are good but that his fatigue still causes a problem.

Step 7. Continue to evaluate and refine the solution. Problem solving is a process. You may have opportunities to apply the same solution again.

How One Student Walked Through a Problem   FIGURE 5.3

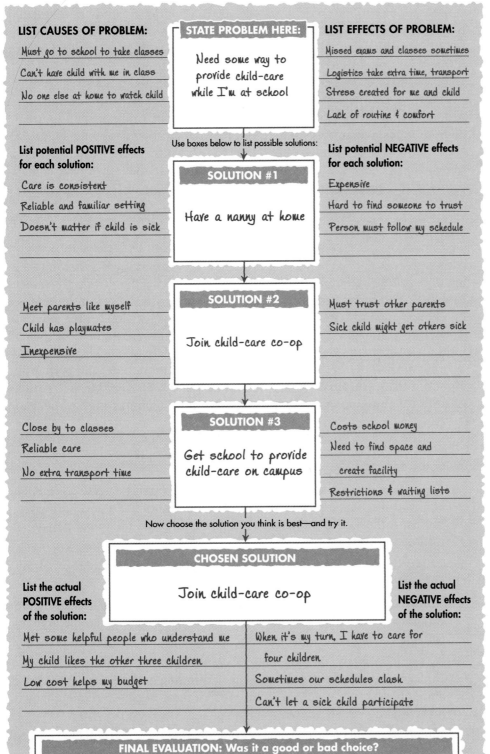

LIST CAUSES OF PROBLEM:

Must go to school to take classes

Can't have child with me in class

No one else at home to watch child

STATE PROBLEM HERE:

Need some way to provide child-care while I'm at school

LIST EFFECTS OF PROBLEM:

Missed exams and classes sometimes

Logistics take extra time, transport

Stress created for me and child

Lack of routine & comfort

Use boxes below to list possible solutions:

List potential POSITIVE effects for each solution:

Care is consistent

Reliable and familiar setting

Doesn't matter if child is sick

SOLUTION #1

Have a nanny at home

List potential NEGATIVE effects for each solution:

Expensive

Hard to find someone to trust

Person must follow my schedule

Meet parents like myself

Child has playmates

Inexpensive

SOLUTION #2

Join child-care co-op

Must trust other parents

Sick child might get others sick

Close by to classes

Reliable care

No extra transport time

SOLUTION #3

Get school to provide child-care on campus

Costs school money

Need to find space and

create facility

Restrictions & waiting lists

Now choose the solution you think is best—and try it.

CHOSEN SOLUTION

Join child-care co-op

List the actual POSITIVE effects of the solution:

Met some helpful people who understand me

My child likes the other three children

Low cost helps my budget

List the actual NEGATIVE effects of the solution:

When it's my turn, I have to care for

four children

Sometimes our schedules clash

Can't let a sick child participate

FINAL EVALUATION: Was it a good or bad choice?

All in all, I think this is the best I could do on my budget. There are times when I have to stay home with a sick child, but I'm mostly able to stay committed to both parenting and school.

Learning Styles Tip
Visually depicting the steps in a problem-solving plan will be especially helpful to logical-mathematical and visual-spatial learners.

Evaluate repeatedly, making changes that you decide make the solution better (i.e., more reflective of the causes of the problem).

Sample problem: The student may decide to continue to study more regularly but, after a few weeks of tutoring, could opt to trade in the tutoring time for some extra sleep. He may decide to take what he has learned from the tutor so far and apply it to his increased study efforts.

Using this process will enable you to solve school, work, and personal problems in a thoughtful, comprehensive way. The think link in Figure 5.2 demonstrates a way to visualize the flow of problem solving. Figure 5.3 shows how one person used this plan to solve a problem. It represents the same plan as Figure 5.2 but with space to write in so that it can be used in the problem-solving process.

Decision Making

Although every problem-solving process involves making a decision (deciding on a solution), not all decisions involve problems. Decisions are choices. Making a choice, or decision, requires thinking critically through the possible choices and evaluating which will work best for you and for the situation.

Before you begin the process, evaluate the decision. Some decisions are little day-to-day considerations that you can take care of quickly (what books to bring to class). Others require thoughtful evaluation, time, and perhaps the input of others you trust (whether to quit a good job). The following is a list of steps for thinking critically through the more complex kind of decision.

1. Decide on a goal. Why is this decision necessary? What result do you want from this decision, and what is its value? Considering the *effects* you want can help you formulate your goal.

   Sample decision: A student currently attends a small private college. Her goal is to become a physical therapist. The school has a good program, but her father has changed jobs and the family can no longer pay the tuition and fees.

2. Establish needs. *Recall* the needs of everyone (or everything) involved in the decision. Consider all who will be affected.

   Sample decision: The student needs a school with a full physical therapy program; she and her parents need to cut costs; she needs to be able to transfer credits.

3. Name, investigate, and evaluate available options. Brainstorm possible choices, and then look at the facts surrounding each. *Evaluate* the good and bad effects of each possibility. Weigh these effects and judge which is the best course of action.

   Sample decision: Here are some possibilities that the student might consider:
   - Continue at the current college. **Positive effects:** I wouldn't have to adjust to a new place or to new people. I could continue my course work as planned. **Negative effects:** I would have to find a way to finance most of my tuition and costs on my own, such as through loans, grants, or work. I'm not sure I could find time to work as

Teaching Tip
Students should try to visualize the long-term consequences of change and anticipate how a decision will affect different areas of their lives. For example, they might ask themselves how taking a job with heavy travel will affect their family as well as their career.

much as I would need to, and I don't think I would qualify for as much aid as I now need.

- **Transfer to the state college.** **Positive effects:** I could reconnect with people there that I know from high school. Tuition and room costs would be cheaper than at my current school. I could transfer credits. **Negative effects:** I would still have to work some or find minimal financial aid. The physical therapy program is small and not very strong.

- **Transfer to the community college.** **Positive effects:** They have many of the courses I need to continue with the physical therapy curriculum. The school is close by, so I could live at home and avoid paying housing costs. Credits will transfer. The tuition is extremely reasonable. **Negative effects:** I don't know anyone there. I would be less independent. The school doesn't offer a bachelor's degree.

4. **Decide on a plan and take action.** Make a choice based on your evaluation, and act on it.

   Sample decision: In this case, the student might decide to go to the community college for two years and then transfer back to a four-year school to earn a bachelor's degree in physical therapy. Although she might lose some independence and contact with friends, the positive effects are money saved, opportunity to spend time on studies rather than working to earn tuition, and the availability of classes that match the physical therapy program requirements.

5. **Evaluate the result.** Was it useful? Not useful? Some of both? Weigh the positive and negative effects. If the student decides to transfer, she may find that it can be hard being back at home, although her parents are adjusting to her independence and she is trying to respect their concerns. Fewer social distractions result in her getting more work done. The financial situation is favorable. All things considered, she evaluates that this decision was a good one.

Students listen to a lecture.

Making important decisions can take time. Think through your decisions thoroughly, considering your own ideas as well as those of others you trust, but don't hesitate to act once you have your plan. You cannot benefit from your decision until you follow through on it.

HOW DO YOU CONSTRUCT AND EVALUATE ARGUMENTS?

In this case, "argument" refers to a persuasive case that you make to prove or disprove a point. It is a set of connected ideas supported by examples. Anytime a statement is presented and supported—such as in textbooks, newspaper articles, or lectures—an argument is taking place.

Persuade

To convince someone through argument or reasoning to adopt a belief, position, or course of action.

Premise

Something supposed as a basis of argument; a preliminary assumption.

Learning Styles Tip
Advise students with bodily-kinesthetic and interpersonal intelligences to role play their position with a friend or relative who takes a devil's advocate role.

Constructing an Argument

You will often encounter situations in which your success depends on your ability to **persuade** someone, either verbally or in writing, to agree with you. You may need to write a paper persuading the reader that a particular historical event changed the world, for example, or you may need to persuade a prospective employer that you are the one for the job.

An argument is based on a particular topic and issue. It starts with an idea or **premise,** gives examples to support that premise, and finally asserts a conclusion. See Figure 5.4 for an example of an argument.

To construct an argument, follow these steps:

1. *Establish the premise.* Define what you want to argue. Establish the topic of your argument (the subject) and the issue at hand (the question that your argument will answer in a certain way).

2. *Gather examples in support.* Gather evidence that supports your premise, and then put it into logical order. You might want to use "chain-link support"—a set of reasons that build on one another.

3. *Anticipate questions and points against you.* What might you be asked to explain? What could someone say that argues against you? Decide what you will say to address questions and opposing points.

4. *Draw a conclusion.* Formulate a conclusion that summarizes how this evidence supports your initial premise. Keep your goal in mind, and make sure that your conclusion reflects that goal.

As an example, here is one way to present an argument for a raise and promotion at work.

Your topic: Job status

Your issue: What role you should have at this point in your career.

FIGURE 5.4 A Sample Argument

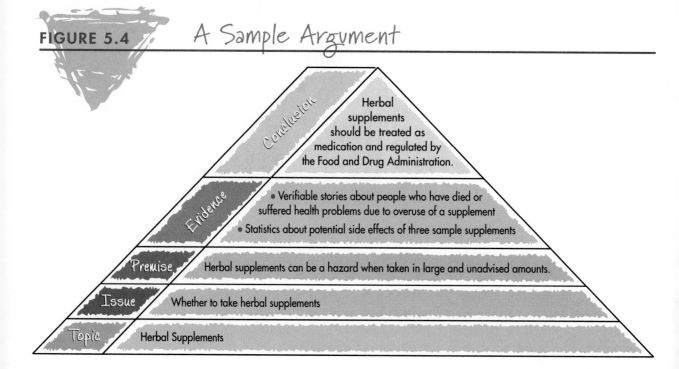

Your premise: You deserve a raise and promotion.

Your audience: Your supervisor (who may or may not be receptive, depending on your relationship).

Your evidence, or examples, that support your idea: You are a solid, creative performer. You feel that your experience and high level of motivation will have positive effects for the company.

Questions you anticipate: "What have you achieved in your current position?" "What do you know about the position you want to take?" "What new and creative ideas do you have?"

Potential counterarguments: Your supervisor might say that you may not be able to handle the new position's hours because of your school schedule. In preparation, you could look into what it would take to reschedule classes and make adjustments in your other commitments.

Your conclusion: Promoting you would have positive effects for both you and the company.

Above all, be flexible. You never know what turn a conversation will take or how a written argument will be interpreted. Keep your mind active and ready to address any surprises that come your way.

Evaluating an Argument

It's easy—and common—to accept or reject an argument outright, according to whether it fits with one's own opinions and views. If you ask questions about an argument, however, you will be able to determine its validity and will learn more from it. Furthermore, critical thinking will help you avoid accepting opinions and assumptions that are not supported by evidence.

Thinking critically about an argument involves a two-part evaluation:

- evaluating the quality of the evidence itself
- evaluating whether the evidence adequately supports the premise

These two considerations will give you a pretty good idea of whether the argument works. If good quality evidence (true input) combines with good quality use of evidence (valid reasoning), you get a solid argument (true output).

Evidence Quality

Ask the following questions in order to see whether the evidence itself is valid.

- What type of evidence is it—fact or opinion?
- How is the evidence similar to, or different from, what I already believe to be true?
- Where is the evidence from? Are those sources reliable and free of bias? (Examples of sources include intuition, authorities, personal experience, and observation.)

Support Quality

Ask these questions to determine whether you think the evidence successfully makes the argument:

- Do examples logically follow from ideas and ideas logically lead to given examples?

- Does the evidence show similarity to what I consider common sense?

- Are there enough pieces of evidence to support the conclusion well?

- Do I know of any competing views or pieces of evidence that differ from this evidence?

- Has the argument evaluated all of the positive and negative effects involved? Are there any negative effects to what the conclusion is arguing that haven't been considered?

The more you read and listen to arguments, the more adept you will become at evaluating them. Read a newspaper. Listen to public radio. Pay attention to the views of people around you. Make an effort not to take anything as true or false without spending some time asking questions about it first.

HOW DO YOU THINK LOGICALLY?

Logical thinking involves questioning the truth and accuracy of information in order to find out whether it is true or reliable. Logical thinking includes these two primary tasks: distinguishing fact from opinion and identifying and evaluating assumptions.

Distinguishing Fact from Opinion

Fact, according to the dictionary, is information presented as objectively real and verifiable. *Opinion* is defined as a belief, conclusion, or judgment and is inherently difficult, if not impossible, to verify. Being able to distinguish fact from opinion is crucial to your understanding of reading material and your ability to decide what information to believe and put to use. See Table 5.2 for some more examples of factual statements versus statements of opinion; note that facts refer to the observable or measurable, while opinions involve cause-and-effect exploration.

Teaching Tip
Reinforce the need to distinguish between fact and opinion by encouraging students to question their teachers' views as well as the views of family and friends.

Characteristics of Facts and Opinions

Following are some indicators that will help you determine what is fact and what is opinion.[2]
Indicators of opinion are:

- **Statements that show evaluation.** Any statement of value, such as "Television is bad for children," indicates an opinion. Words such as *bad, good, pointless,* and *beneficial* indicate value judgments.

- **Statements that predict future events.** Nothing that will happen in the future can be definitively proven in the present. Most statements that discuss something that may happen in the future are opinions.

- **Statements that use abstract words.** While "one gallon" can be defined, "love" has no specific definition. **Abstract** words—*strength, misery, success*—usually indicate an opinion.

Abstract
Theoretical; disassociated from any specific instance.

Examples of Facts and Opinions

TABLE 5.2

TOPIC	FACTUAL STATEMENT	STATEMENT OF OPINION
Stock market	In 1999 the Dow Jones Industrial average rose above 10,000 for the first time.	The Dow Jones Industrial average will continue to grow throughout the first decade of the 21st century.
Weather	It's raining outside.	This is the worst rainstorm yet this year.
Cataloging systems	Computer databases have replaced card catalogs in most college libraries.	Computer databases are an improvement over card catalogs.

- **Statements that use emotional words.** Emotions are by nature unverifiable. Chances are that statements using such words as *delightful, nasty, miserable,* or *wonderful* will present an opinion.
- **Statements that use qualifiers.** Absolute qualifiers such as *all, none, never,* and *always* can point to an opinion. For example, "All students need to work while in school" is an opinion.

Indicators of fact are:

- **Statements that deal with actual people, places, objects, events.** If the existence of the elements involved can be verified through observation, chances are that the statement itself can also be proven true or false. "Jimmy Carter was a peanut farmer in Georgia" is an example of this principle.
- **Statements that use concrete words or measurable statistics.** Any statement that uses concrete, measurable terms and avoids the abstract is likely to be a fact. Examples include "Thirty-six inches constitute a yard" and "There are 2,512 full-time students enrolled this semester."

When you find yourself feeling that an opinion is fact, it may be because you agree strongly with the opinion. Don't discount your feelings; "not verifiable" is not the same as "inaccurate." Opinions are not necessarily wrong even if you cannot prove them.

Qualifier
A word that changes the meaning of another word or word group.

Have a "hot topic" with your friends, professor, or study group. Discuss alternatives to the death penalty or a cure for cancer. Ask each person to distinguish between fact and opinion when they present their views.

Using Questions to Investigate Truth and Accuracy

Once you label a statement as a fact or opinion, explore its degree of truth. Because both facts and opinions can be true or false—for example, "There are 25 hours in a day" is a false factual statement—both require investigation through questioning. Critical-thinking experts Sylvan Barnet and Hugo Bedau state that when you test for the truth of a statement, you "determine whether what it asserts corresponds with reality; if it does, then it is true, and if it doesn't, then it is false."[3] In order to determine to what degree a statement "corresponds with reality," ask questions such as the following:

- What facts or examples provide evidence of truth?
- How does the maker of the statement know this to be true?
- Is there another fact that disproves this statement or information, or shows it to be an opinion?
- How reliable are the sources of information?
- What about this statement is similar to or different from other information I consider fact?

Another crucial step in determining the truth is to question the assumptions that you and others hold, which are the underlying force in shaping opinions.

Identifying and Evaluating Assumptions

Assumption

An idea or statement accepted as true without examination or proof.

"If it's more expensive, it's better." "You should study in a library." These statements reveal assumptions—evaluations or generalizations influenced by values and based on observing cause and effect—that can often hide within seemingly truthful statements. An **assumption** can influence choices—you may assume that you should earn a certain degree or own a car. Many people don't question whether their assumptions make sense, nor do they challenge the assumptions of others.

Assumptions come from sources such as parents or relatives, television and other media, friends, and personal experiences. As much as you think such assumptions work for you, it's just as possible that they can close your mind to opportunities and even cause harm. Investigate each assumption as you would any statement of fact or opinion, analyzing its causes and effects.

The first step in uncovering the assumptions that underlie a statement is to look at the cause-and-effect pattern of the statement, seeing if the way reasons move to conclusions is supported by evidence or involves a hidden assumption. See Figure 5.5 for questions you can ask to evaluate an assumption.

For example, here's how you might use these questions to investigate the following statement: "The most productive schedule involves getting started early in the day." First of all, a cause-and-effect evaluation shows that this statement reveals the following assumption: "The morning is when people have the most energy and are most able to get things done." Here's how you might question the assumption:

Career Connection

At work, students should encourage all the members of their work team to challenge assumptions along with them. If they take this approach alone, others may see them as a troublemaker rather than as a critical thinker and problem solver.

Be a Team

Ask students, working in groups of four, to challenge the assumptions that underlie the following statement: "All school buses should be equipped with seat belts to save the lives of young children."

- This assumption may be true for people who have good energy in the morning hours. But the assumption may be not true for people who work best in the afternoon or evening hours.
- Society's basic standard of daytime classes and 8:00 A.M. to 5:00 P.M. working hours supports this assumption. Therefore, the assumption may work for people who have early jobs and classes. It may not work, however, for people who work other shifts or who take evening classes.
- Maybe people who believe this assumption were raised to start their days early. Or, perhaps they just go along with what seems to be society's standard. Still, there are plenty of people who operate on a different schedule and yet enjoy successful, productive lives.
- Taking this assumption as fact could hurt people who don't operate at their peak in the earlier hours. In situations that favor their particular

Questioning an Assumption

FIGURE 5.5

In what cases is this assumption valid or invalid? What examples prove or disprove it?

What is the source of this assumption? How reliable is the source—can it be counted on to have investigated this assumption?

What harm could be done by always taking this assumption as fact?

What positive and negative effects has this assumption had on me or others?

characteristics—later classes and jobs, career areas that don't require early morning work—such people have just as much potential to succeed as anyone else.

Be careful to question all assumptions, not just those that seem problematic from the start. Form your opinion after investigating the positive and negative effects of any situation.

WHY SHOULD YOU EXPLORE PERSPECTIVES?

Perspective is complex and unique to each individual. You have your own way of looking at everything that you encounter, from your big-picture perspective on the world to your general opinion on ideas, activities, people, and places. However, seeing the world *only* from your perspective—and resisting any challenges to that perspective—can be inflexible, limiting, and frustrating to both you and others. You probably know how difficult it can be when someone cannot understand your point of view. Perhaps an instructor doesn't like that you leave early on Thursdays for physical therapy, or a friend can't understand why you would date someone of a race different from yours.

Perspective

A mental point of view or outlook, based on a cluster of related assumptions, incorporating values, interests, and knowledge.

Evaluating Perspective

The most effective way to evaluate perspectives involves taking in information, evaluating it with questions, and then acting upon it in whatever way seems appropriate. Exploring perspectives critically will introduce you to new ideas, improve your communication with others, and encourage mutual respect.

Take In New Information

The first step is to take in new perspectives and simply acknowledge that they exist without immediately judging, rejecting, or even accepting them. It's easy to feel so strongly about a topic—for example, whether the government should allow capital punishment—that you don't even give a chance to anyone with an opposing view. Resist your own strong opinions and listen. A critical thinker is able to allow for the existence of perspectives that differ from, and even completely negate, his or her own.

Evaluate the Perspective

Asking questions will help you maintain flexibility and openness.

- What is similar and different about this perspective and my own perspective and about this person and me? What personal experiences have led to our particular perspectives?
- What examples, evidence, or reasons could be used to support or justify this perspective? Do some reasons provide good support even if I don't agree with the reasons?
- What effects may come from this way of being, acting, or believing? Are the effects different on different people and different situations? Even if this perspective seems to have negative effects for me, how might it have positive effects for others and therefore have value?
- What can I learn from this different perspective? Is there anything I could adopt that would improve my life? Is there anything I wouldn't do but that I can still respect and learn from?

Accept and Perhaps Take Action

On the one hand, perhaps your evaluation will lead you simply to a recognition and appreciation of the other perspective, even if you decide that it is not right for you. On the other hand, thinking through the new perspective may lead you to feel that it would be worthwhile to try it out or to adopt it as your own. You may feel that what you have learned has led you to a new way of seeing yourself or your life.

The Value of Seeing Other Perspectives

Seeing beyond one's own perspective can be difficult. Why put in the effort? Here are some of the very real benefits of being able to see and consider other perspectives.

Improved communication. When you consider another person's perspective, you open the lines of communication. For example, if you want to add or drop a course and your advisor says it's impossible before listening to you, you might not feel much like explaining. But if your advisor asks to hear your perspective, you may sense that your needs are respected and be ready to talk.

Mutual respect.   When someone takes the time and energy to understand how you feel about something, you probably feel respected and in return offer respect to the person who made the effort. When people respect one another, relationships become stronger and more productive, whether they are personal, work-related, or educational.

Continued learning.   Every time you shift your perspective, you can learn something new. There are worlds of knowledge and possibilities outside your experience. You may find different yet equally valid ways of getting an education, living as a family, or relating to others. Above all else, you may see that each person is entitled to his or her own perspective, no matter how foreign it may be to you.

By being able to recognize perspectives, the connection that you foster with others may mean the difference between success and failure in today's world. This becomes more true as the Information Age introduces you to an increasing number of perspectives every day.

The Wheel of Thinking   FIGURE 5.6

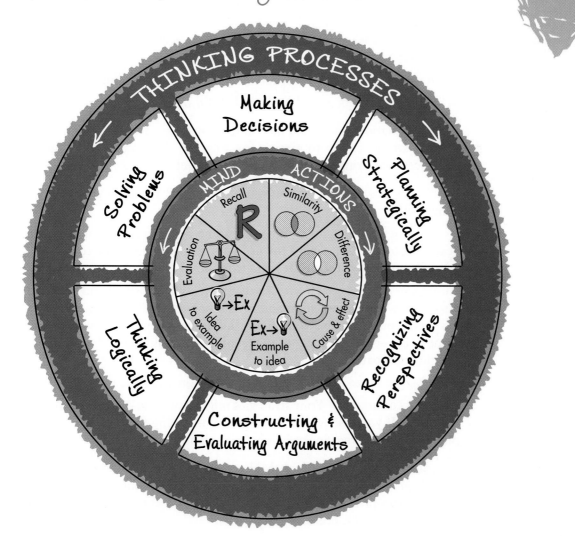

WHY PLAN STRATEGICALLY?

If you've ever played a game of chess, participated in a martial arts match, or made a detailed plan of how to reach a particular goal, you have had experience with **strategy.** Strategy is the plan of action, that is, the method or the "how," behind any goal you want to achieve.

Strategic planning means looking at the next week, month, year, or 10 years and exploring the future positive and negative effects that current choices and actions may have. As a student, you have planned strategically by deciding that the effort of school is a legitimate price to pay for the skills and opportunities you will receive. Being strategic means using decision-making skills to choose how to accomplish tasks. It means asking questions.

Strategy and Critical Thinking

In situations that demand strategy, think critically by asking questions like these:

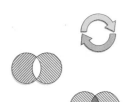

- If you aim for a certain goal, what actions may cause you to achieve that goal?

- What are the potential effects, positive or negative, of different actions or choices?

- What can you learn from previous experiences that may inspire similar or different actions?

- What can you recall about what others have done in similar situations?

- Which set of effects would be most helpful or desirable to you?

For any situation that would benefit from strategic planning, from getting ready for a study session to aiming for a career, these steps will help you make choices that bring about the most positive effects.

1. **Establish a goal.** What do you want to achieve? When do you want to achieve it?

2. **Brainstorm possible plans.** What are some ways that you can get where you want to go? What steps toward your goal will you need to take 1 year, 5 years, 10 years, or 20 years from now?

3. **Anticipate all possible effects of each plan.** What positive and negative effects may occur, both soon and in the long term? What approach may best help you to achieve your goal? Talk to people who are where you want to be—professionally or personally—and ask them what you should anticipate.

4. **Put your plan into action.** Act on the decision you have made.

5. **Evaluate continually.** Your strategies might not have the effects you predicted. If you discover that things are not going the way you planned, for any reason, reevaluate and change your strategy.

The most important critical-thinking question for successful strategic planning begins with "how." *How* do you remember what you learn? *How* do you develop a productive idea at work? The process of strategic planning, in a nutshell, helps you find the best answer.

Benefits of Strategic Planning

Strategic planning has many important positive effects, including the following:

School and work success. A student who wants to do well in a course needs to plan study sessions. A lawyer needs to anticipate how to respond to points raised in court. Strategic planning creates a vision into the future that allows the planner to anticipate possibilities and to be prepared for them.

Successful goal setting. Thinking strategically helps you to see how to achieve goals over time. For example, a student might have a part-time job to work toward the goal of paying tuition.

Keeping up with technology. Technological developments have increased workplace change. Thinking strategically about job opportunities may lead you to a broader range of courses or a major and career in a growing career area, making it more likely that your skills will be in demand when you graduate.

Strategic planning means using critical thinking to develop a vision of your future. Although you can't predict with certainty what will happen, you can ask questions about the potential effects of your actions. With what you learn, you can make plans that will bring the best possible effects for you and others.

Career Connection
Strategic thinking is also important for career advancement. Employees should take in-house training courses to keep up with technological changes that affect their job. They should also try to chart career moves that will enhance their value to future employers.

HOW CAN YOU DEVELOP YOUR CREATIVITY?

Everyone is creative. Although the word *creativity* may inspire images of art and music, creativity comes in many other forms. A creation can be a solution, idea, approach, tangible product, work of art, system, or program. Creative innovations introduced by all kinds of people continually expand and change the world. Here are some that have had an impact:

Creativity
The ability to produce something new through imaginative skill.

- Harold Cohen, biology teacher at College of DuPage, helps his students gain hands-on experience by linking them up with aquariums and animal rehabilitation centers.

- Rosa Parks refused to give up her seat on the bus to a white person, setting off a chain of events that gave rise to the civil rights movement.

- Jody Williams and the group she founded, International Campaign to Ban Landmines, have convinced nearly 100 countries to support a treaty that would end land mine production and sales.

- Art Fry and Spencer Silver invented the Post-it® in 1980, enabling people to save paper and protect documents by using removable notes.

Even though these particular innovations had wide-ranging effects, the characteristics of these influential innovators can be found in all people who exercise their creative capabilities. Creativity can be as down-to-earth as planning how to coordinate your work and class schedules.

Be a Team
Ask students to write their own list of creative people and the reasons for their choices. Then ask them to share their list with a partner, comparing and contrasting the types of creativity on which they focused.

Characteristics of Creative People

Career Connection

Companies try to identify creative job candidates through questions that reveal how they think. For example, students may be asked to describe a major challenge they overcame in order to succeed.

Creative people combine ideas and information in ways that form new solutions, ideas, processes, or products. "I've found that the hallmark of creative people is their mental flexibility," says creativity expert Roger van Oech. "Like race-car drivers who shift in and out of different gears depending on where they are on the course, creative people are able to shift in and out of different types of thinking depending on the needs of the situation at hand."[4] See Figure 5.7 for some primary characteristics of creative people.

FIGURE 5.7

Characteristics of Creative People

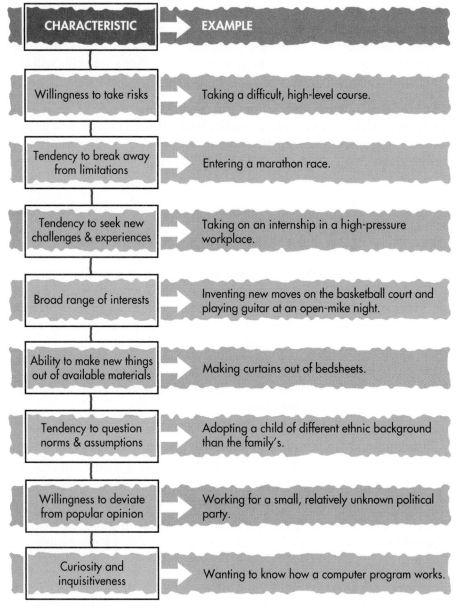

CHARACTERISTIC	EXAMPLE
Willingness to take risks	Taking a difficult, high-level course.
Tendency to break away from limitations	Entering a marathon race.
Tendency to seek new challenges & experiences	Taking on an internship in a high-pressure workplace.
Broad range of interests	Inventing new moves on the basketball court and playing guitar at an open-mike night.
Ability to make new things out of available materials	Making curtains out of bedsheets.
Tendency to question norms & assumptions	Adopting a child of different ethnic background than the family's.
Willingness to deviate from popular opinion	Working for a small, relatively unknown political party.
Curiosity and inquisitiveness	Wanting to know how a computer program works.

Source: Adapted from T. Z. Tardif and R. J. Sternberg, "What Do We Know About Creativity?" in *The Nature of Creativity,* ed., R. J. Sternberg (London: Cambridge University Press, 1988).

Enhancing Your Creativity

Following are some ways to enhance your natural creativity, adapted from material by J. R. Hayes.[5]

Take the broadest possible perspective. At first, a problem may look like "My child won't stay quiet when I study." If you take a wider look, you may discover hidden causes or effects of the problem, such as "We haven't had time together, so he feels lonely."

Choose the best atmosphere. T. M. Amabile says that people are more creative and imaginative when they spend time around other creative folk.[6] Hang out with people whose thinking inspires you.

Give yourself time. Rushing can stifle your creative ability. When you allow time for thoughts to percolate or you take breaks when figuring out a problem, you may increase your creative output.

Gather varied input. The more information and ideas you gather as you think, the more material you have to build a creative idea or solution. Every new piece of input offers a new perspective.

Here are a few additional creativity tips from van Oech:[7]

Don't get hooked on finding the one right answer. There can be lots of "right answers" to any question. The more possibilities you generate, the better your chance of finding the best one.

Don't always be logical. Following strict logic may cause you to miss analogies or ignore your hunches.

Break the rules sometimes. All kinds of creative breakthroughs have occurred because someone bypassed the rules. Women and minorities can vote and hold jobs because someone broke a rule—a law—many years ago. When necessary, challenge rules with creative ideas.

Let yourself play. People often hit upon their most creative ideas when they are exercising or just relaxing. Often when your mind switches into play mode, it can more freely generate new thoughts.

Let yourself go a little crazy. What seems like a crazy idea might be a brilliant discovery. For example, the idea for Velcro came from examining how a burr sticks to clothing.

Don't fear failure. Even Michael Jordan got cut from the basketball team as a high school sophomore in Wilmington, North Carolina. If you insist on getting it right all the time, you may miss out on the creative path—often paved with failures—leading to the best possible solution.

Brainstorming combines many of these strategies. Use brainstorming for problem solving, decision making, writing a paper, or whenever you need to free your mind for new possibilities.

Brainstorming Toward a Creative Answer

You are brainstorming when you approach a problem by letting your mind free-associate and come up with as many possible ideas, examples, or solutions as you can, without immediately evaluating them as good or bad.

"Learning to let yourself create is like learning to walk. . . .

Progress, not perfection, is what we should be asking of ourselves."

Julia Cameron

Teaching Tip
Emphasize to students that creative solutions often evolve over time and that patience is a necessary virtue. Expecting an immediate flow of creative ideas may lead to disappointment.

e-mail

E-mail or talk to one of your close friends about a problem or issue you are trying to resolve. Work with them to brainstorm as many options as possible. Notice how much further you get when you see someone else's mind at work in addition to your own.

Springboard
Ask students to discuss why teenagers find it especially hard to deviate from the ideas that are popular among their peers.

Brainstorming is also referred to as *divergent thinking;* you start with the issue or problem and then let your mind diverge, or go in as many different directions as it wants, in search of ideas or solutions. Following are two general guidelines for successful brainstorming:[8]

Don't evaluate or criticize an idea right away. Write down your ideas so that you remember them. Evaluate them later, after you have had a chance to think about them. Try to avoid criticizing other people's ideas as well. Students often become stifled when their ideas are evaluated during brainstorming.

Focus on quantity; don't worry about quality until later. Generate as many ideas or examples as you can. The more thoughts you generate, the better the chance that one may be useful. Brainstorming works well in groups. Group members can become inspired by, and make creative use of, one another's ideas.

Remember, creativity can be developed if you have the desire and patience. Nurture your creativity by being accepting of your own ideas. Your creative expression will become more free with practice.

Creativity and Critical Thinking

Critical thinking is inherently creative because it requires you to use given information to come up with ideas or solutions to problems. For example, if you were brainstorming to generate possible causes of fatigue in afternoon classes, you might come up with lack of sleep, too much morning caffeine, or an instructor who doesn't inspire you. Through your consideration of causes and solutions, you have been thinking both creatively and critically.

Creative thinkers and critical thinkers have similar characteristics—both consider new perspectives, ask questions, don't hesitate to question accepted assumptions and traditions, and persist in the search for answers. You use critical-thinking mind actions throughout everything you do in school and in your daily life. In this chapter and in some of the other study skills chapters, you will notice mind action icons placed where they can help you to understand how your mind is working.

One particularly important area in which you will benefit from thinking critically is in how you approach the media that you encounter on a daily basis.

WHAT IS MEDIA LITERACY?

Media
The agencies of mass communication—television, film, and journalism (magazines and newspapers).

Do you believe everything you read, see on television, or find on the Internet? Think about it for a moment. If you trusted every advertisement, you would believe that at least four fast-food restaurants serve "the best burger available." If you agreed with every magazine article, you would know that Elvis passed away many years ago and yet still believe that he was shopping for peanut butter last week in Oklahoma. It is impossible to believe it all without becoming completely confused about what is real.

If literacy refers to the ability to read, media literacy can be seen as the ability to read the **media.** Media literacy—the ability to respond with critical

How do I solve the problem of getting the classes I want?

Edhilvia Campos, Parkland Community College, Champaign, Illinois, Microbiology Major

Every semester it's a challenge to figure out what classes I will need. I am majoring in Microbiology, so I need a lot of science courses, and the ones I want aren't always available. Also, I eventually want to transfer to the University of Illinois. The processes for registering and figuring out what credits will transfer seem complicated.

When I came to the states for college, only a few of my math credits transferred because the math classes I had taken in high school in Venezuela were not acceptable credits for college.  My freshman year I took two algebra classes and later found out that they couldn't be applied to my major, which made me feel like I wasted my time. I also don't want to pay for classes that I don't need. Trying to regulate the number of classes you take isn't easy either. One thing I have learned to do is to take at least one fun class each semester. Last semester I had to take chemistry and calculus, so I decided to take music, too, which was a nice break for me.

I may want to go back to Venezuela during the summers. I've considered taking classes then, but the Venezuelan universities don't really offer my major. Once again, I'm trying to find out what classes are available that apply to my major. Do you have suggestions for what I can do to make this process more efficient?

Shera Chantel Caviness, University of Memphis, Early Childhood Education Major, Graduate

First and foremost, hang in there. I know that things seem hard now, but it will pay off. Attending college is similar to a "micro" real world. Throughout college, you will have to face problems that must be solved. I understand that you feel you wasted time and money taking certain classes. But some classes are not always transferable, and unfortunately extra money has to be utilized to take certain courses before entering a degree program.

To prepare to trans-  fer, get acquainted with an academic counselor at the University of Illinois (preferably one in your major) who can help you. He or she can tell you what will transfer so that you will not have to repeat or take unnecessary classes. While at Parkland, find an academic counselor in your field who can guide you toward appropriate courses for that degree. Use the undergraduate catalog to stay informed (and to inform your counselors) of the necessary classes for your major.

Get to know the professors in your field because they can help. Your interest will show that you have the will to achieve. If some classes are not available for one semester, gather at least 8 to 10 students to voice their concern about opening a section for that class. The class schedule is done at the beginning of the previous semester, and professors are often unaware of the demand for certain courses because students do not speak up.

If you do plan to return to Venezuela for the summer, only take courses that will apply to your degree or take some general lower-division classes that are transferable. Make sure you check with the counselors at Parkland and the University of Illinois before signing up. All in all, keep your determination alive and do not let things discourage you. Always find something valuable within each course you take because this will help you become more well-rounded. Remember to think positive; this is only a "micro" real-world experience, helping to prepare you for the R-E-A-L world.

thinking to the media that you encounter—is essential for a realistic understanding of the information that bombards you daily. It means that instead of accepting anything a newspaper article, TV commercial, or Internet site says is fact, you take time to question the information, using your mind actions and critical-thinking processes.

The people who founded the Center for Media Literacy work to encourage others to think critically about the media. They have put forth the following, which they call the "Five Core Concepts of Media Literacy":[9]

All media are constructions. Any TV show or advertisement, for example, is not a view of actual life or fact but rather a carefully constructed presentation that is designed to have a particular effect on the viewer—to encourage you to feel a certain emotion, develop a particular opinion, or buy the product advertised. For example, an article that wants the reader to feel good about the president will focus on his strengths rather than his shortcomings.

Media use unique "languages." The people who produce media carefully choose wording, background music, colors, images, timing, and other factors to produce a desired effect. When watching a movie, listen to the music that plays behind an emotional scene or a high-speed chase.

Different audiences understand the same media message differently. Individual people understand media in the context of their own unique experiences. For this reason, people may often interpret media quite differently. A child who has not experienced violence personally but who watches it on TV may not understand that violence brings pain and suffering. In contrast, a child who has witnessed or experienced violence firsthand may react to it with fear for his or her personal safety.

Taking time out to think.

Media have commercial interests. Media are driven by the intent to sell you something, not by the need to tell the truth. Television and radio stations, newspapers, magazines, and commercial Web sites make sure that the advertisers who support them get a chance to convey a message to the consumer. Advertising is chosen so that it appeals to those most likely to encounter that particular kind of media; for example, ads for beer and cars dominate the airwaves during major sports events.

Media have embedded values and points of view. Any media product carries the values of the people who created it. For example, even by choosing the topics on which to write articles, a magazine's editor conveys an opinion that those topics are important. *Runner's World* thinks that how to stay warm on a winter run is important, for example.

To be media literate is to approach what you see, hear, and read with thought and consideration. Use your critical-thinking processes to analyze the media and develop an informed opinion.

Ask questions based on the mind actions. Is what you read in a newspaper similar to something you already know to be true? Do you evaluate a magazine article to be useful or not? Do you agree with the causes or effects that are cited?

Evaluate the truth of the argument.   If a TV ad argues that a certain kind of car is the best on the road, evaluate this information the way that you would any argument. With what facts do they back up their claims? Are the claims opinion? Does assuming their claims to be true cause any harm? What strategies are they using to persuade you to adopt their idea?

Recognize perspective.   It is just as important to avoid rejecting the media automatically as it is to avoid accepting them automatically. Any media offering has its own particular perspective, coming from the person or people who created it. Explore this perspective, asking what positive and negative effects it might have. For example, if a Web site encourages you to adopt the perspective that you should dislike a particular ethnic group, this may have harmful effects.

Becoming media literate will help you become a smart consumer of the media, one who ultimately is responsible for his or her actions. Don't let a TV ad or a Web banner tell you what to do. Evaluate the message critically and make your own decision. Media literacy is a key to a responsible, self-powered life.

Κριvειv

The word *critical* is derived from the Greek word *krinein,* which means to separate in order to choose or select. To be a mindful, aware critical thinker, you need to be able to separate, evaluate, and select ideas, facts, and thoughts.

Think of this concept as you apply critical thinking to your reading, writing, and interaction with others. Be aware of the information you take in and of your thoughts, and be selective as you process them. Critical thinking gives you the power to make sense of life by deliberately selecting how to respond to the information, people, and events that you encounter.

Name   Date

BUILDING SKILLS FOR COLLEGE, CAREER, AND LIFE SUCCESS

Critical Thinking
Applying Learning to Life

Make an Important Decision

In this series of exercises you will use the seven mind actions and the five decision-making steps. First, write here the decision you need to make. Choose an important decision that needs to be made soon.

_____

_____

Step 1 Decide on a Goal

Be specific: What goal, or desired effects, do you seek from this decision? For example, if your decision is a choice between two jobs, the effects you want might be financial security, convenience, experience, or anything else that is a priority to you. It could also be a combination of these effects. Write down the desired effects that together make up your goal. Note priorities by numbering the effects in order of importance.

_____

_____

_____

Step 2 Establish Needs

Who and what will be affected by your decision? If you are deciding how to finance your education and you have a family to support, you must take into consideration their financial needs as well as your own when exploring options.

List here the people, things, or situations that may be affected by your decision and indicate how your decision will affect them.

_____

_____

_____

Step 3 Name, Investigate, and Evaluate Available Options

Look at any options you can imagine. Consider options even if they seem impossible or unlikely; you can evaluate them later. Some decisions only have two options (to move to a new apartment or not; to get a new roommate or not); others have a wider selection of choices.

   List two possible options for your decision. Then evaluate the potential good and bad effects of each.

Option 1 _____

Positive effects _____

Negative effects _____

Option 2 _____

Positive effects _____

Negative effects _____

Have you or someone else ever made a decision similar to the one you are about to make? Can you learn anything from that decision that may help you?

_____

_____

_____

Step 4 Decide on a Plan and Take Action

Taking your entire analysis into account, decide what to do. Write your decision here.

_____

_____

_____

Next is perhaps the most important part of the process: *Act on your decision.*

Step 5 Evaluate the Result

After you have acted on your decision, evaluate how everything turned out. Did you achieve the effects you wanted to achieve? What were the effects on you? On others? On the situation? To what extent were they positive, negative, or some of both?

   List three effects here. Name each effect, circle whether it was positive or negative, and explain your evaluation.

Effect _____
                Positive   Negative
Why? _____

Effect _____
                Positive   Negative
Why? _____

Effect _____

      Positive   Negative

Why? _____

 Final evaluation: Write one statement in reaction to the decision you made. Indicate whether you feel the decision was useful or not useful, and why. Indicate any adjustments that could have made the effects of your decision more positive.

_____

_____

_____

Brainstorming on the Idea Wheel

Your creative mind can solve problems when you least expect it. Many people report having sudden ideas while exercising, driving, showering, upon waking, or even when dreaming. When the pressure is off, the mind is often more free to roam through uncharted territory and bring back treasures.

To make the most of this "mind float," grab ideas right when they surface. If you don't, they roll back into your subconscious as if on a wheel. Because you never know how big the wheel is, you can't be sure when that particular idea will roll to the top again. That's why writers carry notebooks—they need to grab thoughts when they come to the top of the wheel.

Name a long-term goal for which you need to do some strategic planning. Do a brainstorm without the time limit. Be on the lookout for ideas, causes, effects, or related short-term goals coming to the top of your wheel. The minute it happens, grab this book and write down your thought. Look at your ideas later and see how your creative mind may have pointed you toward some original and workable solutions. You may also want to keep a book by your bed to catch ideas that pop up before, during, or after sleep.

Goal: _____

Ideas: _____

_____

_____

Arguments, Assumptions, and Perspectives

Name an assumption that you know is common or that you have made yourself. It can be about anything—people, lifestyles, education, differences, money, relationships, and so forth. Write it here:

_____

Now you will construct two arguments: one that supports the assumption and one that disputes it. Use your mind actions to ask important questions as you construct your arguments—think of cases or examples that fit and don't fit the assumption, positive and negative effects of believing the assumption, similar and different assumptions, and what experiences might cause the assumption.

Argument supporting _____

_____

_____

Argument disputing _____

_____

_____

Analyze each argument in your mind. Which perspective seems more open-minded? Which works better for situations in your life? Which perspective is closer to yours? Note here which perspective is farther from your own and write one thing that you have learned from exploring that side of the argument.

_____

_____

_____

_____

Teamwork
Combining Forces

Group Problem Solving As a class, brainstorm a list of problems in your lives. Write the problems on the board or on a large piece of paper attached to an easel. Include any problems you feel comfortable discussing with others. Such problems may involve school, relationships, jobs, discrimination, parenting, housing, procrastination, and others. Divide into groups of two to four with each group choosing or being assigned one problem to work on. Use the empty problem-solving flowchart on p. 155 to fill in your work.

1. Identify the problem. As a group, state your problem specifically, without causes ("I'm not attending all of my classes" is better than "lack of motivation"). Then, explore and record the causes and effects that surround it. Remember to look for "hidden" causes (you may perceive that traffic makes you late to school, but getting up too late might be the hidden cause).

2. **Brainstorm possible solutions.** Determine the most likely causes of the problem; from those causes, derive possible solutions. Record all the ideas that group members offer. After 10 minutes or so, each group member should choose one possible solution to explore independently.

3. **Explore each solution.** In thinking independently through the assigned solution, each group member should (a) weigh the positive and negative effects, (b) consider similar problems, and (c) describe how the solution affects the causes of the problem. Evaluate your assigned solution. Is it a good one? Will it work?

4. **Choose your top solution(s).** Come together again as a group. Take turns sharing your observations and recommendations, and then take a vote: Which solution is the best? You may have a tie or may want to combine two different solutions. Either way is fine. Different solutions suit different people and situations. Although it's not always possible to reach agreement, try to find the solution that works for most of the group.

5. **Evaluate the solution you decide is best.** When you decide on your top solution or solutions, discuss what would happen if you went through with it. What do you predict would be the positive and negative effects of this solution? Would it turn out to be a truly good solution for everyone?

Writing
Discovery Through Journaling

To record your thoughts, use a separate journal or the lined page at the end of the chapter.

Media Literacy Choose a magazine you read, a Web site you visit, a TV program you watch, or any other media source with which you come into contact. Evaluate this media source according to what you know about media literacy. What effect does this media intend to have on you? Does it use particular language or images to create that effect? Is it trying to sell something? What values does it convey? And most importantly, how do you feel about its intentions and effects?

Career Portfolio
Charting Your Course

Investigate a Career Choose one career that interests you. Use your critical-thinking processes to think through all aspects of this career strategically. Be an investigator. Find out as many facts as you can, and evaluate all opinions based on what you already know.

Problem-Solving Flowchart

LIST CAUSES OF PROBLEM:

_____
_____
_____
_____
_____

STATE PROBLEM HERE:

LIST EFFECTS OF PROBLEM:

_____
_____
_____
_____
_____

List potential POSITIVE effects for each solution:

Use boxes below to list possible solutions:

List potential NEGATIVE effects for each solution:

SOLUTION #1

_____
_____
_____
_____

_____
_____
_____
_____

SOLUTION #2

_____
_____
_____
_____
_____

_____
_____
_____
_____
_____

SOLUTION #3

_____
_____
_____
_____
_____

_____
_____
_____
_____
_____

Now choose the solution you think is best—and try it.

CHOSEN SOLUTION

List the actual POSITIVE effects of the solution:

List the actual NEGATIVE effects of the solution:

_____
_____
_____
_____

FINAL EVALUATION: Was it a good or bad choice?

Performance counts!

- What are the different kinds of jobs available in this career?
- What is the condition of the industry—growing, lagging, or holding steady?
- Does this career require you to live in a certain area of the country or world?
- Who can you talk to to find out more information about this career?
- What are the pros and cons (positive and negative effects) of working in this area?
- What types of people tend to succeed in this career, and what types tend not to do well?
- What are the opinions of those around you about this career?
- What preparation—in school and/or on the job—does this career require?

Your ability to investigate will be central to success in any career you pursue, whether you're analyzing and discovering new opportunities, or finding your competitor's soft spots. Honing this skill now as it applies to your personal development will help you greatly in the long run.

Then, write up your findings in a report. Use each question as a separate heading. Keep your research in your portfolio. Write a conclusion about your prospects in this career area based on what you learned in your investigation.

Journal Entry

Name _____   Date _____

Reading, Studying, and Using the Library

Maximizing Written Resources

In this chapter, you will explore answers to the following questions:

- What are some challenges of reading?
- Why define your purpose for reading?
- How can SQ3R help you own what you read?
- How can you respond critically to what you read?
- How and why should you study with others?
- How can you make the most of the library?

Your reading background—your past as a reader—may not necessarily prepare you for the new challenges of college reading. In high school, you generally had more time to read less material, with less necessity for deep-level understanding. In college, however, your reading will often be complex, and you may experience an overload of assignments. College reading and studying require a step-by-step approach aimed at the construction of meaning and knowledge. The material in this chapter will present techniques that can help you read and study as efficiently as possible while still having time left over for other things. Using the library is also a focus of this chapter. Through informed use of the library, you will be able to access resources that can help you learn and reach your potential.

Teaching Tip
See the following helpful Web site:
- Study Web - www.studyweb.com/

WHAT ARE SOME CHALLENGES OF READING?

Everyone has reading challenges, such as difficult texts, distractions, a lack of speed and comprehension, or insufficient vocabulary. Following are some ideas about how to meet these challenges. Note that if you have a reading disability, if English is not your primary language, or if you have limited reading skills, you may need additional support. Most colleges provide services for students through a reading center or tutoring program. Take the initiative to seek help if you need it. Many accomplished learners have benefited from help in specific areas.

Working Through Difficult Texts

Although many textbooks are useful learning tools, some may be poorly written and organized, perhaps written by experts who may not explain information in the friendliest manner for nonexperts. Because texts are often written to challenge the intellect, even well-written texts may be difficult to read.

Generally, the further you advance in your education, the more complex your required reading is likely to be. You may feel at times as though you are reading a foreign language as you encounter new concepts, words, and terms. Assignments can also be difficult when the required reading is from *primary sources*—original documents rather than another writer's interpretation of these documents—or from academic journal articles and scientific studies that don't define basic terms or supply a wealth of examples. Primary sources include:

■ historical documents

■ works of literature (novels, poems, and plays)

■ scientific studies, including lab reports and accounts of experiments

■ journal articles

The following strategies may help you make your way through difficult reading material:

Approach your reading assignments head-on. Be careful not to prejudge them as impossible or boring before you even start to read.

Accept the fact that some texts may require some extra work and concentration. Set a goal to make your way through the material and learn, whatever it takes.

> "No barrier of the senses shuts me out from the sweet, gracious discourse of my book friends. They talk to me without embarrassment or awkwardness."
>
> Helen Keller

When a primary source does not explain concepts, define them on your own. Ask your instructor or other students for help. Consult reference materials in that subject area, other class materials, dictionaries, and encyclopedias. You may want to create your own minilibrary at home. Collect reference materials that you use often, such as a dictionary, a thesaurus, a writer's style handbook, and maybe an atlas or computer manual (many of these are available as computer software or CD-ROMs). "If you find yourself going to the library to look up the same reference again and again, consider purchasing that book for your personal or office library," advises library expert Sherwood Harris.[1]

Look for order and meaning in seemingly chaotic reading materials. The information you will find in this chapter on the SQ3R reading technique and on critical reading will help you discover patterns and achieve a greater depth of understanding. Finding order within chaos is an important skill, not just in the mastery of reading but also in life. This skill can give you power by helping you "read" (think through) work dilemmas, personal problems, and educational situations.

Managing Distractions

With so much happening around you, it's often hard to focus on your reading. Some distractions are external: the telephone or a child who needs attention. Other distractions come from within, as thoughts arise about various topics; for example, a paper due in art history or a Web site that you want to visit.

Identify the Distraction and Choose a Suitable Action

Pinpoint what's distracting you before you decide what to do. If the distraction is *external* and *out of your control,* such as outside construction or a noisy group in the library, try to move away from it. If the distraction is *external* but *within your control,* such as the television or telephone, take action; for example, turn off the television or let the answering machine answer the phone. Figure 6.1 explores some ways that parents or other people caring for children may be able to maximize their study efforts.

e-mail

We all have distractions. Talk with or write one of your close friends about the proactive way in which you are dealing with your distractions. Solicit your friend's perspective on how he or she handles similar issues.

If the distraction is *internal,* different strategies may help you clear your mind. You may want to take a study break and tend to one of the issues that worries you. Physical exercise may relax and refocus you. For some people, studying while listening to music helps to quiet a busy mind. For others, silence may do the trick. If you need silence to read or study and cannot find a truly quiet environment, consider purchasing sound-muffling headphones or even earplugs.

Find a Study Place and Time That Promote Success

Any reader needs focus and discipline in order to concentrate on the material. Finding a place and time to study that minimizes outside distractions will help you achieve that focus. Here are some suggestions:

Read alone unless you are working with other readers. Family members, friends, or others who are not in a study mode may interrupt your concentration. If you prefer to read alone, establish a relatively interruption-proof place and time, such as an out-of-the-way spot at the library or an after-class hour in an empty classroom. If you study at home and live with others, try putting a "Quiet" sign on the door.

Find a comfortable location. Many students study at a library desk. Others prefer an easy chair at the library or at home, or even the floor. Choose a spot comfortable enough for hours of reading but not so cushy that you fall asleep. Make sure that you have adequate lighting and aren't too hot or cold.

FIGURE 6.1 Exploring Options and Solutions

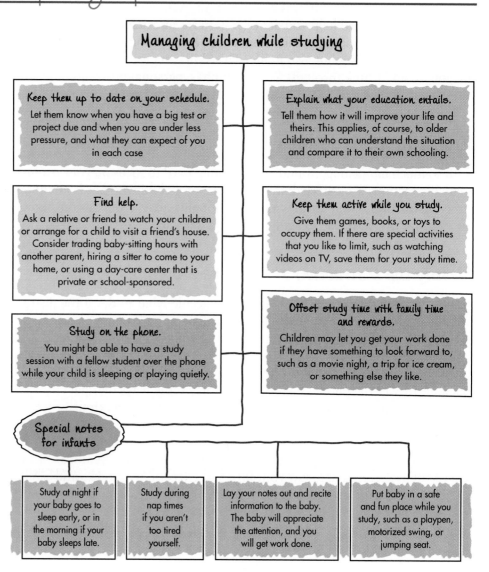

Managing children while studying

Keep them up to date on your schedule. Let them know when you have a big test or project due and when you are under less pressure, and what they can expect of you in each case

Explain what your education entails. Tell them how it will improve your life and theirs. This applies, of course, to older children who can understand the situation and compare it to their own schooling.

Find help. Ask a relative or friend to watch your children or arrange for a child to visit a friend's house. Consider trading baby-sitting hours with another parent, hiring a sitter to come to your home, or using a day-care center that is private or school-sponsored.

Keep them active while you study. Give them games, books, or toys to occupy them. If there are special activities that you like to limit, such as watching videos on TV, save them for your study time.

Study on the phone. You might be able to have a study session with a fellow student over the phone while your child is sleeping or playing quietly.

Offset study time with family time and rewards. Children may let you get your work done if they have something to look forward to, such as a movie night, a trip for ice cream, or something else they like.

Special notes for infants

Study at night if your baby goes to sleep early, or in the morning if your baby sleeps late.

Study during nap times if you aren't too tired yourself.

Lay your notes out and recite information to the baby. The baby will appreciate the attention, and you will get work done.

Put baby in a safe and fun place while you study, such as a playpen, motorized swing, or jumping seat.

Learning Styles Tip
It might help students with musical intelligence to play music that sets the right mood for the material they are reading.

Choose a regular reading place and time. Choose a spot or two that you like, and return often. Also, choose a time when you feel alert and focused. Try reading just before or after the class for which the reading is assigned, if you can. Eventually, you will associate preferred places and times with focused reading.

Turn off the television. For most people, reading and television don't mix.

Building Comprehension and Speed

Most students lead busy lives, carrying heavy academic loads while perhaps working a job or even caring for a family. It's difficult to make time to study at all, let alone handle the reading assignments for your classes. Increasing your reading comprehension and speed will save you valuable time and effort. Because greater comprehension is the primary goal and actually promotes faster reading, make comprehension your priority over speed.

Methods for Increasing Reading Comprehension

Following are some specific strategies for increasing your understanding of what you read:

Continually build your knowledge through reading and studying. What you already know before you read a passage will determine your ability to understand and remember important ideas. Previous knowledge, including vocabulary, facts, and ideas, gives you a **context** for what you read.

Establish your purpose for reading. When you establish what you want to get out of your reading, you will be able to determine what level of understanding you need to reach and, therefore, on what you need to focus. A detailed discussion of reading purposes follows later in this chapter.

Remove the barriers of negative self-talk. Instead of telling yourself that you cannot understand, think positively. Tell yourself: *I can learn this material. I am a good reader.*

Think critically. Ask yourself questions. Do you understand the sentence, paragraph, or chapter you just read? Are ideas and supporting examples clear? Could you explain what you just read to someone else? Take in the concepts that titles, headings, subheadings, figures, and photographs communicate to you.

Methods for Increasing Reading Speed

The average American adult reads between 150 and 350 words per minute, and faster readers can be capable of speeds up to 1,000 words per minute.[2] However, the human eye can only move so fast; reading speeds in excess of 350 words per minute involve "skimming" and "scanning" (see p. 166). The following suggestions will help increase your reading speed:

- Try to read groups of words rather than single words.
- Avoid pointing your finger to guide your reading, because this will slow your pace.
- When reading narrow columns, focus your eyes in the middle of the column. With practice, you'll be able to read the entire column width as you read down the page.
- Avoid *vocalization*—speaking the words or moving your lips—when reading.
- Avoid thinking each word to yourself as you read it, a practice known as subvocalization.

Expanding Your Vocabulary

Vocabulary is a work in progress—part of lifelong learning is continually learning new words. A strong vocabulary increases reading speed and comprehension; when you understand the words in your reading material, you don't have to stop as often to think about what they mean. Improve your vocabulary by reading and writing words in context and by using a dictionary.

Learning Styles Tip
Drawing pictures of what they are reading may help improve the reading comprehension of visual-spatial learners.

Context
Written or spoken knowledge that can help to illuminate the meaning of a word or passage.

Teaching Tip
When students fail because they did not understand the required reading, they should not belittle their intelligence. Instead of telling themselves, "I'll never learn this. I'm stupid," they should ask, "What can I learn from this failure that will help me in the future?"

Teaching Tolerance
If anyone with a reading disability is in your class, he or she may never become a rapid reader. Be tolerant as you work with the person to gather information via discussion, tapes, and text summaries that focus on important material.

Reading and Writing Words in Context: Natural Language Development

Most people learn words best when they read and use them in written or spoken language. Although a definition tells you what a word means, it may not include a context. Using a word in context after defining it will help to anchor the information so that you can remember it and continue to build on it. Here are some strategies for using context to solidify your learning of new vocabulary words.

Use new words in a sentence or two right away. Do this immediately after reading their definitions while everything is still fresh in your mind.

Reread the sentence where you originally saw the word. Go over it a few times to make sure that you understand how the word is used.

Use the word over the next few days whenever it may apply. Try it while talking with friends, writing letters or notes, or in your own thoughts.

Consider where you may have seen or heard the word before. When you learn a word, going back to sentences you previously didn't "get" may solidify your understanding. For example, most children learn the Pledge of Allegiance by rote without understanding what "allegiance" means. Later, when they learn the definition of "allegiance," the pledge provides a context that helps them better understand the word.

Seek knowledgeable advice. If after looking up a word you still have trouble with its meaning, ask an instructor or friend to help you figure it out.

Use a Dictionary

When reading a textbook, the first "dictionary" to search is the glossary. The definitions there are usually limited to the meaning of the term as it is used in the text. Standard dictionaries provide broader information such as word origin, pronunciation, part of speech, and multiple meanings. Using a dictionary whenever you read will increase your comprehension. Buy a standard dictionary, keep it nearby, and consult it for help in understanding passages that contain unfamiliar words.

You may not always have time to use the following suggestions, but when you can use them, they will help you make the most of your dictionary.

Read every meaning of a word, not just the first. Think critically about which meaning suits the context of the word in question, and choose the one that makes the most sense to you.

Substitute a word or phrase from the definition for the word. Use the definition you have chosen. Imagine, for example, that you read the following sentence and do not know the word *indoctrinated*:

The cult indoctrinated its members to reject society's values.

In the dictionary, you find several definitions, including *brainwashed* and *instructed*. You decide that the one closest to the correct meaning is *brainwashed*. With this term, the sentence reads as follows:

The cult brainwashed its members to reject society's values.

Facing the challenges of reading is only the first step. The next important step is to examine why you are reading any given piece of material.

WHY DEFINE YOUR PURPOSE FOR READING?

As with other aspects of your education, asking questions will help you make the most of your efforts. When you define your purpose, you ask yourself *why* you are reading a particular piece of material. One way to do this is by completing this sentence: "In reading this material, I intend to define/learn/answer/achieve . . ." With a clear purpose in mind, you can decide how much time and what kind of effort to expend on various reading assignments.

Achieving your reading purpose requires adapting to different types of reading materials. Being a flexible reader—adjusting your reading strategies and pace—will help you to adapt successfully.

A student puts in a late night of studying.

Purpose Determines Reading Strategy

When you know why you are reading something, you can decide how best to approach it. Following are four reading purposes. You may have one or more for any "reading event":

Purpose 1: Read for understanding. In college, studying involves reading for the purpose of comprehending the material. The two main components of comprehension are *general ideas* and *specific facts or examples*. These components depend on each other. Facts and examples help to explain or support ideas, and ideas provide a framework that helps the reader to remember facts and examples.

> *General ideas.* Reading for a general idea is rapid reading that seeks an overview of the material. You search for general ideas by focusing on headings, subheadings, and summary statements.

> *Specific facts or examples.* At times, readers may focus on locating specific pieces of information—for example, the stages of intellectual development in children. Often, a reader may search for examples that support or explain general ideas—for example, the causes of economic recession. Because you know exactly what you are looking for, you can skim the material quickly.

Purpose 2: Read to evaluate critically. Critical evaluation involves understanding. It means approaching the material with an open mind, examining causes and effects, evaluating ideas, and asking questions that test the writer's argument and search for assumptions. Critical reading brings an understanding of material that goes beyond basic information recall (see p. 171 for more on critical reading).

(see p. 171 for more on critical reading)

Critical Thinking

Are computers making Purpose 3 out-moded? Instead of reading a manual in a linear way to learn how to do something, computer savvy people point and click for specific solutions to specific problems. Ask students to use their own experiences to argue for or against this view.

Purpose 3: Read for practical application. A third purpose for reading is to gather usable information that you can apply toward a specific goal. When you read a computer manual or an instruction sheet for assembling a gas grill, your goal is to learn how to do something. Reading and action usually go hand in hand. Remembering the specifics requires a certain degree of general comprehension.

Purpose 4: Read for pleasure. Some materials you read for entertainment, such as *Sports Illustrated* magazine or the latest John Grisham courtroom thriller. Recreational reading may also go beyond materials that seem obviously designed to entertain. Whereas some people may read a Jane Austen novel for comprehension, as in a class assignment, others may read her books for pleasure.

Purpose Determines Pace

George M. Usova, senior education specialist and graduate professor at Johns Hopkins University, explains: "Good readers are flexible readers. They read at a variety of rates and adapt them to the reading purpose at hand, the difficulty of the material, and their familiarity with the subject area."[3] For example, you may need to read academic and/or unfamiliar materials more slowly, whereas you will increase reading speed for journalism, nonfiction and fiction books, magazines, and on-line publications.

So far, this chapter has focused on reading as a deliberate, purposeful process of meaning construction. Recognizing obstacles and defining reading purposes lay the groundwork for effective studying—the process of mastering the concepts and skills contained in your texts.

HOW CAN SQ3R HELP YOU OWN WHAT YOU READ?

When you study, you take ownership of the material you read. You learn it well enough to apply it to what you do. For example, by the time students studying to be computer-hardware technicians complete their course work, they should be able to analyze hardware problems that lead to malfunctions. On-the-job computer technicians use the same study technique to keep up with changing technology. Studying to understand and learn also gives you mastery over concepts. For example, a dental hygiene student learns the causes of gum disease, and a business student learns about marketing.

SQ3R is a technique that will help you grasp ideas quickly, remember ideas, and review effectively for tests. SQ3R stands for *survey, question, read, recite,* and *review*—all steps in the studying process. Developed in the 1940s by Francis Robinson, the technique is still being used today because it works.[4] It is particularly helpful for studying all kinds of textbooks.

Moving through the stages of SQ3R requires that you know how to skim and scan. **Skimming** involves rapid reading of chapter elements, including introductions, conclusions, and summaries; the first and last lines of para-

Skimming

Rapid, superficial reading of material that involves glancing through it to determine central ideas and main elements.

graphs; boldfaced or italicized terms; pictures, charts, and diagrams. The goal of skimming is a quick construction of the main ideas. In contrast, **scanning** involves the careful search for specific facts and examples. You might use scanning during the review phase of SQ3R when you need to locate particular information (such a formula in a chemistry text).

Scanning

Reading material in an investigative way, searching for specific information.

Survey

When reading textbooks, surveying can help you learn. *Surveying* refers to the process of previewing, or pre-reading, a book before you actually study it. Most textbooks include devices that give students an overview of the text as a whole, as well as of the contents of individual chapters. As you look at Figure 6.2, think about how many of these devices you already use when you read.

Question

Your next step is to examine the chapter headings and, on a separate piece of paper, to write *questions* linked to them. If your reading material has no headings, develop questions as you read. These questions focus your attention and increase your interest, helping you build comprehension and relate new ideas to what you already know. You can take questions from the textbook or from your lecture notes, or come up with them on your own when you survey, based on what ideas you think are most important.

Here is how this technique works. In Table 6.1, the column on the left contains primary-level headings from a section of *Business,* a text by Ricky W. Griffin and Ronald J. Ebert (Prentice Hall, 1996). The column on the right rephrases these headings in question form.

Text and Chapter Previewing Devices **FIGURE 6.2**

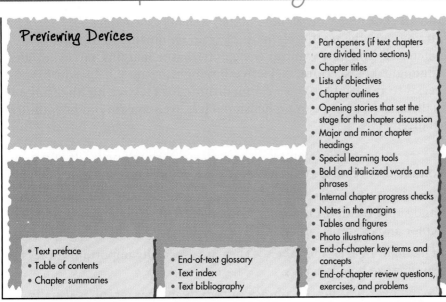

Previewing Devices

- Part openers (if text chapters are divided into sections)
- Chapter titles
- Lists of objectives
- Chapter outlines
- Opening stories that set the stage for the chapter discussion
- Major and minor chapter headings
- Special learning tools
- Bold and italicized words and phrases
- Internal chapter progress checks
- Notes in the margins
- Tables and figures
- Photo illustrations
- End-of-chapter key terms and concepts
- End-of-chapter review questions, exercises, and problems

- Text preface
- Table of contents
- Chapter summaries

- End-of-text glossary
- Text index
- Text bibliography

At the beginning of the text or chapters

At the end of the text

In the middle, linked to specific chapters

Rephrasing in the Form of a Question

1. The Consumer Buying Process	1. What Is the Consumer Buying Process?
A. Problem/Need Recognition	A. Why must consumers first recognize a problem or need before they buy a product?
B. Information Seeking	B. What is information seeking and who answers consumers' questions?
C. Evaluation of Alternatives	C. How do consumers evaluate different products to narrow their choices?
D. Purchase Decision	D. Are purchasing decisions simple or complex?
E. Postpurchase Evaluations	E. What happens after the sale?

There is no "correct" set of questions. Given the same headings, you could create your own particular set of questions. The more useful kinds of questions engage the critical thinking mind actions and processes found in Chapter 5.

Read

Your questions give you a starting point for *reading,* the first R in SQ3R. Read the material with the purpose of answering each question you raised. Pay special attention to the first and last lines of every paragraph, which should tell you what the paragraph is about. As you read, record key terms, phrases, and concepts in your notebook. Some students divide the notebook into two columns, writing questions on the left and answers on the right. This method is called the Cornell note-taking system (see Chapter 7).

If you own the textbook, marking it up will help you to make sense of the material. You may want to write notes in the margins, circle key ideas, or highlight key sections. Selective highlighting may help you pinpoint material to review before an exam, although excessive highlighting may actually interfere with comprehension. Here are some tips on how to strike a balance.

Mark the text after you read the material through once. If you do it on the first reading, you may mark less important passages.

Highlight key terms and concepts. Mark the examples that explain and support important ideas. You might try highlighting ideas in one color and examples in another.

Highlight figures and tables. They are especially important if they summarize text concepts.

Avoid overmarking. A phrase or two in any paragraph is usually enough. Set off long passages with brackets rather than marking every line.

Write notes in the margins. Comments like "main point" and "important definition" will help you find key sections later on.

Be careful not to mistake highlighting for learning. You will not learn what you highlight unless you review it carefully. Additional benefit will come from writing the highlighted information into your notes.

One critical step in the reading phase is to divide your reading into digestible segments. Pace your reading so that you understand as you go. If you find you are losing the thread of the ideas you are reading, you may want to try smaller segments, or you may need to take a break and come back to it later. Try to avoid reading in mere sets of time—such as, "I'll read for 30 minutes and then quit"—or you may destroy the meaning by stopping in the middle of a key explanation.

Recite

Once you finish reading a topic, stop and answer the questions you raised in the Q stage of SQ3R. You may decide to *recite* each answer aloud, silently speak the answers to yourself, tell the answers to another person as though you were teaching him or her, or write your ideas and answers in brief notes. Writing is often the most effective way to solidify what you have read because writing from memory checks your understanding. Use whatever techniques best suit your learning styles (see Chapter 4).

After you finish one section, read the next. Repeat the question-read-recite cycle until you complete the entire chapter. If during this process you find yourself fumbling for thoughts, you may not yet "own" the ideas. Reread the section that's giving you trouble until you master its contents. Understanding each section as you go is crucial because the material in one section often forms a foundation for the next.

Review

Review soon after you finish a chapter. Here are some techniques for reviewing.

- Skim and reread your notes. Then try summarizing them from memory.

- Answer the text's end-of-chapter review, discussion, or application questions.

- Quiz yourself using the questions you raised in the Q stage. If you can't answer one of your own or one of the text's questions, go back and scan the material for answers.

- Review and summarize in writing the sections and phrases you have highlighted or bracketed.

- Create a chapter outline in standard outline form or as a think link.

- Reread the introduction, headings, tables, and summary.

- Recite important concepts to yourself, or record important information on a cassette tape and play it on your car's tape deck or your portable cassette player.

Learning Styles Tip
Encourage logical-mathematical students to create a chart that lists the personal traits of characters in the novels they read.

Chat with one of your professors or your study group to solicit feedback on what you feel the main points are in one of your text passages. Did you miss something someone else picked up? What did others learn from your observations?

- Make flash cards that have an idea or word on one side and examples, a definition, or other related information on the other. Test yourself.

- Think critically: Break ideas down into examples, consider similar or different concepts, recall important terms, evaluate ideas, and explore causes and effects.

- Make think links that show how important concepts relate to one another.

Be a Team
Ask groups of students to identify and discuss people they know (class-mates, friends, relatives) who have mastered the skills of active reading. Suggest that they make these people reading role models by observing their reading habits and incorporat-ing them into their own reading.

If you need help clarifying your reading material, ask your instructor. Pinpoint the material you want to discuss, schedule a meeting with him or her during office hours, and bring a list of questions.

Repeating the review process renews and solidifies your knowledge. Set up regular review sessions, for example, once a week. As you review, remember that refreshing your knowledge is easier and faster than learning it the first time. Reviewing in as many different ways as possible increases the likelihood of retention.

As you can see in Figure 6.3, using SQ3R is part of being an active read-er. Active reading involves the specific activities that help you retain what you learn.

FIGURE 6.3   Use SQ3R to Become an Active Reader

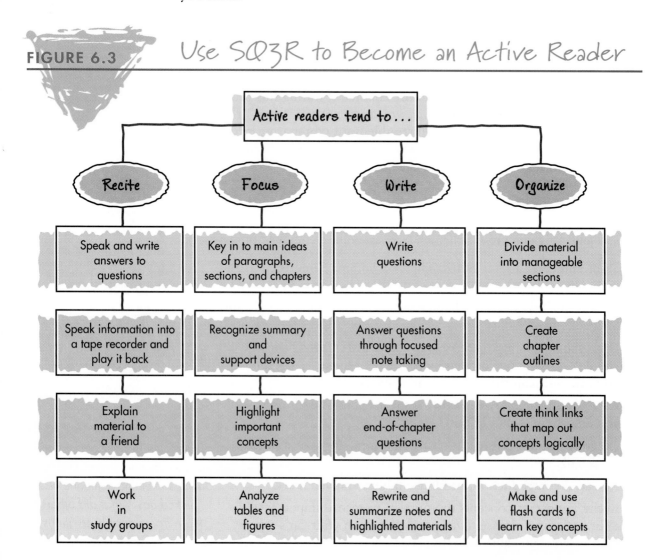

Active readers tend to...

Recite	Focus	Write	Organize
Speak and write answers to questions	Key in to main ideas of paragraphs, sections, and chapters	Write questions	Divide material into manageable sections
Speak information into a tape recorder and play it back	Recognize summary and support devices	Answer questions through focused note taking	Create chapter outlines
Explain material to a friend	Highlight important concepts	Answer end-of-chapter questions	Create think links that map out concepts logically
Work in study groups	Analyze tables and figures	Rewrite and summarize notes and highlighted materials	Make and use flash cards to learn key concepts

HOW CAN YOU RESPOND CRITICALLY TO WHAT YOU READ?

Textbook features often highlight important ideas and help you determine study questions. As you advance in your education, however, many reading assignments—especially primary sources—will not be so clearly marked. You will need critical-reading skills to select important ideas, identify examples that support them, and ask questions about the text without the aid of any special features.

Critical reading enables you to develop a thorough understanding of reading material. A critical reader is able to discern the central idea of a piece of reading material, as well as identify what in that piece is true or accurate, such as when choosing material as a source for an essay. A critical reader can also compare one piece of material to another and evaluate which makes more sense, which proves its thesis more successfully, or which is more useful for the reader's purposes.

Engage your critical-thinking processes by using the following suggestions for critical reading.

Use SQ3R to "Taste" Reading Material

Sylvan Barnet and Hugo Bedau, authors of *Critical Thinking, Reading, and Writing: A Brief Guide to Argument,* suggest that the active reading of SQ3R will help you form an initial idea of what a piece of reading material is all about. Through surveying, skimming for ideas and examples, highlighting and writing comments and questions in the margins, and reviewing, you can develop a basic understanding of its central ideas and contents.[5]

Summarizing, part of the SQ3R review process, is one of the best ways to develop an understanding of a piece of reading material. To construct a summary, focus on the central ideas of the piece and the main examples that support them. A summary does not contain any of your own ideas or your evaluation of the material. It simply condenses the material, making it easier to focus on the structure and central ideas of the piece when you go back to read more critically. At that point, you can begin asking questions, evaluating the piece, and introducing your own ideas. Using the mind actions described in Chapter 5 will help you.

Summary

A concise restatement of the material, in your own words, that covers the main points.

Ask Questions Based on the Mind Actions

The essence of critical reading, as with critical thinking, is asking questions. Instead of simply accepting what you read, seek a more thorough understanding by questioning the material as you go along. Using the mind actions to formulate your questions will help you understand the material.

What parts of the material you focus on will depend on your purpose for reading. For example, if you are writing a paper on the causes of World War II, you might look at how certain causes fit your thesis. If you are comparing two pieces of writing that contain opposing arguments, you may focus on picking out their central ideas and evaluating how well the writers use examples to support them.

You can question any of the following components of reading material:

- the central idea of the entire piece
- a particular idea or statement
- the examples that support an idea or statement
- the proof of a fact
- the definition of a concept

Following are some ways to critically question reading material. Apply them to any component you want to question by substituting the component for the words *it* and *this*.

 Similarity

What does this remind me of, or how is it similar to something else I know?

 Difference

What different conclusions are possible?

How is this different from my experience?

 Cause and Effect

Why did this happen, or what caused this?

What are the effects or consequences of this?

What effect does the author want to have, or what is the purpose of this material?

What effects support a stated cause?

 Example to Idea

How would I classify this, or what is the best idea to fit this example?

How would I summarize this, or what are the key ideas?

What is the thesis or central idea?

 Idea to Example

What evidence supports this, or what examples fit this idea?

 Evaluation

How would I evaluate this? Is it useful or well constructed?

Does this example support my thesis or central idea?

Is this information or point of view important to my work? If so, why?

Engage Critical-Thinking Processes

Certain thinking processes from Chapter 5 can help to deepen your analysis and evaluation of what you read. These processes are thinking logically, evaluating an argument, and recognizing perspective. Within these processes you will ask questions that use the mind actions.

Thinking Logically

With what you know about logical thinking, you can evaluate any statement in your reading material, identifying it as fact, opinion, or assumption and challenging how it is supported. Evaluate statements, central ideas, or entire pieces of reading material, using questions such as the following:

- Is this fact? Is the factual statement true? How does the writer know?
- Is this opinion? How could I test its validity?
- What assumptions underlie this?
- What else do I know that is similar to or different from this?
- What information that I already know supports or disproves this?
- What examples disprove this as fact or do not fit this assumption?

For example, imagine that a piece of writing states, "The dissolving of the family unit is the main cause of society's ills." You may question this statement by looking at what facts and examples support it. You may question the writer's sources. You could find hidden assumptions within this statement, such as an assumed definition of what a family is. You could also find examples that do not fit this assumption, such as successful families that don't fit the traditional definition of family used by the writer.

Evaluating an Argument

As you read in Chapter 5, an argument is a persuasive case that seeks to prove or disprove a point. When reading material contains one or more arguments, use what you know about arguments to evaluate whether the writer has constructed his or her argument effectively. Ask questions like the following:

- Do I believe this argument? How is the writer trying to persuade me?
- If the author uses cause-and-effect reasoning, does it seem logical?
- Do the examples adequately support the central idea of the argument?
- Is the evidence fact or opinion? Is it true or verifiable?
- What different and perhaps opposing arguments seem just as valid?
- If I'm not sure whether I believe this, how could I construct an opposing argument?

Don't rule out the possibility that you may agree wholeheartedly with an argument. However, use critical thinking to make an informed decision rather than accepting the argument outright.

Recognizing Perspectives

This critical thinking process will help you understand that many reading materials are written from a particular perspective. For example, if both a recording artist and a music censorship advocate were to write a piece about a controversial song created by that artist, their different perspectives would result in two very different pieces of writing.

To analyze perspective, ask questions like the following:

What perspective is guiding this? What are the underlying ideas that influence this material?

Who wrote this and with what intent? For example, promotional materials on a new drug, written by the manufacturer, may differ from a doctor's or consumer advocate's evaluation of the drug.

Critical Thinking
Establishing truth often involves researching an author's background to learn if previous works are biased for or against a subject. For example, a well-known Republican who writes a book on politics is likely to view the subject from a Republican perspective.

Teaching Tip
Point out the difference between correlation and cause. Two variables may be related to one another (correlation), but have no cause-and-effect relationship. For example, while heart disease and obesity are linked, there is no evidence that obesity causes the problem.

"In books, I could travel anywhere, be anybody, understand worlds long past and imaginary colonies in the future."

Rita Dove

How does the material's source affect its perspective? For example, an article on health maintenance organizations (HMOs) published in an HMO newsletter may be more favorable than one published in the *New York Times*.

How is this perspective supported? Examine what examples, evidence, or reasons are used to justify the position taken by this piece of writing. See if you think the support is valid, whether or not you feel comfortable with the perspective.

Be Media Literate

Everything that you learned about media literacy in Chapter 5 applies to your college reading material. Even seemingly objective textbooks are written by a person or persons who have particular points of view, which may influence the information they include or how they include it. For example, the growing awareness of the multicultural heritage of the United States has prompted revision of many history texts that previously ignored or shortchanged topics such as Native American history. In all your reading, especially primary sources, remember the following:

- Your reading materials are created by people who have particular perspectives.
- Authors may use particular wording or tone to create an effect on a reader.
- Different readers may have different interpretations of a piece of reading material, depending on individual perspective and experience.
- Users of media may intend to market a product to you.
- Any written material carries the values of the people who created it and is influenced, to varying degrees, by the perspectives and intents of the authors.

As a media literate reader, you have the ability to stay aware of these realities and to sift through your materials critically so that you gain from them what is most useful to you.

Seek Understanding

The fundamental purpose of all college reading is to understand the material. Reading critically allows you to reach the highest possible level of understanding. Think of your reading process as an archaeological dig. The first step is to excavate a site and uncover the artifacts, which corresponds to your initial survey and reading of the material. As important as the excavation is, the process would be incomplete if you took home a bunch of dirt-covered items and stopped there. The second half of the process is to investigate each item, evaluate what each one means, and derive new knowledge and ideas from what you discover. Critical reading allows you to complete that crucial second half of the process.

Remember that critical reading takes time and focus. Give yourself a chance to be a successful critical reader by finding a time, place, and purpose for your reading. Take advantage of the opportunity to learn from others by working in pairs or groups whenever you can.

HOW AND WHY SHOULD YOU STUDY WITH OTHERS?

Everything you know and will learn comes from your interaction with the outside world. Often this interaction takes place between you and one or more people. You learn from listening to them, reading what they write, observing them, and trying to do what they do. In school you listen to instructors and other students, you read materials that people have written, and you model yourself after the behavior and ideas of those whom you most trust and respect.

Learning takes place the same way in your career and personal life. Today's workplace puts the emphasis on work done through team effort. Companies value the ideas, energy, and cooperation that results from a well-coordinated team.

Strategies for Study Group Success

Not all study groups work the same way. The way you operate your group may depend on the members' personalities, the subject you study, the location of the group, and the size of the group. No matter what your particular group's situation, though, certain general strategies will help.

Teaching Tolerance
People from Asian and Eastern cultures, particularly women, may be less willing than Americans to participate actively in study groups. It is important that students not confuse a culturally based reserve with lack of preparation.

Choose a leader for each meeting. Rotating the leadership helps all members take ownership of the group. Be flexible. If a leader has to miss class for any reason, choose another leader for that meeting.

Set meeting goals. At the start of each meeting, compile a list of questions you want to address.

Adjust to different personalities. Respect and communicate with members whom you would not necessarily choose as friends. The art of getting along will serve you well in the workplace, where you don't often choose your coworkers.

Share the workload. The most important factor is a willingness to work, not a particular level of knowledge.

Set general goals. Determine what the group wants to accomplish over the course of a semester.

Set a regular meeting schedule. Try every week, every two weeks, or whatever the group can manage.

Create study materials for one another. Give each group member the task of finding a piece of information to compile, photocopy, and review for the other group members.

Help each other learn. One of the best ways to solidify your knowledge of something is to teach it to someone else. Have group members teach certain pieces of information; make up quizzes for each other; go through flash cards together.

Pool your note-taking resources. Compare notes with your group members and fill in any information you don't have. Try other note-taking styles: For example, if you generally use outlines, rewrite your notes in a think link. If you tend to map out ideas in a think link (see Chapter 7 for more on note taking).

Benefits of Working with Others

If you apply this information to your schoolwork, you will see that studying with a partner or in a group can enhance your learning in many ways. You will benefit from shared knowledge, solidified knowledge, increased motivation, and increased teamwork ability.

Shared knowledge. Each student has a unique body of knowledge and individual strengths. Students can learn from one another. To have individual students pass on their knowledge to each other in a study group requires less time and energy than for each of those students to learn all of the material alone.

Solidified knowledge. When you discuss concepts or teach them to others, you reinforce what you know and strengthen your critical thinking. Part of the benefit comes from simply repeating information aloud and rewriting it on paper, and part comes from how you think through information in your mind before you pass it on to someone else.

Increased motivation. When you study by yourself, you are accountable to yourself alone. In a study group, however, others will see your level of work and preparation, which may increase your motivation.

Increased teamwork ability. The more you understand the dynamics of working with a group and the more experience you have at it, the more you will build your ability to work well with others. This is an invaluable skill for the workplace, and it will contribute to your personal marketability.

No matter where or how you prefer to study, your school's library (or libraries) can provide many useful services to help you make the most of classes, reading, studying, and assignments.

Career Connection
In the workplace, team members have different skills, abilities, and responsibilities. Often, there is little overlap in team assignments. Yet, members must learn to work together to design the project, assign tasks, and put the project pieces together when they are complete.

HOW CAN YOU MAKE THE MOST OF THE LIBRARY?

A library is a home for information; consider it the "brain" of your college. Libraries contain a world of information—your job is to find what you need as quickly and efficiently as you can.

Career Connection
Many large companies have their own corporate library for employees who do research. Students may find themselves using many of the research skills they learned in college in the workplace.

Start with a Road Map

Most college libraries are bigger than high school and community libraries. You may feel lost on your first visit, or even a few visits after that. Make your life easier right away by learning how your library is organized. Although every library has a different layout, all libraries have certain areas in common.

Reference area. Here you'll find reference books, including encyclopedias, public- and private-sector directories, dictionaries, almanacs, and

How can I cope with my learning disabilities?

Darrin Estepp, Ohio State University, Columbus, Ohio, Major Undeclared

In elementary school I needed extra help with reading. By high school, I was having a hard time keeping up, and I felt stupid. A test I took showed I had dyslexia. Study assistance helped, but I attended high school for an extra year to improve my record. Then I enrolled in community college and worked part-time as a nursing home cook. I transferred to Ohio State after two years.

I wanted to major in Special Education so I could help people with learning disabilities, but the classes were too much of a struggle. I still want to help others—I can see myself being on the lookout for the early signs of disabilities like mine. Recently I was diagnosed with another learning disability. I have always had trouble sitting still for long periods of time. About 45 minutes into a 2 1/2-hour history class I found I couldn't remain seated. I kept standing up. Later I took a test which showed that I have attention deficit hyperactivity disorder (ADHD).

I have trouble with spelling, too. In class, by the time I figure out how to spell a word for my notes, I'm far behind. I  learn best by hearing, seeing, and doing all at once. If I just hear something, it doesn't sink in very well. Not long ago I went to see my learning disability counselor because it seems no matter how hard I try it's never enough. I keep hanging in there though because I want to prove that I can graduate from a major university. What suggestions do you have for how I can cope with my learning disabilities?

Morgan Paar, Graduate Student, Academy of Art College, San Francisco, California

I remember dreading to read out loud to my fourth-grade class. Other students would laugh. Fortunately, this is when my disability was discovered. One thing I learned in college was that there is more than one way to succeed, even if I couldn't keep up with the reading. First, I attended every single class without exception. Second, if I got behind in my note taking (and I often did), I would borrow a friend's notes and rewrite mine, combining them with theirs. I knew spelling would get me behind, so in class I would just write away and figure it out when I got home. Third, I made friends with my teachers, and they would help me during their office hours.

One incident showed me that anything was possible. A friend worked for a newspaper and asked me to write a story. I laughed—  I said I could barely spell my name, never mind write an article. He said, "Come on, computers have spell checkers." I labored through it; my friend loved the writing (though he did say that I had used some very creative grammar), and it appeared as a two-part story in the travel section. I have since had 17 articles published.

It never gets easy—but one route to success is to do something you love. I write travel stories because I love traveling and sharing stories. I am now a filmmaker, and I am studying film in graduate school so I can someday teach it. Darrin, you already know the skills you need to achieve your goals, though maybe they are deep in your subconscious mind. I was 27 years old before I knew what I really wanted to do. Just keep following your passions, never give up, figure out what you need to do to achieve your goals, and know that there is more than one path to your destination. If you truly love what you do, there is nothing that can stop you.

A student uses his laptop computer in the campus library.

Periodicals

Magazines, journals, and newspapers that are published on a regular basis throughout the year.

Microfilm

A reel of film on which printed materials are photographed at greatly reduced size.

Microfiche

A card or sheet of microfilm that contains a considerable number of pages of printed text and/or photographs in reduced form.

Teaching Tip

Computers have changed the very nature of library research. On-line, including Internet links, and CD-ROMs enable students to find information faster and more efficiently than ever before. This has increased student productivity.

atlases. You'll also find librarians and/or other library employees who can help direct you to the information you need. Computer terminals, containing the library's catalog of holdings as well as on-line bibliographic and full-text databases, are usually part of the reference area.

Book area. Books—and, in many libraries, magazines and journals in bound or boxed volumes—are stored in the *stacks*. A library with "open stacks" will allow you to search for materials on your own. In a "closed-stack" system, a staff member will retrieve materials for you.

Periodicals area. Here you'll find recent issues of popular and scholarly magazines, journals, and newspapers. Most college libraries collect **periodicals,** ranging from *Time* to *Advertising Age* to the *New England Journal of Medicine*.

Audiovisual materials areas. Many libraries have specialized areas for video, art, photographic, and recorded music collections.

Computer areas. Computer terminals, linked to databases and the Internet, are increasingly found in libraries and may be scattered throughout the building or set off in special areas. You may be able to access these databases and the Internet from the college's computer labs and writing centers, or even from your own computer if you have one.

Microform areas. Most libraries have microform reading areas or rooms. Microforms are materials printed on film, either **microfilm** or **microfiche,** that is read through special viewing machines. Many microform reading machines can print hard copies of stored images and text.

To learn about your college library, take a library tour or a training session. Almost all college libraries offer some kind of orientation on how to use their books, periodicals, databases, and Internet hookups. You might also ask for a pamphlet that describes the layout, and then take some time for a self-tour.

Learn How to Conduct an Information Search

The most successful library research involves following a *search strategy*—a step-by-step method for finding information that takes you from general to specific sources. Starting with general sources usually works best because they provide an overview of your research topic and can lead you to more specific information and sources. For example, an encyclopedia article on the Dead Sea Scrolls—manuscripts written between 250 B.C. and A.D. 68 that trace the roots of Judaism and Christianity—may mention an important book on the subject, *Understanding the Dead Sea Scrolls,* edited by Hershel Shanks (New York: Random House, 1992). This book, in turn, will lead you to 13 experts, the authors who wrote chapters in the book.

Defining your exact topic is critical to the success of your search. Although "the Dead Sea Scrolls" may be too broad for your research paper, some possibilities of narrower topics may include the following:

- how the Dead Sea Scrolls were discovered by Bedouin shepherds in 1947
- the historical origins of the scrolls
- the process archaeologists used to reconstruct scroll fragments

Conducting a Keyword Search

A *keyword search*—a search for information through the use of specific words and phrases associated with your search subject—will help you narrow your topic. Use your library's computer database for keyword searches. For example, instead of searching through the broad category *Art*, use a keyword search to narrow your focus to *French Art* or more specifically to *French Art in the 19th century*.

Keyword searches are relatively easy because you use natural language rather than specialized classification vocabulary. Figure 6.4 includes some tips that will help you use the keyword system.

As you search, keep in mind that

- Quotation marks around a word or phrase will locate the term exactly as you entered it ("financial aid").
- Using upper or lower case will not affect the search (*Scholarships* will find *scholarships*).
- Singular terms will find the plural (*scholarship* will find *scholarships*).

Real World Link
The nature of keyword searches is continually changing along with technology. Students may want to consult the librarian for the most up-to-date search methods and terms.

How to Perform an Effective Keyword Search FIGURE 6.4

If you are searching for . . .	Do this	Example
A word	Type the word normally	aid
A phrase	Type the phrase in its normal word order (use regular word spacing) or surround the phrase with quotation marks	financial aid or "financial aid"
Two or more keywords without regard to word order	Type the words in any order, surrounding the words with quotation marks (use *and* to separate the words)	"financial aid" and "scholarships"
Topic A or topic B	Type the words in any order, surrounding the words with quotation marks (use *or* to separate the words)	"financial aid" or "scholarships"
Topic A but not topic B	Type topic A first, within quotation marks, and then topic B, within quotation marks (use *not* to separate the words)	"financial aid" not "scholarships"

FIGURE 6.5 Library Search Strategy

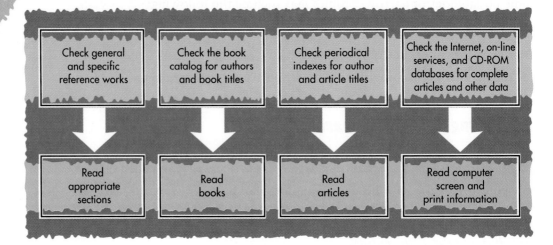

Conduct Research Using a Search Strategy

Knowing where to look during each phase of your search will help you find information efficiently. A successful search strategy often starts with general reference works, then moves to more specific reference works, books, periodicals, and electronic sources, including the Internet (see Figure 6.5).

Use General Reference Works

Begin your research with *general reference works*. These works cover hundreds—and sometimes thousands—of different topics in a broad, nondetailed way. General reference guides are often available on-line or on **CD-ROM.** General reference works include:

- encyclopedias such as the multivolume *Encyclopedia Americana*
- almanacs such as the *World Almanac and Book of Facts*
- yearbooks such as the *McGraw-Hill Yearbook of Science and Technology*
- dictionaries such as *Webster's New World College Dictionary*
- biographical reference works such as *American Writers* and *Who's Who*
- bibliographies such as *Books in Print* (especially the *Subject Guide to Books in Print*)

Scan these sources for an overview of your topic. Bibliographies at the end of encyclopedia articles may also lead to other important sources.

Search Specialized Reference Works

After you have an overview of your topic, specialized reference works will help you find more specific facts. The short summaries you will find in such

CD-ROM

A compact disc, containing words and images in electronic form, that can be read by a computer (CD-ROM stands for "compact disc read-only memory").

works focus on critical ideas and on the keywords you will need to research further. Bibliographies that accompany the articles point to the names and works of recognized experts. Examples of specialized reference works, organized by subject, include the following:

■ history, such as the *Encyclopedia of American History*

■ science and technology, such as the *Encyclopedia of Computer Science and Technology*

■ social sciences, such as the *Dictionary of Education*

■ current affairs, such as the *Social Issues Resources Series (SIRS)*

Browse Through Books on Your Subject

Use the *library catalog* to find books and other materials on your topic. The catalog tells you which publications the library owns and where they can be found. Most card catalogs have been replaced by on-line computerized catalogs. When general and specialized reference works lead to a dead end, the catalog may provide a good topic overview.

The library catalog contains a list of every library holding, searchable by author, title, and subject. For example, a library that owns *The Artist's Way: A Spiritual Path to Higher Creativity* by Julia Cameron may list the book in the author catalog under Cameron, Julia (last name first); in the title catalog, under *Artist's Way* (articles such as *the, a,* and *an* are dropped from the beginnings of titles and subjects); in the subject catalog under "Creative Ability—problems, exercises, etc.," "Self-actualization—psychology," and "Creation—literary, artistic, etc."

Library Classification Systems

Each catalog listing refers to the library's classification system, which tells you exactly where the publication can be found. Taking a moment to familiarize yourself with your library's system will help save time in your research because you will more quickly know where to go to find what you need. The Dewey decimal and Library of Congress systems are among the most common classification systems.

The *Dewey decimal system* classifies materials into 10 major subject categories and assigns each library holding a specific *call number.* For example, publications with call numbers from 100 to 199 deal with philosophy. Successive numbers and decimal points divide each major category into subcategories. The more specific the call number, the more targeted your search. For example, a book with a call number of 378 falls into the general social science category and into the subcategory of higher education. Student finances, a narrower topic, uses the call number 378.3.

The *Library of Congress System* uses a letter-based classification system to divide library holdings according to subject categories (Figure 6.6 shows the call letters that correspond to each category). Each category is divided further into specialized subgroups through the addition of letters and numbers.

FIGURE 6.6 The Library of Congress Subject Classification System

Call Letter	Main Classification Category	Call Letter	Main Classification Category
A	General works	N	Fine arts
B	Philosophy and religion	P	Language - Literature (nonfiction)
C	History - Auxiliary sciences	Q	Sciences
D	History - Topography	R	Medicine
E–F	American history - Topography	S	Agriculture
G	Geography - Anthropology	T	Technology
H	Social sciences	U	Military science
J	Political sciences	V	Naval science
K	Law	Z	Bibliography and library science
L	Education	P–Z	Literature (fiction)
M	Music		

Use Periodical Indexes to Search for Periodicals

Because of their frequent publication, periodicals are a valuable source of current information. *Journals* are periodicals written for readers with special knowledge and expertise. Whereas *Newsweek* magazine may run a general-interest article on AIDS research, the *Journal of the American Medical Association* may print the original scientific study and direct the article to physicians and scientists. Many libraries display periodicals that are up to a year or two old and convert older copies to microfilm or microfiche. Many full-text articles are also available on computer databases.

Periodical indexes lead you to specific articles. The *Reader's Guide to Periodical Literature,* available on CD-ROM and in book form, provides general information. The *Reader's Guide* indexes articles in more than 240 general-interest magazines and newspapers. Many libraries also carry the *Reader's Guide Abstracts,* which include article summaries. Look in the *Infotrac* family of databases, on-line or on CD-ROM, for other periodical indexes such as *Health Reference Center* and *General Business File.*

Because there is no all-inclusive index for technical, medical, and scholarly journal articles, you'll have to search indexes that catalog articles in narrow subject areas. For example, the *Business Periodicals Index* lists business articles. Many specialized indexes also include *abstracts* (article summaries) and can be found in electronic or book form. You may find separate newspaper indexes at your library in print, microform, CD-ROM, or on-line.

In addition, journals not found in your library or on-line may be available through *interlibrary loan.* Interlibrary loan is a process by which you can have your library request materials from another library. You can then use the materials at your library, but you must return them by a specified date. Interlibrary loans can be helpful, but the amount of time you will have to wait for the materials can be unpredictable and may stretch out for weeks.

Teaching Tip
While periodicals provide the most recent information, they lack the comprehensiveness that is found in many books.

Search the Internet

In many ways, the Internet is a researcher's dream come true. You'll find sites that teach you how to write a business plan; others that list job openings at major companies; others that provide health, wellness, and nutritional information; and still others that analyze different theories of child development. Navigating the constantly changing Internet can be challenging. Consult one of the guides mentioned in the Bibliography for advice on how to find the information you need.

Springboard
Discuss with students their experiences using the Internet for research. How has Internet access changed the research process and the library experience?

Ask the Librarian

Librarians are information experts who can help you solve research problems. They can help you locate unfamiliar or hard-to-find sources as well as navigate computer catalogs and databases. Say, for example, you are researching a gun-control bill that is currently before Congress, and you want to contact organizations on both sides of the issue. The librarian may lead you to the *Encyclopedia of Associations,* which lists the National Rifle Association, a pro-gun lobbying organization, and Handgun Control Inc., a gun-control group. By calling or e-mailing these groups or visiting their Web sites, you can find their information on current legislation.

Note that librarians are not the only helpful people in the library. For simplicity's sake, this book will use the word *librarian* to refer to both librarians and other staff members who are trained to help.

Among the specific services librarians provide are the following:

Search services. Here are some tips on getting the best advice:
- Be prepared. Know what you're looking for. Instead of asking for information on the American presidency, focus on your paper's specific topic, for example, how President Franklin D. Roosevelt's physical disability may have affected his leadership during World War II.
- Be willing to reach out. You don't have to do it all yourself. Librarians will help you with sources or more difficult problems. Asking questions is a sign of willingness to learn, not weakness.
- Ask for help when you can't find a specific source. For example, when a specific book is not on the shelf, the librarian may direct you to another source that will work just as well.

Information services. Most libraries answer phone inquiries that can be quickly researched. For example, if you forget to write down the publisher and date of publication of Renee Blank and Sandra Slipp's book, *Voices of Diversity: Real People Talk about Problems and Solutions in a Workplace Where Everyone Is Not Alike,* call a staff member and tell them the title and author, and they can look it up for you.

Interlibrary loans. If a publication is not available in your library, the librarian can sometimes arrange for an interlibrary loan.

Use Critical Thinking to Evaluate Every Source

If all information were equal, you could trust the accuracy of every book and article, and information from the Internet home page of the National Aeronautics and Space Administration (NASA) would have the same value as

"With one day's reading a man may have the key in his hands."

Ezra Pound

information from "Bob's Home Page on Aliens and Extraterrestrials." Because that isn't the case, use critical-thinking skills to evaluate research sources. Here are some critical-thinking questions to ask about every source:

Is the author a recognized expert? A journalist who writes his or her first article on child development may not have the same credibility as an author of three child development texts.

Does the author write from a particular perspective? An article evaluating liberal democratic policies written by a Republican conservative would almost certainly have a bias.

Is the source recent enough for your purposes? Whereas a history published in 1990 on the U.S. Civil War will probably be accurate in the year 2005, a 1990 analysis of current computer technology would be hopelessly out of date long before then.

Are the author's sources reliable? Where did the author get the information? Check bibliography and footnotes for the number of sources listed and for their quality. Find out whether they are reputable, established publications. If the work is based on *primary evidence,* the author's original work or direct observation, does solid proof support the conclusions? If it is based on *secondary evidence,* an analysis of the works of others, are the conclusions supported by evidence?

Critical-thinking skills are especially important when using the Internet. Accepting information you find there on face value—no matter what the source—is often a mistake and may lead to incorrect conclusions. Anyone, without being screened or evaluated, can post any kind of information on the Internet. It is up to you to discern whether the information you find is accurate, from a reliable source, and useful.

The library is one of your college's most valuable resources, so take advantage of it. Your library research and critical-thinking skills will give you the ability to collect information, weigh alternatives, and make decisions. These skills will last a lifetime.

Be a Team
Ask student groups to discuss ways in which they may use their library research skills after graduation to pursue personal interests, community activities, and career information.

читать

This word may look completely unfamiliar to you, but anyone who can read the Russian language and knows the alphabet will know that it means "read." People who read languages that use different kinds of characters, such as Russian, Japanese, or Greek, learn to process those characters as easily as you process the letters of your native alphabet. Your mind learns to process individually each letter or character you see. This ability enables you to move to the next level of understanding—making sense of those letters or characters when they are grouped to form words, phrases, and sentences.

Think of this concept when you read. Remember that your mind processes immeasurable amounts of information so that you can understand the concepts on the page. Give your mind the best opportunity to succeed by reading often and by focusing on all of the elements that help you read to the best of your ability.

Name _____   Date _____

Critical Thinking
Applying Learning to Life

Studying a Text Page

The following page is from the chapter "Groups and Organizations" in the sixth edition of John J. Macionis's *Sociology,* a Prentice Hall text.[6] Using what you learned in this chapter about study techniques, complete the questions that follow the reading (you can also mark the page itself).

SOCIAL GROUPS

Virtually everyone moves through life with a sense of belonging; this is the experience of group life. A **social group** refers to *two or more people who identify and interact with one another.* Human beings continually come together to form couples, families, circles of friends, neighborhoods, churches, businesses, clubs, and numerous large organizations. Whatever the form, groups encompass people with shared experiences, loyalties, and interests. In short, while maintaining their individuality, the members of social groups also think of themselves as a special "we."

Groups, Categories, and Crowds

People often use the term "group" imprecisely. We now distinguish the group from the similar concepts of category and crowd.

Category

A *category* refers to people who have some status in common. Women, single fathers, military recruits, homeowners, and Roman Catholics are all examples of categories.

Why are categories not considered groups? Simply because, while the individuals involved are aware that they are not the only ones to hold that particular status, the vast majority are strangers to one another.

Crowd

A *crowd* refers to a temporary cluster of individuals who may or may not interact at all. Students sitting in a lecture hall do engage one another and share some common identity as college classmates; thus, such a crowd might be called a loosely formed group. By contrast, riders hurtling along on a subway train or bathers enjoying a summer day at the beach pay little attention to one another and amount to an anonymous aggregate of people. In general, then, crowds are too transitory and impersonal to qualify as social groups.

The right circumstances, however, could turn a crowd into a group. People riding in a subway train that crashes under the city streets generally become keenly aware of their common plight and begin to help one another. Sometimes such extraordinary experiences become the basis for lasting relationships.

Primary and Secondary Groups

Acquaintances commonly greet one another with a smile and the simple phrase, "Hi! How are you?" The response is usually a well scripted "Just fine, thanks. How about you?" This answer, of course, is often more formal than truthful. In most cases, providing a detailed account of how you are *really* doing would prompt the other person to beat a hasty and awkward exit.

Sociologists classify social groups by measuring them against two ideal types based on members' genuine level of personal concern. This variation is the key to distinguishing *primary* from *secondary* groups.

According to Charles Horton Cooley (1864–1929), who is introduced in the box, a **primary group** is *a small social group whose members share personal and enduring relationships.* Bound together by primary relationships, individuals in primary groups typically spend a great deal of time together, engage in a wide range of common activities, and feel that they know one another well. Although not without periodic conflict, members of primary groups display sincere concern for each other's welfare. The family is every society's most important primary group.

Cooley characterized these personal and tightly integrated groups as *primary* because they are among the first groups we experience in life. In addition, the family and early play groups also hold primary importance in the socialization process, shaping attitudes, behavior, and social identity.

Source: Sociology, 6/e, by John J. Macionis, © 1997. Reprinted by permission of Prentice-Hall, Inc., Upper Saddle River, NJ.

1. Identify the headings on the page and the relationship among them. Which headings are primary-level headings? Which are secondary? Which are tertiary (third-level heads)? Which heading serves as an umbrella for the rest?

2. What do the headings tell you about the content of the page?

3. After reading the chapter headings, write three study questions.

a.

b.

c.

4. Using a marker pen, highlight key phrases and sentences. Write short marginal notes to help you review the material at a later point.

5. After reading this page, list three key concepts that you would need to study.

a.

b.

c.

Building Your Vocabulary

Look again at the textbook page you just worked with. Are there any words that are new to you? If so, write them below and look them up in the dictionary. Write the definition next to the word, and then include the word in a sentence you write. If there are no unfamiliar words in this page, choose three words from any reading assignment you have this week.

1.

2.

3.

Focusing on Your Purpose for Reading

Read the following paragraphs on kinetic and potential energy and the first law of thermodynamics taken from *Life on Earth* by Teresa Audesirk and Gerald Audesirk.[7] When you have finished, answer the questions that follow.

Among the fundamental characteristics of all living organisms is the ability to guide chemical reactions within their bodies along certain pathways. The chemical reactions serve many functions, depending on the nature of the organism: to synthesize the molecules that make up the organism's body, to reproduce, to move, even to think. Chemical reactions either require or release **energy**, which can be defined simply as *the capacity to do work*, including synthesizing molecules, moving things around, and generating heat and light. In this chapter we discuss the physical laws that govern energy flow in the universe, how energy flow in turn governs chemical reactions, and how the chemical reactions within living cells are controlled by the molecules of the cell itself. Chapters 7 and 8 focus on photosynthesis, the chief "port of entry" for energy into the biosphere, and glycolysis and cellular respiration, the most important sequences of chemical reactions that release energy.

Energy and the Ability to Do Work

As you learned in Chapter 2, there are two types of energy: **kinetic energy** and **potential energy**. Both types of energy may exist in many different forms. Kinetic energy, or *energy of movement*, includes light (movement of photons), heat (movement of molecules), electricity (movement of electrically charged particles), and movement of large objects. Potential energy, or *stored energy*, includes chemical energy stored in the bonds that hold atoms together in molecules, electrical energy stored in a battery, and positional energy stored in a diver poised to spring (Fig. 4-1). Under the right conditions, kinetic energy can be transformed into potential energy, and vice versa. For example, the diver converted kinetic energy of movement into potential energy of position when she climbed the ladder up to the platform; when she jumps off, the potential energy will be converted back into kinetic energy.

To understand how energy flow governs interactions among pieces of matter, we need to know two things: (1) the quantity of available energy and (2) the usefulness of the energy. These are the subjects of the laws of thermodynamics, which we will now examine.

The Laws of Thermodynamics Describe the Basic Properties of Energy

All interactions among pieces of matter are governed by the two **laws of thermodynamics**, physical principles that define the basic properties and behavior of energy. The laws of thermodynamics deal with "isolated systems," which are any parts of the universe that cannot exchange either matter or energy with any other parts. Probably no part of the universe is completely isolated from all possible exchange with every other part, but the concept of an isolated system is useful in thinking about energy flow.

The First Law of Thermodynamics States That Energy Can Neither Be Created nor Destroyed

The **first law of thermodynamics** states that within any isolated system, energy can neither be created nor destroyed, although it can be changed in form (for example, from chemical energy to heat energy). In other words, within an isolated system *the total quantity of energy remains constant*. The first law is therefore often called the law of conservation of energy. To use a familiar example, let's see how the first law applies to driving your car (Fig. 4-2). We can consider that your car (with a full tank of gas), the road, and the surrounding air roughly constitute an isolated system. When you drive your car, you convert the potential chemical energy of gasoline into kinetic energy of movement and heat energy. The total amount of energy that was in the gasoline before it was burned is the same as the total amount of this kinetic energy and heat.

An important rule of energy conversions is this: Energy always flows "downhill," from places with a high concentration of energy to places with a low concentration of energy. This is the principle behind engines. As we described in Chapter 2, temperature is a measure of how fast molecules move. The burning gasoline in your car's engine consists of molecules moving at extremely high speeds: a high concentration of energy. The cooler air outside the engine consists of molecules moving at much lower speeds: a low concentration of energy. The molecules in the engine hit the piston harder than the air molecules outside the engine do, so the piston moves upward, driving the gears that move the car. Work is done. When the engine is turned off, it cools down as heat is transferred from the warm engine to its cooler surroundings. The molecules on both sides of the piston move at the same speed, so the piston stays still. No work is done.

Source: Life on Earth by Audesirk/Audesirk, ©1997. Reprinted by permission of Prentice-Hall, Inc., Upper Saddle River, NJ.

1. *Reading for critical evaluation.* Evaluate the material by answering these questions:

   a. Were the ideas clearly supported by examples? If you feel one or more were not, give an example.

   _____

   _____

   _____

   b. Did the author make any assumptions that weren't examined? If so, name one or more.

   _____

   _____

   _____

   c. Do you disagree with any part of the material? If so, which part, and why?

   _____

   _____

   _____

2. *Reading for practical application.* Imagine you have to give a presentation on this material the next time the class meets. On a separate sheet of paper, create an outline or think link that maps out the key elements you would discuss.

3. *Reading for comprehension.* Answer the following questions to determine the level of your comprehension:

   a. Name the two types of energy.

   _____

   _____

   b. Which one "stores" energy? _____

   c. Can kinetic energy be turned into potential energy? _____

   d. What term describes the basic properties and behaviors of energy? _____

   e. Mark the following statements as true (T) or false (F).

   _____ Within any isolated system, energy can be neither created nor destroyed.

   _____ Energy always flows downhill, from high concentration levels to low.

   _____ All interactions among pieces of matter are governed by two laws of thermodynamics.

   _____ Some parts of the universe are isolated from other parts.

Teamwork
Combining Forces

Reading and Group Discussion Divide into small groups of three or four. Take a few minutes to preview an article or other short section of reading material assigned to you for this class (other than your textbook). Then, as a group, write down the questions that came up during the preview. Each person should select one question to focus on while reading (no two people should have the same question). Group members should then read the material on their own, using critical-thinking skills to explore their particular questions as they read, and finally, they should write down answers to their questions.

When you answer your question, focus on finding ideas that help to answer the question and examples that support them. Consider other information you know, relevant to your question, that may be similar to or different from the material in the passage. If your questions look for causes or effects, scan for them in the passage. Be sure to make notes as you read.

When you have finished reading critically, gather as a group. Each person should take a turn presenting the question, the response and/or answer that was derived through critical reading, and any other ideas that came up while reading. The group then has an opportunity to present any other ideas to add to the discussion. Continue until each person has had a chance to present what they worked on.

Writing
Discovery Through Journaling

To record your thoughts, use a separate journal or the lined page at the end of the chapter.

Reading Challenges What is your most difficult college reading challenge? A challenge might be a particular kind of reading material, a reading situation, or the achievement of a reading goal. Considering the tools that this chapter presents, make a plan that addresses this challenge. What techniques might be able to help, and how will you test them? What positive effects do you anticipate they may have?

Career Portfolio
Charting Your Course

Reading and Research Skills on the Job The society you live and work in revolves around the written word. Although the growth of computer technology may seem to have made technical knowledge more important than reading, the focus on word processing and computer handling of documents

has actually increased the need for literate employees. As a 1996 *Condition of Education* report states, "In recent years, literacy has been viewed as one of the fundamental tools necessary for successful economic performance in industrialized societies. Literacy is no longer defined merely as a basic threshold of reading ability, but rather as the ability to understand and use printed information in daily activities, at home, at work, and in the community."[8]

Reading plays a fundamental role in job performance and overall life options. Whether you are reading Consumer Reports *before purchasing that expensive washer and dryer, or you are reading the paper to keep up on the stock market, reading keeps you versatile, active, and informed.*

On a separate sheet of paper, do the following: For each of the skill areas below, list all of the ways you know of in which you use that skill on the job or know you will need to use it in your future career. Then, also for each skill, rate your ability on a scale from 1 to 10, with 10 being highest. Finally, on the same sheet of paper, circle the two skills that you think will be most important for your career.

- Ability to define your reading purpose
- Reading speed
- Reading comprehension
- Vocabulary building
- Identification and use of text-surveying devices
- Evaluating reading material with others
- Ability to understand and use visual aids
- Ability to track down information using research strategies

For the two skill areas in which you rated yourself lowest, think about how you can improve your abilities. Make a problem-solving plan for each (use a flowchart like the one on p. 155).

Journal Entry

Name _____ Date _____

EMPOWER

Note Taking and Writing

Harnessing the Power of Words and Ideas

7

In this chapter, you will explore answers to the following questions:

- How can you make the most of note taking?
- Which note-taking system should you use?
- How can you write faster when taking notes?
- Why does good writing matter?
- What are the elements of effective writing?
- What is the writing process?

Words, joined to form ideas, are tools that have enormous power. Whether you write an essay, a memo to a supervisor, or a love letter sent by e-mail, words allow you to take your ideas out of the realm of thought and give them a form that other people can read and consider. Set a goal for yourself: Strive continually to improve your knowledge of how to use words to construct understandable ideas. This chapter will teach you the note-taking skills you need to record information successfully. It will show you how to express your written ideas completely and how good writing is linked to clear thinking. In class or at work, taking notes and writing well will help you truly understand what you learn.

Teaching Tip

Helpful Web sites include:

- Online Writing Lab - Purdue University - owl.english.purdue.edu
- Researchpaper.com - www.researchpaper.com

HOW CAN YOU MAKE THE MOST OF NOTE TAKING?

COMPANION WEBSITE

Notes help you learn when you are in class, doing research, or studying. Since it is virtually impossible to take notes on everything you hear or read, the act of note taking encourages you to decide what is worth remembering, and it has many more positive effects:

- Your notes provide material that helps you study information and prepare for tests.

- When you take notes, you listen better and become more involved in class.

- Notes help you think critically and organize ideas.

- The information you learn in class may not appear in any text; you will have no way to study it without writing it down.

- If it is difficult for you to process information while in class, having notes to read can help you process and learn the information.

- Note taking is a skill for life that you will use on the job, in community activities, and in your personal life.

Springboard

Discuss the following statement with students: The act of taking notes forces them to become actively involved with the material, to struggle to understand it, to put it in the context of what they already know, and to agree or disagree with what is being said.

Recording Information in Class

Your notes have two purposes: First, they should reflect what you heard in class, and second, they should be a resource for studying, writing, or comparing with your text material.

Preparing to Take Class Notes

Taking good class notes depends on good preparation.

- Preview the text (or any other assigned reading material) to become familiar with the topic and any new concepts that it introduces. Visual familiarity helps note taking during lectures.

- Use separate pieces of 8½-by-11-inch paper for each class. If you use a three-ring binder, punch holes in handouts and insert them immediately following your notes for that day.

- Find a comfortable seat where you can easily see and hear—sitting near the front may be your best bet. Be ready to write as soon as the instructor begins speaking.

- Choose a note-taking system that helps you handle the instructor's style. (You'll probably be able to determine this style after a few classes.) For example, whereas one instructor may deliver organized lectures at a normal speaking rate, another may jump from topic to topic or talk very quickly.

- For each class, set up a support system with two students. That way, when you are absent, you can get the notes you missed (having two "buddies" instead of one helps make it likely that at least one person will be in class on any given day).

"Omit needless words. . . . This requires not that the writer make all his sentences short, or that he avoid all detail and treat his subjects only in outline, but that every word tell."

William Strunk Jr.

What to Do During Class

Because no one has time to write down everything he or she hears, the following strategies will help you choose and record what you feel is important in a format that you can read and understand later. This is not a list of "musts." Rather, it is a list of ideas to try as you work to find the note-taking system that works best for you. Experiment with these strategies until you feel that you have found a successful combination. Keeping your learning styles in mind, choose strategies that seem to make the most of your strong points and help boost your weaker areas.

Remember that the first step in note taking is to listen actively; you can't write down something that you don't hear. Use the listening strategies in Chapter 8 to make sure you are prepared to take in the information that comes your way during class.

- Date and identify each page. When you take several pages of notes during a lecture, add an identifying letter or number to the date on each page: for example, 11/27 A, 11/27 B, or 11/27—1 of 3, 11/27—2 of 3. This will help you keep track of the order of your pages. Add the specific topic of the lecture at the top of the page. For example:

    11/27—U.S. Immigration Policy After World War II

- If your instructor jumps from topic to topic during a single class, try starting a new page for each new topic.

- Ask yourself critical-thinking questions as you listen: Do I need this information? Is the information important or just a digression? Is the information fact or opinion? If it is opinion, is it worth remembering? (Chapter 5 discusses how to distinguish between fact and opinion.)

- Record whatever an instructor emphasizes (see Figure 7.1 for specifics on how an instructor might call attention to particular information).

Real World Link
An Internet service hires college students to take course notes and post them, free of charge, on the Internet. Critics fear that students will stop taking their own notes and attending class. Supporters say that the system helps students who learn best by reading.

How to Pick Up on Instructors' Cues   **FIGURE 7.1**

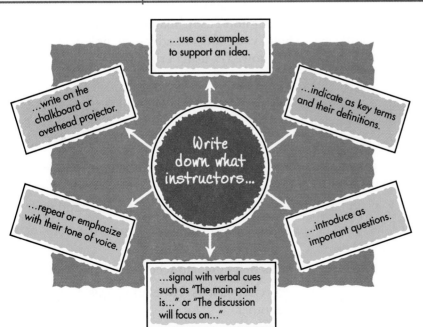

Teaching Tip
Emphasize the connection between reviewing and remembering. For most people, hearing something once is not enough to commit it to memory. Also, during an after-class review, students may recall important details they did not record during the lecture.

- Continue to take notes during class discussions and question-and-answer periods. What your fellow students ask about may help you as well.

- Leave one or more blank spaces between points. This white space will help you review your notes because information will appear in self-contained sections.

- Draw pictures and diagrams that help illustrate ideas.

- Indicate material that is especially important with a star, with underlining, with a highlighting marker, or by writing words in capital letters.

- If you don't understand something, leave space and place a question mark in the margin. Then take advantage of your resources—ask the instructor to explain it after class, discuss it with a classmate, or consult your textbook—and fill in the blank when the idea is clear.

- Take notes until the instructor stops speaking. If you stop writing a few minutes before the class is over, you might miss critical information.

- Make your notes as legible and organized as possible—you can't learn from notes that you can't read or understand. But don't be too fussy; you can always rewrite and improve your notes.

- Consider that your notes are part but not all of what you need to learn. Using your text to add to your notes after class makes a superior, "deeper and wider" set of information to study.

Make Notes a Valuable Reference: Review and Revise Your Notes

Class notes are a valuable study tool when you review them regularly. Begin your review within a day of the lecture. Review the notes to learn information, clarify points, write out abbreviations, fill in missing information, and underline or highlight key ideas. Try to review each week's notes again at the end of the week. Think critically about the material in writing, in study group discussions, or during reflective thought.

Revising and adding to your notes using material from your print sources is one of the best ways to build your understanding and link new information to information you already know. Try using critical-thinking actions to add on to your notes in the following ways:

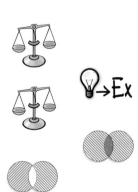

Evaluate, and perhaps work to improve, your ability to recall the facts and figures in your notes.

Brainstorm and write down examples that illustrate central ideas.

Evaluate how important the ideas are, and highlight or rewrite the most important ones.

Think of similar facts or ideas that will help you understand your notes.

Consider what in your class notes might differ from your book notes, and why.

Write down any new ideas that come up when reviewing your notes.

Look at cause-and-effect relationships. Note how ideas, facts, and examples relate to one another.

Writing a summary of your notes is another important review technique. Summarizing involves critically evaluating which ideas and examples are most important and writing them in a shortened form, focusing on those important ideas and examples. You may prefer to summarize as you review your notes, although you might also try summarizing your notes from memory after you review them.

You can take notes in many ways. Different note-taking systems suit different people and situations. Explore each system and choose what works for you.

E-mail or discuss in person with your professor any points that weren't clear from your lecture notes. Get these points clarified as soon as you can so that you will have the foundation on which to build more sophisticated concepts.

WHAT NOTE-TAKING SYSTEM SHOULD YOU USE?

You will benefit most from the system that feels most comfortable to you and makes the most sense for the type of content covered in any given course. For example, you might take notes in a different style for a history class than for a foreign language class. The most common note-taking systems include outlines, the Cornell system, and think links.

As you consider each system, remember your learning styles from Chapter 4. In any given class, choose a system that takes both your learning style and the class material into account. For example, a visual learner may take notes in think link style most of the time but may find that only the Cornell style works well for a particular chemistry course. Experiment to discover what works best in any situation.

Teaching Tolerance
Help students accept that different instructors have different lecture styles by helping them learn to use various systems of note-taking. For example, while an outline will probably fail with a disorganized speaker who moves back and forth among topics, a think link will enable students to follow the instructor's remarks.

Taking Notes in Outline Form

When a reading assignment or lecture seems well organized, you may choose to take notes in outline form. When you use an outline, you construct a line-by-line representation, with certain phrases set off by varying indentations, showing how ideas relate to one another and are supported by facts and examples.

Formal outlines indicate ideas and examples using Roman numerals, capital and lowercase letters, and numbers. When you are pressed for time, such as during class, you can use an informal system of consistent indenting and dashes instead. Formal outlines also require at least two headings on the same level—that is, if you have a IIA you must also have a IIB. Figure 7.2 shows an outline on civil rights legislation.

Critical Thinking
Ask students whether they think it is important to take notes on everything an instructor says. When is it okay to take partial notes, recording only the details they consider important?

Guided Notes

From time to time, an instructor may give you a guide, usually in the form of an outline, to help you take notes in the class. This outline may be on a page that you receive at the beginning of the class, on the board, or on an overhead projector.

Although guided notes help you follow the lecture and organize your thoughts, they do not replace your own notes. Because they are more of a basic outline of topics than a comprehensive coverage of information, they

FIGURE 7.2   Sample Formal Outline

> Civil Rights Legislation: 1860–1968
>
> I. Post-Civil War Era
>   A. Fourteenth Amendment, 1868: equal protection of the law
>   for all citizens
>   B. Fifteenth Amendment, 1870: constitutional rights of citizens
>   regardless of race, color, or previous servitude
> II. Civil Rights Movement of the 1960s
>   A. National Association for the Advancement of Colored People (NAACP)
>   1. Established in 1910 by W.E.B. DuBois and others
>   2. Legal Defense and Education fund fought school segregation
>   B. Martin Luther King Jr., champion of nonviolent civil rights action
>   1. Led bus boycott: 1955–1956
>   2. Marched on Washington, D.C.: 1963
>   3. Awarded NOBEL PEACE PRIZE: 1964
>   4. Led voter registration drive in Selma, Alabama: 1965
>   C. Civil Rights Act of 1964: prohibited discrimination in voting,
>   education, employment, and public facilities
>   D. Voting Rights Act of 1965: gave the government power to enforce
>   desegregation
>   E. Civil Rights Act of 1968: prohibited discrimination in the sale
>   or rental of housing

require that you fill in what they do not cover in detail. If your mind wanders because you think that the guided notes are all you need, you may miss important information.

When you receive guided notes on paper, write directly on the paper if there is room. If not, use a separate sheet and copy the outline categories that the guided notes suggest. If the guided notes are on the board or overhead, copy them, leaving plenty of space in between for your own notes.

Using the Cornell Note-Taking System

The Cornell note-taking system, also known as the T-note system, was developed more than 45 years ago by Walter Pauk at Cornell University.[1] The system is successful because it is simple—and because it works. It consists of three sections on ordinary notepaper:

- *Section 1,* the largest section, is on the right. Record your notes here in informal outline form.

- *Section 2,* to the left of your notes, is the *cue column.* Leave it blank while you read or listen; then fill it in later as you review. You might fill it with comments that highlight main ideas, clarify meaning, suggest examples, or link ideas and examples. You can even draw diagrams.

■ *Section 3,* at the bottom of the page, is the *summary area,* where you use a sentence or two to summarize the notes on the page. When you review, use this section to reinforce concepts and provide an overview.

When you use the Cornell system, create the note-taking structure before class begins. Picture an upside-down letter T and use Figure 7.3 as your guide. Make the cue column about 2½ inches wide and the summary area 2 inches tall. Figure 7.3 shows how a student used the Cornell system to take notes in an introductory business course.

Sample Cornell System Notes

FIGURE 7.3

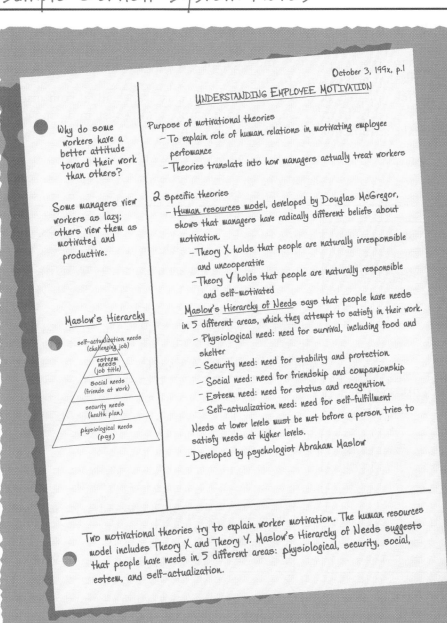

October 3, 199x, p.1

UNDERSTANDING EMPLOYEE MOTIVATION

Why do some workers have a better attitude toward their work than others?

Some managers view workers as lazy; others view them as motivated and productive.

Purpose of motivational theories
- To explain role of human relations in motivating employee performance
- Theories translate into how managers actually treat workers

2 specific theories
- Human resources model, developed by Douglas McGregor, shows that managers have radically different beliefs about motivation
  - Theory X holds that people are naturally irresponsible and uncooperative
  - Theory Y holds that people are naturally responsible and self-motivated
Maslow's Hierarchy of Needs says that people have needs in 5 different areas, which they attempt to satisfy in their work.
- Physiological need: need for survival, including food and shelter
- Security need: need for stability and protection
- Social need: need for friendship and companionship
- Esteem need: need for status and recognition
- Self-actualization need: need for self-fulfillment
Needs at lower levels must be met before a person tries to satisfy needs at higher levels.
- Developed by psychologist Abraham Maslow

Maslow's Hierarchy
- self-actualization needs (challenging job)
- esteem needs (job title)
- social needs (friends at work)
- security needs (health plan)
- physiological needs (pay)

Two motivational theories try to explain worker motivation. The human resources model includes Theory X and Theory Y. Maslow's Hierarchy of Needs suggests that people have needs in 5 different areas: physiological, security, social, esteem, and self-actualization.

Learning Styles Tip
Emphasize that the cue column helps visual learners absorb the material. The visual nature of a think link also facilitates this learning style.

Creating a Think Link

A *think link,* also known as a mind map, is a visual form of note taking. When you draw a think link, you diagram ideas by using shapes and lines that link ideas and supporting details and examples. The visual design makes the connections easy to see, and the use of shapes and pictures extends the material beyond just words. Many learners respond well to the power of **visualization.** You can use think links to brainstorm ideas for paper topics as well.

Visualization

The interpretation of verbal ideas through the use of mental visual images.

One way to create a think link is to circle your topic in the middle of a sheet of paper. Next, draw a line from the circled topic and write the name of one major idea at the end of the line. Circle that idea also. Then jot down specific facts related to the idea, linking them to the idea with lines. Continue the process, connecting thoughts to one another by using circles, lines, and words. Figure 7.4 shows a think link on a sociology concept called social stratification. This is only one of many think link styles; other examples include stair steps (showing connecting ideas that build to a conclusion) and a tree shape (roots as causes and branches as effects). You can design any think link that makes sense to you.

A think link may be tough to construct in class, especially if your instructor talks quickly. In this case, use another note-taking system during class. Then make a think link as you review your notes.

FIGURE 7.4 Sample Think Link

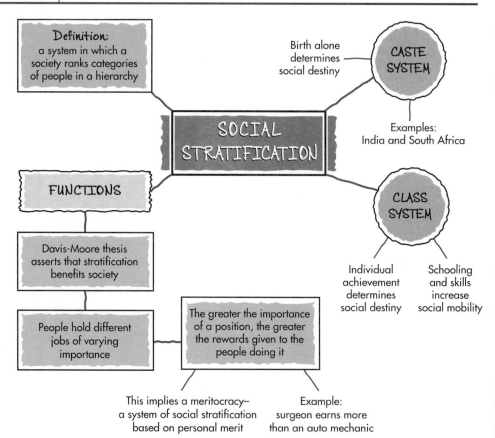

Using Other Visual Note-Taking Strategies

Several other note-taking strategies will help you organize your information and are especially useful to visual learners. These strategies may be too involved to complete quickly during class, so you may want to use them when taking notes on a text chapter or when rewriting your notes for review:

Time lines. A time line can help you organize information—such as dates of French Revolution events or eras of different psychology practices—into chronological order. Draw a vertical or horizontal line on the page and connect each item to the line, in order, noting the dates.

Tables. You will notice tables throughout this text that show information through vertical or horizontal columns. Use tables to arrange information according to particular categories.

Hierarchy charts. Charts showing the hierarchy of information can help you understand that information in terms of how each piece fits into the hierarchy. A hierarchy chart could show levels of government, for example, or levels of scientific classification of animals and plants.

> **Hierarchy**
> A graded or ranked series.

Once you choose a note-taking system, your success will depend on how well you use it. Personal shorthand will help you make the most of whatever system you choose.

HOW CAN YOU WRITE FASTER WHEN TAKING NOTES?

When taking notes, many students feel that they can't keep up with the instructor. Using some personal shorthand (not standard secretarial shorthand) can help you push your pen faster. *Shorthand* is writing that shortens words or replaces them with symbols. Because you are the only intended reader, you can misspell and abbreviate words in ways that only you understand.

The only danger with shorthand is that you might forget what your writing means. To avoid this problem, review your shorthand notes while your abbreviations and symbols are fresh in your mind. If there is any confusion, spell out words as you review.

Here are some suggestions that will help you master this important skill:

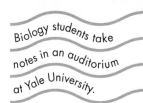

Biology students take notes in an auditorium at Yale University.

1. Use the following standard abbreviations in place of complete words:

w/	with	cf	compare, in comparison to
w/o	without	ff	following
→	means; resulting in	Q	question
←	as a result of	p.	page
↑	increasing	*	most importantly
↓	decreasing	<	less than

"Clear a space for the writing voice . . . you cannot will this to happen. It is a matter of persistence and

faith and hard work. So you might as well just go ahead and get started."

Anne Lamott

∴	therefore	>	more than
∵	because	=	equals
≈	approximately	%	percent
+ or &	and	∧	change
—	minus; negative	2	to; two; too
No. or #	number	vs.	versus; against
i.e.	that is,	e.g.	for example
etc.	and so forth	c/o	care of
ng	no good	lb	pound

2. Shorten words by removing vowels from the middle of words:

   prps   =   purpose

   Crvtte   =   Corvette (as on a vanity license plate for a car)

3. Substitute word beginnings for entire words:

   assoc   =   associate; association

   info   =   information

4. Form plurals by adding s:

   prblms   =   problems

   prntrs   =   printers

5. Make up your own symbols and use them consistently:

   b/4   =   before

   2thake   =   toothache

6. Use key phrases instead of complete sentences ("German-nouns capitalized" instead of "In the German language, all nouns are capitalized.")

While note taking focuses on taking in ideas, writing focuses on expressing them. Next you will explore the roles that writing can play in your life.

WHY DOES GOOD WRITING MATTER?

Almost any course will require you to communicate your knowledge and thought processes by writing essays or papers. To express yourself successfully, you need good writing skills. Knowing how to express your ideas in writing is essential outside of school as well. People who see your writing judge your thinking ability based on what you write and how you write it. Over the next few years you may write papers, essays, answers to essay test questions, job application letters, résumés, business proposals and reports, memos to coworkers, and letters to customers and suppliers. Good writing skills will help you achieve the goals you set out to accomplish with each writing task.

Good writing depends on and reflects clear thinking. Therefore, a clear thought process is the best preparation for a well-written document, and a well-written document shows the reader a clear thought process. Good writing also depends on reading. Exposing yourself to the work of other writers helps you learn words, experience concepts, and discover different ways to express ideas. In addition, critical reading generates new ideas you can use in your writing. The processes of reading and writing are interrelated; the skills in one process tend to enhance the skills in the other..

WHAT ARE THE ELEMENTS OF EFFECTIVE WRITING?

Every writing situation is different, depending on three elements. Your goal is to understand each element before you begin to write:

- **Your purpose:** What do you want to accomplish with this particular piece of writing?
- **Your topic:** What is the subject about which you will write?
- **Your audience:** Who will read your writing?

Figure 7.5 shows how these elements depend on one another. As a triangle needs three points to be complete, a piece of writing needs these three elements. Consider purpose and audience even before you begin to plan. Topic will come into play during the planning stage (the first stage of the writing process).

Audience
The reader or readers of any piece of written material.

Writing Purpose

Writing without having a clear purpose is like driving without deciding where you want to go. You'll get somewhere, but chances are it won't be the right place. Therefore, when you write, always decide what you want to accomplish before you start. Although there are many different writing purposes, the two you will most commonly use for school and on the job are to inform and to persuade.

The purpose of *informative writing* is to present and explain ideas. A research paper on how hospitals use donated blood to save lives informs readers without trying to mold opinions. The writer presents facts in an unbiased way without introducing a particular point of view. Most newspaper articles, except on the opinion and editorial pages, are examples of informative writing.

The Three Elements of Writing   **FIGURE 7.5**

Persuasive writing has the purpose of convincing readers to adopt your point of view. For example, as a member of the student health committee, you write a newspaper column attempting to persuade readers to give blood. Examples of persuasive writing include newspaper editorials, business proposals, and books and magazine articles with a point of view.

Knowing Your Audience

In almost every case, a writer creates written material so that others can read it. The writer and audience are partners in this process. Knowing who your audience is will help you communicate successfully.

Key Questions About Your Audience

In school, your primary audience is your instructors. For many assignments, instructors will want you to assume that they are typical readers. Writing for "typical readers" usually means that you should be as complete as possible in your explanations. You may also write for "informed readers" who know a great deal about your topic. In every case, ask yourself some or all of the following questions to help you define your readers' needs:

- What are my readers' ages, cultural backgrounds, interests, and experiences?
- What are their roles? Are they instructors, students, employers, or customers?
- How much do they know about my topic? Are they experts in the field or beginners?
- Are they interested, or do I have to convince them to read what I write?
- Can I expect my audience to have open or closed minds?

Learning Styles Tip
To define audience characteristics, logical-mathematical learners might draw a graph with audience analysis data.

After you answer the questions about your audience, take what you have discovered into consideration as you write.

Your Commitment to Your Audience

Be a Team
Have student teams write a survey with demographic and attitudinal questions, distribute it to the class, and compile the results. The goal is to develop a profile that will guide written communication to the class.

Your goal is to communicate—to organize your ideas so that readers can follow them. Suppose, for example, you are writing an informative research paper for a nonexpert audience on using Internet job banks to get a job. One way to accomplish your goal is first to explain what these employment services are and the kinds of help they offer, then to describe each service in detail, and finally to conclude with how these services will change job hunting in the 21st century.

Effective and successful writing involves following the steps of the writing process.

WHAT IS THE WRITING PROCESS?

The writing process provides an opportunity for you to state and refine your thoughts until you have expressed yourself as clearly as possible. Critical thinking plays an important role every step of the way. The four main parts of the process are planning, drafting, revising, and editing.

Planning

Planning gives you a chance to think about what to write and how to write it. Planning involves brainstorming for ideas, defining and narrowing your topic by using prewriting strategies, conducting research if necessary, writing a thesis statement, and writing a working outline. Although these steps are listed in sequence, in real life the steps overlap one another as you plan your document.

Open Your Mind Through Brainstorming

Whether your instructor assigns a partially defined topic (novelist Amy Tan) or a general category within which you make your own choice (women authors), you should brainstorm to develop ideas about what you want to write. Brainstorming is a creative technique that involves generating ideas about a subject without making judgments (see pp. 145–146).

First, let your mind wander. Write down anything on the assigned subject that comes to mind, in no particular order. Then, organize that list into an outline or think link that helps you see the possibilities more clearly. To make the outline or think link, separate list items into general ideas or categories and subideas or examples. Then associate the subideas or examples with the ideas they support or fit. Figure 7.6 shows a portion of an outline that student Michael B. Jackson constructed from his brainstorming list. The assignment is a five-paragraph essay on a life-changing event. Here, only the subject that Michael eventually chose is shown broken down into different ideas.

Narrow Your Topic Through Prewriting Strategies

When your brainstorming has generated some possibilities, narrow your topic. Focus on the subideas and examples from your brainstorming session. Because they are relatively specific, they will be more likely to point you toward possible topics. Choose one or more subideas or examples that you like and explore them by using prewriting strategies such as brainstorming, freewriting, and asking journalists' questions.[2] Prewriting strategies will help you decide which of your possible topics you would most like to pursue.

Brainstorming. The same process you used to generate ideas will also help you narrow your topic further. Generate thoughts about the possibility you have chosen and write them down. Then, organize them into categories, noticing any patterns that appear. See if any of the subideas or examples seem as if they might make good topics.

Freewriting. Another technique that encourages you to put ideas on paper as they occur to you is called *freewriting*. When you freewrite, you write whatever comes to mind without censoring ideas or worrying about grammar, spelling, punctuation, or organization. Freewriting helps you think creative-

Prewriting strategies
Techniques for generating ideas about a topic and finding out how much you already know before you start your research and writing.

Learning Styles Tip
Putting their ideas into pictures may help students with visual-spatial intelligence plan a document.

Springboard
Discuss why withholding judgment is the hardest part of brainstorming. Ask students for suggestions for ways to open their mind to new ideas and approaches and to bury their internal censor.

e-mail

Select a topic for a paper. Brainstorm as many ideas as you can think of and then e-mail a friend and ask for his or her ideas. What did you miss that they thought of?

FIGURE 7.6 *Part of a Brainstorming Outline*

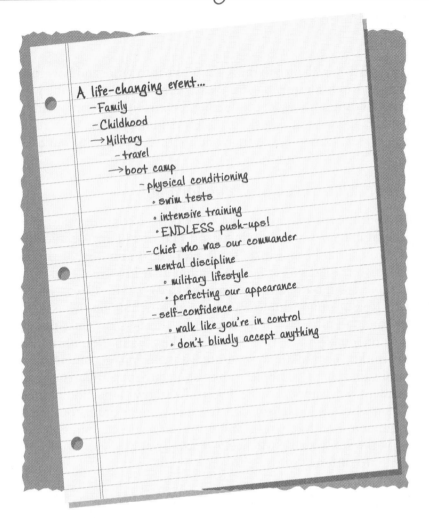

A life-changing event...
- Family
- Childhood
→ Military
  - travel
  → boot camp
    - physical conditioning
      · swim tests
      · intensive training
      · ENDLESS push-ups!
    - Chief who was our commander
    - mental discipline
      · military lifestyle
      · perfecting our appearance
    - self-confidence
      · walk like you're in control
      · don't blindly accept anything

ly and gives you an opportunity to begin weaving in information you know. Freewrite on the subideas or examples you have created to see if you want to pursue any of them. Here is a sample of freewriting:

> Boot camp for the Coast Guard really changed my life. First of all, I really got in shape. We had to get up every morning at 5 A.M., eat breakfast, and go right into training. We had to do endless military-style push-ups—but we later found out that these have a purpose, to prepare us to hit the deck in the event of enemy fire. We had a lot of aquatic tests, once we were awakened at 3 A.M. to do one in full uniform! Boot camp also helped me to feel confident about myself and be disciplined. Chief Marzloff was the main person who made that happen. He was tough but there was always a reason. He got angry when I used to nod my head whenever he would speak to me, he said that made it seem like I was blindly accepting whatever he said, which was a weakness. From him I have learned to keep an eye on my body's movements when I communicate. I learned a lot more from him too.

Asking journalists' questions. When journalists begin work on a story, they ask themselves: Who? What? Where? When? Why? and How? You can use these *journalists' questions* to focus your thinking. Ask these questions about any subidea or example to discover what you may want to discuss.

Who?   Who was at boot camp? Who influenced me the most?

What?   What about boot camp changed my life? What did we do?

When?   When in my life did I go to boot camp, and for how long? When did we fulfill our duties?

Where?   Where was camp located? Where did we spend our day-to-day time?

Why?   Why did I decide to go there? Why was it such an important experience?

How?   How did we train in the camp? How were we treated? How did we achieve success?

A certified nursing student uses a dictionary while studying.

As you prewrite, keep an eye on paper length, assignment due date, and any other requirements (such as topic area or purpose). These requirements influence your choice of a final topic. For example, if you have a month to write an informative 20-page paper on a learning disability, you might discuss the symptoms, effects, and treatment of attention deficit hyperactivity disorder (ADHD). If you have a week to write a five-page persuasive essay, you might write about how elementary students with ADHD need special training.

Prewriting will help you develop a topic broad enough to give you something with which to work but narrow enough to be manageable. Prewriting also helps you see what you know and what you don't know. If your assignment requires more than you already know, you may need to do research.

Conduct Research

Some college writing, such as an opinion essay or exam essay, will rely on what you already know about a subject. In these cases, prewriting strategies may generate all the ideas and information you need. In other writing situations, outside sources are necessary. Try doing your research in stages. In the first stage, look for a basic overview that can lead to a thesis statement. In the second stage, go into more depth, tracking down information that will help you fill in gaps and complete your thoughts.

Teaching Tip
Thanks to the Internet and computer links between students and the school library, students can usually conduct preliminary research quickly and efficiently, often without leaving their room.

Write a Thesis Statement

Your work up until this point has prepared you to write a thesis statement, the central message you want to communicate. The thesis statement states your subject and point of view, reflects your writing purpose and audience, and acts as the organizing principle of your paper. It tells your readers what they should expect to read. Here is an example from Michael's paper:

Topic	Coast Guard boot camp
Purpose	To inform

Audience	Instructor with unknown knowledge about the topic
Thesis statement	Chief Marzloff, our Basic Training Company Commander at the U. S. Coast Guard Basic Training Facility, shaped our lives through physical conditioning, developing our self-confidence, and instilling strong mental discipline.

A thesis statement is just as important in a short document, such as a letter, as it is in a long paper. For example, when you write a job application letter, a clear thesis statement will help you tell the recruiter why you deserve the job.

Write a Working Outline

The final step in the preparation process is writing a working outline. Use this outline as a loose guide instead of a final structure. As you draft your paper, your ideas and structure may change many times. Only by allowing changes and refinements to occur can you get closer to what you really want to say. Some students prefer a more formal outline structure, while others like to use a think link. Choose whatever form suits you best.

Create a Checklist

Use the checklist in Table 7.1 to make sure your preparation is complete. Under "Date Due," create your own writing schedule, giving each task an intended completion date. Work backward from the date the assignment is due and estimate how long it will take to complete each step. Refer to Chapter 3 for time-management skills that will help you schedule your writing process.

As you develop your schedule, remember that you'll probably move back and forth between tasks. You might find yourself doing two and even three things on the same day. Stick to the schedule as best you can—while balancing the other demands of your busy life—and check off your accomplishments on the list as you complete them.

TABLE 7.1

Preparation Checklist

DATE DUE	TASK	IS IT COMPLETE?
	Brainstorm	
	Define and narrow	
	Use prewriting strategies	
	Conduct research if necessary	
	Write thesis statement	
	Write working outline	
	Complete research	

Drafting

Some people aim for perfection when they write a first draft. They want to get everything right—from word choice to tone to sentence structure to paragraph organization to spelling, punctuation, and grammar. Try to resist this tendency because it may lead you to shut the door on ideas before you even know they are there.

A *first draft* involves putting ideas down on paper for the first time—but not the last. You may write many different versions of the assignment until you create one you like. Each version moves you closer to communicating exactly what you want to say in the way you want to say it. It is as if you started with a muddy pond and gradually cleared the mud away until your last version became a clear body of water, showing the rocks and the fish beneath the surface. Think of your first draft as a way of establishing the pond before you start clearing it up.

The process of writing a first draft includes freewriting, crafting an introduction, organizing the ideas in the body of the paper, formulating a conclusion, and citing sources. When you think of drafting, it might help you to imagine that you are creating a kind of "writing sandwich." The bottom slice of bread is the introduction, the top slice is the conclusion, and the sandwich stuffing is made of central ideas and supporting examples (see Figure 7.7).

Teaching Tip

One of the biggest challenges students face is to turn their freewritten draft into a logically organized, linear product. Emphasize that while freewriting is for the writer's eyes only, the final draft is for the reader.

Freewriting Your Draft

If the introduction, body, and conclusion are the three parts of the sandwich, freewriting is the process of searching the refrigerator for the ingredients and laying them all on the table. Taking everything that you have developed in the planning stages, freewrite a very rough draft. Don't censor yourself. For now, don't consciously think about your introduction, con-

The "Writing Sandwich"   **FIGURE 7.7**

clusion, or structure within the paper's body. Focus on getting your ideas out of the realm of thought and onto the paper in whatever form they prefer to be at the moment.

When you have the beginnings of a paper in your hands, you can start to shape it into something with a more definite form. First, work on how you want to begin.

Writing an Introduction

The introduction tells your readers what the rest of the paper will contain. A thesis statement is essential. Here, for example, is a draft of an introduction for Michael's paper about the Coast Guard. The thesis statement is underlined at the end of the paragraph:

> Chief Marzloff took on the task of shaping the lives and careers of the youngest, newest members of the U. S. Coast Guard. During my eight weeks in training, he was my father, my instructor, my leader, and my worst enemy. He took his job very seriously and demanded that we do the same. <u>The Chief was instrumental in conditioning our bodies, developing our self-confidence, and instilling mental discipline within us.</u>

When you write an introduction, you might try to draw the reader in with an anecdote—a story that is related to the thesis. You can try other **hooks,** including a relevant quotation, dramatic statistics, and questions that encourage critical thinking. Whatever strategy you choose, link it to your thesis statement. In addition, try to state your purpose without referring to its identity as a purpose. For example, in your introductory paragraph, state "Computer technology is infiltrating every aspect of business" instead of "In this paper, my purpose is to prove that computer technology is infiltrating every aspect of business."

After you have an introduction that seems to set up the purpose of your paper, make sure the body fulfills that purpose.

Hooks

Elements—including facts, quotes, statistics, questions, stories, or statements—that catch the reader's attention and encourage him or her to want to continue to read.

Creating the Body of a Paper

The body of the paper contains your central ideas and supporting evidence. *Evidence*—proof that informs or persuades—consists of the facts, statistics, examples, and expert opinions that you know or have gathered during research.

Look at the array of ideas and evidence in your draft in its current state. Think about how you might group certain items of evidence with the particular ideas they support. Then, try to find a structure that helps you to organize such evidence groups into a clear pattern. Here are some strategies to consider:

Arrange ideas by time. Describe events in order or in reverse order.

Arrange ideas according to importance. You can choose to start with the idea that carries the most weight and move to ideas with less value or influence. You can also move from the least important to the most important idea.

Arrange ideas by problem and solution. Start with a specific problem; then discuss one or more solutions.

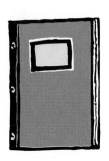

Writing the Conclusion

Your conclusion is a statement or paragraph that communicates that your paper is complete. Summarize the information that is in the body of your paper and critically evaluate what is important about it. Try one of the following strategies:

- Summarize main points (if material is longer than three pages).
- Relate a story, statistic, quote, or question that makes the reader think.
- Call the reader to action.
- Look to the future.

As you work on your conclusion, try not to introduce new facts or restate what you feel you have proved ("I have successfully proven that violent cartoons are related to increased violence in children"). Let your ideas as they are presented in the body of the paper speak for themselves. Readers should feel that they have reached a natural point of completion.

Crediting Authors and Sources

When you write a paper using any materials other than your own thoughts and recollections, the ideas you gathered in your research become part of your own writing. This does not mean that you can claim these ideas as your own or fail to attribute them to someone. To avoid **plagiarism,** you need to credit authors for their ideas and words.

Writers own their writings just as a computer programmer owns a program that he or she designed or a photographer owns an image that he or she created. A piece of writing and its ideas are the writer's products, or "intellectual property." Using an idea, phrase, or word-for-word paragraph without crediting its author is the same as using a computer program without buying it or printing a photograph without paying the photographer. It is just as serious as any other theft and may have unfavorable consequences. Most colleges have stiff penalties for plagiarism, as well as for other cheating offenses.

To avoid plagiarism, learn the difference between a quotation and a paraphrase. A *quotation* refers to a source's exact words, which are set off from the rest of the text by quotation marks. A *paraphrase* is a restatement of the quotation in your own words, using your own sentence structure. Restatement means to completely rewrite the idea, not just to remove or replace a few words. A paraphrase may not be acceptable if it is too close to the original. Figure 7.8 demonstrates these differences.

Plagiarism often begins by accident when you research. You may forget to include quotation marks around a word-for-word quotation from the source, or you may intend to cite it or paraphrase but never find the time to do so. To avoid forgetting, try writing something like "Quotation from original; rewrite later" next to quoted material, and note at that time the specifics of the original document (title, author, source, page number, etc.), so you don't spend hours trying to locate it later.

Even an acceptable paraphrase requires a citation of the source of the ideas within it. Take care to credit any source that you quote, paraphrase, or use as evidence. To credit a source, write a footnote or endnote that describes

Plagiarism
The act of using someone else's exact words, figures, unique approach, or specific reasoning without giving appropriate credit.

Springboard
Ask students if they agree that plagiarism is a serious offense. How do students benefit when they are forced to put another writer's ideas into their own words?

FIGURE 7.8

Avoid Plagiarism by Learning How to Paraphrase[3]

QUOTATION

"The most common assumption that is made by persons who are communicating with one another is . . . that the other perceives, judges, thinks, and reasons the way he does. Identical twins communicate with ease. Persons from the same culture but with a different education, age, background, and experience often find communication difficult. American managers communicating with managers from other cultures experience greater difficulties in communication than with managers from their own culture."[4]

UNACCEPTABLE PARAPHRASE

(The underlined words are taken directly from the quoted source.)

When we communicate, we assume that the person to whom we are speaking perceives, judges, thinks, and reasons the way we do. This is not always the case. Although identical twins communicate with ease, persons from the same culture but with a different education, age, background, and experience often encounter communication problems. Communication problems are common among American managers as they attempt to communicate with managers from other cultures. They experience greater communication problems than when they communicate with managers from their own culture.

ACCEPTABLE PARAPHRASE

Many people fall into the trap of believing that everyone sees the world exactly as they do and that all people communicate according to the same assumptions. This belief is difficult to support even within our own culture as African-Americans, Hispanic-Americans, Asian-Americans, and others often attempt unsuccessfully to find common ground. When intercultural differences are thrown into the mix, such as when American managers working abroad attempt to communicate with managers from other cultures, clear communication becomes even harder.

it. Use the format preferred by your instructor. Writing handbooks, such as Modern Language Association's *MLA Style Manual and Guide to Scholarly Publishing* (1998) contain acceptable formats.

Continue Your Checklist

Create a checklist for your first draft (see Table 7.2). The elements of a first draft do not have to be written in order. In fact, many writers prefer to write the introduction after they complete the body of the paper, so the introduc-

First Draft Checklist

TABLE 7.2

DATE DUE	TASK	IS IT COMPLETE?
	Freewrite a draft	
	Plan and write the introduction	
	Organize the body of the paper	
	Include research evidence in the body	
	Plan and write the conclusion	
	Check for plagiarism and rewrite passages to avoid it	
	Credit your sources	

tion will reflect the paper's content and tone. Whatever order you choose, make sure your schedule allows you to get everything done—with enough time left over for revisions.

Revising

When you revise, you critically evaluate the word choice, paragraph structure, and style of your first draft. Any draft, no matter how good, can always be improved. Be thorough as you add, delete, replace, and reorganize words, sentences, and paragraphs. You may want to print out your draft and then make notes and corrections on the hard copy before you make changes on a typewritten or computer-printed version. Figure 7.9 shows a paragraph from Michael's first draft with revision comments added.

Teaching Tip
Reading a paper aloud helps students hear the sound of language and change sections that are awkward or unclear.

In addition to revising on your own, some classes may include peer review (having students read one another's work and offer suggestions). A peer reviewer can tell you what comes across well and what seems confusing. Having a different perspective on your writing is extremely valuable. Even if you don't have an organized peer review system, you may want to ask a classmate to review your work as a favor.

The elements of revision include being a critical writer, evaluating paragraph structure, and checking for clarity and conciseness.

Being a Critical Writer

Critical thinking is as important in writing as it is in reading. Thinking critically when writing will help you move beyond restating what you have researched and learned. Of course, your knowledge is an important part of your writing. What will make your writing even more important and unique, however, is how you use critical thinking to construct your own new ideas and knowledge from what you have learned.

"See revision as 'envisioning again.' If there are areas in your work where there is a blur or vagueness, you can simply see the picture again and add the details that will bring your work closer to your mind's picture."
Natalie Goldberg

WINDOWS ON THE WORLD
Real Life Student Issues

How can I become more confident about my writing?

Beverly Andre, Triton College, River Grove, Illinois, Continuing Education

The best thing I ever wrote was in the sixth grade. My teacher let us pick a topic, and I chose to write about riding horses because I loved to do it and knew a lot about it. In high school, writing was okay because my English teacher was helpful. On the other hand, writing college papers has been a real challenge. For one thing, I don't think I'm very original when it comes to topic ideas. I also feel like I have to come up with college-level vocabulary, and mine is not that advanced. If a professor assigns a topic that I know nothing about, I usually don't have as much interest as I do when I'm writing on something I already know about.

One of the reasons I don't like to write is because I don't like looking up information. Knowing how to begin the research gets con-

fusing because there's so much to choose from. Once I do manage to pull the information together, I can't seem to expand on an idea without being redundant. I also have trouble sticking to the point, so I go off on all sorts of tangents. Occasionally, I come up with something a professor thinks is interesting. I'm always a little surprised when that happens. The bottom line is that I find it difficult to put my thoughts to paper. Can you help me become a better writer?

Raymond Montolvo, Jr., Writers Program, University of Southern California, Los Angeles, California

No matter what your writing goal, in most cases the person you are writing for, your instructor, wants you to improve. Keeping this in mind may help you concentrate on trying to improve your skills instead of worrying about getting a good grade.

I suggest a two-pronged approach to better writing. The first step is to read. Read novels, the newspaper, and nonfiction articles. Reading will help you learn to organize your thoughts, and it increases your vocabulary. If you want to study a specific area, such as what you plan to major in, read publications in that area on your own. Create file folders for pieces of writ-

ing that you like. For example, make a copy of a business letter that you think is well written, and refer to it when you need to write a similar correspondence.

Second, bridge the gap between what you should know and what an instructor can tell you. Ask your instructor what he or she thinks you need to work on. Focus your energy on understanding the assignment and strengthening technical skills such as sentence structure and grammar. Another tip is to read what you've written, sentence by sentence, and think about how you could say it better.

If you don't know where to begin your research, start with what feels comfortable. If you are at ease with computers, use the Internet. If you prefer libraries, start by asking the reference librarian for assistance. The main point with research is to jump right in. Once you read something that relates to your topic, it will refer you to something else.

Finally, don't get frustrated by setbacks. Writing is a process that you learn as you would an exercise. Set goals you can attain. Instead of sitting down and trying to write a 10-page paper, write a 3-page one. Finishing something builds confidence.

Sample First Draft with Revision Comments FIGURE 7.9

Of the changes that ~~happened to us,~~ the physical [military recruits undergo]

transformation is the ~~biggest.~~ [most evident] ~~When we arrived at the~~ [Too much ↗]

~~training facility, it was January, cold and cloudy. At the~~ [Maybe— upon my January arrival at the training facility,]

~~time,~~ I was a little thin, but I had been working out and

thought that I could physically do anything. Oh boy, was

I wrong! The Chief said to us right away: "Get down, [his trademark phrase ←]

maggots!" Upon this command, we ~~all~~ [were] to drop to the

ground and do ~~military-style~~ [endless] push-ups. Water survival

tactics were also part of the training ~~that we had to~~ [unnecessary]

~~complete.~~ Occasionally, my dreams of home were

interrupted at 3 a.m. when we had a surprise aquatic

test. Although we ~~didn't feel too happy about~~ [resented] this

sub-human treatment at the time, we learned to [mention how chief was involved]

appreciate how the conditioning was turning our bodies

into fine-tuned machines. [say more about this (swimming in uniform incident?)]

e-mail

One key to critical writing is asking the question "So what?" For example, if you were writing a paper on nutrition, you might discuss a variety of good eating habits. Asking "So what?" could lead into a discussion of why these habits are helpful or what positive effects they have. If you were writing a paper on egg imagery in the novel *All the King's Men* by Robert Penn Warren, you might list all the examples of it that you noticed. Then, asking "So what?" could lead you to evaluate why that imagery is so strong and what idea you think those examples convey.

Another key to critical writing, if your paper contains an argument, is to make sure that the argument is well constructed and convincing. Using what you know about arguments from the discussion in Chapter 5, think through your ideas and provide solid support for them with facts and examples.

Write or discuss with a friend from your class what you thought the main idea was of a short story or book you were assigned. Find out your friend's opinion and then analyze your two perspectives.

Use mind actions to guide your revision. As you revise, ask yourself questions that can help you think through ideas and examples, come up with your own original insights about the material, and be as complete and clear as possible. Here are some examples of questions you may ask:

Are these examples clearly connected to the idea?

Are there any similar concepts or facts I know of that can add to how I support this?

What else can I recall that can help to support this idea?

In evaluating any event or situation, have I clearly indicated the causes and effects?

What new idea comes to mind when I think about these examples or facts?

How do I evaluate any effect, fact, or situation? Is it good or bad, useful or not?

What different arguments might a reader think of that I should address here?

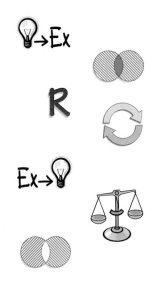

Finally, critical thinking can help you evaluate the content and form of your paper. As you start your revision, ask yourself the following questions:

■ Will my audience understand my thesis and how I've supported it?

■ Does the introduction prepare the reader and capture attention?

■ Is the body of the paper organized effectively?

■ Is each idea fully developed, explained, and supported by examples?

■ Are my ideas connected to one another through logical transitions?

■ Do I have a clear, concise, simple writing style?

■ Does the paper fulfill the requirements of the assignment?

■ Does the conclusion provide a natural ending to the paper?

Evaluating Paragraph Structure

Think of your paragraphs as miniversions of your paper, each with an introduction, a body, and a conclusion. Make sure that each paragraph has a *topic sentence* that states the paragraph's main idea. (A topic sentence does for a paragraph what a thesis statement does for an entire paper.) The rest of the paragraph should support the idea with examples and other evidence. Although some topic sentences may occur just after the first sentence of a paragraph, or even at the end, most occur at the beginning. An example follows:

> <u>Chief Marzloff played an integral role in the development of our self-confidence.</u> He taught us that anything less than direct eye contact was disrespectful to both him and ourselves. He encouraged us to be confident about our own beliefs and to think about what was said to us before we decided whether to accept it. Furthermore, the Chief reinforced self-confidence

Career Connection

Making new connections and creating new ideas is especially important in today's competitive workplace where companies cannot succeed simply by repeating the actions of others.

Teaching Tip

Remind students that instructors raise critical-thinking questions as part of their marking/evaluation process. It is the student's role to try to anticipate and correct any weaknesses in the paper before it is submitted.

Teaching Tip

Have students check also for persuasive language (strong verbs, assertive phrasing) and constructive language (language that takes a positive approach).

through his own example. He walked with his chin up and chest out, like the proud parent of a newborn baby. He always gave the appearance that he had something to do and that he was in complete control.

Examine how your paragraphs flow into one another by evaluating your use of **transitions.** For example, words like *also, in addition,* and *next* indicate that another idea is coming. Similarly, *finally, as a result,* and *in conclusion* tell readers a summary is on its way.

Checking for Clarity and Conciseness

Aim to say what you want to say as clearly and concisely as you can. Try to eliminate extra words and phrases. Rewrite wordy phrases in a more straightforward, conversational way. For example, you can write "if" instead of "in the event that," or "now" instead of "at this point in time." "Capriciously, I sauntered forth to the entryway and pummeled the door that loomed so majestically before me" might become "I skipped to the door and knocked loudly."

Editing

In contrast to the critical thinking of revising, *editing* involves correcting technical mistakes in spelling, grammar, and punctuation, as well as checking style consistency for such elements as abbreviations and capitalizations. Editing comes last, after you are satisfied with your ideas, organization, and style of writing. If you use a computer, you might want to use the grammar-check and spell-check functions to find mistakes. A spell checker helps, but you still need to check your work on your own. Although a spell checker won't pick up the mistake in the following sentence, someone who is reading for sense will:

They are not hear on Tuesdays.

Look also for *sexist language*, which characterizes people according to their gender. Sexist language often involves the male pronoun *he* or *his.* For example, "An executive often spends hours each day going through his electronic mail" implies that executives are always men. A simple change will eliminate the sexist language: "Executives often spend hours each day going through their electronic mail" or "An executive often spends hours each day going through his or her electronic mail." Try to be sensitive to words that leave out or slight women. *Mail carrier* is preferable to *mailman; student* to *coed.*

Proofreading is the last editing stage and happens after your paper is in its final form. Proofreading means reading every word and sentence to make sure they are accurate. Look for technical mistakes, run-on sentences, and sentence fragments. Look for incorrect word usage and unclear references.

Teamwork can be a big help as you edit and proofread because another pair of eyes may see errors that you didn't notice on your own. If possible, have someone look over your work. Ask for feedback on what is clear and what is confusing. Then ask the reader to edit and proofread for errors.

TABLE 7.3

Revising and Editing Checklist

DATE DUE	TASK	IS IT COMPLETE?
	Check the body of the paper for clear thinking and adequate support of ideas	
	Finalize introduction and conclusion	
	Check word spelling, usage, and grammar	
	Check paragraph structure	
	Make sure language is familiar and concise	
	Check punctuation and capitalization	
	Check transitions	
	Eliminate sexist language	
	Get feedback from peers and/or instructor	

Teaching Tip
Like all readers, instructors respond negatively to sloppy documents with smudges and crinkled paper. Students should always put their best face forward by taking pride in how their paper looks.

A Final Checklist

You are now ready to complete your revising and editing checklist. All the tasks listed in Table 7.3 should be complete when you submit your final paper.

Your final paper reflects all the hard work you put in during the writing process. Figure 7.10 shows the final version of Michael's paper.

Suà

Suà is a Shoshone word, derived from the Uto-Aztecan language, meaning "think." Whereas much of the Native-American tradition focuses on oral communication, written languages have allowed Native-American perspectives and ideas to be understood by readers outside of their culture. The writings of Leslie Marmon Silko, N. J. Scott Momaday, and Sherman Alexis have expressed important insights that all readers can consider.

Think of *suà,* and of how thinking can be communicated to others through writing, every time you begin to write. The power of writing allows you to express your own insights so that others can read them and perhaps benefit from knowing them. Explore your thoughts, sharpen your ideas, and remember the incredible power of the written word.

Sample Final Version of Paper

FIGURE 7.10

Michael B. Jackson

BOYS TO MEN

His stature was one of confidence, often misinterpreted by others as cockiness. His small frame was lean and agile, yet stiff and upright, as though every move were a calculated formula. For the longest eight weeks of my life, he was my father, my instructor, my leader, and my worst enemy. His name is Chief Marzloff, and he had the task of shaping the lives and careers of the youngest, newest members of the U. S. Coast Guard. As our Basic Training Company Commander, he took his job very seriously and demanded that we do the same. Within a limited time span, he conditioned our bodies, developed our self-confidence, and instilled within us a strong mental discipline.

Of the changes that recruits in military basic training undergo, the physical transformation is the most immediately evident. Upon my January arrival at the training facility, I was a little thin, but I had been working out and thought that I could physically do anything. Oh boy, was I wrong! The Chief wasted no time in introducing me to one of his trademark phrases: "Get down, maggots!" Upon this command, we were all to drop to the ground and produce endless counts of military-style push-ups. Later, we found out that this exercise prepared us for hitting the deck in the event of enemy fire. Water survival tactics were also part of the training. Occasionally, my dreams of home were interrupted at about 3 a.m. when our company was selected for a surprise aquatic test. I recall one such test that required us to swim laps around the perimeter of a pool while in full uniform. I felt like a salmon swimming upstream, fueled only by natural instinct. Although we resented this sub-human treatment at the time, we learned to appreciate how the strict guidance of the Chief was turning our bodies into fine-tuned machines.

Beyond physical ability, Chief Marzloff also played an integral role in the development of our self-confidence. He would often declare in his raspy voice, "Look me in the eyes when you speak to me! Show me that you believe what you're saying!" He taught us that anything less was an expression of disrespect. Furthermore, he appeared to attack a personal habit of my own. It seemed that whenever he would speak to me individually, I would nervously nod my head in response. I was trying to demonstrate that I understood, but to him, I was blindly accepting anything that he said. He would roar, "That is a sign of weakness!" Needless to say, I am now conscious of all bodily motions when communicating with others. The Chief also reinforced self-confidence through his own example. He walked with his square chin up and chest out, like the proud parent of a newborn baby. He always gave the appearance that he had something to do, and that he was in complete control. Collectively, the methods that the Chief used were all successful in developing our self-confidence.

Perhaps the Chief's greatest contribution was the mental discipline that he instilled in his recruits. He taught us that physical ability and self-confidence were nothing without the mental discipline required to obtain any worthwhile goal. For us, this discipline began with adapting to the military lifestyle. Our day began promptly at 0500 hours, early enough to awaken the oversleeping roosters. By 0515 hours, we had to have showered, shaved, and perfectly donned our uniforms. At that point, we were marched to the galley for chow, where we learned to take only what is necessary, rather than indulging. Before each meal, the Chief would warn, "Get what you want, but you will eat all that you get!" After making good on his threat a few times, we all got the point. Throughout our stay, the Chief repeatedly stressed the significance of self-discipline. He would calmly utter, "Give a little now, get a lot later." I guess that meant different things to all of us. For me, it was a simple phrase that would later become my personal philosophy on life. The Chief went to great lengths to ensure that everyone under his direction possessed the mental discipline required to be successful in boot camp or in any of life's challenges.

Chief Marzloff was a remarkable role model and a positive influence on many lives. I never saw him smile, but it was evident that he genuinely cared a great deal about his job and all the lives that he touched. This man single-handedly conditioned our bodies, developed our self-confidence, and instilled a strong mental discipline that remains in me to this day. I have not seen the Chief since March 28, 1992, graduation day. Over the years, however, I have incorporated many of his ideals into my life. Above all, he taught us the true meaning of the U. S. Coast Guard slogan, "Semper Peratus" (Always Ready).

Name   Date

BUILDING SKILLS FOR COLLEGE, CAREER, AND LIFE SUCCESS

Critical Thinking
Applying Learning to Life

Class vs. Reading

Pick a class for which you have a regular textbook. Choose a set of class notes on a subject that is also covered in that textbook. Read the textbook section that corresponds to the subject of your class notes, taking notes as you go. Compare your reading notes to the notes you took in class.

1. Did you use a different system with the textbook, or the same as in class? Why?

2. Which notes can you understand better? Why do you think that's true?

3. What did you learn from your reading notes that you want to bring to your class note-taking strategy?

Audience Analysis

As a reporter for your college newspaper, you have been assigned the job of writing a story about some part of campus life. You submit the following suggestions to your editor-in-chief:

- The campus parking lot squeeze: Too many cars and too few spaces
- Diversity: How students accept differences and live and work together
- Drinking on campus: Is the problem getting better or worse?

Your editor-in-chief asks you the following questions about reader response (consider that your different "audiences" include students, faculty and administrators, and community members):

1. Which subject would be most likely to appeal to all audiences at your school, and why?

2. How would you adjust your writing according to how much readers know about the subject?

3. For each topic, name the audience (or audiences) that you think would be most interested. If you think one audience would be equally interested in more than one topic, you can name an audience more than once.

   Campus parking lot

   Student diversity

   Drinking on campus

4. How can you make a specific article interesting to a general audience?

Prewriting

Choose a topic you are interested in and know something about—for example, college sports or handling stress. Narrow your topic; then use the following prewriting strategies to discover what you already know about the topic and what you would need to learn if you had to write an essay about the subject for one of your classes (if necessary, continue this prewriting exercise on a separate sheet of paper):

Brainstorm your ideas.

Freewrite.

Ask journalists' questions.

Writing a Thesis Statement

Write two thesis statements for each of the following topics. The first statement should inform the reader, and the second should persuade. In each case, use the thesis statement to narrow the topic:

1. *The rising cost of a college education*
   a. Thesis with an informative purpose:

   b. Thesis with a persuasive purpose:

2. *Taking care of your body and mind*

    a. Thesis with an informative purpose:

    _____

    _____

    b. Thesis with a persuasive purpose:

    _____

    _____

3. *Career choice*

    a. Thesis with an informative purpose:

    _____

    _____

    b. Thesis with a persuasive purpose:

    _____

    _____

Teamwork
Combining Forces

Study Group Notes Evaluation Choose one particular meeting of this class from the last two weeks. Join with two or three other classmates, all of whom were in class that day, and make a temporary study group. Each of you should make enough photocopies of your own notes to pass around one copy to each of the other group members.

    First, look over the sets of notes on your own. Think about:

- readability of handwriting
- information covered
- note-taking systems used
- clarity of the ideas and examples

    Then, gather again and talk through the four topics together, one by one. Approach the notes as though you were in a study group session.

- Can you read each other's handwriting? If not, the information won't be of much use to you.
- Did you cover the same information? If someone missed a topic, someone else can help them fill in the blanks.
- Did you use the same or different note-taking systems? You might gather insight from the way someone else structures their notes.

■ Could you understand what the notes were saying? If you are confused about something in your own notes, someone else might have a helpful perspective. If you don't understand someone else's notes, together you can figure out which information is confusing or missing.

Finally, write one change you plan to make in your note taking based on your study group session.

Writing
Discovery Through Journaling

To record your thoughts, use a separate journal or the lined pages at the end of the chapter.

Affecting Words What piece of powerful writing have you read most recently? Did it make you feel something, think something, and/or do something? If so, why? What can you learn about writing from this piece?

Career Portfolio
Charting Your Course

Writing Sample: A Job Interview Letter To secure a job interview, you may have to write a letter describing your background and explaining your value to the company. To include in your portfolio, write a one-page, three-paragraph cover letter to a prospective employer. (The letter will accompany your résumé.) Be creative—you may use fictitious names, but select a career and industry that interest you. Use the format shown in the sample letter on p. 225.

Introductory paragraph: Start with an attention getter—a statement that convinces the employer to read on. For example, name a person the employer knows who told you to write, or refer to something positive about the company that you read in the paper. Identify the position for which you are applying, and tell the employer that you are interested in working for the company.

Middle paragraph: Sell your value. Try to convince the employer that hiring you will help the company in some way. Center your "sales effort" on your experience in school and the workplace. If possible, tie your qualifications to the needs of the company. Refer indirectly to your enclosed résumé.

Final paragraph: Close with a call to action. Ask the employer to call you, or tell the employer to expect your call to arrange an interview.

Exchange first drafts with a classmate. Read each other's letters and make notes in the margins. Discuss each letter, and make whatever corrections are necessary to produce a well-written, persuasive letter. Create a final draft for your portfolio.

Performance counts!

Your writing is a reflection of how you think. The more you write and practice your writing in college, the more versatile you will be as a writer, as a thinker, and as a communicator on the job.

First name Last name
1234 Your Street
City, ST 12345

January 1, 2000

Ms. Prospective Employer
Prospective Company
5432 Their Street
City, ST 54321

Dear Ms. Employer:

On the advice of Mr. X, career center advisor at Y College, I am writing to inquire about the open position of production assistant at KKKK Radio. I read the description of the job and the company as it was listed on the career center board, and I wish to offer myself as a candidate for the position.

I am a senior at Y College and will graduate this spring with a degree in communications. Since my junior year when I declared my major, I have wanted to pursue a career in radio. For the last year I have worked as a production intern at KCOL Radio, the college's station, and have occasionally filled in as a disc jockey on the evening news show. I enjoyed being on the air, but my primary interest is production and programming. My enclosed résumé will tell you more about my background and experience.

I would be pleased to talk with you in person about the position. You can reach me anytime at 555/555-5555 or by e-mail at xxxx@xx.com. Thank you for your consideration, and I look forward to meeting you.

Sincerely,

(*sign your name here*)

First name Last name

Enclosure(s) (*use this notation if you have included a résumé or other item with your letter*)

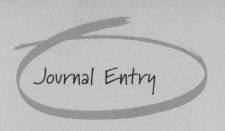

Journal Entry

Name _____   Date _____

Journal Entry

Name _____   Date _____

Listening, Memory, and Test Taking

Taking In, Retaining, and Demonstrating Knowledge

In this chapter, you will explore answers to the following questions:

- How can you become a better listener?
- How does memory work?
- How can you improve your memory?
- How can tape recorders help you listen, remember, and study?
- What types of preparation can improve test performance?
- What strategies can help you succeed on tests?
- How can you learn from test mistakes?

College exposes you daily to facts, opinions, and ideas—your job is to make use of them. Listening helps you take in information, and memory skills enable you to retain it. Then, through test preparation and test taking, you demonstrate knowledge and mastery of what you learn. Compare your skills to using a camera: You start by locating an image through the viewfinder, then you carefully focus the lens (listening), record the image on film (remembering), and produce a print (test taking). Mastery also involves the ability to apply your new knowledge to new situations. In this chapter, you will learn strategies to improve your ability to take in, remember, and show knowledge of what you have learned.

Teaching Tip
Helpful Web sites:
- Algebra Online - www.algebra-online.com
- International Listening Association - www.listen.org/

HOW CAN YOU BECOME A BETTER LISTENER?

Listening

A process that involves sensing, interpreting, evaluating, and reacting to spoken messages.

The act of hearing isn't quite the same as the act of listening. While *hearing* refers to sensing spoken messages from their source, *listening* involves a complex process of communication. Successful listening results in the speaker's intended message reaching the listener. In school and at home, poor listening may cause communication breakdowns and mistakes, whereas skilled listening promotes mutual understanding. Listening is a teachable—and learnable—skill.

Ralph G. Nichols, a pioneer in listening research, studied 200 students at the University of Minnesota over a nine-month period. His findings, summarized in Table 8.1, demonstrate that effective listening depends as much on a positive attitude as on specific skills.[1] Just as understanding the mind actions involved in critical thinking will help you work out problems, understanding the listening process will help you become a better listener.

TABLE 8.1   What Helps and Hinders Listening

LISTENING IS HELPED BY	LISTENING IS HINDERED BY
. . . making a conscious decision to work at listening; viewing difficult material as a listening challenge.	. . . caring little about the listening process; tuning out difficult material.
. . . fighting distractions through intense concentration.	. . . refusing to listen at the first distraction.
. . . continuing to listen when a subject is difficult or dry, in the hope that one might learn something interesting.	. . . giving up as soon as one loses interest.
. . . withholding judgment until hearing everything.	. . . becoming preoccupied with a response as soon as a speaker makes a controversial statement.
. . . focusing on the speaker's theme by recognizing organizational patterns, transitional language, and summary statements.	. . . getting sidetracked by unimportant details.
. . . adapting note-taking style to the unique style and organization of the speaker.	. . . always taking notes in outline form, even when a speaker is poorly organized, leading to frustration.
. . . pushing past negative emotional responses and forcing oneself to continue to listen.	. . . letting an initial emotional response shut off continued listening.
. . . using excess thinking time to evaluate, summarize, and question what one just heard and anticipating what will come next.	. . . thinking about other things and, as a result, missing much of the message.

Teaching Tip
When students actively listen to difficult lectures, they may actually feel tired when the lecture is over. Reassure them that the more experience they get as active listeners, the stronger their skills will become and the easier the task.

Know the Stages of Listening

Listening is made up of four stages that build on one another: sensing, interpreting, evaluating, and reacting. These stages take the message from the speaker to the listener and back to the speaker (see Figure 8.1).

Stages of Listening   **FIGURE 8.1**

SPEAKER DELIVERS MESSAGE TO LISTENER

SENSATION	INTERPRETATION	EVALUATION	REACTION
Listener hears message when ears pick up sound waves	Listener attaches meaning to message	Listener judges message against his or her personal values	Listener provides feedback to speaker through questions and comments

During the *sensation stage* (also known as hearing), your ears pick up sound waves and transmit them to the brain. For example, you are sitting in class and hear your instructor say, "The only opportunity to make up last week's test is Tuesday at 5:00 P.M."

In the *interpretation stage,* listeners attach meaning to a message. This involves understanding what is being said and relating it to what you already know. For example, you relate this message to your knowledge of the test, whether you need to make it up, and what you are doing on Tuesday at 5:00 P.M.

In the *evaluation stage* of listening, you decide how you feel about the message—whether, for example, you like it or agree with it. This involves considering the message as it relates to your needs and values. In this example, if you do need to make up the test but have to work Tuesday at 5 P.M., you may evaluate the message as less than satisfactory.

The final stage of listening involves a *reaction* to the message in the form of direct feedback. Your reaction, in this example, may be to ask the instructor if there is any alternative to that particular makeup test time.

Improving your learning skills also involves managing listening challenges and becoming an active listener. Although good listening will help in every class, it is crucial in subject areas you find difficult.

Springboard
Ask students to discuss the following: Of all the communication skills (listening, speaking, reading, and writing), listening is learned first and used most often throughout life. Despite its importance, it receives the least attention in school and is rarely taught.

"No one cares to speak to an unwilling listener. An arrow never lodges in a stone; often it recoils upon the sender of it."

St. Jerome

Manage Listening Challenges

Classic studies have shown that immediately after listening, students are likely to recall only half of what was said. This is partly due to particular listening

Learning Styles Tip
Try to minimize any environmental sounds that may interfere with listening. Students with musical intelligence are especially sensitive to these distractions.

Career Connection
Effective listening is becoming more difficult in the workplace because of increased productivity demands. Under deadline pressure, employees often do several tasks at once (word processing and talking on the phone, for example), which reduces effective listening.

challenges, including divided attention and distractions, the tendency to shut out the message, the inclination to rush to judgment, and partial hearing loss or learning disabilities.[2] To help create a positive listening environment in both your mind and your surroundings, explore how to manage these challenges.

Divided Attention and Distractions

Imagine you are talking with a coworker in the company cafeteria when you hear your name mentioned across the room. Now you strain to hear what someone might be saying about you and only half listen to your friend. Chances are you hear neither person very well. This situation illustrates the consequences of divided attention. While you are capable of listening to more than one message at the same time, you may not completely hear or understand any of them.

Internal and external distractions often divide your attention. *Internal distractions* include anything from hunger to headache to personal worries. Something the speaker says may also trigger a recollection that causes your mind to drift. In contrast, *external distractions* include noises (e.g., whispering or sirens) and excessive heat or cold. It can be hard to listen in an overheated room in which you are falling asleep.

Your goal is to reduce distractions so that you can focus on what you're hearing. Sitting where you can clearly see and hear will help you to listen. To avoid distracting activity, you may want to sit away from people who might chat or make noise. Dress comfortably, paying attention to the temperature of the classroom, and try not to go to class hungry or thirsty. Work to concentrate on class when you're in class and save worrying about personal problems for later.

Shutting Out the Message

Instead of paying attention to everything the speaker says, many students fall into the trap of focusing on specific points and shutting out the rest of the message. If you perceive that a subject is too difficult or uninteresting, you may tune out. Shutting out the message makes listening harder from that point on, since the information you miss may be the foundation for what goes on in future classes.

Creating a positive listening environment includes accepting responsibility for listening. Although the instructor is responsible for communicating information to you, he or she cannot force you to listen. You are responsible for taking in that information. Instructors often cover material from outside the textbook during class and then test on that material. If you work to take in the whole message in class, you will be able to read over your notes later and think critically about what is most important.

Teaching Tip
During the interpretation stage, we decide, often unconsciously, whether new information contradicts our value system. Cognitive dissonance arises when that information creates stress. To relieve discomfort, we may reject the new idea.

The Rush to Judgment

People tend to stop listening when they hear something they don't like. If you rush to judge what you've heard, making a quick uncritical assumption about it, your focus turns to your personal reaction rather than the content of the message. Judgments also involve reactions to the speakers themselves. If you do not like your instructors or if you have preconceived notions about their ideas or background, you may assume that their words have little value.

Work to recognize and control your judgments by making an effort to listen first without jumping to any conclusions. Ask critical-thinking questions about any assumption (see p. 139). Stay aware of what you tend to judge so that you can avoid rejecting messages that clash with your opinions. Consider education as a continuing search for evidence, regardless of whether that evidence supports or negates your perspective.

Partial Hearing Loss and Learning Disabilities

Good listening techniques don't solve every listening problem. Students who have a partial hearing loss have a physical explanation for listening difficulty. If you have some level of hearing loss, seek out special services that can help you listen in class. You may require special equipment, or you might benefit from tutoring. You may be able to arrange to meet with your instructor outside of class to clarify your notes.

Other disabilities, such as attention deficit hyperactivity disorder (ADHD) or a problem with processing spoken language, can make it hard to focus on and understand oral messages. If you have one of these disabilities, don't blame yourself for your difficulty. Visit your school's counseling or student health center, or talk with your advisor or instructors about getting the help you need to meet your challenges.

Become an Active Listener

On the surface, listening seems like a passive activity; you sit back and listen as someone else speaks. Effective listening, however, is really an active process that involves setting a purpose for listening, asking questions, and paying attention to verbal signposts.

Set purposes for listening. Active listening is only possible if you know (and care) why you are listening. In any situation, establish what you want to achieve through listening, such as greater understanding of the material, or better note taking to make it easier to study for tests. Having a purpose gives you a goal that motivates you to listen.

Ask questions. A willingness to ask questions shows a desire to learn and is the mark of a critical thinker. Some questions are *informational*—seeking information—such as any questions beginning with "Can you explain . . ." Other *clarifying* questions ask if your understanding of something you just heard is correct, such as "So some learning disabilities can be improved with treatment?"

Pay attention to verbal signposts. You can identify important facts and ideas and predict test questions by paying attention to the speaker's specific choice of words. Verbal signposts

e-mail

E-mail one of your friends and let them know your greatest listening weakness (or ask them to tell you, in case it's hard to see yourself clearly). For the next month, observe your behavior on this issue and e-mail your friend on the progress you've made in improving your listening abilities. Be specific!

Learning Styles Tip
Learning styles affect the ability to learn through listening. Verbal learners can absorb spoken information better than visual learners, who remember best what they see.

Verbal signposts
Spoken words or phrases that call your attention to the information that follows.

Medical students discuss scheduling.

often involve transition words and phrases that help organize information, connect ideas, and indicate what is and is not important. Let phrases like those in Table 8.2 direct your attention to the material that follows them.

Listening in order to acquire knowledge is only the first step. The next goal is to remember what you hear, read, and take in through your other senses.

TABLE 8.2 Paying Attention to Verbal Signposts

SIGNALS POINTING TO KEY CONCEPTS	SIGNALS OF SUPPORT
There are two reasons for this . . .	For example, . . .
A critical point in the process involves . . .	Specifically, . . .
Most importantly, . . .	For instance, . . .
The result is . . .	Similarly, . . .
SIGNALS POINTING TO DIFFERENCES	**SIGNALS THAT SUMMARIZE**
On the contrary, . . .	Finally, . . .
On the other hand, . . .	Recapping this idea, . . .
In contrast, . . .	In conclusion, . . .
However, . . .	As a result, . . .

Source: Adapted from George M. Usova, *Efficient Study Strategies: Skills for Successful Learning.* Pacific Grove, CA: Brooks/Cole Publishing, 1989, p. 69.

Critical Thinking
Why is feedback in the form of questions and nonverbal engagement (eye contact, nodding, etc.) important to the speaker as well as the listener? Can students think of examples when feedback helped a speaker redirect or clarify his/her message?

HOW DOES MEMORY WORK?

Teaching Tip
The more neural connections that form for new information, the more likely we are to remember the information. Neural connections are strengthened when they are linked to emotion. Thus, students are more likely to remember their first day of college than their 42nd day.

Your memory enables you to use the knowledge you take in. Human memory works like a computer. Both have essentially the same purpose: to encode, store, and retrieve information.

- During the *encoding stage,* information is changed into usable form. On a computer, this occurs when keyboard entries are transformed into electronic symbols and stored on a disk. In the brain, sensory information becomes impulses that the central nervous system reads and codes. You are encoding, for example, when you study a list of chemistry formulas.

- During the *storage stage,* information is held in memory (the mind's version of a computer hard drive) for later use. In this example, after you complete your studying of the formulas, your mind stores them until you need to use them.

- During the *retrieval stage,* memories are recovered from storage by recall, just as a saved computer program is called up by name and used again. In this example, your mind would retrieve the chemistry formulas when you had to take a test or solve a problem.

Memories are stored in three different storage banks. The first, called *sensory memory,* is an exact copy of what you see and hear and lasts for a second or less. Certain information is then selected from sensory memory and moves into *short-term memory,* a temporary information storehouse that lasts no more than 10 to 20 seconds. You are consciously aware of material in your short-term memory. Whereas unimportant information is quickly dumped, important information is transferred to *long-term memory*—the mind's more permanent information storehouse.

Having information in long-term memory does not necessarily mean that you will be able to recall it when needed. Particular techniques can help you improve your recall.

HOW CAN YOU IMPROVE YOUR MEMORY?

Most forgetting occurs within minutes after memorization. In a classic study conducted in 1885, researcher Herman Ebbinghaus memorized a list of meaningless three-letter words such as CEF and LAZ. Within one hour he measured that he had forgotten more than 50 percent of what he learned. After two days, he knew fewer than 30 percent. Although his recall of the syllables remained fairly stable after that, the experiment shows how fragile memory can be—even when you take the time and energy to memorize information.[3]

People with superior memories may have an inborn talent for remembering. More often, though, they have mastered techniques for improving recall. Remember that techniques aren't a cure-all for memory difficulties, especially for those with learning disabilities. If you have a disability, the following strategies may help but may not be enough. Seek specific assistance if you consistently have trouble remembering.

Be a Team
Have student groups discuss how they think actors remember their lines and then interview people with acting experience to compare the group's ideas with what really happens. What techniques appear on both lists?

Use Memory Improvement Strategies

As a student, your job is to understand, learn, and remember information—everything from general concepts to specific details. The following suggestions will help improve your recall.

Have Purpose and Intention

Why can you remember the lyrics to dozens of popular songs but not the functions of the pancreas? Perhaps this is because you want to remember the lyrics, you connect them to a visual image, or you have an emotional tie to them. To achieve the same results at school or on the job, make sure you have a purpose for what you are trying to remember. When you know why it is important, you will be able to strengthen your intention to remember it.

"The true art of memory is the art of attention."
Samuel Johnson

Understand What You Memorize

Make sure that everything you want to remember makes sense to you. Something that has meaning is easier to recall than something that is gibberish. This basic principle applies to everything you study—from biology and astronomy to history and English literature. If something you need to memorize makes no sense, consult textbooks, fellow students, or an instructor for an explanation.

Recite, Rehearse, and Write

Teaching Tip
Suggest to students that they write information they want to remember in outline form. When they remember the main points, they may also remember the subpoints under it. As they try to recall information, they may actually "see" the outline in their mind's eye.

When you *recite* material, you repeat it aloud to remember it. Reciting helps you retrieve information as you learn it and is a crucial step in studying (see Chapter 6). *Rehearsing* is similar to reciting but is done silently. It is the process of repeating, summarizing, and associating information with other information. *Writing* is rehearsing on paper. The act of writing solidifies the information in your memory.

Separate Main Points from Unimportant Details

Use critical-thinking skills to select and focus on the most important information. Asking questions about what is most crucial to remember, highlight only the most important information in your texts and write notes in the margins about central ideas. When you review your lecture notes, highlight or rewrite the most important information to remember.

Study During Short but Frequent Sessions

Research shows that you can improve your chances of remembering material if you learn it more than once. Study in short sessions followed by brief rest periods rather than studying continually with little or no rest. Even though studying for an hour straight may feel productive, you'll probably remember more from three 20-minute sessions. Try studying between classes or during other breaks in your schedule.

Separate Material into Manageable Sections

Learning Styles Tip
Another helpful memory tool for logical-mathematical thinkers is a timeline to order events.

When material is short and easy to understand, studying it from start to finish may work. With longer material, however, you may benefit from dividing it into logical sections, mastering each section, putting all the sections together, and then testing your memory of all the material.

Use Visual Aids

Be a Team
Have partners in a two-person team share their experiences with flash cards. For what kinds of information were they a helpful memory tool? How did they use the cards to maximize the results?

Any kind of visual representation of study material can help you remember. Try converting material into a think link or outline. Use any visual that helps you recall it and link it to other information.

Flash cards (easily made from index cards) are a great visual memory tool. They give you short repetitive review sessions that provide immediate feedback. Use the front of each card to write a word, idea, or phrase you want to remember. Use the back side for a definition, explanation, and other key facts. Figure 8.2 shows two flash cards for studying psychology.

Here are some additional suggestions for making the most of your flash cards:

- Carry the cards with you and review them frequently.
- Shuffle the cards and learn the information in various order.
- Test yourself in both directions (e.g., first look at the terms and provide the definitions or explanations; then turn the cards over and reverse the process).

Sample Flash Cards

FIGURE 8.2

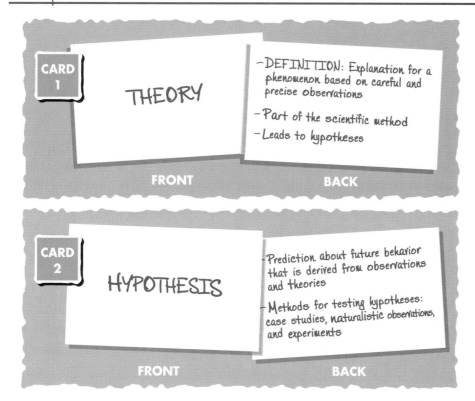

CARD 1

THEORY

FRONT

–DEFINITION: Explanation for a phenomenon based on careful and precise observations
– Part of the scientific method
– Leads to hypotheses

BACK

CARD 2

HYPOTHESIS

FRONT

– Prediction about future behavior that is derived from observations and theories
– Methods for testing hypotheses: case studies, naturalistic observations, and experiments

BACK

Use Critical Thinking

Your knowledge of the critical-thinking mind actions can help you remember information. Many of the mind actions use the principle of *association*—considering new information in relation to information you already know. The more you can associate a piece of new information with your current knowledge, the more likely you are to remember it.

Imagine that you have to remember information about a specific historical event—for example, the signing of the Treaty of Versailles, the agreement that ended World War I. You might put the mind actions to work in the following ways:

Recall everything that you know about the topic.

Think about how this event is *similar* to other events in history, either recent events or events from long ago.

Consider what is *different* and unique about this treaty in comparison to other treaties.

Explore the *causes* that led up to this event, and look at the event's *effects*.

From the general *idea* of treaties that ended wars, explore other *examples* of such treaties.

Think about *examples* of what happened during the treaty signing, and from those examples come up with *ideas* about the tone of the event.

Looking at the facts of the event, *evaluate* how successful you think the treaty was.

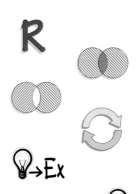

You don't have to use every mind action in every memory situation. Choose the ones that will help you most. The more information and ideas you can associate with the new item you're trying to remember, the more successful at remembering it you will be.

Make the Most of Last-Minute Studying

Career Connection
Cramming may be necessary at work as well as in school. Workers are frequently given new data minutes before a meeting or presentation, and they have to be able to absorb it on the spot.

Last-minute studying, or *cramming,* often results in information going into your head and popping right back out shortly after. Study conditions, however, aren't always ideal. Sometimes a busy week may leave you only a few hours to prepare for a big exam. If you end up with a tight schedule, as most every student does at some point during college, use these hints to make the most of your study time:

- Go through your flash cards, if you have them, one last time.
- Focus on crucial concepts. Don't go through your notes or textbook page by page.
- Create a last-minute study sheet. On a single sheet of paper, write down key facts, definitions, formulas, and so on, in list or think link form. Keep it short and simple.
- Arrive early. Study the sheet or your flash cards until you are asked to clear your desk.

After your exam, evaluate the effects cramming had on your learning. See if you can plan ahead and improve the situation next time.

Use Mnemonic Devices

Mnemonic devices

Memory techniques that involve associating new information with information you already know.

Mnemonic (pronounced neh MAHN ick) **devices** work by connecting information you are trying to learn with simpler information or information that is familiar. Instead of learning new facts by rote (repetitive practice), associations give you a hook on which to hang and retrieve these facts. Mnemonic devices make information familiar and meaningful through unusual, unforgettable mental associations and visual pictures.

Here's an example of the power of mnemonics. Suppose you want to remember the names of the first six presidents of the United States. The first letters of their last names—Washington, Adams, Jefferson, Madison, Monroe, and Adams—together are W A J M M A. To remember them, you might add an E after the J and create a short nonsense word: *wajemma.*

Visual images, idea chains, and acronyms are a few of the more widely used kinds of mnemonic devices. Apply them to your own memory challenges.

Create Visual Images and Associations

Teaching Tip
The strength of visual images explains why students are drawn to movies, television, and computers. These images stay with us far longer than words alone.

Visual images are often easier to remember than images that rely on words alone. The best mental images often involve bright colors, three dimensions, action scenes, inanimate objects with human traits, ridiculousness, and humor.

Turning information into mental pictures helps improve memory, especially for visual learners. To remember that the Spanish artist Picasso painted

The Three Women, you might imagine the women in a circle dancing to a Spanish song with a pig and a donkey (pig-asso). Don't reject outlandish images—as long as they help you.

Use an Idea Chain to Remember Items in a List

An *idea chain* is a memory strategy that involves forming exaggerated mental images of a large group of items. The first image is connected to the second image, which is connected to the third image, and so on. Imagine, for example, that you want to remember the seven mind actions that appear in the critical-thinking discussion in Chapter 5: recall, similarity, difference, cause and effect, example to idea, idea to example, and evaluation. You can use the visual icons to form an idea chain that goes like this:

> The letter R (recall) rolls down a hill and bumps into two similar intersecting circles (similarity) which start rolling and bump into two different intersecting circles (difference). Everything rolls past a sign with two circling arrows on it telling them to keep rolling (cause and effect), and then bump into an "EX" at the bottom of the hill which turns on a light bulb (example to idea). That light bulb shines on another "EX" (idea to example). The two "EX"s are sitting on either side of a set of scales (evaluation).

E-mail or talk in person with your professors and TAs. Ask them if you have actually remembered the main points. Often, they can help you define and crystallize your thoughts. The more you discuss these points with them, the stronger you will become at recognizing and remembering key points.

Create Acronyms

Another helpful association method involves the use of the **acronym.** In history, you can remember the "big-three" Allies during World War II—Britain, America, and Russia—with the acronym BAR. See Figure 8.3 for an acronym that often helps students remember the colors of the spectrum.

Acronym
A word formed from the first letters of a series of words; can be created to help you remember the series.

Spectrum Acronym   **FIGURE 8.3**

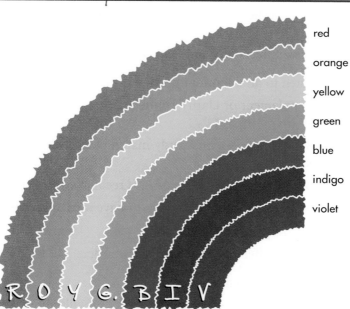

red
orange
yellow
green
blue
indigo
violet

R O Y G. B I V

You can also create an acronym from an entire sentence in which the first letter of each word in the sentence stands for the first letter of each memorized term. When science students want to remember the list of planets in order of their distance from the sun, they learn the sentence: My very elegant mother just served us nine pickles (Mercury, Venus, Earth, Mars, Jupiter, Saturn, Uranus, Neptune, and Pluto).

Improving your memory requires energy, time, and work. By using the specific memory techniques described in this chapter, you will be able to learn more in less time—and remember what you learn long after exams are over.

HOW CAN TAPE RECORDERS HELP YOU LISTEN, REMEMBER, AND STUDY?

The selective use of a tape recorder can reinforce listening and memory skills. It's important, though, not to let tape recording substitute for active participation. Not all students like to use tape recorders, but if you choose to do so, following are some guidelines and a discussion of potential effects.

Guidelines for Using Tape Recorders

- Ask the instructor whether he or she permits tape recorders in class. Some instructors don't mind, whereas others object.

- Use a small portable tape recorder. Sit near the front of the room for best results.

- Participate actively in class. Take notes just as you would if the tape recorder were not there.

- Make your own study tapes. Questions on tape are like audio flash cards. Try using your tape recorder to record study questions, leaving 10 to 15 seconds between questions to answer out loud. Recording the correct answer after the pause gives quick feedback. For example, part of a recording for a writing class might say, "The three elements of effective writing are . . . (10–15 seconds) . . . topic, audience, and purpose."

Potential Positive Effects of Using Tape Recorders

- You can listen to an important portion of the lecture over and over again.

- You can supplement or clarify confusing sections of the lecture or material that you missed.

- Tape recordings can provide study materials to listen to when driving or exercising.

- Tape recordings can help study groups reconcile conflicting notes.

- If you miss class, you might be able to have a friend record the lecture for you.

Potential Negative Effects of Using Tape Recorders

- You may tend to listen less in class.

- You may take fewer notes, figuring that you will rely on your tape.

- It may be time-consuming. When you attend a lecture in order to record it and then listen to the entire recording, you take twice as much time out of your schedule.

- If your tape recorder malfunctions or the recording is hard to hear, you may end up with very little study material, especially if your notes are sparse.

Think critically about using a tape recorder. If you choose to try it, let the tape recorder be an additional resource instead of a replacement for active listening and note taking.

All of the study skills you have read about up to this point—reading, studying, note taking, writing, listening, and memory—will help you to succeed in the final skill discussed in this chapter: test taking.

Springboard

Ask students if they agree or disagree with this statement: The most important factor in evaluating the use of tape recorders is time. Students may be too busy to listen to a recording after class, especially if they are working and raising a family.

WHAT TYPES OF PREPARATION CAN IMPROVE TEST PERFORMANCE?

Exams are preparation for life. For example, when you get a job or work on your budget, you'll have to put your knowledge to work. This is exactly what you do when you take a test. Exams are also part of life; you may encounter them when you apply for a driver's license, interview for a job, or qualify to practice in a particular career (e.g., a state nursing exam).

You can take steps to improve your test-taking skills. Your two goals are to know the material and to convey that knowledge to others.

Career Connection

Tests given in the workplace include pre-employment tests to determine knowledge in a specific work-related area and accreditation exams in such fields as insurance and accounting. These exams may be short answer or essay or a combination of both.

Identify Test Type and Material Covered

Before you begin studying, find out what you can about the test. Try to identify:

- the type of questions on the test (short-answer, essay, or a combination)
- what the test will cover (class lectures and/or readings)
- whether the test deals with material from the whole semester or a more limited topic

Your instructors may answer these questions for you. Even though they may not reveal specific test questions, they might let you know the question format or information covered. Beyond the information they give you, here are a few other strategies for predicting what may be on a test:

Use SQ3R (see Chapter 6) to identify important ideas and facts. Often, the questions you write and ask yourself when you read assigned materials may be part of the test. Textbook study questions are also good candidates.

Examine old tests, if instructors make them available in class or on reserve in the library. If you can't get copies of old tests, use clues from the class to predict test questions. After taking the first exam in the course, you will have a lot more information about what to expect in the future.

Talk to people who took the instructor's course before. Try to find out how difficult the tests are and whether they focus more on assigned readings or class notes. Ask about instructors' preferences—one instructor may emphasize the repetition of facts, another may prioritize applying knowledge, and so on—and study accordingly.

Use Specific Study Strategies

Before you do anything, choose the materials that contain the information you need to study. Go through your notes, texts, and any related readings or handouts. Set aside materials you don't need. Once you are sure you aren't studying anything you don't need to, implement the following strategies:

Make a study plan. Consider the materials you need to study, how many days or weeks until the test, and how much time you can study each day. For example, if the test is in three days and you have no other obligations during that time, you might set two 2-hour sessions each day. If you have two weeks before a test, classes during the day, and work three nights a week, you might spread study sessions over your nights off during those two weeks. A checklist like the one in Figure 8.4 will help you get organized and stay on track.

Prepare through critical thinking. Using techniques from Chapter 5, approach your preparation critically, working to understand rather than just repeat facts. As you study, try to connect ideas to examples, analyze causes and effects, examine assumptions, and look at issues from different perspectives. Critical thinking is especially important for essay tests. Prepare by writing responses to potential essay questions.

Review carefully. Use SQ3R (see pp. 166–170) and study techniques from Chapter 7 (pp. 196–197) to comprehensively review your materials.

Take a pretest. Use textbook study questions to create your own pretest. Choose questions that are likely to appear on the test and answer them under testlike conditions—in quiet, with no books or notes to help you, and with a clock to determine when time is up. If your course doesn't have an assigned text, develop questions from your notes and from assigned readings.

Prepare Physically

When taking a test, you often need to work efficiently under time pressure. If your body is tired or under stress, you will probably not think as clearly or perform as well as you usually do. If you can, get some sleep so that you can be rested and alert. If you tend to press the snooze button in your sleep, try setting two alarm clocks and placing them across the room from your bed.

Eating right is also important. Sugary snacks will bring up your energy, only to send you crashing back down much too soon. Also, too much caffeine can add to your tension and make it difficult to focus. Eating nothing will leave you drained, but too much food can make you sleepy. The best advice is to eat a light, well-balanced meal before a test. When time is short, grab a quick-energy snack such as a banana, some orange juice, or a granola bar.

Pretest Checklist

FIGURE 8.4

Course: _____ Teacher: _____

Date, time, and place of test: _____

Type of test (e.g., Is it a midterm or a minor quiz?): _____

What the instructor has told you about the test, including the types of test questions, the length of the test, and how much the test counts toward your final grade: _____

_____

_____

_____

Topics to be covered on the test in order of importance:

1. _____
2. _____
3. _____
4. _____
5. _____

Study schedule, including materials you plan to study (e.g., texts and class notes) and dates you plan to complete each:

Material	*Date of Completion*
1. _____	_____
2. _____	_____
3. _____	_____
4. _____	_____
5. _____	_____

Materials you are expected to bring to the test (e.g., your textbook, a sourcebook, a calculator): _____

_____

Special study arrangements (e.g., plan study group meetings, ask the instructor for special help, get outside tutoring): _____

_____

_____

Life-management issues (e.g., make child-care arrangements, rearrange work hours): _____

_____

_____

Source: Adapted from Ron Fry, *"Ace" Any Test,* 3rd ed. (Franklin Lakes, NJ: Career Press, 1996), 123–124.

Work Through Test Anxiety

Critical Thinking
How do students think test anxiety compares with the anxiety associated with giving a speech or a musical performance? In each case, the common denominator is "putting yourself on the line." Why do students think this is so difficult even when they are prepared?

A certain amount of stress can be a good thing. Your body is alert, and your energy motivates you to do your best. For some students, however, the time before and during an exam can be miserable for them. Many students have experienced some level of test anxiety at some time during their studies. A bad case of nerves that makes it hard to think or remember, test anxiety can also cause physical symptoms such as sweating, nausea, dizziness, headaches, and extreme fatigue. Work through test anxiety by dealing with its two primary aspects: preparation and attitude.

Preparation

Preparation is the basic defense against anxiety. The more confident you feel about your knowledge of the material, the more you'll feel able to perform on test day. In this way, you can consider all of the preparation and study information in this chapter as test anxiety assistance. Also, finding out what to expect on the exam will help you feel more in control. As mentioned earlier, seek out information about what material will be covered, the question format, the length of the exam, and the points assigned to each question.

Making and following a detailed study plan will help you build the kind of knowledge that can help you fight off anxiety. Divide the plan into a series of small tasks. As you finish each one, you will build your sense of accomplishment, confidence, and control.

Preparation is all about action. Instead of sitting and worrying about the test, put your energy toward concrete, active steps that will help you succeed.

Attitude

Although good preparation will help build your confidence, maintaining a positive *attitude* toward testing is as important as studying. Here are some key ways to maintain an attitude that will help you:

See the test as an opportunity to learn. Sometimes students see a test as an opportunity to fail. Turn this around by focusing on learning. See that a test is an opportunity to show what you have learned, as well as to learn something new about the material and about test taking itself.

See the test as a signpost. It's easy to see a test as a contest to be won or lost. If you pass, or "win" the contest, you might feel no need to retain what you've learned. If you fail, or "lose" the contest, you might feel no need to try again. However, if you see the test as a signpost along the way to a greater goal, you may be more likely to try your best, learn from the experience, and move on. A test is only a small part of your education, and your grade does not reflect your ability to succeed in life.

Give your instructor a positive role. Your instructors don't want to make you miserable. They test you to give you an opportunity to grow and to demonstrate what you have accomplished. They test you so that, in rising to this challenge, you will become better prepared for challenges outside of school.

Seek study partners who challenge you. Your anxiety may get worse if you study with someone who feels just as anxious and unprepared as you do. Find someone who can inspire you to do your best.

Set yourself up for success. Try not to expect failure before you even start. Expect progress of yourself. Take responsibility for creating a setting for success through your preparation and attitude. Know that you are ultimately responsible for the outcome.

Practice relaxation. When you feel test anxiety coming on, take some deep breaths, close your eyes, and visualize positive mental images related to the test, such as getting a good grade and finishing confidently, with time to spare. Do whatever you have to do to ease muscle tension—stretch your neck, tighten and then release your muscles, or take a trip to the rest room to do a couple of forward bends.

Two other important aspects of test anxiety are math anxiety and the specific concerns of the returning adult student.

Coping with Math Anxiety

For many students a special anxiety is associated with taking a math test. As Sheila Tobias, author of *Overcoming Math Anxiety*, explains, math anxiety is linked to the feeling that math is impossible.

> The first thing people remember about failing at math is that it felt like sudden death. Whether it happened while learning word problems in sixth grade, coping with equations in high school, or first confronting calculus and statistics in college, failure was instant and frightening. An idea or a new operation was not just difficult, it was impossible! And instead of asking questions or taking the lesson slowly, assuming that in a month or so they would be able to digest it, people remember the feeling, as certain as it was sudden, that they would never go any further in mathematics.[4]

Students who believe they are no good at math probably won't do well on math tests even if they study. If you are one of these students, here are some steps you can take to begin thinking about math—and math tests—in a different way.

Approach math through critical thinking. Mathematical, or **quantitative,** thinking is at heart a problem-solving discipline. Your critical-thinking skills will help you analyze math problems. For example, the following four-step process in solving word problems reflects the problem-solving plan from Chapter 5.[5]

Quantitative

Of, relating to, or involving the measurement of amount or number.

1. **Understand the individual elements of the problem.** Read the problem carefully. Note what it is asking, what information you have, and what information is missing. Draw a picture, if possible. Translate words into mathematical language (numbers, symbols, formulas).

2. **Name and explore potential solution paths.** Think about similar problems that you understand and how those were solved. Consider whether this problem is an example of a mathematical idea that you know. In your head, try out different ways to solve the problem to see which may work best.

3. **Carry out your plan.** Choose a solution path and solve the problem. Check each of your steps.

4. **Review your result.** Check your answer, if possible. Make sure you've answered the question the problem is asking. Does your result seem logical? Are there other ways to do the problem?

See how math is similar to science. Perhaps you have a higher comfort level in science courses than in math. Science and math actually have many similarities. Science involves a problem-solving process similar to math:

1. **Observation.** Examples (facts) observed lead to questions.

2. **Hypothesis.** From the examples, the observer comes up with an idea (hypothesis) that seems to fit the examples.

3. **Experiment.** The observer attempts, through experimentation, to find examples that prove or disprove the hypothesis. Results are gathered and examined.

4. **Conclusion.** From the evidence gathered through experimentation, the observer accepts or rejects the hypothesis.

See how quantitative thinking can contribute to life success. Working with numbers helps to develop general thinking skills. The calculations and problem solving involved in math help you develop precision, a focus for detail, and a sense of order. Math can also help you address day-to-day issues. For example:

■ Arithmetic (addition, subtraction, etc.) helps you to calculate tips and balance your checkbook.

■ Algebra (determining an unknown value using known values) helps you to figure your GPA or your interest on a loan.

■ Geometry (determining areas and volumes) helps you measure the amount of wallpaper you need in a room or determine how closely you can pass a car.

Think of math as a tool that will help you land a good job. In fields such as engineering and banking, the ability to solve numerical problems is at the heart of the work. In real estate, retail sales, medicine, and publishing, you may use math for such tasks as writing budgets and figuring mortgage rates.

Take basic steps toward success. In math, as with any other subject, the most important factors are preparation, class participation, and reviewing. Read materials before you cover them in class, interacting with them critically by taking notes, drawing sketches, and working through problems on a pad. Ask questions in class. Review notes as soon as possible, comparing your book to your notes. When you do homework, complete as many problems as you can; do more if you still don't feel certain about the concepts. If you get stuck on a problem, go on to another one—or take a break to clear your head.

Don't believe that women can't do math. Tobias says that when male students fail a math quiz, they think they didn't work hard enough; but when female students fail, they are three times more likely to feel that they don't have what it takes.[6] Whether you are a man or a woman, work to overcome this stereotype.

"A little knowledge that acts is worth infinitely more than much knowledge that is idle."

Kahlil Gibran

Career Connection

More jobs are requiring quantitative thinking, even those that, on their face, have little to do with math. A book editor, for example, has to create a budget to produce and market books.

Springboard

Have students discuss the discomfort many women feel with math. Do they think that math anxiety among women is more or less prevalent than it used to be? Ask students to research whether women in other cultures also have this problem.

How can I combat test anxiety?

Peter Changsak, Sheldon-Jackson College, Sitka, Alaska

I am a Yu'pik Eskimo from a village on the Yukon River. Before attending college, I worked for six years as a clerk at the Native Corporation, a gas station and general store. When the manager passed away, the business offered to make me a manager. Even though I knew how to do much of the work, I didn't feel I was ready, so I decided to go to school for more training.

College life is different from what I am accustomed to. The hardest part has been taking tests. I study hard for the exams, but then when I get in class and the test begins, I forget everything. My mind goes blank.

Also, in class, I have a hard time listening. I might be in my math class, but I'm thinking

about the 10-page paper that is due in my social studies class. When I read, I understand what I'm reading, but as soon as I close the book, I can't remember what I just read. My favorite class is biology lab—probably because we can walk around.

I love mechanics and construction. When I worked at the Native Corporation, we built a new building. I felt like I was a success at work, but I don't feel successful as a student. Sometimes I feel like quitting school altogether, but I also think it can help me have more choices if I stick with it. I'm learning how to be a serious student, but it isn't easy. Can you give suggestions about how I can get over my test anxiety?

Tim Nordberg, Executive Director, Chicago Youth Ministries

In many ways my experience in college was similar to yours. I was raised in a car industry town. I was the first person in my family

to go to college, which was intimidating. My first year was hard—I discovered that I read at an 8th grade level. I hated studying and taking tests. During the spring, the college began a building project. Local Amish people came and laid blocks. I wanted to be outside doing manual work, too. I constantly felt a battle going on within me.

Two factors gave me the endurance to go on: One was seeing my old high school buddies, who seemed stuck in the past, and the second factor was my desire to fulfill my goals. I decided that if I fail, it won't be because I haven't given it my best; I'm not going to fail because I refuse to try.

That summer I took a reading class. School was still not easy that fall, but I was not studying as much out of fear or duty; rather, I was studying to do my best. Classes began to take on a different meaning. I was beginning to learn because I enjoyed the challenge. I took tests to see how well I knew the subject. Today, I still love sports and carpentry, but I also love to learn.

Don't fear failure. Just try to do your best. Concentrate on the task at hand. Study to learn, not to take a test. Good test scores will reflect your passion to know what you have studied rather than how good you are at test taking. You are being challenged to survive in new ways, and you are not alone. Ask the student services office to help you through this adjustment process. Ask your advisor if they offer a class that teaches study and test-taking tips.

My advice to you is try to remember why you came to college in the first place—to better equip yourself. As you prepare for classes and tests, spend time reminding yourself what this experience will do for you someday when it is all behind you. Growing in any area of life isn't always fun and may not seem within reach. But if we give up, we may miss out on a part of us that, in time, would have brought greater rewards.

Use the people and resources around you. Get to know your math instructor so you're comfortable asking for help. Join a math study group. Have a pep meeting right before a big test. Look for math anxiety workshops. Seek a tutor who can help you with your skills and build your confidence.

Test Anxiety and the Returning Student

If you're returning to school after 5, 10, or even 20 years, you may wonder if you can compete with younger students or if your mind is still able to learn new material. To counteract these feelings of inadequacy, focus on how your life experiences have given you useful skills. For example, managing work and a family requires strong time-management, planning, and communication skills, which can help you plan your study time, juggle school responsibilities, and interact with students and instructors.

In addition, life experiences give you examples through which you can understand ideas in your courses. For example, your relationships may help you understand psychology concepts; managing your finances may help you understand economics or accounting practices; and work experience may give you a context for what you learn in a business management course. If you let yourself feel positive about your knowledge and skills, you may improve your ability to achieve your goals.

When you have prepared using the strategies that work for you, you are ready to take your exam. Focus on methods that can help you succeed when the test begins.

WHAT STRATEGIES CAN HELP YOU SUCCEED ON TESTS?

Even though every test is different, there are general strategies that will help you handle almost all tests, including short-answer and essay exams.

Write Down Key Facts

Before you even look at the test, write down any key information—including formulas, rules, and definitions—that you studied recently or even just before you entered the test room. Use the back of the question sheet or a piece of scrap paper for your notes (be sure it is clear to your instructor that this scrap paper didn't come into the test room already filled in). Recording this information right at the start will make forgetting less likely.

Begin with an Overview of the Exam

Take a few minutes at the start of the test to examine the kinds of questions you'll be answering, what kind of thinking they require, the number of questions in each section, and their point values. Use this information to schedule your time. For example, if a two-hour test is divided into two sections of equal point value—an essay section with 4 questions and a short-answer section with 60 questions—you can spend an hour on the essays and an hour on the short-answer section.

As you make your calculations, think about the level of difficulty of each section. If you think you can handle the short-answer questions in less than an hour and that you'll need more time for the essays, rebudget your time that way.

Know the Ground Rules

A few basic rules apply to any test. Following them will give you an advantage.

Read test directions. Although a test of 100 true-or-false questions and 1 essay question may look straightforward, the directions may tell you to answer only 80 or that the essay is an optional bonus question. Some questions or sections may be weighted more heavily than others. Try circling or underlining key words and numbers that remind you of the directions.

Begin with the parts or questions that seem easiest to you. Starting with what you know best can boost your confidence and help you save time to spend on the harder parts.

Watch the clock. Keep track of how much time is left and how you are progressing. You may want to plan your time on a piece of scrap paper, especially if you have one or more essays to write. Wear a watch or bring a small clock with you to the test room. Also, take your time. Rushing is almost always a mistake, even if you feel you've done well. Stay until the end so that you can refine and check your work.

Master the art of intelligent guessing. When you are unsure of an answer, you can leave it blank or you can guess. In most cases, guessing will help you. First eliminate all the answers you know—or believe—are wrong. Try to narrow your choices to two possible answers; then choose the one that makes more sense to you. When you recheck your work, decide if you would make the same guesses again, making sure there isn't a qualifier or fact that you hadn't noticed before.

Use Critical Thinking to Avoid Errors

Critical thinking can help you work through each question thoroughly and avoid errors. Use these critical-thinking strategies during a test:

Recall facts, procedures, rules, and formulas. Base your answers on the information you recall. Make sure you recall it accurately.

Think about similarities. If you don't know how to attack a question or problem, consider any similar questions or problems that you have worked on in class or while studying.

Notice differences. Especially with objective questions, items that seem different from the material you have studied may indicate answers you can eliminate.

Think through causes and effects. For a numerical problem, think about how you plan to solve it and see if the answer—the effect of your plan—makes sense. For an essay question that asks you to analyze a condition or situation, consider both what caused it and what effects it has.

Find the best idea to match the example or examples given. For a numerical problem, decide what formula (idea) best applies to the example or examples (the data of the problem). For an essay question, decide what idea applies to, or links, the examples given.

Support ideas with examples. When you put forth an idea in an answer to an essay question, be sure to back up your idea with an adequate number of examples that fit.

Evaluate each test question. In your initial approach to any question, decide what kinds of thinking will best help you solve it. For example, essay questions frequently require cause-and-effect and idea-to-example thinking, and objective questions often benefit from thinking about similarities and differences.

These general strategies also can help you address specific types of test questions.

Objective questions
Short-answer questions that test your ability to recall, compare, and contrast information and to choose the right answer from a limited number of choices.

Subjective questions
Questions that require you to express your answer in terms of your own personal knowledge and perspective.

Master Different Types of Test Questions

Using different approaches, all test questions try to discover how much you know about a subject. Objective questions, such as multiple-choice or true-or-false, test your ability to recall, compare, and contrast information and to choose the right answer from among several choices. Subjective questions, usually essay questions, demand the same information recall, but they require you to use the mind actions to formulate a response and then to organize, draft, and refine it in writing. The following guidelines will help you choose the best answers to both types of questions.

Multiple-Choice Questions

Multiple-choice questions are the most popular type on standardized tests. The following strategies can help you answer them:

Read the directions carefully. While most test items ask for a single correct answer, some give you the option of marking several choices that are correct.

First, read each question thoroughly. Then, look at the choices and try to answer the question.

Underline key words and phrases in the question. If the question is complicated, try to break it down into small sections that are easy to understand.

Be a Team
Ask students if they prefer one test question type over another and to share their thoughts with a partner. For example, while one student likes essay questions (a blank slate), another may prefer multiple-choice questions, which leave little room for interpretation.

Pay special attention to qualifiers such as *only*, *except*, and so on. For example, negative words in a question can confuse your understanding of what the question asks ("Which of the following is *not* . . .").

If you don't know the answer, eliminate those answers that you know or suspect are wrong. Your goal is to narrow down your choices. Ask yourself these questions:

- Is the choice accurate in its own terms? If there is an error in the choice—for example, a term that is incorrectly defined—the answer is wrong.

- Is the choice relevant? An answer may be accurate, but it may not relate to the essence of the question.

- Are there any qualifiers, such as *always, never, all, none,* or *every?* Qualifiers make it easy to find an exception that makes a choice incorrect. For example, the statement that "children *always* begin talking before the age of two" can be eliminated as an answer to the question "When do children generally start to talk?" because some children start later. Choices containing conservative qualifiers (*often, most,* or *rarely*) are often correct.

- Do the choices give clues? Does a puzzling word remind you of a word you know? If you don't know a word, does any part of the word (prefix, suffix, or root) seem familiar to you?

A final exam at a Connecticut state college.

Look for patterns that may lead to the right answer; then use intelligent guessing. Particular patterns in multiple-choice questions, such as the following, may help you.

- Consider the possibility that a choice that is more *general* than the others is the right answer.

- Look for a choice that has a *middle value in a range* (the range can be from small to large or from old to recent). This choice may be the right answer.

- Look for two choices with *similar meanings.* One of these answers is probably correct.

Here are some examples of the kinds of multiple-choice questions you might encounter in an Introduction to Psychology course[7] (the correct answer follows each question):

1. Which of the following has not been shown to be a probable cause of or influence in the development of alcoholism in our society?

   A. intelligence   C. personality

   B. culture   D. genetic vulnerability   *(The correct answer is A)*

2. Geraldine is a heavy coffee drinker who has become addicted to caffeine. If she completely ceases her intake of caffeine over the next few days, she is likely to experience each of the following EXCEPT _____.

   A. depression   C. insomnia

   B. lethargy   D. headaches   *(The correct answer is C)*

Make sure you read every word of every answer. Instructors have been known to include answers that are right except for a single word.

When questions are keyed to a long reading passage, read the questions first. This will help you to focus your reading efforts on the information you need to answer the questions.

True-or-False Questions

True-or-false questions test your knowledge of facts and concepts. Read them carefully to evaluate what they truly say. If you're stumped, guess (unless you're penalized for wrong answers).

Look for qualifiers in true-or-false questions, such as *all, only, always, generally, usually,* and *sometimes,* that can turn a statement that would otherwise be true into one that is false or vice versa. For example: "The grammar rule 'I before E except after C' is always true" is false, whereas "The grammar rule 'I before E except after C' is usually true" is true. The qualifier makes the difference.

Here are some examples of true-or-false questions you might encounter in an Introduction to Psychology course.

Are the following questions true or false?

1. Alcohol use is always related to increases in hostility, aggression, violence, and abusive behavior. *(False)*
2. Marijuana is harmless. *(False)*
3. Simply expecting a drug to produce an effect is often enough to produce the effect. *(True)*

Essay Questions

Teaching Tolerance
Students with illegible handwriting may do poorly on essay questions because their responses cannot be read. These students may have a disability called dysgraphia. Students who are formally diagnosed with this problem may be given permission to respond to essay questions on computer.

An essay question allows you to express your knowledge and views on a topic in a much more extensive manner than any short answer can provide. With the freedom to express your views, though, comes the challenge to both exhibit knowledge and show you have command of how to organize and express that knowledge clearly.

1. **Start by reading the essay questions.** Decide which to tackle (if there's a choice). Then focus on what each question is asking and the mind actions you will need to use. Read directions carefully—some essay questions may contain more than one part.

2. **Watch for action verbs.** Certain verbs can help you figure out how to think. Figure 8.5 explains some words commonly used in essay questions. Underline these words as you read the question, clarify what they mean, and use them to guide your writing.

3. **Budget your time and begin to plan.** Create an informal outline or think link to map your ideas, indicating examples you plan to cite in support. Avoid spending too much time on introductions or flowery language.

4. **Write your essay.** Start with an idea that states your topic and premise. In the first paragraph, introduce key points (subideas, causes, effects, or even examples). Use simple, clear language. Carefully establish your ideas and support them with examples, and look back at your outline or think link to make sure you are covering everything. Wrap it up with a conclusion that is short and to the point. Try to write legibly; if your instructor can't read your ideas, it doesn't matter how good they are.

5. **Reread and revise your essay.** Look for ideas you left out, ideas you didn't support with enough examples, and sentences that might confuse the reader. Check for mistakes in grammar, spelling, punctuation, and usage. No matter what you are writing about, having a command of these factors will make your work more complete and impressive.

Common Action Verbs on Essay Tests FIGURE 8.5

Analyze—Break into parts and discuss each part separately.

Compare—Explain similarities and differences.

Contrast—Distinguish between items being compared by focusing on differences.

Criticize—Evaluate the positive and negative effects of what is being discussed.

Define—State the essential quality or meaning. Give the common idea.

Describe—Visualize and give information that paints a complete picture.

Discuss—Examine in a complete and detailed way, usually by connecting ideas to examples.

Enumerate/List/Identify—Recall and specify items in the form of a list.

Evaluate—Give your opinion about the value or worth of something, usually by weighing positive and negative effects, and justify your conclusion.

Explain—Make the meaning of something clear, often by making analogies or giving examples.

Illustrate—Supply examples.

Interpret—Explain your personal view of facts and ideas and how they relate to one another.

Outline—Organize and present the main examples of an idea or subideas.

Prove—Use evidence and argument to show that something is true, usually by showing cause and effect or giving examples that fit the idea to be proven.

Review—Provide an overview of ideas and establish their merits and features.

State—Explain clearly, simply, and concisely, being sure that each word gives the image you want.

Summarize—Give the important ideas in brief.

Trace—Present a history of the way something developed, often by showing cause and effect.

Springboard

Why are critical thinking techniques important for students as they attempt to understand the differences and similarities among these action verbs?

Here are some examples of essay questions you might encounter in an Introduction to Psychology course. In each case, notice the action verbs from Figure 8.5.

1. Summarize the theories and research on the causes and effects of daydreaming. Discuss the possible uses for daydreaming in a healthy individual.
2. Describe the physical and psychological effects of alcohol and the problems associated with its use.
3. Explain what sleep terrors are, what appears to cause them, and who is most likely to suffer from them.

Use Specific Techniques for Math Problems

Real World Link
Sophisticated calculators and computer applications increasingly are being used in math classrooms and on tests. Students should be completely comfortable with these tools well before test day.

Mathematical test problems, whether on a math or science test, present a special challenge to some students. These strategies may help you overcome any difficulties you might have.

Read through the exam. When you first get an exam, skim through it. Make notes on how you might solve a problem if something occurs to you immediately.

Analyze problems carefully. Categorize problems according to type. Take all the "givens" into account, and write down any formulas, theorems, or definitions that apply before you begin your calculations. Focus on what you want to find or prove, and take your time—precision demands concentration. If some problems seem easier than others, do them first in order to boost your confidence.

Break the calculation into the smallest possible pieces. Go step-by-step and don't move on to the next step until you are clear about what you've done so far.

Recall how you solved similar problems. Past experience can give you valuable clues to how a particular problem should be handled.

Draw a picture to help you see the problem. This can be a diagram, a chart, a probability tree, a geometric figure, or any other visual image that relates to the problem at hand.

Be neat. When it comes to numbers, mistaken identity can mean the difference between a right and a wrong answer. A 4 that looks like a 9 or a 1 that looks like a 7 can make trouble.

Use the opposite operation to check your work. When you come up with an answer, work backward to see if you are right. Use subtraction to check your addition; use division to check your multiplication; and so on. Try to check every problem before you hand in your test.

Look back at the questions to be sure you did everything that was asked. Did you answer every part of the question? Did you show all the required work? Be as complete as you possibly can.

HOW CAN YOU LEARN FROM TEST MISTAKES?

The purpose of a test is to see how much you know, not merely to achieve a grade. Making mistakes, or even failing a test, is human. Rather than ignoring mistakes, examine them and learn from them just as you learn from mistakes on the job and in your relationships. Working through your mistakes will help you avoid repeating them again on another test—or outside of school life.

Try to identify patterns in your mistakes by looking for the following:

- *Careless errors.* In your rush to complete the exam, did you misread the question or directions, blacken the wrong box, skip a question, or use illegible handwriting?

- *Conceptual or factual errors.* Did you misunderstand a concept or never learn it in the first place? Did you fail to master certain facts? Did you skip part of the assigned text or miss important classes in which ideas were covered?

If you have time, rework the questions you got wrong. Based on the feedback from your instructor, try rewriting an essay, recalculating a math problem, or reanswering the questions that follow a reading selection. If you see patterns of careless errors, plan to double-check your work next time. If you pick up conceptual and factual errors, rededicate yourself to better preparation.

When you fail a test, don't throw it away. First, know that a lot of students have been in your shoes and that you have room to grow and improve. Then recommit to the process by seeking a true understanding of why you failed. You may want to ask for an explanation from your instructor. Finally, develop a plan to really learn the material if you didn't understand it in the first place.

In Sanskrit, the classical written language of India and other Hindu countries, the characters above read *sem ma yeng chik*, meaning, "do not be distracted." This advice can refer to focus for a task or job at hand, the concentration required to critically think and talk through a problem, the mental discipline of meditation, or many other situations.

Think of this concept as you strive to improve your listening and memory techniques. Focus on the task, the person, or the idea at hand. Try not to be distracted by other thoughts, other people's notions of what you should be doing, or any negative messages. Be present in the moment to truly hear and remember what is happening around you. Do not be distracted.

Name _____ Date _____

BUILDING SKILLS FOR COLLEGE, CAREER, AND LIFE SUCCESS

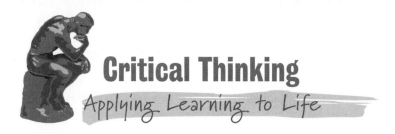

Critical Thinking
Applying Learning to Life

Optimum Listening Conditions

■ Think of a recent situation (this semester or last semester) in which you have been able to understand and retain most of what you heard in the classroom.
Describe the environment (course title, type of classroom setting, etc.):

_____

_____

Describe the instructor's style (lecture, group discussion, Q & A, etc.):

_____

_____

Describe your level of preparation for the class:

_____

_____

Describe your attitude toward the course:

_____

_____

Describe any barriers to listening that you had to overcome in this situation:

_____

_____

■ Now describe a classroom situation you recently experienced where you feel you didn't retain information well.

Describe the environment (course title, type of classroom setting, etc.):

_____

_____

Describe the instructor's style (lecture, group discussion, Q & A, etc.):

Describe your level of preparation for the class:

Describe your attitude toward the course:

Describe any barriers to listening that were present in this situation:

- Examine the two situations. Based on your descriptions, name three conditions that seem crucial for you to listen effectively and retain information.

    1.
    2.
    3.

    Describe one way in which you could have improved your listening and retention in the more difficult situation.

Create a Mnemonic Device

Look back at the memory principles examined in this chapter. Using what you learned about mnemonic devices, create a mnemonic that allows you to remember these memory principles quickly. You can create a mental picture or an acronym. If you are using a mental picture, describe it here and attach a drawing if you like; if you are using an acronym, write it and then indicate what each letter stands for.

Test Analysis

When you get back your next test, take a detailed look at your performance.

1. Write what you think of your test performance and grade. Were you pleased or disappointed? If you made errors, were they careless or due to not knowing facts and concepts?

2. Next, list the test preparation activities that helped you do well on the exam and the activities you wish you had done—and intend to do—for the next exam.

   Actions I took that had positive effects:

   Actions I intend to take next time:

3. Finally, list the activities you don't intend to repeat when studying for the next test.

Learning from Your Mistakes

For this exercise, use an exam on which you made one or more mistakes.

Why do you think you answered the question(s) incorrectly?

Did you try to guess the correct answer? If so, why do you think you made the wrong choice?

Did you feel rushed? If you had had more time, do you think you would have gotten the right answer(s)? What could you have done to budget your time more effectively?

_____

_____

_____

_____

If an essay question was a problem, what do you think went wrong? What will you do differently the next time you face an essay question on a test?

_____

_____

_____

Teamwork
Combining Forces

Boost Your Memory Gather as a class if your class is under 15 people, or divide into two groups if it is larger. Each person in your group should contribute one item to lay on a table (make sure you have as few repeats as possible). When all the items are laid out, allow one minute for everyone to look at them (use a watch with a second hand to time yourselves). Then cover the items, and allow five minutes for each person to individually attempt to list all of the items. Compare lists to see how you did.

   If you have time, go through the same process again, but have each group member choose a specific memory technique to try. For example, two people could use reciting and rehearsing; three could try to make an acronym; two people could try to link images in an idea chain; and the other three could try visual associations. After you evaluate your success, talk about the different techniques and what worked well (or not so well) for whom.

Writing
Discovery Through Journaling

To record your thoughts, use a separate journal or the lined page at the end of the chapter.

Tests Do you experience test anxiety? Describe how tests generally make you feel (you might include an example of a specific test situation and what happened). Identify your specific test-taking fears, and write out your plan to overcome fears and self-defeating behaviors.

Career Portfolio
Charting Your Progress

Listening, Memory, and Testing on the Job This portfolio exercise has two parts. If for any reason no potential career of yours involves tests, complete Part One only.

Part One. Any career that you pursue will make use of your listening and memory skills. Whereas memorizing facts for an anatomy test might not seem particularly crucial, for example, knowing where a particular artery is can make the difference in a life-or-death situation for a doctor.

On a separate sheet of paper, make a list of all of the various listening and memory skills that you can recall from this chapter. Try to write down 12 or more different skills. Then show your list to three different people who are currently in the workforce either part-time or full-time. Ask them to indicate for you the five skills from your list that they consider to be the most important for workplace success.

When you have completed your three interviews, tally the votes and write your three top skills on another sheet of paper (if you have any tie votes, make the choice yourself of which skill you feel is most important). For each skill, write a brief story about a time when this skill was important to you at work or, if you have not yet been employed, in the classroom.

Part Two. Depending on what careers you are considering, you may encounter one or more tests—tests for entry into the field (such as the medical boards), tests on particular equipment (such as a proficiency test on Microsoft Word), or tests that are necessary to move you to the next level of employment (such as a technical certification test). Choose one career you are thinking about, and investigate what tests are involved in entering this particular field. Be sure to look for tests in any of the areas described above. On a separate piece of paper, write down everything you find out about each test involved, for example,

Performance counts!

Your ability to be focused on the job—to remember your priorities and zero in on what's important—is the same skill you're learning right now in college. Ace this now and you'll be one step ahead once you graduate, plus you'll be a much stronger student!

- what it tests you on
- when, in the course of pursuing this career, you would need to take the test
- what preparation is necessary for the test (including course work)
- whether the test will need to be retaken at any time (e.g., airline pilots usually need to be recertified every few years)

Once you have recorded your information, see if there is any possibility of looking at, or even taking, any of the tests you will face if you pursue this particular career. For example, if you will need to be tested on a computer program, your college's career center or computer center may have the test available. As a practice, look at and/or take any test that you can track down.

Journal Entry

Name _____ Date _____

Web Activity
Defining Yourself and Your Goals

Use the Prentice Hall SuperSite to learn more about effective study skills. Go to www.prenhall.com/success and click on the Study Skills section. There is a lot of useful information, so be sure to read carefully.

1. Take the opinion poll. How do your opinions compare to those of other students that have completed the poll?

2. Read the note-taking section on Outline Olivia. How do you take notes? Do you adopt your notes for individual classes, or do you rely on one note-taking style? How does your note-taking style work for you? Are you getting the best grades you possibly can? If not, what can you do to improve your note-taking style? Use the tips in the note-taking article to help you to brainstorm new note-taking strategies.

3. Use each of the steps outlined in the reading link to read two chapters for one of your classes. How do these compare to your usual method for reading? Do these steps help you to retain the information better than if you had used your usual method? How can these steps help you prepare for your next exam?

4. Use your school's library Web site to research one of the topics in Chapters 5–7. Write a one-page report on one of the topics and e-mail it to your instructor. Use the tips in the writing section to help you to write your paper.

5. Read through the questions and answers in the Learning Doctor section; perhaps other students have some of the same questions you do. Submit a question—one that isn't already presented—to the Learning Doctor.

Keys To Success will prepare you to learn while you are in school—and to continue to learn throughout your career. In our competitive, global economy, learning can never stop—even after your formal education is over. In fact, the most successful companies are dynamic learning environments where employees dedicate themselves to mastering the latest knowledge, to continually improving their skills, and to recognizing and relying on the strengths of co-workers who are team members.

As you will see in the following Reading Room selection, Peter M. Senge, founder and director of the Center for Organizational Learning at MIT's Sloan School of Management, contends that organizations are capable of learning if they encourage the creativity and teamwork of their human resources—their employees. Senge points to five separate elements that, together, can build a learning organization that is more than the sum of its parts.

On a cold, clear morning in December 1903, at Kitty Hawk, North Carolina, the fragile aircraft of Wilbur and Orville Wright proved that powered flight was possible. Thus was the airplane invented; but it would take more than thirty years before commercial aviation could serve the general public.

Engineers say that a new idea has been "invented" when it is proven to work in the laboratory. The idea becomes an "innovation" only when it can be replicated reliably on a meaningful scale at practical costs. The Wright Brothers proved that powered flight was possible, but the McDonnell Douglas DC-3 was the first plane that supported itself economically as well as aerodynamically. During those intervening thirty years, myriad experiments with commercial flight had failed. Like early experiments with learning organizations, the early planes were not reliable and cost effective on an appropriate scale.

The DC-3, for the first time, brought together five critical component technologies that formed a successful ensemble. They were the variable-pitch propeller, retractable landing gear, a type of light-weight molded body construction called "monocoque," radial air-cooled engine, and wing flaps. To succeed, the DC-3 needed all five; four were not enough.

Today, I believe, five new "component technologies" are gradually converging to innovate learning organizations. Though developed separately, each will, I believe, prove critical to the others' success, just as occurs with any ensemble. Each provides a vital dimension in building organizations that can truly "learn," that can continually enhance their capacity to realize their highest aspirations.

Systems Thinking. A cloud masses, the sky darkens, leaves twist upward, and we know that it will rain. We also know that after the storm, the runoff will feed into groundwater miles away, and the sky will grow clear by tomorrow. All these events are distant in time and space, and yet they are all connected within the same pattern. Each has an influence on the rest, an influence that is usually hidden from view. You can only understand the system of a rainstorm by contemplating the whole, not any individual part of the pattern.

Business and other human endeavors are also systems. They, too, are bound by invisible fabrics of interrelated actions, which often take years to fully play out their effects on each other. Since we are part of that lacework ourselves, it's doubly hard to see the whole pattern of change. Instead, we tend to focus on snapshots of isolated parts of the system, and wonder why our deepest problems never seem to get solved. Systems thinking is a conceptual framework, a body of knowledge and tools that has been developed over the past fifty years, to make the full patterns clearer, and to help us see how to change them effectively.

Personal Mastery. Personal mastery is the discipline of continually clarifying and deepening our personal vision, of focusing our energies, of developing patience, and of seeing reality objectively. As such, it is an essential cornerstone of the learning organization—the learning organization's spiritual foundation. An organization's commitment to and capacity for learning can be no greater than that of its members.

Mental Models. "Mental models" are deeply ingrained assumptions, generalizations, or even pictures or images that influence how we understand the world and how we take action. Very often, we are not consciously aware of our mental models or the effects they have on our behavior. For example, we may notice that a co-worker dresses elegantly, and say to ourselves, "She's a country club person." About someone who dresses shabbily, we may feel, "He doesn't care about what others think."

The discipline of working with mental models starts with turning the mirror inward; learning to unearth our internal pictures of the world, to bring them to the surface and hold them rigorously to scrutiny. It also includes the ability to carry on "learningful" conversations that balance inquiry and advocacy, where people expose their own thinking effectively and make that thinking open to the influence of others.

Building Shared Vision. If any one idea about leadership has inspired organizations for thousands of years, it's the capacity to hold a shared picture of the future we seek to create. When there is a genuine vision, people excel and learn, not because they are told to, but because they want to.

The practice of shared vision involves the skills of unearthing shared "pictures of the future" that foster genuine commitment and enrollment rather than compliance. In mastering this discipline, leaders learn the counterproductiveness of trying to dictate a vision, no matter how heartfelt.

Team Learning. The discipline of team learning starts with "dialogue," the capacity of members of a team to suspend assumptions and enter into a genuine "thinking together." To the Greeks, *dia-logos* meant a free flowing of meaning through a group, allowing the group to discover insights not attainable individually.

There are striking examples where the intelligence of the team exceeds the intelligence of the individuals in the team, and where teams develop extraordinary capacities for coordinated action. When teams are truly learning, not only are they producing extraordinary results but the individual members are growing more rapidly than could have occurred otherwise.

At the heart of a learning organization is a shift of mind—from seeing ourselves as separate from the world to connected to the world, from seeing problems as caused by someone or something "out there" to seeing how our own actions create the problems we experience. A learning organization is a place where people are continually discovering how they create their reality. And how they can change it. As Archimedes has said, "Give me a lever long enough and single-handed I can move the world."

Source: From *The Fifth Discipline* by Peter M. Senge. Copyright © 1990 by Peter M. Senge. Used by permission of Doubleday, a division of Random House Inc.

Think. Discuss. Talk amongst yourselves.

You'll need good writing skills to do well in college and to succeed in your career. As you will see in the following Reading Room selection, even if you are a technology wizard, poor writing may still hold you back in business because it hampers clear communication with coworkers and customers. This selection will help you see the very real connection between your instructors' emphasis on effective writing and your ability to do well in your career.

No matter how good your technical skills are, you probably won't move up the information technology career ladder unless your writing measures up. "One of the most surprising features of the information revolution is that the momentum has turned back to the written word," says Hoyt Hudson, vice president of [information systems] at InterAccess, an Internet service provider in Chicago. "Someone who can come up with precise communication has a real advantage in today's environment."

Whether you are pitching a business case or justifying a budget, the quality of your writing can determine success or failure. Writing ability is especially important in customer communication. Business proposals, status reports, customer documentation, technical support, or even e-mail replies all depend on clear, written communication.

Alan Cunningham, a manager at Computer Sciences Corp. who is working on a project at NASA's Marshall Space Flight Center, in Huntsville, Ala., says many failed partnerships between business personnel and their information technology counterparts can be directly attributed to lack of communication between the parties.

"Without good communication skills, information technology professionals are little good to business people because there is no common platform," Cunningham says. "Just like all information technology professionals should have to take some elementary finance and accounting courses to better understand business processes and methods, every information technology professional should be able to write cogently and explain technical elements in readable English."

"Knowledge may be power, but communications skills are the primary raw materials of good client relationships," Cunningham adds. Every job description for a new position on his staff includes the following line:

"Required: effective organization and mastery of the English language in written and oral forms."

Clear communication can enhance your reputation as an information technology professional, says Kevin Jetton, executive vice president of the Association of Information Technology Professionals (AITP) and president of GeniSys Consulting Services, in San Antonio. It is especially important to communicate in plain English and not technical jargon when you are talking to a non-information technology business executive.

"You can have the greatest technical skills in the world, but without solid communication skills, who will know and can understand?" Jetton says.

Even if you have limited customer contact, writing skills are essential. Larry McConnell, deputy registrar for information services at the Massachusetts Registry of Motor Vehicles, in Boston, says that unless you can communicate, your career will level off.

Your job efficiency may depend on how well others communicate, as well. Joe Thompson, product support lead at Kesmai, an online games developer in Charlottesville, Va., says his daily work often depends on somebody's writing skills. Whether he's communicating with the test department or with a customer, Thompson sees writing as the key to effective two-way communication.

Even if writing is not your forte, you can improve your skills. Many companies offer onsite writing courses or send their staff to business writing workshops such as those offered by the American Management Association (http://www.amanet.org) and other training organizations.

Pete McGarahan, executive director of the Help Desk Institute, in San Francisco, says one of the best investments of his career was hiring a trainer to teach business writing for information technology professionals.

Check out writing courses at colleges and community education programs, as well. "College-level courses in English composition and creative writing help broaden skills beyond the technical 'myopia' common to many information technology professionals, enabling them to establish rapport and truly communicate with their clients," Cunningham says.

Good writing requires practice. AITP's Jetton suggests becoming involved in community volunteer opportunities or professional societies, where you can work on newsletters or write committee reports. "Communication skills are an ever-evolving skill set," Jetton says. "You never have enough practice."

Good writing will help you advance in your career because it:

- Increases customer satisfaction
- Saves time
- Improves communication across the organization
- Enhances your professional image
- Contributes to business success
- Raises your professional status

Think again . . . talk more!

Part II CROSSWORD REVIEW

Sharpen Your Skills!

MULTIPLECHOICE
AUDIENCE
INSPIRATION
PERIODICALS
MEDIA
QUESTION
SUMMARY

ACROSS

1. A note-taking system, also called the "T-note" system, that divides a piece of paper into three sections
6. The spontaneous, rapid generation of ideas, often undertaken as part of a problem-solving process
8. An idea or statement accepted as true without examination or proof
9. A bad case of nerves, occuring in an exam situation, that makes it difficult to think or remember
11. Magazines, journals, and newspapers, which are published on a regular basis
13. The agents of mass communication—i.e., television, radio, and newspapers
14. The third stage of the writing process, involving the evaluation of word choice, paragraph structure, and style
16. Reading material in an investigative way, searching for information
17. A mind action in which you describe facts, objects, or events
18. A memory device that involves associating something with information you already know

DOWN

2. A type of test question that offers several selections from which you are to choose the one you think is correct
3. The reader or readers of any piece of written material
4. A descriptive word, such as "always," "never," or "often," that changes the meaning of another word or word group
5. A mind action in which you judge whether something is important or unimportant
7. A stream-of-consciousness technique that encourages you to put ideas down on paper as they occur to you, without censoring ideas
10. A plan of action designed to accomplish a specific goal
12. The first stage of listening, in which your ears pick up sound waves and transmit them to the brain
15. A concise restatement of material, in your own words, that covers the main points

Part III Creating Life Success

CHAPTER 9 Relating to Others: Appreciating Your Diverse World

CHAPTER 10 Personal Wellness: Taking Care of Yourself

CHAPTER 11 Managing Career and Money: Reality Resources

CHAPTER 12 Moving Ahead: Building a Flexible Future

C O N N E C T

CONNECT

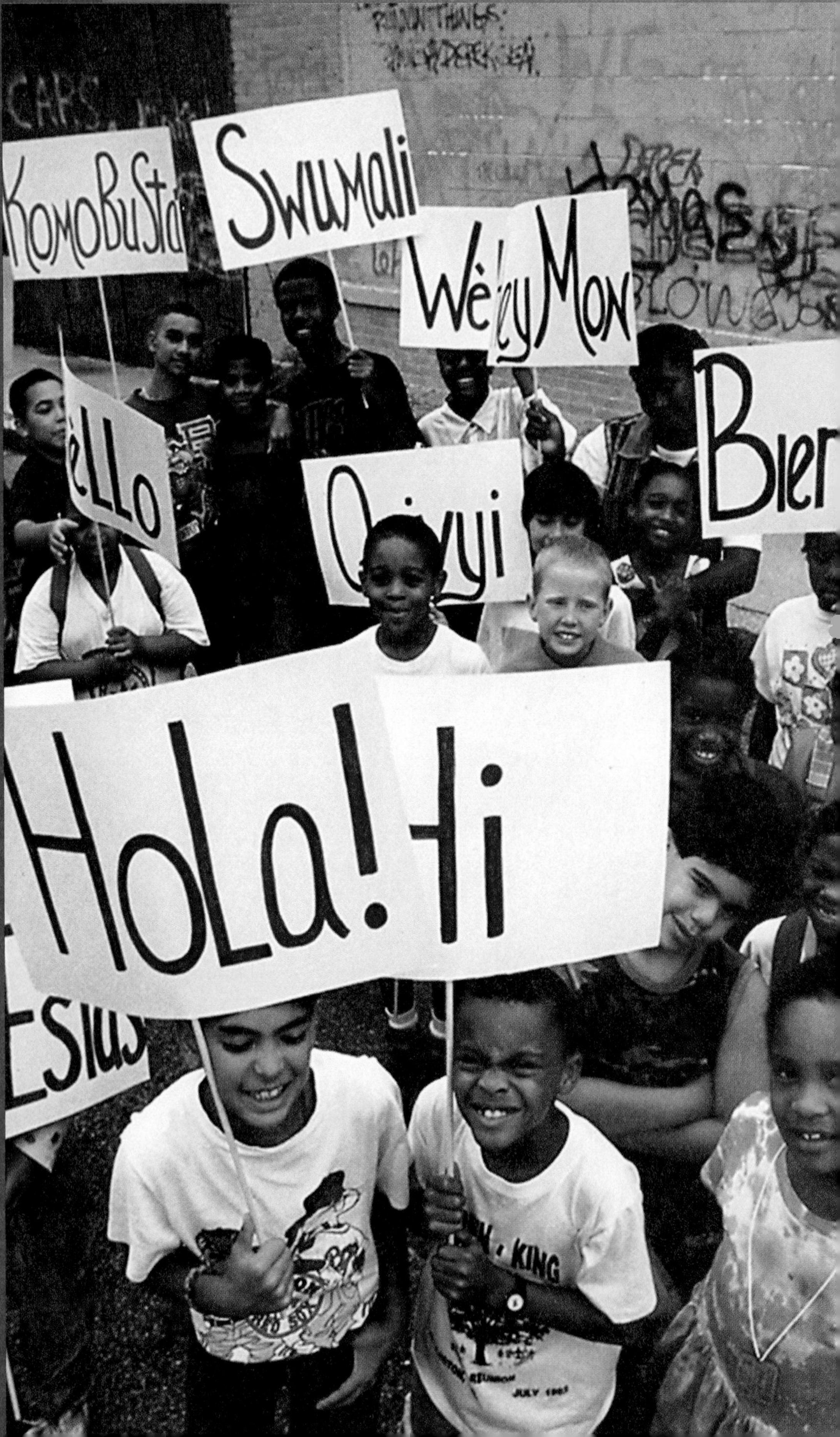

Relating to Others

Appreciating Your Diverse World

In this chapter, you will explore answers to the following questions:

- Why is it important to understand and accept others?
- How can you think critically about diversity?
- How can you express yourself effectively?
- How do your personal relationships define you?
- How can you handle conflict and criticism?
- What role do you play in groups?

The greater part of your waking life involves interaction with people—family and friends, fellow students, coworkers, instructors, and many more. Having a strong network of relationships can help you grow as a person and progress toward your goals. In this chapter you will explore how your ability to open your mind can positively affect the way in which you perceive and relate to others. You will also explore communication styles, personal relationships, and the roles you can play in groups and teams. Finally, you will learn to handle conflict and criticism so that you can learn from your points of vulnerability as well as your strengths.

Teaching Tip

Helpful Web sites:

- Diversity Database, University of Maryland - www.inform.umd.edu/EdRes/Topic/Diversity/
- National Civil Rights Museum - www.civilrightsmuseum.org
- Teaching Tolerance - www.splcenter.org/teachingtolerance/tt-index.html

WHY IS IT IMPORTANT TO UNDERSTAND AND ACCEPT OTHERS?

As your world becomes increasingly diverse, you will encounter people who may be different from anyone you have ever met. Accepting differences—enabled by an open mind and a willingness to learn—will allow you to expand your horizons and create more options in all areas of your life.

Diversity in Your World

For centuries, travel to different countries was seen as part of a complete education. Today, although traveling is still a valuable way to learn, different places and people often come to you. More and more, **diversity** is part of your community, on your television, on your Internet browser, at your school, in your workplace, and in your family. Immigration and intermarriage will continue to increase the ethnic diversity of the United States, as shown in Figure 9.1, which compares the current population with what is projected for the year 2050. Diversity in age is also on the rise—whereas in 1994 only 1 in every 25 persons was older than 65 years of age, it is projected that 1 in 5 will be over 65 by the year 2050 and that the elderly population will have more than doubled.[1]

> **Diversity**
>
> The variety that occurs in every aspect of humanity, involving both visible and invisible characteristics.

Most people used to live in societies with others who seemed very similar to them. Now, differences are often woven into everyday life. You may encounter examples of diversity like these:

- communities with people from different stages of life
- coworkers who represent a variety of ethnic origins

FIGURE 9.1 Growing Diversity

Population distribution of the United States

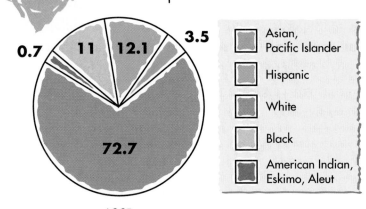
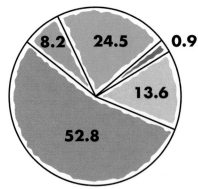

1997
(total population: 267.6 million)

2050 projected
(total population: 393.9 million)

Source: U. S. Bureau of the Census, *Statistical Abstract of the United States 1998,* 118th Ed. (Washington, D.C.: U.S. Government Printing Office, 1998).

Source: U. S. Bureau of the Census, *Current Population Reports,* Series P25-1092 (Washington, D.C.: Government Printing Office, 1992), and *Statistical Abstract of the United States 1994* (Washington, D.C.: U. S. Government Printing Office, 1994).

- classmates who speak a number of different languages
- social situations featuring people from various cultures, with various religions, and with varying sexual orientations
- individuals who marry a person or adopt a child from a different racial or religious background
- diverse restaurants, services, and businesses in the community
- neighborhoods with immigrants from a variety of class backgrounds
- different lifestyles, as reflected in the media and popular culture
- people in the workplace who have a variety of disabilities (physical or emotional)

Each person has a *choice* about how to relate to others—or even whether to relate to them. No one can force you to interact with any other person, or to adopt a particular attitude as being "right." Considering two important responsibilities may help you analyze your options:

Your responsibility to yourself is to make sure your feelings are honest and well considered. Observe your reactions to others. Consider sources; for example, have you heard these ideas from other people, organizations, or the media? Do you agree with them, or does a different approach feel better to you? Through critical thinking you can arrive at decisions about which you feel comfortable and confident.

Your responsibility to others lies in treating people with tolerance and respect. No one will like everyone he or she meets, but acknowledging that others deserve respect and have a right to their opinions, just as you do, will build understanding. The more people accept one another, the more all kinds of relationships will be able to thrive.

The Positive Effects of Diversity

Accepting diversity has very real benefits to people in all kinds of relationships. Acceptance and respect form the basis for any successful interaction. As more situations bring diverse people into relationships, communication will become more and more dependent on mutual acceptance. Understanding and communication in school, work, and personal relationships can help you achieve your goals as you develop positive personal and business relations. Failure to understand and communicate well can have negative effects.

For example, examine the potential effects of reactions to diversity in the following situations. Although each of these situations focuses on the reaction of only one person, it's important to note that both parties need to work together to establish mutual trust and openness.

A student with a learning disability has an Asian instructor. If the student assumes that Asian people are intellectually superior, expecting nothing less than a perfect performance, she may resist the instructor's advice and directions and do poorly in the class or drop it. On the other hand, if the student rejects racial stereotypes about Asians and talks to the instructor about the specific accommodations she needs to succeed in class, the instructor may feel respected and be more encouraging. The

Real World Link
Ask students to cooperate in a poll that defines the diversity of the class. Ask students to define their ethnic/racial backgrounds, age, first language, disabilities, and other characteristics. Analyze the data and report your classroom's world of difference.

Springboard
Cicily Wilson, who is biracial, recalled her first day of college in a predominately white university in the following way: "I realized that I had the job of reeducating these people [about accepting people with one black and one white parent]. Is this my job? I just want to live my life." Ask students to discuss the implications of Cicily's statement.

student may then be more likely to pay attention in class, work hard, and advance in her education.

A Caucasian man has a sister who adopts a biracial child. If the man cuts off contact with his sister because he fears racial differences and doesn't approve of racial mixing, he may deny himself her support and create a rift in the family. On the other hand, if the man can respect his sister's choice, seeing the child as a new family member regardless of color, she may feel more supported and continue to support him in turn. The situation may help to build a close and rewarding family relationship.

Accepting others isn't always easy. Following are some barriers that can hinder your ability to accept and understand others and suggestions for how your problem-solving skills can help you overcome them.

HOW CAN YOU THINK CRITICALLY ABOUT DIVERSITY?

You deserve to feel positive about who you are, where you come from, what you believe, and the others with whom you identify. However, problems arise when people use the power of group identity to put others down or cut themselves off from others. Table 9.1 shows how an open-minded approach can differ from an approach that is characterized by barriers.

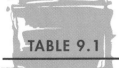

TABLE 9.1 Approaches to Diversity

YOUR ROLE	SITUATION	CLOSE-MINDED APPROACH	OPEN-MINDED APPROACH
Fellow student	For an assignment, you are paired with a student old enough to be your mother.	You assume the student will be closed off to the modern world. You think she might preach to you about how to do the assignment.	You get to know the student as an individual. You stay open to what you can learn from her experiences and knowledge.
Friend	You are invited to dinner at a friend's house. When he introduces you to his partner, you realize that he is gay.	You are turned off by the idea of two men in a relationship. You make an excuse to leave early. You avoid your friend after that evening.	You have dinner with the two men and make an effort to get to know more about what their lives are like and who they are individually and as a couple.
Employee	Your new boss is of a different racial and cultural background than you.	You assume that you and your new boss don't have much in common, and you think he will be distant and uninterested in you.	You rein in your assumptions, knowing they are based on stereotypes, and approach your new boss with an open mind.

Thinking critically can help you to understand and to break down the barriers that prevent different people from communicating successfully with one another. As you explore the following causes and their destructive effects, consider what you can do to prevent these effects in your mind and your environment.

Prejudice

Prejudice occurs when people *prejudge* (make a judgment before they have sufficient knowledge on which to base that judgment). People often form prejudiced opinions on the basis of a particular characteristic—gender, race, sexual orientation, religion, and so on. You may be familiar with the labels for particular prejudices, such as *racism* (prejudice based on race) or *ageism* (prejudice based on age). Any group can be subjected to prejudice, although certain groups have more often been on the receiving end of close-minded attitudes.

Why do people prejudge? Sources of prejudice include the following:

- **Family and culture.** You learn the attitudes of those with whom you grow up. When you encounter different ideas, you may react by thinking that your ideas are superior.

- **Individual experience.** Judging others because of a bad experience is human, especially when a particular characteristic raises strong emotions.

- **Jealousy, insecurity, and fear of failure.** When people feel insecure about their own abilities, they may find it easier to devalue the abilities of others than to take risks themselves. It can be easier to blame others than to take responsibility for your own situation.

The many faces of prejudice often show on college campuses. A student may not want to work with students of another race. Members of campus clubs may reject prospective members who do not share their background. Religious groups may devalue the beliefs of other religions. Groups that gather because of a common characteristic might be harassed by others. Students may find that instructors judge their abilities and attitudes according to their gender. Such attitudes block attempts at mutual understanding.

Prejudice Causes Discrimination

Prejudice can lead people to disrespect, harass, and put down others. In some cases, prejudice may lead to unrealistic expectations of others that aren't necessarily negative, such as if someone were to believe that all Jewish people excel in business. The most destructive effect of prejudice is discrimination.

Discrimination occurs when people deny others opportunities because of their perceived differences in gender, language, race, culture, weight, physical ability, and other factors. Victims of discrimination suffer when they are denied equal employment, educational, and housing

Prejudice
A preconceived judgment or opinion, formed without just grounds or sufficient knowledge.

Career Connection
Point out the prejudices Asian-Americans face in the workplace, including expectations that they will excel in science, be poor leaders, and be deferential to authority. Discuss how these prejudices may hold Asian-Americans back from career advancement.

e-mail

Write to or speak with one of your friends, acknowledging a time when you behaved prejudicially. Be honest about why you think you responded that way. Ask your friend to share a like experience so that you can encourage each other to be honest about past actions and to practice tolerance in the future.

Be a Team

Ask some small groups to research specific laws against workplace discrimination. Ask other groups to focus on laws against discrimination in education. Have each team report, then encourage a discussion on the effectiveness of the laws in preventing discrimination.

"Minds are like parachutes. They only function when they are open."

Sir James Dewar

Springboard

Ask students what they think about the following statement: Many students, who would never knowingly discriminate against the disabled in the classroom, may never invite a disabled person out with friends. Explain that many disabled people feel shunned in informal settings.

Career Connection

When students begin working, they may encounter diversity training programs that help employees accept differences and work as a team. Among the organizations that run these programs are Xerox, Avon, and the Internal Revenue Service.

opportunities and when they are treated as second-class citizens in their access to goods and services. Sheryl McCarthy, an African-American columnist for *New York Newsday,* says: "Nothing is quite so basic and clear as having a cab go right past your furiously waving body and pick up the white person next to you."[2] Even so-called majority populations may now experience the disturbing power of discrimination. For example, a qualified white man may be passed up for a promotion in favor of a female or a culturally diverse employee.

United States federal law states that it is unlawful for you to be denied an education, work, or the chance to apply for work, housing, or basic rights because of your race, creed, color, age, gender, national or ethnic origin, religion, marital status, potential or actual pregnancy, or potential or actual illness or disability (unless the illness or disability prevents you from performing required tasks and unless accommodations for the disability are not possible). Unfortunately, the law is often broken; the result is that many people suffer the impact of discrimination. Some people don't report violations, fearing trouble from those they accuse. Others aren't aware that discrimination has occurred.

Addressing Prejudice and Discrimination

The best and most lasting solutions come from addressing the cause rather than the effect (see Chapter 5). Therefore, fight discrimination by working to eliminate prejudice. First and foremost, be responsible for your own behavior. For example, you find yourself discriminating against a particular student in choosing people for a study group. Ask yourself: Where did I get this prejudice? What are the effects of this prejudice on me or others? How can I reverse this negative thought pattern? Use problem-solving steps to make an adjustment if necessary. As Dr. Martin Luther King, Jr., states in the following quote, critical thinking is the key.

> The tough-minded person always examines the facts before he reaches conclusions: in short, he postjudges. The tender-minded person reaches conclusions before he has examined the first fact; in short, he prejudges and is prejudiced. . . . There is little hope for us until we become tough-minded enough to break loose from the shackles of prejudice, half-truths, and downright ignorance.[3]

When someone you know displays prejudice or discriminates, what can you do? It can be hard to stand up to someone and risk a relationship or, if the person is your employer, a job. Evaluate the situation and decide what choice is most suitable. You can decide not to address it at all. You may drop a humorous hint. You may test the waters with a small comment. Whatever you do, express your opinion respectfully. Whether or not the other person makes a change, you have taken an important stand.

If you want to approach an authority about a discriminatory act that you have seen or experienced, begin by talking to the person who can most directly affect the situation—an instructor or supervisor. The law is clearly on your side. At each decision stage, weigh all the positive and negative effects and evaluate whether the action is feasible for you.

Stereotyping

As you learned in Chapter 5, an assumption is an idea that is accepted without looking for proof. A **stereotype** is a kind of assumption, made about a person or group of people based on one or more characteristics. You may have heard stereotypical assumptions such as these: "Women are too emotional for business"; "African-Americans can run fast and sing well"; "Hispanics are Catholic and have tons of kids"; "White people are cold and power-hungry"; "Gay people sleep around"; "People with learning disabilities can't hold down jobs"; or "Older people can't learn new things." Stereotypes are as common as they are destructive.

What are some sources of stereotypes?

- *A desire for patterns and logic.* Trying to make sense of a complex world is human nature. People often try to find order by using the labels and categories that stereotypes provide.

- *The media.* The more people see stereotypical images—the unintelligent blonde or the funny overweight person—the easier it is to believe that such stereotypes are universal.

- *Laziness.* Making assumptions from observing external characteristics is easier than trying to know people as individuals. Labeling a group according to a characteristic they seem to have in common takes less time and energy than exploring unique qualities within the group.

The "ease" of stereotypes comes at a high price. First and foremost, stereotypes can perpetuate harmful generalizations and falsehoods about others. These false ideas can promote discrimination. For example, if an employer believes that Vietnamese people cannot speak English well, he or she might not even bother to interview a Vietnamese applicant. Second, stereotypes communicate the message that you don't respect others enough to discover who they really are. This may encourage others to stereotype you in return.

Stereotyping Causes Stereotype Vulnerability

When people identify themselves as part of a particular group, they may want to distance themselves from stereotypical qualities associated with that group. *Stereotype vulnerability* occurs when people avoid facing a problem because they think that admitting it will just perpetuate a stereotype.[4] For example, an immigrant to the United States may resist tutoring in English for fear of seeming like just another foreigner. Such avoidance cuts people off from assistance and communication that could connect them with others and thus improve their lives.

Another side of stereotype vulnerability occurs when people refuse help because they believe that others want to help them out of pity: "She considers me disadvantaged because I'm African-American"; "He only wants to help because he looks down on me because of my learning disability." These refusals are based on assumptions. Sometimes, such assumptions may contain a grain of truth. Frequently, though, the person who offers help just wants to help another human being, and the person who refuses it loses out on what may be valuable assistance.

Addressing Stereotypes and Stereotype Vulnerability

Recall from the critical-thinking material in Chapter 5 the questions you can ask about an assumption to examine its validity. Apply these questions to stereotypes:

- In what cases is this stereotype true, if ever? In what cases is it not true?
- Has stereotyping others benefited me? Has it hurt me? In what ways? How would I feel if I were on the receiving end of this stereotype?
- What is the source of this stereotype, and why?
- What harm could be done by always accepting this stereotype as true?

Using these questions, think about the stereotypes that you assume are true, and curb your tendencies to judge according to such stereotypes. When you hear someone use a stereotype and you know something that disproves it, volunteer that information. Encourage others to think through stereotypes and to reject them if they don't hold up under examination. Approach every person as a unique individual who deserves respect.

Furthermore, if you find yourself avoiding help because you don't want to be labeled, don't let stereotypes prevent you from getting assistance. Approach someone who can help you and give that person a chance to get to know your individual needs and problems. Perhaps he or she will see you not as a representative of a group but as an individual who needs and deserves specific attention.

Fear of Differences

It's human instinct to fear the unknown. Many people allow their fears to prevent them from finding out about what's outside their known world. As cozy as that world can be, it also can be limiting, cutting off communication from people who could enrich the world in many different ways.

The fear of differences has many effects. A young person who fears the elderly may avoid visiting a grandparent in a nursing home. A person of one religion might reject friendships with those of other religions. A person might turn down an offer to buy a house in a neighborhood that is populated with people of a different sexual orientation. In each case, the person has denied himself or herself a chance to learn a new perspective, communicate with new individuals, and grow from new experiences.

Fear of Differences Causes Hate Crimes

Hate crime

A crime committed against a person motivated by a hatred of a specific characteristic thought to be possessed by that person.

A **hate crime** is the most extreme effect of the fear of differences. Unfortunately, recent years have brought many unwelcome examples, such as the following:

- In June 1998, an African-American named James Byrd, Jr., was chained to the back of a pickup truck and dragged along the road until he died. One of his convicted murderers is an admitted white supremacist.
- In Wyoming in the fall of 1998, a gay college student named Matthew Shepard was kidnapped and tied to a fence where his captors beat him and abandoned him. He died as a result of the injuries he sustained.

- In April 1999, Eric Harris and Dylan Klebold opened fire in Columbine High School in Littleton, Colorado, killing 12 students and 1 teacher and wounding others. Their writings revealed their intention to harm minorities, athletes, and others different from them.

- In May 1999 in Victor, Colorado, a white man named Mark Dale Butts was beaten by a group of African-American men until he died. The incident started with some racially charged comments made in a bar.

- In August 1999, Buford O. Furrow entered the North Valley Jewish Community Center near Los Angeles, California, and shot three preschool children and two adults because they were Jewish. He then shot and killed a Filipino-American letter carrier because he was not white.

The increase in hate crimes in recent years has prompted a great deal of concern. Organized groups based on hate of a particular race or culture are growing, and many have Internet sites dedicated to their prejudiced ideas. Other Internet sites are developed and maintained by individuals who want to express their racism, anti-Semitism, hatred of gays, misogyny (hatred of women), or other prejudices. Some sites even promote prejudices to kids through games and other interactive formats. Figure 9.2 shows statistics on what motivates people to commit hate crimes.

All of the causes of this devastating trend are not completely understood. What are important is awareness of the problem and a willingness to face it.

Addressing Fear of Differences and Hate Crimes

Diversity doesn't mean that you have to feel comfortable with everyone and their beliefs. If you can gradually broaden your horizons, however, you may avoid limiting your growth through fear. Today's world increasingly presents

Reported Motivations of Hate Crimes  FIGURE 9.2

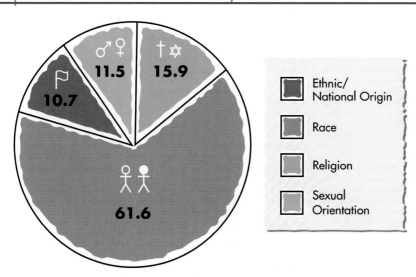

Source: Federal Bureau of Investigation, *1996 Hate Crimes Statistics Press Release* (Washington, D.C.: FBI National Press Office, January 1998).

opportunities for such exposure. You can choose a study partner who has a different ethnic background, expand your knowledge through books or magazines, or attend an unfamiliar religious service with a friend. If you are uncomfortable with even this level of exploration, you can start by respecting people who are different from you and allowing them to live peacefully and privately.

In addition, do whatever you can to promote the lessening of the kind of fear and anger that can lead to hate crimes. Step up your own awareness of such crimes and promote awareness in others. Add your voice to those in protest of these acts of violence. Set an example by practicing kindness and forgiveness and treating people of all cultures and lifestyles with respect. In fact, anything that you do to promote and encourage the positive effects of diversity—including all of the strategies in the following section—will serve to combat the kind of irrational hatred that can lead to violence.

Accepting and Dealing with Differences

Be a Team
Ask partners to react to and discuss this statement: Individual identity is broader than group identity because it is influenced by life experience, personality, occupation, and parenting style. An individual can never be fully defined in terms of group membership.

Successful interaction with the people around you depends upon your ability to accept differences. Realize that the opinions of family, friends, the media, and any group with which you identify may sometimes lead you to adopt attitudes that you haven't completely thought through. Ask yourself important questions about the actions you want to take, and make a choice that feels right.

What can you do to accept and deal with differences?

Avoid judgments based on external characteristics. These include skin color, weight, facial features, physical disability, or gender.

Cultivate relationships with people of different cultures, races, perspectives, and ages. Find out how other people live and think, and see what you can learn from them. Acknowledge that everyone has a right to his or her opinion, whether or not you agree with it.

Leading a focus group.

Educate yourself and others. Read about other cultures and people. "Take advantage of books and people to teach you about other cultures," say Tamera Trotter and Joycelyn Allen in *Talking Justice: 602 Ways to Build and Promote Racial Harmony.* "Empowerment comes through education."[5]

Be sensitive to the needs of others at school and on the job. Think critically and develop empathy. Ask yourself questions about what you would feel and do if you were in another person's shoes.

Help other people, no matter how different they may be. Sheryl McCarthy writes about an African-American who, in the midst of the 1992 Los

Angeles riots, saw a man being beaten and helped him to safety. "When asked why he risked grievous harm to save an Asian man he didn't even know, Williams said, 'Because if I'm not there to help someone else, when the mob comes for me, will there be someone there to save me?' "[6] Continue the cycle of kindness.

Explore your own background, beliefs, and identity. Respect and explore your ethnic and cultural heritage. Share what you learn with others.

Take responsibility for making changes. Avoid blaming problems in your life on certain groups of people.

Learn from history. Remember the atrocities of slavery, the Holocaust, and the "ethnic cleansing" in Kosovo. Cherish your freedom and seek continual improvement at home and elsewhere in the world.

Look for common ground. You might share parenting goals, classes, personal challenges, or interests.

Recognize that people everywhere have the same basic needs. Everyone loves, thinks, hurts, hopes, fears, and plans. Strive to find out what is special about others instead of what you find problematic or distasteful. People are united through their essential humanity.

At the forefront of the list of ways to deal with differences is mutual respect. Respect for yourself and others is essential. Knowing that other people's cultures, behaviors, races, religions, appearances, and ideas deserve as much respect as your own promotes communication and learning.

Expressing your ideas clearly and interpreting what others believe are two crucial keys to communicating in a diverse world. Particular strategies can help you communicate effectively with those around you.

Teaching Tolerance

Ask students for their reactions to the following: "I am not a wheelchair," said a disabled woman. "Yet many people see me only in terms of my chair. I am a lawyer, a daughter, and a mother. I love baseball, politics, and sci-fi novels. All of these—and more—describe who I am."

HOW CAN YOU EXPRESS YOURSELF EFFECTIVELY?

The only way for people to know one another's needs is to communicate as clearly and directly as possible. Successful communication promotes success at school and work and in your personal relationships. Exploring communication styles, paying attention to body language, and addressing specific communication issues will help you express yourself effectively.

Adjusting to Communication Styles

Communication is an exchange between two or more people. The speaker's goal is for the listener (or listeners) to receive the message exactly as the speaker intended. Different people, however, have different styles of communicating. Problems arise when one person has trouble "translating" a message that comes from someone who uses a different style.

Your knowledge of multiple intelligences (see Chapter 4) will help you understand different styles of communication. Particular communication styles tend to accompany dominance in particular intelligences. Recognizing specific styles in yourself and in others will help you communicate more clearly.

The Styles

Teaching Tip
Point out that gender differences may also influence communication. Gender communication studies show, for example, that women tend to focus more on relationships and men focus more on the dynamics of power.

Following are the communication styles that tend to accompany dominance in six of the eight intelligences.

Bodily-kinesthetic communicators are tuned in to the physical. They often use body language to send messages and may be likewise adept at reading the body language of others. They may experience more communication success when speaking in person than when talking on the phone or reading e-mail, because being physically present can help them read a situation comprehensively.

Visual-spatial communicators benefit from visual aids to communication. Reinforcing a message with a visual—for example, accompanying a spoken presentation at work with slides or transparencies—may boost their ability to listen and understand. Visual-spatial communicators may find it helpful to use visual images or aids when communicating to others.

Verbal-linguistic communicators gravitate toward any kind of verbal communication. Whether spoken (oral) or written, they tend to put their messages across in words. They receive best those messages that are communicated verbally. As for their studies, verbal people process reading material well.

Logical-mathematical communicators favor communication that follows a structure or a system. They often explain information in a manner focused more on logic or measurable quantities and less on emotion or other more vague concepts. They also receive best any communication that has clear structure and a logical emphasis.

Interpersonal communicators prefer personal contact. They tend to receive information most effectively and communicate information most clearly when interacting directly with others. Interpersonal communicators also tend to focus on, and respond to, emotion in their interactions.

Intrapersonal communicators often need additional time to process communication. They may prefer to spend time alone thinking through information before communicating it. They may also need similar processing time after receiving communication, whether written on paper or spoken in person.

You may shift from style to style according to the situation, particularly when trying to communicate with someone who prefers a style different from yours. Shifting, however, is not always easy or possible. The most important task is to try to understand the different styles and to help others understand yours. No one style is any better than another. Each has its own positive effects that enhance communication and negative effects that can hinder it, depending on the situation.

While musical and naturalistic intelligences are not primary influences on communication, they may still be a factor for those who have a strong dominance in either or both intelligences. For example, a musical learner may prefer to communicate an emotion through writing and performing a song, while a naturalistic learner may prefer to walk outdoors while having an important discussion or may find that he or she understands communication better when it is explained using metaphors from nature.

Identifying Your Styles

As with the intelligences themselves, people may possess characteristics from more than one category or may shift dominance depending on the situation, but for most people one, two, or perhaps three styles are most prominent. Thinking about your dominant intelligences will help you to determine your most comfortable communication style or styles. Consider which settings or strategies seem to have positive or negative effects on your ability to give or receive communication.

When you know what works best for you, try to create the best situation for you and for those with whom you communicate. Step back from your emotions and try to be as objective as possible. You can make adjustments both as the communicator and as the receiver.

Adjusting to the Receiver's Style

When you are the speaker, you will benefit from an understanding of both your own style and the styles of your receivers or listeners. It doesn't matter how clear you think you are being if the person you are speaking to can't "translate" your message due to a difficulty in understanding your style. Try to take your listener's style into consideration when you communicate.

Following is an example of how adjusting to the listener can aid communication.

An interpersonal instructor to a logical-mathematical student: "I didn't get any sense of your individual writing voice from your essay." The student's reply: "What do you mean?"

■ **Without adjustment:** If the interpersonal instructor doesn't take note of the logical student's need for detail and examples, he or she may continue with a string of general and/or emotion-focused ideas that might further confuse or turn off the student. "You need to elaborate more. Try writing from the heart. You're not considering your audience."

■ **With adjustment:** If the instructor shifts toward a focus on detail, the student may begin to understand, and the lines of communication can open. "You've supported your central idea clearly, but you didn't move beyond the facts into your personal interpretation of what they mean. Your essay reads like a research paper—the language is technical and doesn't sound like it is coming directly from you. I've seen you put more of yourself into your work before."

Adjusting to the Communicator's Style

As a facet of communication, listening is just as important as speaking. When you are the listener, try to stay aware of the communication style of the speaker. Observe how that style satisfies or fails to meet your needs. Work to understand the speaker in the context of his or her style and translate the message into one that makes sense to you.

Following is an example of how adjusting to the communicator can boost understanding.

A bodily-kinesthetic employee to a verbal-linguistic supervisor: "I'm really upset about the e-mail memo you sent to me. I don't think you've been fair in not addressing the situation with me in person. I don't feel I've had a chance to defend myself."

■ **Without adjustment:** If the supervisor becomes annoyed with the employee's focus on direct personal contact, he or she may put up an even stronger barrier. "I told you clearly and specifically what needs to be done, and my language wasn't hurtful. I don't know what else there is to discuss."

■ **With adjustment:** If the supervisor considers that a different approach will help the employee better understand the situation, he or she could respond in a way that incorporates the in-person communication that the employee understands best. "Let's meet after lunch so you can explain to me why you're upset and how we can improve the situation."

Words are only one aspect of communication style. People also use their bodies in different ways to communicate messages to one another.

The Power of Body Language

Your actions—not your words—are the most basic form of communication. Even people who cannot speak each other's language can communicate ideas and feelings physically. Nonverbal communication, also called *body language,* includes gestures, eye movement, facial expression, body positioning and posture, touching behavior, and use of personal space. Understanding how body language works will help you use it to your advantage as you communicate more effectively.

How Body Language Works

Body language can reinforce or contradict verbal statements. When body language contradicts verbal language, the message conveyed by the body is dominant. Consider, for example, if someone were to ask you how you feel, and you said "Fine" although you don't feel fine at all. In such a case your posture, eye contact, and other body signs would convey the real message loud and clear.

Nonverbal cues also color what you communicate. Consider this statement: "This is the best idea I've heard all day." If you were to say this three different ways—in a loud voice while standing up, quietly while sitting with arms and legs crossed and looking away, and while maintaining eye contact and taking the receiver's hand—you might send three different messages.

Although differences occur from person to person and from culture to culture, some specific types of body language may have particular meanings. See Figure 9.3 for some examples.

Nonverbal communication strongly influences a first impression. Although first impressions emerge from a combination of nonverbal cues, tone of voice, and choice of words, nonverbal elements (cues and tone) usually come across first and strongest. When you meet someone, you tend to make assumptions based on nonverbal behavior such as posture, eye contact, gestures, and speed and style of movement.

Possible Meanings of Body Language

FIGURE 9.3

Firm handshake	Body turned away	Hands on hips	Open sitting posture
capability, friendliness	lack of interest	readiness, toughness	interest or agreement

Using Body Language to Your Advantage

The following strategies can help you maximize your awareness and use of body language.

Become aware. Pay attention to what other people communicate non-verbally. If a friend compliments you with strong eye contact and a natural smile, you might feel flattered. If the same friend speaking the same words doesn't look you in the eye and is physically closed off from you, there might be something left unsaid. Know that your nonverbal communication affects your messages.

Match your words with your body language. A nonverbal message that goes against what you speak can cause confusion. The receiver, unsure of which to believe, may tend to go with the nonverbal message. For example, if you say to your supervisor at work, "The new assignment is fine with me," with a tense tone of voice and an aggressive posture, the supervisor may wonder whether to believe what you say.

Note cultural differences. In some cultures, casual acquaintances stand close together when speaking; in others, the same distance may be used only in very intimate, personal conversations. In the United States, direct and steady eye contact may show attention and respect, while in Asian countries, respect is often conveyed by avoiding direct eye contact.[7] Within any conversation, you can discover what seems appropriate by paying attention to what the other person does on a consistent basis. You may also want to read about the nonverbal differences in communication styles that characterize other cultures.

Addressing Communication Issues

Communication can be complicated; people filter information through their own perspectives and interpret it in different ways. Some of the most common communication issues follow, along with strategies to help you address them.

Be a Team

Ask students to shake hands and greet as many classmates as possible in a given period of time. After dividing the class into groups, ask students to choose the person in the class with the best greeting skills and to discuss the specific verbal and nonverbal factors that influenced their choice.

Critical Thinking

Ask students whether they have ever met anyone from a different culture who uses nonverbal cues that are not common in the United States. If they met several people from the same culture, did they share the same nonverbal patterns? Have they noticed differences in the nonverbal language of men and women?

Have a discussion with your professor or your study group about some of the cultural differences each of you have learned about first-hand through interacting with people from other countries.

Issue: Unclear or incomplete explanation

Solution: Support ideas with examples

Teaching Tip
Suggested research project: Research the relationship between culture and communication in Mexico, Japan, Germany, and Saudi Arabia.

When you clarify a general idea with supporting examples that illustrate how it works and what effects it causes, you will help your receiver understand what you mean, and therefore you will have a better chance to hold his or her attention. Be clear, precise, and to the point as you link your ideas to examples.

For example, if you tell a friend to take a certain class, that person might not take you seriously until you explain why. If you then communicate the positive effects of taking that class (progress toward a major, an excellent instructor, and friendly study sessions), you may get your message across. If at work you assign a task without explanation, you might get a delayed response or find mistakes in an employee's work. If, however, you explain potential positive effects of the task, you'll have better results.

Issue: Limited knowledge of audience

Solution: Target your message to your listeners and the situation

Teaching Tip
Meeting the audience's needs requires speakers to adopt a "you" attitude, which focuses on the listener, rather than the speaker. Suggest that students orient their explanations around listeners' questions.

As with writing a paper, considering your audience will improve communication. Ask yourself questions that will help you clarify what is appropriate for your audience. Tailor your words, tone, and level of formality to the person and the situation. Even with the same person, your communication style may change from situation to situation. For example, if you have a good relationship with a supervisor, you may have a more informal communication style when the two of you are alone than when you are with others in a work setting. Be sensitive, stay aware, and make adjustments as necessary.

Issue: Choosing when to communicate

Solution: Choose optimum listening conditions

Even a perfectly worded message won't get through to someone who isn't ready to receive it. If you try to talk to your instructor when she is rushing out the door, your message probably won't come across too well. If someone tries to communicate with you when you are distracted with work or children, you may not hear accurately. Pay attention to mood as well. If a friend has had an exhausting or difficult week, you might want to wait before asking a favor.

Communication will also benefit from good timing. When you have something to say, choose a time when you feel ready to focus and express yourself clearly. Spoken too soon, ideas can come out sounding nothing like you intended. Left to simmer too long, your feelings can spill over into other issues. Take the time you need to think through what you want to say, and then speak promptly. Rehearsing mentally or talking your thoughts through with a friend can help you choose the best combination of words.

> "Do not use a hatchet to remove a fly from your friend's forehead."
>
> Chinese proverb

Issue: Attacking the receiver

Solution: Send "I" messages

When a conflict arises, often the first instinct is to pinpoint what someone else did wrong: "You didn't lock the door!" "You never called last night!" Making an accusation, especially without proof, puts the other person on the defensive and shuts down the lines of communication.

Using "I" messages will help you communicate your own needs rather than focusing on what you think someone else should do differently: "I felt uneasy when I came to work and the door was unlocked." "I became worried about you when I didn't hear from you last night." "I" statements soften the conflict by highlighting the effects that the other person's actions have had on you, rather than the person or the actions themselves. When you focus on your own response and needs, your receiver may feel more free to respond, perhaps offering help and even acknowledging mistakes.

Issue: Passive or aggressive communication styles

Solution: Become assertive

Among the three major communication styles—aggressive, passive, and assertive—the one that conveys a message in the clearest, most productive way is the **assertive** style. The other two, although commonly used, throw the communication out of balance. Assertive behavior strikes a balance between aggression and passivity. If you can be an assertive communicator, you will be more likely to get your message across while assuring that others have a chance to speak as well. Table 9.2 compares some characteristics of each kind of communicator.

Aggressive communicators focus primarily on their own needs. They can become angry and impatient when those needs are not immediately satisfied. To become more assertive, aggressive communicators might try to take time to think before speaking, avoid ordering people around, use "I" statements, and focus on listening to what the other person has to say.

Assertive
Able to declare and affirm one's own opinions while respecting the rights of others to do the same.

Aggressive, Passive, and Assertive Styles

TABLE 9.2

AGGRESSIVE	PASSIVE	ASSERTIVE
Loud, heated arguing	Concealing one's own feelings	Expressing feelings without being nasty or overbearing
Physically violent encounters	Denying one's own anger	Acknowledging emotions but staying open to discussion
Blaming, name-calling, and verbal insults	Feeling that one has no right to express anger	Expressing oneself and giving others the chance to express themselves equally
Walking out of arguments before they are resolved	Avoiding arguments	Using "I" statements to defuse arguments
Being demanding: "Do this . . ."	Being noncommittal: "You don't have to do this unless you really want to . . ."	Asking and giving reasons: "I would appreciate it if you would do this, and here's why . . ."

Springboard
Discuss how language sometimes communicates weakness. For example, what words communicate weakness in the following: "I'm sorry to interrupt, but..." "I may not have the right to say this, but..."? How would students change these phrases to make them more assertive, but not aggressive?

Passive communicators deny themselves the power that aggressive people grab. They focus almost exclusively on the needs of others instead of on their own needs, often experiencing unexpressed frustration and tension. To become more assertive, passive communicators might try to acknowledge anger or hurt more often, speak up when they feel strongly about something, realize that they have a right to make requests, and know that their ideas and feelings are as important as anyone else's.

Good communication skills will come in handy when you have to communicate in more formal situations. Remember these communication strategies as you read the next section on public speaking.

Speaking/Oral Presentations

Speaking in front of others involves special preparation, strategy, and confidence. Whether you are giving group project results to your class or making a presentation to coworkers, think critically in order to make your communication as effective as it can be. Use the strategies that follow.

Compare Speaking to Writing

If you think of speaking as a verbal equivalent to writing, you can apply writing strategies to speaking. Here are some strategies that apply to both activities:

> Think through what you want to say and why. What is your purpose—to make or refute an argument, present information, entertain? Have a goal for your speech.

> Plan. Get organized beforehand. Brainstorm your topic—narrow it with prewriting strategies, determine your central idea or argument, and write an outline. Do research if you need to.

> Draft your thoughts. It's important to get your thoughts organized for both speaking and writing. Instead of writing out complete sentences, make a draft using "trigger" words or phrases that will remind you of what you want to say.

> Use clear thinking. Illustrate ideas with examples, and show how examples lead to ideas. As in writing, have a clear beginning and end. Begin with an attention-getter and end with a wrap-up that summarizes your thoughts and leaves your audience with something to remember.

Springboard
Ask students whether they think written language and spoken language are the same. That is, will a document intended for reading be successful as a speech?

Think Critically About Your Audience

Your speech will be most effective if it takes your audience into consideration. As in writing, take time to think about who your listeners are and how you expect them to respond. Consider the following about your audience:

- profile (ages, backgrounds, interests)
- roles (instructors, students, coworkers, customers)
- expected knowledge base (experts, beginners, in between)

- expected response (in agreement, in disagreement, open- or close-minded)
- issues or questions you expect they may have

When you have developed a picture of your listeners, tailor your speech to them. For example, a presentation to coworkers who know a lot about a computer system will not require an elementary explanation of the system, whereas a presentation to a class of beginners will emphasize the basics.

Practice Your Performance

The element of performance distinguishes speaking from writing. Use the following strategies to combat any performance anxiety you may have.

Model after good speakers. Observe people whom you consider to be successful oral communicators. Watch them live, on TV, or on videotape. Listen to them on the radio. Think about what elements draw you in, keep your attention, and inspire you to consider ideas.

Know the parameters. How long do you have? What topics do you have to choose from? Make sure you stick to the guidelines that your instructor gives you. Where will you be speaking? Be aware of the physical setting—where your audience will be, where you will be, and what you may have around you to use (a podium, table, chair, or blackboard, for example).

Use index cards or notes. It's helpful to have notes to refer to. However, keep them out of your face; it's tempting to hide behind them. Use visuals if they help you to illustrate ideas.

Pay attention to the physical. Your body positioning, your voice, and what you wear contribute to the impression you make. Look good and sound good. Walk around if you like to talk that way. Above all, make eye contact with your audience. You are speaking to them—be sure to look at them.

Practice ahead of time. Do a test run with friends or alone. If you can, practice in the room where you will speak. Audiotape or videotape yourself practicing, and use the tapes to evaluate yourself. Give yourself a positive image—envision yourself delivering the speech successfully and skillfully.

Be Yourself

When you write, you express your personality through your particular style of putting words together. When you speak, you do the same—plus, you add the element of your presence. First of all, if you have a choice of topic, choose something that moves or interests you. Then, don't be afraid to add your own bits of humor or style to the presentation. Finally, take deep breaths. Smile. Know that you can communicate successfully and that, in most situations, your audience has the very same hope for you.

Knowing who you are and being yourself isn't just useful for making oral presentations. It will also help you make the most of your personal relationships.

HOW DO YOUR PERSONAL RELATIONSHIPS DEFINE YOU?

The relationships you have with friends, family members, and significant others often take center stage. The people with whom you share your life help to define who you are. Since birth, you have acquired knowledge from their verbal and nonverbal language. Those with whom you live, play, study, and work are primary sources of ideas, beliefs, and ways of living.

These influential relationships can affect other areas of your life. On one hand, you may have experienced conflict that caused you to be unable to sleep, eat, or get work done. On the other hand, a successful relationship can have positive effects on your life, increasing your success at work or at school.

Relationship Strategies

If you can feel good about your personal relationships, other areas of your life will benefit. Here are some strategies for improving your personal relationships:

Real World Link
Have students discuss the pluses and minuses of Internet relationships, which begin in chat rooms or with e-mail. Stress the role fantasy plays in these relationships. Ask students if they consider these relationships as real and meaningful as traditional friendships.

Make personal relationships a high priority. Nurture the ones you have and be open to new ones. Life is meant to be shared. In some marriage ceremonies, the bride and groom share a cup of wine, symbolizing that the sweetness of life is doubled by tasting it together and the bitterness is cut in half when shared by two. Any personal relationship can benefit from the experience of this kind of sharing.

Invest time. You devote time to education, work, and the other priorities in your life. Relationships need the same investment of attention. In addition, spending time with people you like can relieve everyday stress and strain. When you make time for others, everyone benefits.

Spend time with people you respect and admire. Life is too short to hang out with people who bring you down, encourage you to participate in activities you don't approve of, or behave in ways that upset you. Develop relationships with people who you respect, whose choices you admire, and who inspire you to fulfill your potential.

Getting to know one another.

Work through tensions. Negative feelings can multiply when left unspoken. Unexpressed feelings about other issues may cause you to become disproportionately angry over a small issue. Get to the root of the problem. Discuss it, deal with it, and move on.

Refuse to tolerate violence. People may tolerate violence out of a belief that it will end, a desire to keep their families together, a self-esteem so low that they believe they deserve what they get, or a fear that trying to leave may lead to greater violence. No level of violence is acceptable. If you find that you are either an aggressor or a victim, do your best to get help. See Chapter 10 for more information on domestic violence.

Show appreciation. In this fast-moving world, people don't thank each other often enough. If you think of something positive, say it. Thank someone for a service or express your affection with a smile. A little positive reinforcement goes a long way toward nurturing a relationship.

If you want a friend, be a friend. If you treat a friend with the kind of loyalty and support that you appreciate yourself, you are more likely to receive the same in return.

Take risks. It can be frightening to reveal your deepest dreams and frustrations, to devote yourself to a friend, or to fall in love. However, giving is what makes a relationship grow. If you take the plunge, you stand to gain the incredible benefits of companionship, which for most people outweigh the risks.

Don't force yourself into a pattern that doesn't suit you. Some students date exclusively and commit early. Some students prefer to socialize in groups. Some students date casually and like to maintain a distance from the people they date. Be honest with yourself—and with those with whom you socialize—about what is right for you at any given time. Don't let public opinion about the "right" way to behave get in the way of your needs.

Keep personal problems in their place. Solve personal problems with the people directly involved. If at all possible, try not to bring your emotions into class or work. Doing so may hurt your performance while doing nothing to help your problem.

If a relationship doesn't work out, find ways to cope. Everyone experiences strain and breakups in intimate relationships, friendships, and family ties. Be kind to yourself, and use coping strategies that help you move on. Some people need time alone; others need to spend time with friends and family. Some seek counseling. Some people throw their energy into a project, job, class, or a new workout regimen. Some just need to cry it out. Some write in a journal. Do what's right for you, and believe that sooner or later you can emerge from the experience stronger and with new perspective.

Now and again, your personal relationships will be in conflict. Following are ideas for how to deal with conflict and criticism in a productive and positive way.

Springboard
Discuss how the following will help defuse an argument: (1) Spending more time listening than talking; (2) Focusing on feelings, not thoughts; (3) Sticking to the point; (4) Never trying to hurt the other person by attacking weaknesses.

Career Connection
Many large corporations have Employee Assistance Programs (EAPs) to help workers manage personal problems including childcare, divorce, addiction, and mental illness. EAPs offer confidential counseling and are run by trained professionals.

HOW CAN YOU HANDLE CONFLICT AND CRITICISM?

Conflict and criticism, as unpleasant as they can be, are natural elements in the dynamic of getting along with others. It's normal to want to avoid people or situations that cause distress. However, if you can face your fears and think about them critically, you can gain valuable insight into human nature—your own and that of others. You may be able to make important changes in your life based on what you learn.

Conflict Strategies

Conflicts, both large and small, arise when there is a clash of ideas or interests. You may have small conflicts with a housemate over a door left unlocked or a bill that needs paying. On the other end of the spectrum, you might encounter major conflicts with your partner about finances or with an instructor about a failing grade.

Conflict can create anger and frustration, shutting down communication. The two most destructive tendencies are to avoid the conflict altogether (a passive tactic) or to let it escalate into a huge fight (an aggressive tendency). Avoidance doesn't make the problem go away—in fact, it will probably worsen; however, a shouting match gives no one an opportunity or desire to listen.

If calmly and intelligently handled, conflict can shed light on new ideas and help to strengthen bonds between those involved. The primary keys to conflict resolution are calm communication and critical-thinking skills. Think through any conflict, using what you know about problem solving.

1. **Identify and analyze the problem.** Determine the severity of the problem by looking at its effects on everyone involved. Then, find and analyze its causes.

2. **Brainstorm possible solutions.** Consider as many angles as you can, without judgment. Explore what ideas you can come up with from what you or others have done in a similar situation.

3. **Explore each solution.** Evaluate the positive and negative effects of each solution. Why might each work, not work, or work partially? What would take into account everyone's needs? What would cause the least stress? Make sure everyone has a chance to express an opinion.

4. **Choose, carry out, and evaluate the solution you decide is best.** When you have implemented your choice, evaluate its effects. Decide whether you feel it was a good choice.

One more hint: Use "I" statements. Focus on the effects the problem has had on you rather than focusing on someone who caused it.

Dealing with Criticism and Feedback

No one gets everything right all the time. People use constructive criticism and **feedback** to communicate what went wrong and to suggest improvements. Consider any criticism carefully. If you always interpret criticism as a threat, you will close yourself off from learning. Even if you eventually decide that you disagree, you can still learn from exploring the possibility.

Criticism can be either **constructive** or nonconstructive. Criticism is considered constructive when it is offered supportively and contains useful suggestions for improvement. In contrast, nonconstructive criticism focuses on what went wrong, doesn't offer alternatives or help, and is often delivered in a negative or harsh manner. Whereas constructive criticism can promote a sense of hope for improvement in the future, nonconstructive criticism can create tension, bad feelings, and defensiveness.

Any criticism can be offered constructively or nonconstructively. Consider a case in which someone has continually been late to work. A supervisor can offer criticism in either of these ways:

Constructive. The supervisor talks privately with the employee: "I've noticed that you have been late to work a lot. Other people have had to do some of your work. Is there a problem that is keeping you from being on time? Is it something that I or someone else can help you with?"

Feedback
Evaluative or corrective information about an action or process.

Constructive
Promoting improvement or development.

Learning Styles Tip
Students with a highly developed musical intelligence may be especially sensitive to the vocal qualities of nonconstructive, critical speech.

Nonconstructive. The supervisor watches the employee slip into work late. The supervisor says, in front of other employees, "Nice to see you could make it. If you can't start getting here on time, I might look for someone else who can."

How might you react? Think about which situation you consider to have more positive effects. If you can learn to give constructive criticism and deal with whatever criticism comes your way from others, you will improve your relationships and your productivity. When offered constructively and carefully considered, criticism can bring about important changes.

Giving Constructive Criticism

When you offer criticism, use the following strategies to communicate clearly and effectively:

- **Criticize the behavior rather than the person.** Make sure the behavior you intend to criticize is changeable. Chronic lateness can be changed; a physical inability to perform a task cannot.

- **Define specifically the behavior you want to change.** Try not to drag any side issues into the conversation.

- **Limit the behaviors you will criticize to one.** If you have others, discuss them later, one at a time. People can hear criticism better if they are not hit with several issues at once.

- **Balance criticism with positive words.** Alternate critical comments with praise in other areas.

- **Stay calm and be brief.** Avoid threats, ultimatums, or accusations. Use "I" messages; choose positive, nonthreatening words so the person knows that your intentions are positive.

- **Explain the effects caused by the behavior.** Talk about options in detail. Compare and contrast the effects of the current behavior with the effects of a potential change.

- **Offer help in changing the behavior.** Lead by example.

Receiving Criticism

When you find yourself on the receiving end of criticism, use the following coping techniques:

- **Listen to the criticism first.** Resist the desire to defend yourself until you've heard all the details. Decide if the criticism is offered in a constructive or nonconstructive manner.

- **Think the criticism through critically.** Evaluate it carefully. Is it constructive? Does it come from a desire to help, or has it emerged from a place of jealousy or frustration? It may be best to let nonconstructive criticism go without a response.

- **If the criticism is constructive, ask for suggestions on how to change the criticized behavior.** You could ask, "How would you handle this if you were in my place?"

How can I deal with diversity?

Richard Pan, Columbia University, New York City, Engineering Major

I was born in Taiwan and came to the United States when I was 12. At my high school in Santa Barbara, California, everyone mingled well. Caucasian kids hung out with Asians and African-Americans, and we all got along fine. Then, when I started college at Columbia University, I noticed a difference. The Asian kids hung out only with other Asians, and the Caucasians did the same. I'm used to hanging out with all sorts of people, and I like that. Now I feel this tension. It's as if the Asian kids are thinking, "Why is he bothering to hang out with them?"

During a summer work program at Harvard, I roomed with a Chinese-American who advised me to avoid being friends with

people from different ethnic groups. Although I don't feel comfortable with his advice, I do think you get judged by all sides when you try to be friends with everybody. Sometimes if I'm with a Caucasian person and other Caucasian people approach us, they aren't as friendly, talking only to the other Caucasian kid like I'm not there. Whenever I've tried to talk to my Asian friends about this problem, they respond jokingly, saying something like, "Rich, you're just better at doing that [mingling with other groups] than I am."

Sometimes I feel like I'm having an identity crisis. I ask myself, "Which side am I on?" I'm not really Asian-American because I wasn't born here, but I have become accustomed to America and I like living here. I think overall I've handled the situation pretty well, but I am open to suggestions. Do you have any ideas about how I could do a better job managing this problem?

Jo Anne Roe, Spanish Instructor, Oak Park–River Forest High School, Illinois

It is wonderful that you have developed the ability to mingle with and enjoy the company of people from diverse backgrounds. This is a skill that many people do not possess; it is a skill that will be immensely valuable for your personal and professional future. Your comfort in a multicultural setting reflects self-assurance, maturity, and a clearly defined sense of identity.

The problem that you face—prejudice—does not originate within you but rather is being imposed upon you. To accuse one specific group of having a monopoly on this practice would be a denial of the truth. Misunderstanding of, apprehension toward, and nonacceptance of others who are different are facets of an elemental and, sadly, universal flaw in the human psyche. And because it is so painful, it is natural for people to guard themselves against its damage.

Perhaps some Caucasians display insensitivity out of fear of being rejected by their peers. Or, perhaps these same students believe they accept you so completely that not to show that they are aware of your presence is evidence that you are "one of the guys." I imagine that the other Asian-Americans are advising you out of sincere concern for you not to be hurt by people with whom they have had negative encounters in the past. The bottom line is that you are not at fault!

The best advice that I can offer to you is the "Golden Rule": Treat other people the way you want them to treat you. In following the wisdom of this refrain, you neither compromise your own outlook on life nor give in to the fears and insecurities of other people, and you maintain human dignity in general. Continue as you are and be patient. Eventually you will begin to see gradual and positive changes in the actions of your friends, directly due to the impact you will have made on them through your positive, accepting attitude.

- **Summarize the criticism and your response to it.** Repeat it back to the person who offered it. Make sure both of you understand the situation in the same way.
- **Plan a specific strategy.** Think over how you might change your behavior and what you might learn from the change.

Remember that the most important feedback you will receive in school is from your instructors, and the most important on-the-job feedback will come from your supervisors, more experienced peers, and occasionally clients. Making a special effort to take in this feedback and consider it carefully will help you learn many important lessons. Furthermore, knowing how to handle conflict and criticism will help you define your role and communicate with others when you work in groups.

WHAT ROLE DO YOU PLAY IN GROUPS?

Group interaction is an important part of your educational, personal, and working life. With a team project at work or a cooperative learning exercise in school, for example, being able to work well together is necessary to accomplish a goal.

A group or team can be coworkers, fellow students, a family, or any other people who need to accomplish a goal together. Because everyone has a vested interest in the outcome, all group members should have the opportunity to voice opinions and to participate in reaching the desired goal.

The two major roles in the group experience are those of participant and leader. Any group needs both to function successfully. Become aware of the role you tend to play, and try different roles to evaluate where you can be most effective. The following strategies are linked to either participating or leading.[8] Keep in mind that for many groups, the lines may blur: Members may perform some leadership tasks and some participant tasks at the same time, or the leadership of the group may shift frequently.

Learning Styles Tip
To enhance interpersonal intelligence in a group setting and to encourage a flow of ideas, suggest that group meetings take place at a round table.

Being an Effective Participant

Some people are happiest when participating in group activities that someone else leads and designs. They don't feel comfortable in a position of control. They prefer to take on an assigned role in the project. Participants need to remember that they are "part owners" of the process. Each team member has a responsibility for, and a stake in, the outcome. The following strategies will help a participant to be effective.

Critical Thinking
Why is an effective leader, necessary—but not sufficient—for group success? Can students think of an example in which a leader and participants shared responsibility for the success of the group's efforts?

Participation Strategies

Get involved. If the rest of the group makes a decision you don't like and you don't speak up, you have no one to blame but yourself for the group's poor choice. Let people know your views.

Be organized. When you participate, stay focused and organized. The more organized your ideas are, the more people will listen, take them into consideration, and be willing to try them.

Be willing to discuss. Everyone has an equal right to express his or her ideas. Even as you enthusiastically present your opinions, be willing to consider those of others.

Keep your word. Do what you say you're going to do. Let people know what you have accomplished. If you bring little or nothing to the process, your team members may feel as if you weigh them down rather than pulling your own weight.

Focus on ideas, not people. One of the easiest ways to start an argument is for participants to attack people instead of discussing their ideas. Separate the person from the idea, and keep the idea in focus.

Play fairly. Give everyone a chance to participate. Be respectful of other people's ideas. Don't dominate the discussion or try to control or manipulate others.

Being an Effective Leader

Teaching Tolerance
Students from Asian and Far Eastern backgrounds may be reluctant to be group leaders because of cultural taboos that discourage assertive behavior.

Some people prefer to initiate the action, make decisions, and control how things proceed. They have ideas they want to put into practice and enjoy explaining them to others. They are comfortable giving directions to people and guiding group outcomes. Leaders often have a "big picture" perspective; it allows them to see how all of the different aspects of a group project can come together. In any group the following strategies will help a leader succeed.

Leadership Strategies

Critical Thinking
Can a leader be effective without a powerful vision? Is the ability to inspire others an important part of leadership? Does being a leader imply going it alone, or do great leaders recruit others to help achieve goals? Ask students for examples to support their opinions.

Define and limit projects. One of the biggest ways to waste time and energy is to assume that a group will know its purpose. The leader should define the purpose of the gathering and limit tasks so the group doesn't take on too much. Some common purposes are giving/exchanging information, brainstorming, making a decision, delegating tasks, or collaborating on a project.

Map out who will perform which tasks. A group functions best when everyone has a particular contribution to make. You can help different personalities work together by exploring who can do what best. Give people specific responsibilities, trusting that they will do their jobs.

Set the agenda. The leader is responsible for establishing and communicating the goal of the project and how it will proceed. Without a plan, it's easy to get off track. Having a written agenda to which group members can refer is helpful. A good leader invites advice from others when determining group direction.

Focus progress. Even when everyone knows the plan, it's still natural to wander off the topic. The leader should do his or her best to keep everyone to the topic at hand. When challenges arise midstream, the leader may need to help the team change direction.

Set the tone. Setting a positive tone helps to bring the group together and motivate people. When a leader values diversity in ideas and backgrounds and sets a tone of fairness, respect, and encouragement, group members may feel more comfortable contributing their ideas.

Evaluate results. The leader should determine whether the team is accomplishing its goals. If the team is not moving ahead, the leader needs to make changes and decisions.

If you don't believe that you fit into the traditional definition of a leader, remember that there are other ways to lead that don't involve taking charge of a group. You can lead others by setting an honorable example in your actions, choices, or words. You can lead by putting forth an idea that takes a group in a new direction. You can lead by being the kind of person who others would like to be.

Considering Cultural Differences

Even if you are equipped with all kinds of information about successful group interaction, unexpected issues can arise due to cultural differences. People from different cultural backgrounds may have different ways of interacting or even different ideas of what constitutes a leadership or participatory role.

The kinds of cultural differences that affect group interaction are the same differences that affect any communication among people of different cultures. Two people may behave in very different ways or may have different opinions of the same idea or thing. Here are some examples:[9]

- Your biology study group is scheduled to meet at 8 A.M. sharp to prepare for a big test the following day. Everyone is on time except one classmate who shows up 45 minutes late—not because he is rude but because punctuality does not have a high value in his culture.

- A classmate in one of your collaborative work groups keeps staring at you for prolonged periods. Insulted by his rudeness, you are about to say something when another group member who senses your discomfort tells you that natives of his country of origin often believe that extended eye contact will reveal what is in a person's heart.

In their book *CrossTalk: Communicating in a Multicultural Workplace*, Sherron B. Kenton and Deborah Valentine report, "The increasingly multicultural environment where we live and work creates a proportionately complex communication challenge. Our employers expect us to communicate effectively in complex situations to people who are often very different from ourselves."[10] This observation certainly applies to educational environments as well. Use the following guidelines, based on Kenton and Valentine's communication model, to ask yourself important questions about any situation in which you need to communicate with people notably different from you:

1. **Consider the environment.** Who are you talking to? What is the atmosphere in which you will be communicating? What choices will be most favorable to this audience in this situation?

2. **Choose your options.** How can you send your message so that this particular group will understand? When will the message be most successfully received?

3. **Collect and organize your information.** What kinds of information and which communication structure will be most effective?

Real World Link
Ask students to think about the meetings they attended recently in school, at work, or in voluntary activities and to identify the strengths and weaknesses of meeting leaders. Ask the class for their reactions to these qualities.

"I have a dream that one day on the red hills of Georgia the sons of former slaves and the sons of former slave owners will be able to sit down together at the table of brotherhood."
Martin Luther King, Jr.

4. **Deliver your message.** What mode of delivery will be make your message most accessible to this audience?

5. **Confirm evaluation for success.** What feedback have you received from your audience? Did they receive the message you intended to send?

Many different details define any given group of people. Your success depends not on the details themselves but on whether you have adequately investigated those details and incorporated your knowledge into your communication choices. The best communicators reach out to their audiences with understanding and respect, not with judgment.

It takes the equal participation of all group members to achieve a goal. Whatever role works best for you, know that your contribution is essential. You may even play different roles with different groups. You might be a participator at school and a leader in a self-help group. You could enjoy leading a religious group but prefer to take a backseat at work. Find a role that feels comfortable. The happier each group member is, the more effectively the group as a whole will function.

Kente

The African word *kente* means "that which will not tear under any condition." *Kente* cloth is worn by men and women in African countries such as Ghana, Ivory Coast, and Togo. There are many brightly colored patterns of *kente,* each beautiful, unique, and special.

Think of how this concept applies to being human. Like the cloth, all people are unique, with brilliant and subdued aspects. Despite any mistreatment or misunderstanding by the people you encounter in your life, you need to remain strong so that you don't tear and give way to disrespectful behavior. This strength can help you to endure, stand up against any injustice, and fight peacefully but relentlessly for the rights of all people.

BUILDING SKILLS FOR COLLEGE, CAREER, AND LIFE SUCCESS

Critical Thinking
Applying Learning to Life

Diversity Discovery

Express your own personal diversity. Describe yourself in response to the following questions:

How would you identify yourself (write words or short phrases that describe you)?

_____

_____

_____

Name one or more facts about yourself that would not be obvious to someone who has just met you.

_____

_____

Name two values or beliefs that govern how you live, what you pursue, and/or with whom you associate.

_____

_____

What choices have you made that tell something about who you are?

_____

_____

_____

Now, join with a partner in your class. Try to choose someone you don't know well. Your goal is to communicate what you have written to your partner, and for your partner to communicate to you in the same way. Talk to each other for 10 minutes, and take notes on what the other person says. At the end of that period, join together as a class. Each person will describe his or her partner to the class.

What did you learn about your partner that surprised you?

_____

_____

What did you learn that went against any assumptions you may have made about that person based on his or her appearance, background, or behavior?

_____

_____

_____

Has this exercise changed the way you see this person or other people? Why or why not?

_____

_____

_____

Prejudice

Name an incorrect assumption others may have about you.

_____

_____

Why would others assume this?

_____

_____

Now, describe a prejudice that you have, or have had, that is directed toward another group.

_____

_____

Think critically about this prejudice. In what ways is this unfair or illogical?

_____

_____

How do you plan to work to gain perspective about your prejudice?

_____

Your Communication Style

Look back at the communication styles on p. 282. Which describes you the best? Write the three styles that fit you best, listing them from most to least dominant.

1. _____
2. _____
3. _____

Of the two styles that best fit you, which one has more positive effects on your ability to communicate? What are those effects?

_____
_____

Which style has more negative effects? What are they?

_____
_____

To determine whether you are primarily passive, aggressive, or assertive, read the following sentences and circle the ones that sound like something you would say to a peer.

1. Get me the keys.
2. Would you mind if I stepped out just for a second?
3. Don't slam the door.
4. I'd appreciate it if you would have this done by two o'clock. The client is coming at three.
5. I think maybe it needs a little work just at the end, but I'm not sure.
6. Please take this back to the library.
7. You will have a good time if you join us.
8. Your loss.
9. If you think so, I'll try it.
10. Let me know what you want me to do.
11. Turn it this way and see what happens.
12. We'll try both our ideas and see what works best.
13. I want it on my desk by the end of the day.
14. Just do what I told you.
15. If this isn't how you wanted it to look, I can change it. Just tell me and I'll do it.

Aggressive communicators would be likely to use sentences 1, 3, 8, 13, and 14.
Passive communicators would probably opt for sentences 2, 5, 9, 10, and 15.
Assertive communicators would probably choose sentences 4, 6, 7, 11, and 12.

From which category did you choose the most sentences? _____

If you scored as an assertive communicator, you are on the right track. If you scored in the aggressive or passive categories, analyze your style. What are the effects? Give an example in your own life of the effects of your style.

_____

_____

Turn back to p. 287 to review suggestions for aggressive or passive communicators. What can you do to improve your skills?

_____

Teamwork
Combining Forces

Problem Solving Close to Home Divide into small groups of two to five students. Assign one group member to take notes. Discuss the following questions, one by one:

1. What are the three largest problems my school faces with regard to how people get along with and accept others?
2. What could my school do to deal with these three problems?
3. What can each individual student do to deal with these three problems? (Talk about what *you* specifically feel that you can do.)

When you are finished, gather as a class and hear each group's responses. Observe the variety of problems and solutions. Notice whether more than one group came up with one or more of the same problems. You may want to assign one person in the class to gather all of the responses together. That person, together with your instructor, could put these responses into an organized document that you can give to the upper-level administrators at your school.

Writing
Discovery Through Journaling

To record your thoughts, use a separate journal or the lined page at the end of the chapter.

New Perspective[11] Imagine that you have no choice but to change either your gender or your racial, ethnic, or religious group. Which would you change and why? What do you anticipate would be the positive and negative effects of the change—in your social life, in your family life, on the job, and at school? How would what you know and experience before the change affect how you would behave after it?

Career Portfolio
Charting Your Course

Compiling a Résumé What you have accomplished in various work and school situations will be important for you to emphasize as you strive to land your ideal job. Whether on the job, in school, in the community, or at home, your roles help you gain knowledge and experience.

Use two pieces of paper. On one, list your education and skills information. On the other, list job experience. For each job record your job title, the dates of employment, and the tasks that this job entailed (if the job had no particular title, come up with one yourself). Be as detailed as possible— it's best to write down everything you remember. When you compile your résumé, you can make this material more concise. Keep this list current by adding experiences and accomplishments to it as you go along.

Using the information you have gathered and Figure 9.4 as your guide, draft a résumé for yourself. Remember that there are many ways to construct a résumé; consult other resources (such as those listed in the bibliography) for different styles. You may want to reformat your résumé according to a style that your career counselor or instructor recommends, that best suits the career area you plan to enter, or that you like best.

Don't discount non-workplace accomplishments when putting together your resume or deciding what to talk about in an interview. The hands-on experience of volunteering with cancer patients or the coordination skills it takes to run a household can be as valuable to an employer as any paying work you've done.

Keep your résumé draft on hand—and on a computer disk. When you need to submit a résumé with a job application, check the draft, update it if necessary, and print it out on high-quality paper.

Here are some general tips for writing a résumé:

- Always put your name and contact information at the top. Make it stand out.

- State an objective if it is appropriate—that is, if your focus is specific and/or you are designing this résumé for a particular interview or career area.

- List your post-secondary education, starting from the latest and working backwards. This may include summer school, night school, and seminars.

- List jobs in reverse chronological order (most recent job first). Include all types of work experience (full-time, part-time, volunteer, internship, and so on).

- When you describe your work experience, use action verbs and focus on what you have accomplished, rather than on the description of assigned tasks.

- Have references listed on a separate sheet. You may want to put "References upon request" at the bottom of your résumé.

- Use formatting (larger font sizes, different fonts, italics, bolding, and so on) and indents selectively to help the important information stand out.

- Get people to look at your résumé before you send it out. Other readers will have ideas that you haven't thought of, and may pick up errors that you have missed.

FIGURE 9.4 *Sample Résumé*

DÉSIRÉE WILLIAMS
237 Custer Street, San Francisco, CA 92017 • 650/555-5252 (W) or 415/555-7865 (H)
fax: 707/555-2735 e-mail: desiree@zzz.com

EDUCATION

1997 to present **San Francisco State University, San Francisco, CA**
Pursuing a B.A. in the Spanish BCLAD (Bilingual, Cross-Cultural Language Acquisition Development) Education and Multiple Subject Credential Program. Expected graduation: June, 2001

PROFESSIONAL EMPLOYMENT

10/98 to present **Research Assistant, Knowledge Media Lab**
Developing ways for teachers to exhibit their inquiry into their practice of teaching in an online, collaborative, multimedia environment.

5/99 to present **Webmaster/ Web Designer**
Worked in various capacities at QuakeNet, an Internet Service Provider and Web Commerce Specialist in San Mateo, CA. Designed several sites for the University of California, Berkeley, Graduate School of Education, as well as private clients such as A Body of Work and Yoga Forever.

9/97 to 6/98 **Literacy Coordinator**
Coordinated, advised, and created literacy curriculum for an America Reads literacy project at Prescott School in West Oakland. Worked with non-reader 4th graders on writing and publishing, incorporating digital photography, internet resources, and graphic design.

8/97 **Bilingual Educational Consultant**
Consulted for Children's Television Workshop, field-testing bilingual materials. With a research team, designed bilingual educational materials for an ecotourism project run by an indigenous rain forest community in Ecuador.

1/97 to 6/97 **Technology Consultant**
Worked with 24 Hours in Cyberspace, an on-line worldwide photojournalism event. Coordinated participation of schools, translated documents, and facilitated public relations.

SKILLS

Languages: Fluent in **Spanish.**
Proficient in **Italian** and **Shona** (majority language of Zimbabwe).

Computer: Programming ability in **HTML, Javascript, Pascal,** and **Lisp.**
Multimedia design expertise in **Adobe Photoshop, Netobjects Fusion, Adobe Premiere, Macromedia Flash,** and many other visual design programs.

Personal: Perform professionally in Mary Schmary, a women's a cappella quartet. Have climbed Mt. Kilimanjaro.

Name

Date

B A L A N C E

Personal Wellness
Taking Care of Yourself

In this chapter, you will explore answers to the following questions:

- How can you maintain a healthy body?
- How do you nurture a healthy mind?
- How are alcohol, tobacco, and drugs used and abused?
- What should you consider when making sexual decisions?

Your physical and mental health affect your ability to succeed in school. It doesn't matter how great your classes are if you aren't physically healthy enough to get to them or mentally healthy enough to focus and learn while you're there. In this chapter you will examine both the physical and mental aspects of wellness, looking at how to maintain your health as well as how to identify and work through particular health problems that many students face. You will also explore substance use and abuse and sexuality as they relate to your personal wellness.

Teaching Tip

Helpful Web sites:

- Centers for Disease Control National Prevention Information Network - www.cdcnpin.org/
- Food and Nutrition Information Center - www.nalusda.gov/fnic
- Duke University Health Devil Online - gilligan.mc.duke.edu/h-devil/
- Healthwise - www.goaskalice.columbia.edu/
- Suicide Awareness\Voices of Education - www.save.org
- National Clearinghouse for Alcohol and Drug Information - www.health.org
- QuitNet - A Free Resource To Quit Smoking - www.quitnet.org

HOW CAN YOU MAINTAIN A HEALTHY BODY?

Although your daily schedule may leave you little time to take care good of yourself, it's important to take time to focus on yourself. The healthier you are, the more energy you'll have both for yourself and for those who share your life. Eating right, exercising, getting enough sleep, and taking advantage of medical care will help you maintain a healthy body. For each of these aspects of your health, think critically about your choices and consider them in light of what you know about yourself.

Eating Right

Be a Team
Have 4-person teams research the health benefits of the following foods and report their findings to the class: milk, broccoli, tomatoes, soy, whole grains, red grapes, garlic, and omega-3 oils (found in cold-water fish).

The food and drink you take in help build and maintain your body. If you eat well, you are more likely to be strong and healthy. If you take in too much fat, sugar, processed foods, and other less-than-nutritional substances, your body will operate at reduced power. Learning to make healthier choices about what you eat on a daily basis can lead to more energy, better general health, and an enriched quality of life.

The U. S. Departments of Agriculture and of Health and Human Services have developed a publication called *Dietary Guidelines for Americans*, which lists seven important rules of healthy eating.

1. Eat a variety of foods.
2. Maintain a healthy weight.
3. Choose a diet low in fat and cholesterol.
4. Choose a diet with plenty of vegetables, fruits, and grain products.
5. Use sugars in moderation.
6. Use salt and sodium only in moderation.
7. If you drink alcoholic beverages, do so in moderation.

Teaching Tip
Help students be conscious of foods with "hidden" sugar content, such as yogurt with fruit on the bottom of the cup, which contains up to 9 teaspoons of sugar per cup.

Maintaining balance and eating in moderation can help you maintain a healthy diet.

Maintaining Balance

If you vary your diet with foods from the different food groups—meats and meat substitutes, dairy, breads and grains, and fruits and vegetables—you are more likely to take in the different nutrients that your body needs. Figure 10.1 shows the servings that the U. S. Department of Agriculture recommends.

Maintaining balance also means limiting foods that are potential health hazards. From time to time a piece of cake, a cup of coffee, or an order of French fries can add to life's enjoyment and probably won't hurt you. In excess, though, sugar, fats, salt, and caffeine have the potential to damage your health.

Critical Thinking
Can you conclude that because Americans are eating more vegetables, their diets are healthier than they've ever been? Why is it important to know which vegetables they are eating? (In fact, Americans' favorite veggie is the French fried potato, which is laden with fat and calories.)

- Sugar gives you quick energy but lets you down fast.
- Fats pile on extra pounds that overburden your system.
- Too much salt can raise your blood pressure to dangerous levels.
- Caffeine can irritate your stomach and overstimulate your heart and nervous system.

Food Guide Pyramid

FIGURE 10.1

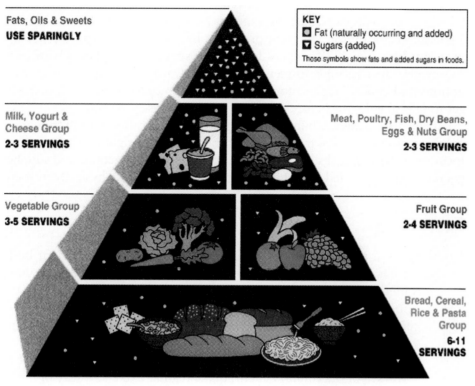

KEY
- ☐ Fat (naturally occurring and added)
- ☑ Sugars (added)

These symbols show fats and added sugars in foods.

Fats, Oils & Sweets
USE SPARINGLY

Milk, Yogurt &
Cheese Group
2-3 SERVINGS

Meat, Poultry, Fish, Dry Beans,
Eggs & Nuts Group
2-3 SERVINGS

Vegetable Group
3-5 SERVINGS

Fruit Group
2-4 SERVINGS

Bread, Cereal,
Rice & Pasta
Group
**6-11
SERVINGS**

Source: U. S. Department of Agriculture and the U. S. Department of Health and Human Services.

Many people develop addictive behavior around these substances—primarily caffeine, which is a drug. If you think you overdo any of these, try cutting back for a couple of weeks and evaluate how you feel (you may actually feel worse for a time—caffeine **withdrawal,** for example, can cause severe headaches). If you feel better eventually, continue to limit intake or cut out the substance entirely. You will reap the benefits in the long run.

Withdrawal

The discontinuance of the use of a drug, including attendant side effects.

Eating in Moderation

Although your best move is to practice moderation when you eat, college doesn't always make moderation easy. You may be taking snack breaks during late-night study sessions. You may frequent a cafeteria where one price buys all you can eat. You may have fast-food options available at all hours of the day or night. Such opportunities can be hard to resist.

Overeating may lead to health problems; being significantly overweight can aggravate ailments and diseases such as digestive problems, arthritis, diabetes, and cancer. Weight gain, however, isn't always just a medical issue. Many people eat to find comfort and escape problems, seeking to fill the gaps that problems in personal life, school, or work can create. Judith Linsey Palken, in *The Wellness Book,* suggests: "If you tend to make poor food choices, try to determine what triggers the problem. Only by understanding the emotions and situations that lead you to overeat can you begin to make changes."[1]

Learning Style Tip

This diagram will help visual learners master this material. To help verbal learners, repeat the concepts on this diagram during a class lecture.

Teaching Tip

Help students link what they eat now to their future health. For example, stress the relationship between calcium and the prevention of osteoporosis—a debilitating bone-thinning disease—in women. While the average adult woman needs at least 1,000 mg of calcium per day, she takes in only about 600 mg.

Springboard

Have students discuss how they can apply the principles of goal setting they learned in Chapter 3 to weight management. Encourage a discussion of short- and long-term goals and procrastination in this context.

Teaching Tolerance

Many obese people face societal and workplace discrimination. They may have trouble getting a job and making new friends.

Try to moderate your food intake according to one basic measure: Don't eat more than your body can use. If you think you need to examine your eating habits, check out books in your library, look in the Yellow Pages under Weight Control Services, surf Web sites or newsgroups on the Internet, or ask a counselor for advice. Different programs have different purposes. While a program like Weight Watchers lays out a specific diet plan, Overeaters Anonymous focuses on your mental attitude toward food. Explore all of your options and choose one or more that serve your needs. Above all, don't forget to talk to a doctor before starting any weight-loss program.

If you are exhausted, hungry, jittery from sugar or caffeine, or ill from poor nutrition, you may have trouble concentrating. Eating right helps your mind focus on important tasks because it reduces potential distractions and supplies good energy. A well-fed body frees the mind, and so does a physically fit body.

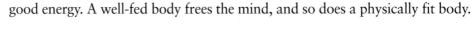

e-mail

Write or talk to one of your friends about a goal you would like to set that will achieve better all-around health for you. Ask them if there is a goal they would like to set for themselves, so that you can provide mental support for one another.

Exercising

Good physical fitness increases your energy efficiency. An efficient body system has more energy and more ability to direct that energy toward problem solving and the fulfillment of goals. A fit body also helps the mind handle stress. During physical activity, the brain releases endorphins, chemical compounds that have a positive and calming effect on the body.

Your body's physical power can decrease unless you put it to work. For maximum benefit, make regular exercise a way of life. If you haven't been exercising regularly, start slowly. Walking, for example, is one of the most beneficial and available forms of exercise. If you exercise frequently and are already relatively fit, you may prefer a more intense or longer workout. Always check with a physician before beginning any exercise program, and adjust your program to your physical type and fitness level.

Types of Exercise

Springboard

Discuss these exercise-related facts with students. Ask for their personal experiences: (1) Rather than stimulate hunger, exercise curbs hunger and helps dieters eat less; (2) Exercise helps compensate for the slower metabolism that accompanies weight loss.

Career Connection

Bodily-kinesthetic learners can turn their love of movement into a career in dance, theater, exercise physiology, physical therapy, teaching, etc.

The type of exercise you choose depends on factors such as time available, physical limitations, preferences, available facilities, cost, and level of fitness. For example, someone who wants to lose fat may take long walks, while someone who wants to gain muscle may work out with weights. Types of exercise fall into three main categories.

- *Cardiovascular training* is exercise that strengthens your heart muscles and lung capacity. Examples include running, swimming, in-line skating, aerobic dancing, and biking.

- *Strength training* is exercise that strengthens any of many different muscle groups. Examples include using weight machines and free weights and doing pushups and abdominal crunches.

- *Flexibility training* is exercise that maintains and increases muscle flexibility. Examples include various stretches and forms of yoga.

Some exercises, such as lifting weights or biking, fall primarily into one category. Others combine elements of two or all three, such as astanga yoga, which requires constant movement (cardiovascular), stretching (flexibility), and the support of body weight (strength). For maximum benefit and a comprehensive workout, try alternating your exercise methods through **cross training.** For example, if you lift weights, you could use a stationary bike or stair machine for cardiovascular work.

Making Exercise a Priority

Student life, both in school and out, is crammed with responsibilities. You can't always make a nice, neat plan that gets you to the gym three days a week for two hours each time. You also may not have the money for an expensive health club. Be sure to check into your school's fitness opportunities—they may be low cost or even be included in your tuition. The following suggestions will help you make exercise a priority, even in the busiest weeks and on the tightest budgets:

- Walk to classes and meetings on campus.
- Choose the stairs rather than the elevator or escalator.
- Purchase exercise tapes for use at home.
- Do strenuous chores, if your doctor approves, such as shoveling snow, raking, or mowing.
- Play team recreational sports with your school's intramural program or at a local YMCA club.
- Use home exercise equipment such as weights, a treadmill or stair machine, or a mat.
- Work out with a friend or family member to combine socializing and exercise.

Exercise is a key component of a healthy mind and body, as is adequate rest.

Getting Enough Sleep

No one can function well without adequate sleep. During sleep, your body repairs itself while your mind sorts through problems and questions. A lack of sleep, or poor sleep, causes poor concentration and irritability, which can mean a less-than-ideal performance at school and at work. Irritability can also put a strain on personal relationships. Making up for lost sleep with caffeine may raise your anxiety and stress level and leave you more tired than before.

While the average recommended for adults is seven to seven-and-one-half hours of sleep per night, people in their late teens and early twenties may need eight to nine hours. Gauge your needs by evaluating how you feel. If you aren't fatigued or irritable during the day, you may have slept adequately. On the other hand, if you are groggy in the morning or doze off at various times during the day, you may be sleep-deprived.

Barriers to a Good Night's Sleep

College students often get inadequate sleep. Long study sessions may keep you up late, and early classes may get you up early. Socializing, eating, and

---

Cross training
Alternating types of exercise and combining elements from different types of exercise.

Teaching Tip
Sticking to a program involves goal setting and time management. To be successful, busy people who have trouble fitting exercise into their schedules must anticipate setbacks, including exhaustion and aches and pains, and learn to deal with them without giving up.

Be a Team
Research has shown that 30 minutes of exercise a day helps people stay fit. Ask students to list the ways in which they accumulate exercise time and share the list with a partner. Urge them to try to apply their partner's suggestions to their own life.

Springboard
Encourage students to link priority setting and time management (see Chapter 3) with their struggle to get enough sleep. Ask students if all their commitments are essential or if they can eliminate activities to give them flexibility.

Developing physical fitness and inner calm through yoga.

Teaching Tip
Students may find that vigorous exercise in the late evening may actually keep them awake at night.

Critical Thinking
Millions of people in their twenties and thirties see no need for health insurance because they are at low risk for serious health problems. Ask students whether they agree with this position. How do short- and long-term goals and priorities affect the decision to buy health coverage?

drinking may make it hard to settle down. Some barriers to sleep are within your control, and some are not.

What is out of your control? Barriers such as outside noise and your children's needs require you to do what you can to address the situation and then try to get as much sleep as possible. Try using earplugs or playing relaxing music in your room to counteract outside noise.

What is within your control? Late nights out, what you eat and drink, and your study schedule are often (although not always) within your power to change. Schedule your studying so that it doesn't all pile up at the last minute. Avoid a late dinner the night before a big test. Respectfully ask the people you live with to keep the noise down when you need to rest. Be willing to do the same for them.

Tips for Quality Sleep

Sleep expert Gregg D. Jacobs recommends the following steps to better sleep:[2]

- **Reduce consumption of alcohol and caffeine.** Caffeine may keep you awake. Alcohol causes you to sleep more lightly, making you feel less rested and refreshed when you awaken.
- **Exercise regularly.** Studies show that regular exercise, especially in late afternoon or early evening, promotes good sleep because it raises body temperature and then allows it to fall.
  - **Complete tasks an hour or more before you sleep.** Getting things done some time before you turn in gives you a chance to wind down and calm your brain activity.
  - **Establish a comfortable sleeping environment.** Little or no light usually facilitates sleep. Some people like to have quiet, while some prefer the noise of a fan or air conditioner.

Another advantage of adequate sleep is that it can help you fight off illnesses. If you do get sick, however, you will want to have access to effective medical care.

Taking Advantage of Medical Care

Even the healthiest people cannot always avoid situations where medical care is needed. You can protect yourself from the cost of medical care with health insurance, and you can protect yourself from disease through immunizations.

Health Care Providers

Health care comes in different packages and at varied cost. Following is a brief list of options: Explore them using the library, Internet, student health center, and your network of family and friends. Then, evaluate what you can best afford and secure as much protection as possible for yourself and your family.

Health Maintenance Organizations (HMOs). An HMO offers care at its own facilities and with its own medical personnel, and requires a monthly or quarterly payment, which varies according to the HMO and the state of which you are a resident. Often there is a nominal "copayment"—$10 to $15—each time you visit a doctor. Any visit to a doctor outside the HMO will require an additional payment.

Paid Provider Organizations (PPOs). A PPO allows you to receive services from a selected network of independent providers (doctors) in your area. PPO membership requires monthly or quarterly payment, and individual doctor visits may require a copayment.

School-sponsored health plan. Many schools offer full or partial coverage to students for the duration of their status as full-time students. However, students on a less-than-full-time basis may have to pay a stipend to receive health care benefits through the school. Health services may be available at the school's health center or at a nearby facility by arrangement with an HMO or PPO.

E-mail or join a discussion group about a health issue that you'd like to improve. You may want to do some research on the Web first, then seek support and advice from those who are in a position to help.

Work-sponsored health plan. Some companies and organizations provide full or partial health care coverage for free or for a reduced cost. You are usually eligible for this coverage as long as you maintain the work commitment that your company requires.

Government-sponsored health programs. Programs such as Medicaid (available to welfare recipients) or Medicare (available to U. S. citizens over the age of 65) are sponsored by the U. S. government. You must fulfill certain requirements to be eligible, and you must use health centers, hospitals, and doctors who participate in the program to which you belong.

Do not underestimate the importance of having some kind of health care coverage. You need to be prepared for health emergencies that may arise through no fault of your own, such as car accidents or contagious illnesses. Play it safe and make sure you and your family are covered.

"To keep the body in good health is a duty . . . otherwise we

shall not be able to keep our mind strong and clear."

Buddha

Adult Immunizations

Making sure your immunizations are updated is an important part of your health. Immunizations are not just for kids; adults often need them for particular circumstances or because they didn't receive a full course of shots as children. Immunizations are important in order to prevent influenza, hepatitis B, tetanus, diphtheria, measles, mumps, rubella (German measles), and meningitis (recently on the rise on college campuses).

Table 10.1 shows some basic information on what immunizations you should receive (or should have received) and when. Consult your doctor find out whether you still need shots and when you should receive them. People with immune disorders should check with their doctors before receiving any vaccine. In addition, pregnant women should only receive vaccines in three instances: when risk of disease exposure is high, when infection poses significant risk to mother or fetus, and when the vaccine is unlikely to cause harm.

One illness not protected by immunization, but worth mentioning here, is *mononucleosis*, also known as "mono." Mono is caused by a virus that is passed through saliva. It is fairly common on college campuses and often transmitted through kissing or sharing a glass. Major symptoms are fever,

TABLE 10.1 Immunizations

VACCINE	WHEN	WHO	IMPORTANT INFORMATION
Meningococcal (prevents meningococcal meningitis)	When entering college, ideally, or anytime during college (meningitis outbreaks have been attributed to close proximity in living and work situations).	College students (the bacteria is spread via direct contact—such as sharing a glass—or indirect contact—such as sneezing—with an infected individual).	• Meningitis can lead to permanent and serious disabilities and even death. • Vaccine should not be given to pregnant women or any individual sensitive to thimerosal.
Influenza (flu)	Each year before flu season (optimal time is mid-Oct. through mid-Nov.).	All adults over 65 should receive the vaccine. Recommended for younger adults who are likely to be in high-risk areas during flu season.	Pregnant women may receive vaccine after 14 weeks of pregnancy and should receive it if they are pregnant during flu season.
Diphtheria, pertussis, and tetanus (DPT)	If all three childhood shots received, booster at 50 years. If childhood shots not completed, booster every 10 years.	All adults; either a booster at 50 years of age or when having received any sort of wound.	Recommended for people with immune system disorders. Only for pregnant women if situation calls for it.
Hepatitis B	One course of immunization (three doses) in childhood or later.	Any adult not immunized in childhood, especially those in homosexual relationships, with multiple partners, or injection drug users.	Person with immune system disorders may need larger doses. Use in pregnant women only if high risk.
Measles, mumps, and rubella (MMR)	One course of immunization (two doses) in childhood.	Nonimmune adults born after 1956; also adults who received the "killed" virus (1963–1967).	Not to be given to pregnant women.
Pneumococcal (prevents meningitis, pneumonia)	One dose followed by booster after 6 years in childhood.	Anyone over 65 or in high-risk conditions (such as health care workers).	Only for pregnant women who are high risk.
Varicella (chickenpox)	Two doses 4–8 weeks apart in childhood.	Any adult with increased risk of exposure, especially adults who never had it as a child (most adults are immune).	Not to be given to pregnant women or persons with immune system disorders.

sore throat, swollen lymph glands, and fatigue. Mono can last as little as a few days or as long as a few months. The only treatment is rest, fluids, and a balanced diet. Protect yourself against mono by being careful about your interactions with fellow students and housemates.

Following are important ways to maintain mental health. Think holistically about your health. Your body and mind function together. The better each feels, the better you will feel overall.

HOW DO YOU NURTURE A HEALTHY MIND?

Your success depends on your mental health. Learning some ways to handle stress and preventing or working through emotional disorders are two important steps to a healthy mind.

Stress

When you hear the word stress, you may think of tension, hardship, problems, anger, and other negative thoughts and emotions. However, stress can have good results as well as bad. Stress is an effect of life change. It refers not to the change itself, but to how you react to the change. For this reason, even positive events, such as a wedding, can cause stress. Reactions vary; an event that causes one person great anxiety may cause only a mild reaction in another.

Almost any change in your life can create some level of stress. The Holmes-Rahe Social Readjustment Scale, developed by two psychologists, assigns to various life changes a number value indicating the capability of causing stress (a higher number means higher stress). See Table 10.2 for dif-

Be a Team
Have students keep a journal of their stressful life events based on Table 10.2 (entries can be compiled over 1–2 weeks) and share it with a partner. Partners can then brainstorm stress-reduction techniques.

The Holmes-Rahe Scale

TABLE 10.2

EVENT	VALUE	EVENT	VALUE
Death of spouse or partner	100	Son or daughter leaving home	29
Divorce	73	Trouble with in-laws	29
Marital separation	65	Outstanding personal achievement	28
Jail term	63	Spouse begins or stops work	26
Personal injury	53	Starting or finishing school	26
Marriage	50	Change in living conditions	25
Fired from work	47	Revision of personal habits	24
Marital reconciliation	45	Trouble with boss	23
Retirement	45	Change in work hours, conditions	20
Changes in family members' health	44	Change in residence	20
Pregnancy	40	Change in schools	20
Sex difficulties	39	Change in recreational habits	19
Addition to family	39	Change in religious activities	19
Business readjustment	39	Change in social activities	18
Change in financial status	38	Mortgage or loan under $10,000	17
Death of a close friend	37	Change in sleeping habits	16
Change to different line of work	36	Change in number of family gatherings	15
Change in number of marital arguments	35	Change in eating habits	15
Mortgage or loan over $10,000	31	Vacation	13
Foreclosure of mortgage or loan	30	Christmas season	12
Change in work responsibilities	29	Minor violation of the law	11

Source: Reprinted with permission from *Journal of Psychosomatic Research,* 11 (2), T. H. Holmes and R. H. Rahe, "The social readjustment rating scale," 1967, with permission from Elsevier Science Inc.

ferent changes along with their corresponding stress levels. To find your score, add the values of the events that you have experienced in the past year. Scoring over 300 points means that you are at a high risk of illness or injury due to stress. If you score between 150 and 299, your risk is reduced by 30 percent, and if you score under 150, you have only a very small chance of illness or injury.

Positive Effects of Stress

What you feel in a stressful situation, such as the time before a test—increased energy, perhaps, and a heightened awareness that may make you feel on edge—can have positive effects. In fact, moderate levels of stress can actually improve performance and efficiency. Too little stress may result in boredom or inactivity, and too much stress may cause an unproductive anxiety level. Figure 10.2, based on research by Drs. Robert M. Yerkes and John D. Dodson, illustrates this concept.

Control over your responses is essential to maintaining a helpful level of stress. You can exercise some level of control by attempting to respond to stressful situations as positively as possible. Perceiving stress as good encourages you to push the boundaries of your abilities. For example, a student who responds positively to the expectations of college instructors might be encouraged to improve study skills and to work on time management in order to have more study time.

Being able to control how you respond will help you deal with the negative effects of stress as well.

FIGURE 10.2 Yerkes–Dodson Law

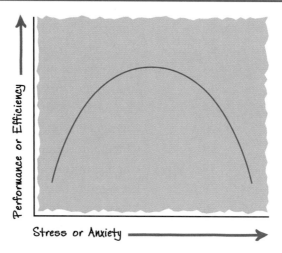

Source: From YOUR MAXIMUM MIND by Herbert Benson, M.D. with William Proctor. Copyright © 1987 by Random House, Inc. Reprinted with permission of Times Books, a division of Random House, Inc.

Teaching Tip

Negative effects can also be categorized in terms of: (1) emotional factors: sadness, irritability, anxiety; (2) physical factors: head, back, stomach pain; (3) intellectual factors: poor concentration; (4) behavioral factors: more drinking or smoking, less sleep.

Negative Effects of Stress

If you perceive stress as bad, you may pour your energy into unproductive anxiety rather than problem solving. For example, a student who responds negatively to instructor expectations may become distracted and may skip class or avoid studying. Negative stress may have dangerous physical and psychological effects. Physically, you may experience a change in appetite, body aches, or increased vulnerability to illnesses. Psychologically, you may feel depressed, unable to study or focus in class, unhappy, or anxious. Both kinds of problems may affect your relationships and responsibilities.

Negative reactions to excessive stress are an increasing phenomenon on the job. The American Institute of Stress and the American Psychological Association report that job stress costs companies an estimated $200 billion a year.[3] Pressure for companies to succeed, downsizing with its resulting layoffs, and increasing numbers of two-career households all contribute to job stress.

Managing Stress

Thinking critically, you can use your problem-solving skills to cope with stressful life changes. First, try to adjust the cause of the stress, using the following strategies.

- **Address issues specifically.** When a situation at school or work is causing stress, think through the details and decide on a plan of attack. For example, if you have a problem with course work, set up a meeting with the instructor. If your work environment is stressful, brainstorm about ways to change it.

- **Break jobs into smaller pieces.** Goals will appear more manageable when approached as a series of smaller steps. Perform a smaller task well rather than a larger one not so well.

- **Set reasonable, manageable goals.** Trying to achieve something that is out of your reach will cause more stress than success.

- **Avoid procrastination.** The longer you wait to do something, the more difficulty you may have doing it.

- **Be thorough.** Loose ends can be irritating. Many people find that only when they finish something completely can they enjoy a feeling of accomplishment. Finish the job and move on.

- **Set boundaries and learn to say "no."** Don't take responsibility for everyone and everything. Stop stress before it starts by delegating what can be or should be taken care of by someone else.

Sometimes a cause lies beyond your control such as an illness. In these cases, address its effect on you. The following are techniques that can help you adjust to the effects of a stressful situation:

- **Exercise, eat right, and get adequate sleep.** Physical health promotes clear thinking.

- **Do something relaxing.** Take breaks regularly: Play music, take a nap, read a book, go for a drive, take a walk outside, or see a movie. Recreation restores your mind and body.

- **Change your surroundings.** Getting away from situations and locations you associate with stress can lighten the effect it has on you and help you place problems in perspective.

Positive thinking and taking action can help you control stress. In some cases, however, an emotional disorder may make stress difficult to handle without special treatment.

"God grant me the serenity to accept things I cannot change, courage to change things I can, and wisdom to know the difference."

Reinhold Niebuhr

Career Connection

Workers who exercise little control over their schedule experience greater stress than those with time flexibility, even if the latter also have more responsibility. For example, a bus driver may have more stress-related complaints than the head of the bus company.

Learning Style Tip

To encourage intrapersonal intelligence, ask students to draw pictures in a journal that describe how they are feeling.

Teaching Tip

Help students master the simple answer, "Let me think about it. I'll get back to you soon," before making a commitment. Making a decision on the spot without thinking critically about its added responsibility may be a set-up for stress.

Springboard

Discuss the connection between saying no and being assertive. For example, people with less stress at work tend to ask for help on projects or to extend deadlines while those who feel overwhelmed are reluctant to tell others that they need help or more time.

Emotional Disorders

Everyone encounters the ups and downs of life. Some people have emotional disorders that interfere with their ability to cope. Following are descriptions of disorders that affect people in all walks of life.

Depression

Almost everyone has experienced the sadness or melancholy that life's troubles can cause. However, as many as 10 percent of Americans will experience a major depression at some point in their lives that is more than temporary blues. A depressive disorder is an illness; it is not a sign of weakness or a mental state that can be escaped by just trying to "snap out of it." This illness requires medical evaluation and is treatable.

A depressive disorder is "a 'whole-body' illness, involving your body, mood, and thoughts."[4] You may experience a combination of symptoms, which may include some of the following:

- feeling constantly sad, worried, or anxious
- loss of interest in classes, people, or activities that you normally like
- constant fatigue
- sleeping too much or too little
- eating too much or too little
- low motivation
- crying
- hopeless feelings and thoughts of suicide
- low self-esteem
- physical aches and pains
- difficulty with decisions or concentration

Depression can stem from genetic, psychological, physiological, or environmental causes, or even a combination of different causes. Table 10.3 describes these causes along with other strategies helpful for depression.

If you recognize yourself anywhere in this discussion of depression, the most important thing to do is to seek help. Start with your school's counseling office or student health program. People at these offices may be able to help or refer you to someone who can.

Clinical depression requires medical treatment. A doctor will help you sort through your symptoms, examine family history, and determine a treatment plan. Treatment can involve therapy or medications or both. For some people, adequate sleep, a regular exercise program, and a healthier diet may be part of the solution. If you see a doctor and are diagnosed with depression, know that your condition is nothing to be ashamed of, and be proud that you have taken a step toward recovery.

If you know someone who suffers from depression, see that the person gets immediate medical attention and evaluation, especially if you sense that the person is contemplating suicide. SA\VE (Suicide Awareness\Voices of Education), an organization dedicated to educating the public about suicide prevention, advises that you be understanding and patient with a depressed friend or family member. Don't make too many demands or tell the person

Important Information About Depression

TABLE 10.3

POSSIBLE CAUSES OF DEPRESSION	HELPFUL STRATEGIES
■ A genetic trait that makes its carrier more likely to suffer depression.	■ Do the best you can, and don't have unreasonable expectations of yourself.
■ A chemical imbalance in the brain.	■ Try to be with others rather than alone.
■ Seasonal affective disorder, which occurs when a person becomes depressed in reaction to reduced daylight during autumn and winter.	■ Don't expect your mood to change right away; feeling better will take time.
■ Highly stressful situations such as financial trouble, a failure of a test or class, a death in the family.	■ Try to avoid making major life decisions until your condition improves. ■ Remember not to blame yourself for your condition.
■ Illnesses, injuries, lack of exercise, poor diet.	
■ Reactions to medications.	

Source: National Institutes of Health, Publication No. 94-3561, National Institutes of Health, 1994.

that he or she should "get over it." SA\VE offers the following suicide warning signs to be aware of:

- Statements about hopelessness or worthlessness: "The world would be better off without me."
- Loss of interest in people, things, or activities that the person cares about.
- Preoccupation with suicide or death.
- Making arrangements, such as visiting or calling close friends and relatives, giving things away.
- Sudden sense of happiness or calm. (A decision to commit suicide often brings a sense of relief. For this reason, others often may say that the person "seemed to be on an upswing.")

Post-Traumatic Stress Disorder

Also called "shell shock" and "post-rape syndrome," post-traumatic stress disorder (PTSD) may affect people who have gone through traumatic incidents such as rape, war, domestic violence, child abuse, and natural disasters. PTSD is an illness requiring medical treatment and can include depression or suicidal tendencies. Symptoms include flashbacks (reexperiencing the incident and the emotions), becoming numb and disconnected from others, sudden fear of anything that recalls the incident, irritable behavior, insomnia, and panic attacks (increased breathing and heart rate, nausea, dizziness).

If you have experienced a traumatic incident, PTSD could make school, work, and family issues difficult to deal with. Seek medical help so that you can begin to work through the trauma and reclaim control over your life. A psychiatrist can offer treatment that helps the sufferer restore a sense of safe-

Real World Link
Students who survive school shootings, including the 1999 shooting at Colorado's Columbine High School, may suffer from PTSD. Realizing this, school systems routinely bring in teams of psychologists to help students cope.

ty and control, although the effects of the incident may never completely go away. PTSD sufferers need to confront what happened and learn to accept the trauma as part of the past. Group therapy may also help.[5]

Eating Disorders

Be a Team
Have 4-person teams cut out news-papers and magazine fashion ads featuring female models and discuss the effect of these ads on the devel-opment of eating disorders in young women. Broaden the discussion to the other media, including TV and movies.

Millions of people develop serious and sometimes life-threatening eating dis-orders every year. The most common disorders are anorexia nervosa, bulim-ia, and binge eating.

Anorexia nervosa. Some people develop such a strong desire to be thin that it creates unnatural self-starvation. This condition—anorexia nervosa—occurs mainly in young women, although men and older women can also be affected. People with anorexia lose an extreme amount of weight and look painfully thin, although they feel that they are overweight. In order to reach their unreasonable weight goals, they refuse to eat, exercise constantly, use laxatives, and develop obsessive rituals around food. An estimated 5 to 7 per-cent of college undergraduates in the United States suffer from anorexia.[6]

The causes of anorexia are not fully known. The desire to emulate an "ideal" body type is one factor, and genetics may be involved (eating disor-ders tend to run in families). Victims of anorexia are also often perfectionists, critical of themselves, and low in self-esteem. Effects of anorexia-induced starvation include loss of menstrual periods in women, impotence in men, organ damage, heart failure, and death.

Bulimia. People who binge on excessive amounts of food, usually sweets and fattening foods, and then purge through self-induced vomiting have bulimia. They may also use laxatives or exercise obsessively. Bulimia can be hard to notice because bulimics are often able to maintain a normal appearance. Lee Hoffman of the National Institutes of Mental Health emphasizes, "Because many individuals with bulimia 'binge and purge' in secret and maintain nor-mal or above normal body weight, they can often successfully hide their problem from others for years."[7]

The causes of bulimia, like those of anorexia, can be rooted in a desire to fulfill a body-type ideal or can come from genetically inherited chemical imbalances. Bulimia patients are also often suffering from depression or other psychiatric illnesses. Effects of bulimia include damage to the digestive tract, stomach rupture, and even heart failure due to the loss of important minerals.

Critical Thinking
Ask students why they think eating disorders are so common on campus. How would they help a friend with this problem? Would they call her parents or notify a health counselor? Or would they consider these actions an invasion of privacy?

Binge eating. Like bulimics, people with binge eating disorder eat large amounts of food and have a hard time stopping. However, they do not purge afterwards. Binge eaters are often overweight and feel that they cannot con-trol their eating. As with bulimia, depression and other psychiatric illnesses may be partially responsible for binge eating disorder. The effects are similar to the effects of obesity, such as high blood pressure, increased stress on the body, and high cholesterol.

Eating disorders can go untreated for a long time because the sufferer may hide the disease or may deny the problem. Given these descriptions, if you recognize a friend or relative or yourself, know that there are people and resources that can help. Because eating disorders are a common problem on college campuses, most student health centers and campus counseling centers can provide both medical and psychological help. Treatment can involve any combination of psychotherapy, medical treatments, drug therapy, and even hospitalization or residence in a treatment center.

Food is only one of several possible addictions. Following is an exploration of the use and abuse of other potentially addictive substances.

HOW ARE ALCOHOL, TOBACCO, AND DRUGS USED AND ABUSED?

Alcohol, tobacco, and drug users comprise men and women from all socioeconomic levels, racial and cultural groups, and areas of the country. Substance abuse can cause financial struggles, emotional traumas, health problems, and even death. Think critically as you read the following sections. Carefully consider the potential positive and negative effects of your actions, and take the time to make decisions that are best for you.

Alcohol

Alcohol is a drug as much as it is a beverage. People receive mixed messages about it as they grow up: "Alcohol is fun." "Alcohol is dangerous." "Alcohol is for adults only." These conflicting ideas can make drinking appear more glamorous, secretive, and exciting than it really is.

When used in moderation, for many people alcohol may not cause a problem. Many people drink only occasionally, and many others choose not to drink at all. The key is to be in control and to ask yourself why you drink. If you drink once in a while at a social gathering or because you like the taste, you are more likely to drink moderately than someone who drinks to escape problems or to fit in with the crowd.

The National Institute on Alcohol Abuse and Alcoholism (NIAAA) offers these statistics about college students and alcohol:[8]

A therapist talks to patients in a group therapy session.

Real World Link
With more than 4 out of 10 students describing themselves as "binge drinkers," colleges are using media campaigns to help curb the problem. These campaigns use peers, instead of authority figures, to warn students about the dangers of alcohol.

- An overwhelming majority of college students—88 percent—have used alcohol.

- Greater alcohol use is connected to sexual aggression. Students on campuses reporting high levels of binge drinking experience more incidents of assault and unwanted sexual advances as a result of drinking than do students at campuses with fewer binge drinkers.

- Drinking with a group and serving one's own drinks may contribute to greater consumption of alcohol. Both of these situations are common at large gatherings such as fraternity parties.

Of all alcohol consumption, **binge drinking** has the most problematic effects. Here are the statistics:

Binge drinking
Having five or more drinks at one sitting.

- From a survey of a random sampling of students, 43 percent said they are binge drinkers, and 21 percent said that they binge drink frequently.[9]

- Of students who do not binge drink, 80 percent surveyed reported experiencing one or more secondhand effects of binge drinking (vandalism, sexual assault or unwanted sexual advances, interrupted sleep or study).[10]

■ Students who binge drink are more likely to miss classes, be less able to work, have hangovers, become depressed, engage in unplanned sexual activity, and ignore safer sex practices.[11]

The bottom line is that heavy drinking causes severe problems. The NIAAA estimates that alcohol contributes to the deaths of 100,000 people every year through both alcohol-related illnesses and accidents involving drunk drivers.[12] Heavy drinking can damage the liver, the digestive system, and brain cells and can impair the central nervous system. Indeed, as *The New Wellness Encyclopedia* states, "chronic, excessive use of alcohol can seriously damage every function and organ of the body."[13] Prolonged use also can cause **addiction,** making it seem impossibly painful for the user to stop drinking.

Figure 10.3, a self-test, will help you determine if your drinking habits may cause problems.

Tobacco

College students do their share of smoking. The National Institute on Drug Abuse (NIDA) found that 38.8 percent of college students reported smoking at least once in the year before they were surveyed, and 24.5 percent had smoked once within the month before. Nationally, about 60 million people are habitual smokers.[14] The choice to smoke—often influenced by advertising directed at young people—shortly may turn into a harmful addiction.

When people smoke they inhale nicotine, a highly addictive drug found in all tobacco products. Nicotine's immediate effects may include an increase in blood pressure and heart rate, sweating, and throat irritation. Long-term effects may include high blood pressure, bronchitis, emphysema, stomach ulcers, and heart conditions. Pregnant women who smoke run an increased risk of having infants with low birth weight, premature births, or stillbirths.

Inhaling tobacco smoke damages the cells that line the air sacs of the lungs. Smoking has long been thought to cause lung cancer, and in late 1996 researchers found a definitive link. They exposed lung cells to tobacco smoke and saw that the damage done to the genes of the cells mirrors the damage they've seen in lung tumors. Lung cancer causes more deaths in the United States than any other type of cancer. Smoking also increases the risk of mouth, throat, and other cancers.[15]

Smoking also creates a danger to nonsmokers. Environmental tobacco smoke, or ETS, also called "secondhand smoke," causes about 3,000 lung cancer deaths per year in nonsmokers.[16] ETS is especially harmful to children, who are exposed to smoke in the nearly 50 percent of U. S. homes that house at least one smoker.

Quitting smoking is extremely difficult; even so, if you have smoked regularly, you can quit through motivation and perseverance. Half of all people who have ever smoked have quit. Suggestions for quitting include the following:[17]

■ Try a nicotine patch or nicotine gum, and be sure to use them consistently.

Career Connection
Federal law classifies alcoholism as a disease. As a result, employees who are in a rehabilitation program are generally protected from dismissal.

Addiction
Compulsive physiological need for a habit-forming substance.

Real World Link
Bidis, a skinny cigarette from India, are becoming popular among teenagers and young adults. Because of their sweet flavoring, smokers may not realize that bidis have much higher nicotine content than cigarettes made in the U.S.

Substance Use and Abuse Self-Test

FIGURE 10.3

Even one *yes* answer may indicate a need to evaluate your substance use. Answering yes to three or more questions indicates that you may benefit from discussing your use with a counselor.

WITHIN THE LAST YEAR:

1. Have you tried to stop drinking or taking drugs but found that you couldn't do so for long?

2. Do you get tired of people telling you they're concerned about your drinking or drug use?

3. Have you felt guilty about your drinking or drug use?

4. Have you felt that you needed a drink or drugs in the morning—as an "eye-opener"—in order to improve a hangover?

5. Do you drink or use drugs alone?

6. Do you drink or use drugs every day?

7. Have you found yourself regularly thinking or saying, "I need" a drink or any type of drug?

8. Have you lied about or concealed your drinking or drug use?

9. Do you drink or use drugs to escape worries, problems, mistakes, or shyness?

10. Do you find you need increasingly larger amounts of drugs or alcohol in order to achieve a desired effect?

11. Have you forgotten what happened while drinking or using drugs (had a blackout)?

12. Have you been surprised by how much you were using alcohol or drugs?

13. Have you spent a lot of time, energy, and/or money getting alcohol or drugs?

14. Has your drinking or drug use caused you to neglect friends, your partner, your children, or other family members, or caused other problems at home?

15. Have you gotten into an argument or a fight that was alcohol- or drug-related?

16. Has your drinking or drug use caused you to miss class, fail a test, or ignore schoolwork?

17. Have you rejected planned social events in favor of drinking or using drugs?

18. Have you been choosing to drink or use drugs instead of performing other activities or hobbies you used to enjoy?

19. Has your drinking or drug use affected your efficiency on the job or caused you to fail to show up at work?

20. Have you continued to drink or use drugs despite any physical problems or health risks that your use has caused or made worse?

21. Have you driven a car or performed any other potentially dangerous tasks while under the influence of alcohol or drugs?

22. Have you had a drug- or alcohol-related legal problem or arrest (possession, use, disorderly conduct, driving while intoxicated, etc.)?

Source: Adapted from the "Criteria for Substance Dependence and Criteria for Substance Abuse," in the *Diagnostic and Statistical Manual of Mental Disorders, Fourth Edition,* published by the American Psychiatric Association, Washington, D. C., and from materials entitled "Are You An Alcoholic?" developed by Johns Hopkins University.

- Get support and encouragement from a health care provider, a "quit smoking" program, a support group, and friends and family.

- Avoid situations that cause you to want to smoke, such as being around other smokers, drinking alcohol, and highly stressful encounters or events.

- Find other ways of lowering your stress level, such as exercise or other activities you enjoy.

- Set goals. Set a quit date and tell friends and family. Make and keep medical appointments.

The positive effects of quitting—increased life expectancy, greater lung capacity, and more energy—may inspire any smoker to consider making a lifestyle change. Quitting provides financial benefits as well. In fact, one study reports that if a one-pack-a-day smoker who paid $1.75 a pack for 50 years had put that money in the bank instead, he or she would have $169,325. A three-pack-a-day smoker would have saved $507,976.[18] Weigh your options and make a responsible choice. In order to evaluate the level of your potential addiction, you may want to take the self-test in Figure 10.3, replacing the words "alcohol" or "drugs" with "cigarettes" or "smoking."

Drugs

The NIDA reports that 31.4 percent of college students have used illicit drugs at least once in the year before being surveyed, and 16 percent in the month before.[19] Drug users rarely think through the possible effects when choosing to take a drug. However, many of the so-called "rewards" of drug abuse are empty. Drug-using peers may accept you for your drug use and not for who you are. Problems and responsibilities may multiply when you emerge from a high. Long-term drug use can do painful damage to your body. Table 10.4 shows the most commonly used drugs and their potential effects.

You are responsible for thinking critically about what to introduce into your body. Ask questions like the following: Why do I want to do this? What positive and negative effects might it have? If others want me to do it, why? Do I respect those people? How does this substance affect other drug users? How would my drug use affect the people in my life? The more informed you are, the better able you will be to make choices that benefit you and avoid choices that harm you.

Drug use violates federal law. You can injure your reputation, your student status, or your employment possibilities if you are caught using drugs or if drug use impairs your performance in school or on the job. These days many companies test both employees and job applicants for drug use. One report indicates that alcohol and drug use combined costs employers over $40 billion a year in reduced productivity.[20]

Identifying and Overcoming Addiction

People with addictions have lost their control for any number of reasons, including chemical imbalances in the brain, hereditary tendencies, or stressful life circumstances. When you observe others or yourself, remember that

How Drugs Affect You

TABLE 10.4

DRUG CATEGORY	DRUG TYPES	HOW THEY MAKE YOU FEEL	PHYSICAL EFFECTS	DANGER OF PHYSICAL DEPENDENCE	DANGER OF PSYCHOLOGICAL DEPENDENCE
Stimulants	Cocaine, amphetamines	Alert, stimulated, excited	Nervousness, mood swings, stroke or convulsions, psychoses, paranoia, coma at large doses	Relatively strong	Strong
Depressants	Alcohol, Valium-type drugs	Sedated, tired, high	Cirrhosis, impaired blood production, greater risk of cancer, heart attack, and stroke, impaired brain function	Strong	Strong
Opiates	Heroin, codeine, other pain pills	Drowsy, floating, without pain	Infection of organs, inflammation of the heart, hepatitis	Yes, with high dosage	Yes, with high dosage
Cannabinols	Marijuana, hashish	Euphoria, mellowness, little sensation of time	Impairment of judgment and coordination, bronchitis and asthma, lung and throat cancers, anxiety, lack of energy and motivation, reduced ability to produce hormones	Moderate	Relatively strong
Hallucinogens	LSD, mushrooms	Heightened sensual perception, hallucinations, confusion	Impairment of brain function, circulatory problems, agitation and confusion, flashbacks	Insubstantial	Insubstantial
Inhalants	Glue, aerosols	Giddiness, lightheadedness	Damage to brain, heart, liver, and kidneys	Insubstantial	Insubstantial

Source: Adapted from Marc Alan Schuckit, *Educating Yourself about Alcohol and Drugs: A People's Primer,* New York: Plenum Press, 1998.

many addicts hide their addictions well. For every obvious alcoholic or drug user, there is someone who abuses substances quietly, continuing to appear functional and controlled. Although they are less likely to be substance abusers, women tend to conceal substance problems more carefully than men do.[21]

If you think you may be addicted, compare the positive and negative effects of your habits and decide if they are worth it. Although others can make suggestions, you are the only one who can truly take the initiative to change.

Facing Addiction

Addiction is incredibly hard to face and overcome alone. Because substances often cause physical and chemical changes, quitting often requires guiding your body through a painful withdrawal. Even substances that don't cause chemical changes create psychological dependence that is tough to break. Asking for help isn't an admission of failure but a courageous move to reclaim a valuable life.

Using the self-test in Figure 10.3, evaluate your behavior to see if you may need help. Even one "yes" answer may indicate that you need to evaluate your alcohol and/or drug use and to monitor it more carefully. If you answered yes to three or more questions, you may benefit from talking to a professional about your use and the problems it may be causing for you.

Working Through Addiction

If you determine that you need to make some changes, there are many resources that can help you along the way. Seek out any combination of the following suggestions:

Teaching Tip
Overcoming addiction often requires the kind of personal insight that is an inherent part of intrapersonal intelligence.

Counseling and medical care. You can find help from school-based, private, government-sponsored, or workplace-sponsored resources. Check with your school's counseling or health center, your personal physician, or a local hospital. If you don't find an appropriate program, a medical professional can refer you to one. Check in the Yellow Pages under Drug Abuse and Addictions for services in your area.

Detoxification ("detox") centers. If you have a severe addiction, you may need a controlled environment in which to separate yourself completely from the substance that you abuse. Some are outpatient facilities that you visit periodically. Other programs provide a 24-hour home-away-from-home for you until you have gotten through the critical period of withdrawal.

Springboard
Substance-abuse support groups are common on the Internet. Discuss with students what they think are the advantages and disadvantages of these groups compared to traditional meeting-based groups.

Support groups. You can derive help and comfort from sharing your experiences with others. Alcoholics Anonymous (AA) is the premier support group for alcoholics. Based on a 12-step recovery program, AA membership costs little or nothing—members may donate one dollar at meetings if they can afford it. AA has led to many other support groups for addicts such as Overeaters Anonymous and Narcotics Anonymous. Many schools have AA, NA, or other group sessions on campus.

When people address their problems directly instead of avoiding them through substance abuse, they can begin to grow and improve. Working through substance-abuse problems can lead to a restoration of both health and self-respect.

Substance Abuse Affects Others

People involved in an abuser's life are often drawn into the addiction, becoming codependents. Melody Beattie, in *Codependent No More,* defines codependents as "people whose lives had become unmanageable as a result of living in a committed relationship with an alcoholic."[22] This definition holds true for any kind of addiction. Codependent spouses, parents, or children of an addict

Springboard
Discuss with students how addictions can destroy families. If they are willing, encourage them to talk about how addiction has affected their own families and friends.

- become overwhelmingly preoccupied with the happiness of the addict
- expend boundless energy caring for the addict, feeling increasingly alone and drained
- become so involved with the addict's life that they lose sight of their own, resulting in low self-esteem and resentment
- may believe that they have caused the addict to abuse substances

Codependency prevents change. An addict often will not change until a codependent detaches, ending any support actions that prevent the addict from facing problems. Examples of detaching include a husband or wife who stops trying to explain away his alcoholic spouse's behavior or a parent who stops making excuses to instructors or employers for an addicted child. If you don't have an abuse problem but have a friend, significant other, child, or parent who does, think about how it affects you. Look into programs, on campus or off, that can help you cope. Al-Anon, Ala-Teen, Co-Dependents Anonymous, and Adult Children of Alcoholics (ACOA), all based on the AA model, can help codependents reclaim their own lives.

WHAT SHOULD YOU CONSIDER WHEN MAKING SEXUAL DECISIONS?

Sexual relationships involve both body and mind on many different levels. Forming your opinions about sexuality takes some thought. In this section, you will explore sexual decision making, birth control options, sexually transmitted diseases, and sexual harassment and abuse.

Sex and Critical Thinking

What sexuality means to you and the role it plays in your life are your own private business. However, the physical act of sex goes beyond the private realm. Individual sexual conduct can have consequences such as unexpected pregnancy and the transmission of sexually transmitted diseases (STDs). These consequences affect everyone involved in the sexual act.

WINDOWS ON THE WORLD
Real Life Student Issues

How do I know if I have a substance abuse problem? Where can I go for help?

Anonymous

I'm a freshman at a large university. At first I was afraid of fitting in because I come from a small town, but I've found some great friends to hang out with. In fact, I'm so busy most of the time, I hardly have time to keep up with my schoolwork. We all share a house near the campus. It's great because it keeps the costs down, and I always have plenty of friends around. Lately, though, it seems like all we do is party. I'm getting kind of worried about how much I'm drinking. I'm sure I can handle it, but I've been waking up with hangovers pretty regularly. I figured out that this last month I didn't go even one day without a drink. I'm feeling like I may have a problem. I just don't want anyone to know.

Laura Brinckerhoff, Program Director— Nonprofit Organization, University of Arizona—Graduate

I started drinking and using drugs when I was in junior high school. It wasn't until my last year of college, though, that I finally got some help. It's amazing that I lasted so long. Part of my cover-up was to give the illusion that everything was fine. If I was in school and doing well, maybe no one would notice that my life was falling apart. The turning point for me was the realization that I'd die if I continued down the same path. I finally asked for help from my doctor. This was a big step for me because I thought that I was in control. I put my life into his hands and began the journey to recovery. It hasn't been easy though. I've had to let go of unhealthy relationships. I've had to change the way I think about my life. I've had to be humble enough to say, "I need help." But, I'm so glad I did. My life is much more meaningful and rich now.

I believe that most people who are successful at overcoming addictions engage in a regular recovery pro- gram. I attend AA meet- ings, practice the 12 steps, and lead a spiritu- ally directed life. I don't know of anything that works as well. Another part of staying sober is to serve others who may be struggling with an addiction. That's why I agreed to tell you my story. If you think you're dependent on alcohol or drugs, I rec- ommend you go to an AA meeting right away. By listening to other people's stories, you should be able to tell fairly soon if you have a problem. Try to attend 5 to 10 meet- ings before you completely make up your mind. Also, if your family or friends have been telling you that you have a problem, then they're probably right. As difficult as it is to hear, listen to them. Their support can help save you a lot of agony. But, regardless of the program you choose, if you're not willing to change the unhealthy patterns in your life or your core beliefs, staying sober will be very difficult. You may end up being a dry drunk—not drinking, but not really happy.

Like me, you may be scared to take the steps to change your life, but it's worth it. I never dreamed that life could be so wonder- ful and fun. It's the greatest gift God's ever given me.

Your self-respect depends on making choices that maintain your own health and safety as well as those of any person with whom you are involved. Think critically about sexual issues, asking important questions and weighing the positive and negative effects of any action before you make a decision. You may ask yourself questions, such as the following:

- Do I feel ready?
- Is this the right person/moment/situation?
- Do I have what I need to prevent pregnancy and exposure to STDs? If not, what may be the consequences? Can I live with those consequences (pregnancy or disease)? Are they worth it?
- Does this person truly care for me and not just for what we might be doing?
- Is this what I really want? Does it fit with my values?
- Will this enhance our emotional relationship or cause problems later?

Critical thinking can help you consider the effects of sexual activity. One of the possible effects is pregnancy. Birth control methods are designed to prevent this particular effect.

Birth Control

Using birth control is a choice, and it is not for everyone. For some, using any kind of birth control is against their religious beliefs. Others may want to have children. Many sexually active people, however, choose one or more methods of birth control.

In addition to preventing pregnancy, some birth control methods also protect against sexually transmitted diseases. Table 10.5 describes the most established methods of birth control, with effectiveness percentages and STD prevention based on proper and regular use.

Evaluate the positive and negative effects of each method, for yourself as well as for your partner. Consider cost, ease of use, convenience, reliability,

Methods of Birth Control

TABLE 10.5

METHOD	APPROXIMATE EFFECTIVENESS	PREVENTS STDs?	DESCRIPTION
Abstinence	100%	Only if no sexual activity occurs	Just saying no. No intercourse means no risk of pregnancy. However, alternative modes of sexual activity can still spread STDs.
Condom (male)	94%	Yes, if made of latex	A sheath that fits over the penis and prevents sperm from entering the vagina.
Condom (female)	90%	Yes	A sheath that fits inside the vagina, held in place by two rings, one of which hangs outside. Can be awkward. It is relatively new and may not be widely available.

(continued)

TABLE 10.5 Methods of Birth Control (continued)

METHOD	APPROXIMATE EFFECTIVENESS	PREVENTS STDs?	DESCRIPTION
Diaphragm or cervical cap	85%	No	A bendable rubber cap that fits over the cervix and pelvic bone inside the vagina (the cervical cap is smaller and fits over the cervix only). Both must be fitted initially by a gynecologist and used with a spermicide.
Oral contraceptive (the "pill")	97%	No	A dosage of hormones taken daily by a woman, preventing the ovaries from releasing eggs. Side effects can include headaches, weight gain, and increased chances of blood clotting. Various brands and dosages; must be prescribed by a gynecologist.
Spermicidal foams, jellies, inserts	84% if used alone	No	Usually used with diaphragms or condoms to enhance effectiveness; they have an ingredient that kills sperm cells (but not STDs). They stay effective for a limited period of time after insertion.
Intrauterine device (IUD)	94%	No	A small coil of wire inserted into the uterus by a gynecologist (who must also remove it). Prevents fertilized eggs from implanting in the uterine wall. Possible side effects include bleeding.
Norplant	Nearly 100%	No	A series of up to five small tubes implanted by a gynecologist into a woman's upper arm, preventing pregnancy for up to five years. Can be tough to remove. Possible side effects may resemble those of oral contraceptives. Must be removed by a doctor.
Depo-Provera	Nearly 100%	No	An injection that a woman must receive from a doctor every few months. Possible side effects may resemble those of oral contraceptives.
Tubal ligation	Nearly 100%	No	Surgery for women that cuts and ties the fallopian tubes, preventing eggs from traveling to the uterus. Difficult and expensive to reverse. Recommended for those who don't want children.
Vasectomy	Nearly 100%	No	Surgery for men that blocks the tube that delivers sperm to the penis. Like tubal ligation, difficult to reverse and only recommended for those who don't want children.
Rhythm method	Variable	No	Abstaining from intercourse during the ovulation segment of the woman's menstrual cycle. Can be difficult to time and may not account for cycle irregularities.
Withdrawal	Variable	No	Pulling the penis out of the vagina before ejaculation. Unreliable, because some sperm can escape in the fluid released prior to ejaculation. Dependent on a controlled partner.

comfort, and protection against STDs. Communicate with your partner and together make a choice that is comfortable for both of you. For literature on this subject, check your library or bookstore, talk to your doctor, ask a counselor at your student health center, or call a helpful organization.

Sexually Transmitted Diseases

Table 10.6 shows some basic information about common STDs. Each one of these diseases is spread through sexual contact (intercourse or other sexual activity that involves contact with the genitals). All are highly contagious. The only birth control methods that protect against them are those that prevent skin-to-skin contact—the male and female condom (latex or polyurethane only). Most of these STDs can also spread to infants of infected mothers dur-

Sexually Transmitted Diseases

TABLE 10.6

DISEASE	SYMPTOMS	HEALTH PROBLEMS IF UNTREATED	TREATMENTS
Chlamydia	Discharge, painful urination, swollen or painful joints, change in menstrual periods for women	Can cause pelvic inflammatory disease (PID) in women, which can lead to sterility or ectopic pregnancies; infection; miscarriage or premature birth.	Curable with full course of antibiotics; avoid sex until treatment is complete.
Gonorrhea	Discharge, burning while urinating	Can cause PID, swelling of testicles and penis, arthritis, skin problems, infections.	Usually curable with antibiotics; however, certain strains are becoming resistant to medication.
Genital herpes	Blisterlike itchy sores in the genital area, headache, fever, chills	Symptoms may subside and then reoccur, often in response to high stress levels; carriers can transmit the virus even when it is dormant.	No cure; some medications such as acyclovir reduce and help heal the sores and may shorten recurring outbreaks.
Syphilis	A genital sore lasting one to five weeks, followed by a rash, fatigue, fever, sore throat, headaches, swollen glands	If it lasts over four years, it can cause blindness, destruction of bone, insanity, or heart failure; can cause death or deformity of an infant born to an infected woman.	Curable with full course of antibiotics.
Human papilloma virus (HPV, or genital warts)	Genital itching and irritation, small clusters of warts	Can increase risk of cervical cancer in women; virus may remain in body even when warts are removed and cause recurrences.	Treatable with drugs applied to warts or various kinds of wart removal surgery.
Hepatitis B	Fatigue, poor appetite, vomiting, jaundice, hives	Some carriers will have few symptoms; others may develop chronic liver disease, which may lead to other diseases of the liver.	No cure; some will recover, some will not. Bed rest may help ease symptoms.

ing birth. Have a doctor examine any irregularity or discomfort—the sooner you are treated, the less the chance of permanent damage. Women should have an annual Pap smear to check for diseases or irregularities.

AIDS and HIV

The most serious of the STDs is AIDS (acquired immune deficiency syndrome), brought on by the spread of the contagious human immunodeficiency virus (HIV). Not everyone who tests positive for HIV will develop AIDS, but AIDS currently has no cure and results in eventual death. Figure 10.4 shows some recent statistics on AIDS.

AIDS disarms the body's immune system, making it unable to fight viruses that it normally would kill. HIV can lie undetected in the body for up to 10 years before surfacing, and a carrier can spread it during that time. Although AIDS was at first associated with male homosexuals, anyone who is sexually active can contract it. AIDS is growing fastest among heterosexual populations, especially women and children. Medical science continues to develop drugs to combat AIDS and its related illnesses. However, the drugs can cause severe side effects, many have not been thoroughly tested, and none are proven cures.

HIV is transmitted through two types of bodily fluids: fluids associated with sex (semen and vaginal fluids) and blood. People have been known to acquire HIV through sexual relations, by sharing hypodermic needles for drug use, and by receiving infected blood transfusions. You cannot become infected with the virus unless one of those fluids is involved. Therefore, it is unlikely you would contract HIV from toilet seats, hugging, kissing, or sharing a glass.

Springboard
Medical advances are prolonging the lives of people with AIDS. Discuss how this has lulled many people into believing that AIDS is no longer the danger it once was and that safe-sex precautions are unnecessary. Emphasize that AIDS is still a fatal disease.

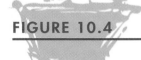

FIGURE 10.4 Recent AIDS Statistics

In the United States, 702,748 cases of AIDS have been reported to the Centers for Disease Control (CDC) by June 1999. More than 62% of those people have died. AIDS is the leading cause of death in the United States for people from the ages of 25 to 44.

Although most AIDS cases are traceable to male-to-male sexual contact or intravenous drug use, heterosexual transmission has increased from 2.5% to 10% of all AIDS cases from 1985 to 1999.

AIDS cases among women increased from 7% to 16% of all AIDS cases from 1985 to 1999. In 1998–1999, women accounted for 32% of cases of adult HIV infection.

As of June 1999, more than 8,000 cases of AIDS in children under 13 had been reported to CDC.

Although AIDS deaths decreased 42% from 1996 to 1997, they decreased only 20% from 1997 to 1998, indicating that the decrease is slowing. The number of persons living with AIDS continues to rise; it increased 10% from 1997 to 1998.

Source: Centers for Disease Control and Prevention, *HIV/AIDS Surveillance Report,* 1999: 11 (no. 1): [1–4].

The best defense against AIDS is not having sex. The U. S. Department of Health and Human Services reports:

> THERE'S ABSOLUTELY NO GUARANTEE EVEN WHEN YOU USE A CONDOM. But most experts believe that the risk of getting AIDS and other sexually transmitted diseases can be greatly reduced if a condom is used properly. . . . Sex with condoms ISN'T totally "safe sex," but it IS "less risky" sex.[23]

Always use a latex condom, because natural skin condoms may let the virus pass through. If a lubricant is used, use K-Y Jelly or a spermicide, because petroleum jelly can destroy the latex in condoms and diaphragms. Although some people dislike using condoms, it's a small price for preserving your life.

To be safe, have an HIV test done at your doctor's office or at a government-sponsored clinic. Your school's health department may also administer HIV tests. Recently, home HIV tests became available over the counter. If you are infected, first inform any recent sexual partners and seek medical assistance. Then contact support organizations in your area or call the National AIDS Hotline at 1-800-342-AIDS.

Sexual Harassment and Abuse

Your sexuality is a private matter for you to express when, where, and to whom you choose. Sexual abuse occurs when someone violates that privacy or tries to interfere with or take away your choices. It can range from an offensive sexual comment or display to spousal abuse and rape. This section describes different types of sexual abuse and offers strategies for coping and prevention.

Sexual Harassment

The facts. Sexual harassment covers a wide range of behavior, which has been divided into the following two types:

- **Quid pro quo harassment** refers to a request for some kind of sexual favor or activity in exchange for something else. It is a kind of bribe or threat ("If you don't do X for me, I will fail you/fire you/make your life miserable").

- **Hostile environment harassment** indicates any situation where sexually charged remarks, behavior, or displayed items cause discomfort. Harassment of this type ranges from lewd conversation or jokes to display of pornography.

Both men and women can be victims of sexual harassment, although the more common situation involves a woman subjected to harassment by a man. Unfortunately, even as women continue to gain equality, **sexism** remains alive. Sexist attitudes can create an environment where men feel they have the right to use words, ideas, and attitudes that degrade women. Even though physical violence is not involved, the fear and mental trauma that such harassment can cause are extremely harmful.

Career Connection
Concerned about multi-million-dollar lawsuits, corporations have strict rules against sexual harassment and dismiss employees who harass others. Harassment victims should report the situation to a manager or to the company's employee relations department.

Sexism
Behavior or attitudes, especially against women, that promote gender-based stereotypes or that discriminate based on sex.

How to cope. Sexual harassment can be difficult to identify and monitor because what offends one person may seem acceptable to another. If you feel degraded by anything that goes on at school or work, address the person whom you believe is harassing you; if that makes you uncomfortable, speak to another authority. Try to avoid assumptions—perhaps the person simply had no idea that his or her behavior could be perceived as offensive. On the other hand, the person may have dishonorable intentions toward you. Either way, you are entitled to request that the person put an end to what has offended you.

Rape and Date Rape

The facts. Any sexual act (intercourse or anal/oral penetration) by a person against another person's will is defined as rape. Rape is primarily a violent act, not a sexual one. It is an expression of power and control. Figure 10.5 shows some current statistics on rape.

Rape is a problem on many campuses, especially acquaintance rape, also called date rape. Any sexual activity during a date that is against one partner's will constitutes date rape, including situations where one partner is too drunk or drugged to give consent. Most date rape victims do not report the incidents. Victims may believe that they can't prove it, that they might have asked for it, that they should be ashamed if drugs or alcohol were involved, or that their assailants may seek revenge if accused.

Beyond the physical harm, rape has serious effects on mental health. Campus Advocates for Rape Education (C.A.R.E.), an organization at Wheaton College in Massachusetts, describes the specific harms of date rape. "One's trust in a friend, date, or acquaintance is also violated. As a result, a victim's fear, self-blame, guilt, and shame are magnified because the assailant is known."[24] Approximately 31 percent of all rape victims develop rape-related post-traumatic stress disorder (see page 319).

How to cope. No kind of rape is deserved or permissible. If you are raped, get medical attention immediately. Try not to shower or change your clothing,

Date rape
Sexual assault perpetrated by the victim's escort during an arranged social encounter.

Be a Team
Ask students to think about the kind of campus-wide program that would discourage date rape and to list its main points. Then ask them to share these points with a partner and come up with a program they both endorse.

FIGURE 10.5 Rape Statistics

- An estimated 868 rapes or attempted rapes are committed every day. This means 36 per hour, or one rape or attempted rape every 1.6 minutes.
- Nearly three-fourths of rape and sexual assault survivors know their attackers.
- It is estimated that 68 percent of rape survivors do not report the crime to the police. The most common reason given for not reporting is that the attack was a "personal matter."
- More than half of rape or sexual assault incidents are reported to have occurred either within one mile of the victim's home or at the home.

Source: Bureau of Justice Statistics, *Criminal Victimization 1998, Changes 1997–1998 with Trends 1993–98*, NCJ-176353 (Washington, D. C.: U. S. Department of Justice, 1999), and *Sex Offenses and Offenders*, NCJ-163392 (Washington, D. C.: U. S. Department of Justice, 1997).

because doing so will destroy evidence. Next, talk to a close friend or counselor. Consider reporting the incident to the police, or to campus officials if it occurred on campus. Finally, consider pressing charges, especially if you can identify your assailant and if there is a chance the police can find the person. Whether or not you press charges or report the incident, don't stop getting help. Continue counseling, join a rape survivor group, or use a hotline.

Domestic Abuse

The facts. The abuse of a spouse or partner isn't always of a sexual nature. However, it occurs within the context of a relationship that may have a sexual dimension, such as a married or closely involved couple. Although men may sometimes experience abuse, women are the primary victims. The Family Violence Prevention Fund reports these sobering statistics on domestic abuse in the United States[25]:

- Almost four million women were physically abused by husbands or boyfriends last year.
- A woman is abused every nine seconds.
- Two-thirds of attacks on women are committed by someone the victim knows.

Because victims often hide the effects, abuse is more common than people would think. Very few victims want anyone to know that the partner they have chosen is subjecting them to abuse, especially if they love or have loved the abuser. They may also believe that they have done something wrong and deserve the abuse in return. Therefore, they may try to endure it alone, hoping that it will end if they can give more to the relationship.

How to cope. If you are being abused, your safety and sanity depend on your seeking help. When you are alone, call a shelter or abuse hotline and talk to someone who understands what you are going through. Seek counseling at your school or at a center in your community. If you need medical attention, get to a clinic or hospital. If you feel that your life is in danger, get out and take any children with you. Through your local police department, you can get a restraining order that will require your abuser to stay away from you.

Career Connection
Domestic abuse is also a problem in the workplace when women are victimized by husbands or partners. This is one of the reasons that large companies require all visitors to sign in before admission to the workplace.

Staying Safe

No matter how safe you feel in any situation, you can never be too sure. Take steps to prevent incidents, sexual or otherwise, from occurring.

Avoid situations that present clear dangers. Don't walk or exercise alone at night or in neglected areas—travel with one or more people. Don't work or study alone in a building. If someone looks suspicious to you, contact security or someone else who can help you.

Avoid use of drugs or overuse of alcohol. Anything that reduces or obliterates your judgment will make you more vulnerable to any kind of assault.

Watch your belongings. Keep your keys with you at all times—but don't attach them to anything that could identify them as yours (ID, credit cards, etc.). Carry bags or backpacks close to your body. If someone tries to snatch it, let it go rather than risk injury.

Avoid people who make you uneasy. If there is a fellow student or coworker who puts you on your guard, avoid situations in which you would need to work with him or her. Speak to an instructor or supervisor if you feel threatened.

Communicate. Be clear about what you want from people you associate with (personally or professionally) and why. Don't assume that others want what you want or even know what you want. If you have a request, make it respectfully and invite a response.

Joie de vivre

The French have a phrase that has become commonly used in the English language as well: *joie de vivre,* which literally means "joy of living." A person with *joie de vivre* is one who finds joy and optimism in all parts of life, who is able to enjoy life's pleasures and find something positive in its struggles. Without experiencing difficult and sometimes painful challenges, people might have a hard time recognizing and experiencing happiness and satisfaction.

Think of this concept as you examine your level of personal wellness. If you focus on what is positive about yourself, that attitude can affect all other areas of your life. Give yourself the gift of self-respect so that you can nourish your body and mind every day, in every situation. Through both stressful obstacles and happy successes, you can find the joy of living.

Name   Date

Critical Thinking
Applying Learning to Life

Health Habits

Put your critical-thinking skills to work in improving your physical health. The two key steps to take when making choices for your version of healthy living are as follows:

1. Ask questions to determine the options available to you.
2. Consider what you know about yourself (personality type, multiple intelligences, habits, abilities, etc.) to determine which of these options will work best for who you are.

For each of the following issues—food, exercise, and sleep—follow these two steps.

Food. Think critically about your eating habits. What could change for the better? Below, write three options available to you for changes you could make. Broaden your thinking to cover all kinds of changes—you could change when you eat, where you eat, the combination of foods you take in at a meal, the type of foods you eat (meat, vegetarian foods, etc.), the balance of food groups, whether you cook or not, how much sugar, caffeine, or fat you take in, and so on.

1. _____

2. _____

3. _____

Next, considering your self-knowledge, choose one option that you feel you can carry out.

Option: _____

What about who you are makes this a good choice? _____

_____

What positive effects might this change have on you? _____

_____

Exercise. Now consider your exercise habits. Brainstorming all the possibilities—kinds of exercise, when and where you exercise, with whom you exercise, how long you exercise—come up with three possible changes.

1. _____

2. _____

3. _____

Then, considering your self-knowledge, choose one option that makes sense and is doable.

Option: _____

What about who you are makes this a good choice? _____

_____

What positive effects might this change have on you? _____

_____

Sleep. Finally, think critically about your sleep habits—when you sleep, where you sleep, for how long, and so on. Name three possible changes you could make in how you approach sleep.

1. _____

2. _____

3. _____

Then, considering your self-knowledge, name an option you feel you could reasonably execute.

Option: _____

What about who you are makes this a good choice? _____

_____

What positive effects might this change have on you? _____

_____

Early Warning Signs of Stress

Step 1 Check any items that you have experienced at least once in the last three months. Under the Behavioral column, "compulsive behaviors" are behaviors that are repeated excessively, such as constant handwashing.

PHYSICAL	PSYCHOLOGICAL	BEHAVIORAL
☐ Indigestion	☐ Irritability	☐ Forgetfulness
☐ Diarrhea/constipation	☐ Excessive anger	☐ Poor concentration
☐ Nausea or vomiting	☐ Worry	☐ Distorted perception
☐ Appetite problems	☐ Depression	☐ Compulsive behaviors
☐ Headaches	☐ Excessive crying	☐ Decrease in productivity
☐ Neck or back pain	☐ Aggressiveness	☐ Decrease in creativity
☐ Allergies	☐ Isolation	☐ Living in the past
☐ Hair loss	☐ Boredom	☐ Drinking more
☐ Colds, flu, cold sore	☐ Decreased sense of humor	☐ Smoking more
☐ Teeth grinding	☐ Critical of self/others	☐ Decreased sex drive
☐ Problems sleeping	☐ Decreased motivation	☐ Acting "antsy"
☐ Fatigue	☐ Decreased self-esteem	☐ Accident prone

Step 2 Circle the three items that usually occur as early warning signs of stress for you.

Step 3 From what you know about relieving stress, describe the steps you plan to take when you experience any of the three items you circled as early warning signs.

_____

_____

_____

_____

Note: Discuss any early warning signs with a doctor. Some of the symptoms listed above could also signify a condition that requires medical treatment.

Staying Safe

Consider your current personal safety habits and the effects they have on your life. Some may help keep you safe—others may put you in unnecessary danger. List two of each below.

Habits that have positive effects on your safety:

1. _____

2. _____

Habits that have negative effects on your safety:

1. _____

2. _____

Discuss one change that would increase your personal safety—either adding a habit that has positive effects or changing or eliminating one that has negative effects. Explain why the change would help.

_____

_____

_____

_____

Teamwork
Combining Forces

Actively Dealing with Stress By yourself, make a list of stressors—whatever events or factors cause you stress. As a class, discuss the stressors you have listed. Choose the five most common. Divide the class into five groups according to who would choose what stressor as his or her most important (redistribute some people if the group sizes are unbalanced). Each group should discuss its assigned stressor, brainstorming solutions and strategies. List your best coping strategies and present them to the class. You may want to make copies of the lists so that every member of the class has five, one for each stressor.

Writing
Discovery Through Journaling

To record your thoughts, use a separate journal or the lined pages at the end of the chapter.

Addiction Describe how you feel about the concept of addiction in any form—to alcohol, drugs, food, a person, or even an unhealthy behavior. How has it touched your life, if at all? How did you deal with it? If you have never faced an addiction or been close to someone who did, describe how you would face it if it ever happened to you.

Career Portfolio
Charting Your Course

Your Health Record Just as your health affects your success at school, it also affects how you perform on the job. When you apply for many jobs, especially those that require physical activity, you may be asked questions about your health and physical condition. Companies that provide health benefits to their employees may be especially interested in hiring people who take care of their health. You will benefit from (1) being aware of your health status and (2) working to improve any conditions that you have.

On a separate sheet of paper, draw up a "medical record" for yourself. Include the following:

- health insurance plan and policy numbers
- phone numbers of physicians and clinics; phone numbers of who to call in a medical emergency
- immunizations: ones you have completed and any you have yet to receive
- surgeries you have had (include reason)
- hospital stays (include reason)

- illnesses and/or diseases
- family health history (parents, grandparents, siblings)
- chronic health problems (arthritis, tendonitis, ulcer, etc.)
- vision and/or hearing statistics, if applicable
- prescriptions used regularly and why
- other

Highlight any conditions you feel you could improve with work or treatment. Choose one and draw up a problem-solving plan for making that improvement a reality.

Look again at the self-test on p. 323. Make a copy of the questions and answer them on a separate sheet to keep with your portfolio. If you feel that your score indicates a problem, write on the sheet what steps you intend to take, and get help.

Consider the positive side of your health as well. Make a list of the areas in which you enjoy very good health. For each, describe briefly how you maintain it.

Keep these lists up to date so you can monitor your health. If you change health plans or apply for a new job, for example, you may need to furnish information about your health record. You'll have many opportunities to refer to this information.

A good bill of health—mental, emotional, and physical—is another asset that employers look for in those they hire. Begin now to lead a healthy life so that when you transition from college to career, you are already adjusted to a healthy, positive mode.

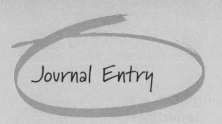

Journal Entry

Name _____ Date _____

Name _____   Date _____

Managing Career and Money

Reality Resources

11

In this chapter, you will explore answers to the following questions:

- How can you plan your career?
- How can you juggle work and school?
- What should you know about financial aid?
- How can strategic planning help you manage money?
- How can you create a budget that works?
- What should you know about banking and credit cards?

M any people either love their jobs but don't make much money or dislike their jobs but are paid well. Still other people have neither job satisfaction nor a good paycheck to show for their work. The ideal career inspires passion and motivation in you *and* pays you enough to live comfortably. Career exploration, job-hunting strategy, and money management can work together to help you find that ideal career, whether it is being a teacher in Minnesota, an attorney in Manhattan, an archaeologist in northern Africa, or anything else that fits your dreams. In this chapter, you will first look at career exploration and how to balance work and school. Then, you will explore how to bring in money with financial aid and how to manage the money you have.

Teaching Tip

Helpful Web sites:

- U.S. Department of Education - Financial Aid - www.ed.gov/finaid.html
- Hope Scholarship and Lifetime Learning Credits - www.ed.gov/offices/OPE/PPI/HOPE/
- Women's Wire - www.womenswire.com/work
- 1st Steps in the Hunt: Daily News for Online Job Hunters - interbiznet.com/hunt/
- College Grad Job Hunter - www.collegegrad.com

HOW CAN YOU PLAN YOUR CAREER?

College is an ideal time to investigate careers because so many different resources are available to you. Students are in different stages when it comes to thinking about careers. Like many people, you may not have thought too much about it yet. You may have already had a career for years and are looking for a change. You may have decided on a particular career but are now having second thoughts. Regardless of your starting point, now is the time to make progress.

Everything you read and work on in this book is geared toward workplace success. Critical thinking, teamwork, writing skills, and long-term planning all prepare you to thrive in any career.

Define a Career Path

Aiming for a job in a particular area requires planning the steps that can get you there. Whether these steps take months or years, they help you focus your energies on your goal. Defining a career path involves investigating yourself, exploring potential careers, staying current on the state of the working world, and building knowledge and experience.

Investigate Yourself

When you explore your learning style in Chapter 4, evaluate your ideal note-taking system in Chapter 7, or look at how you relate to others in Chapter 9, you build self-knowledge. Gather everything that you know about yourself, from this class or from life experiences, and investigate. Ask the following questions:

- What do you know best, do best, and enjoy best?
- Out of jobs you've had, what did you like and not like to do?
- How would you describe your learning style and personality?
- What kinds of careers could make the most of everything you are?

If you don't know exactly what you want to do, you are not alone. Many students who have not been in the workplace—and even some who have—don't know what career they want to pursue. Give yourself permission to change your mind as you take courses and find out more about different careers. Taking the Campbell Interest and Skill Survey, in this book's appendix, will help to give you ideas.

Don't discount any of your likes when considering what you may want to do for a career. Something that seems like it has nothing to do with the working world may serve you well. For example, Mike Lazzo, vice president of programming at the Cartoon Network, turned his lifelong cartoon devotion into a career as a network executive. He started in the shipping department at Turner Broadcast Network and worked his way up to his present position. You never know where your favorite activities will take you.

Explore Potential Careers

Career possibilities extend far beyond what you can imagine. Brainstorm about career areas. Ask instructors, relatives, and fellow students about careers that they have or know about. Check your library for books on careers or biographies of people who worked in fields that interest you. Explore careers you discover through movies, newspapers, novels, or nonfiction.

Use your critical-thinking skills to broaden your questions beyond just what tasks you perform for any given job. Many other factors will be important to you. Look at Table 11.1 for some of the kinds of questions you might ask as you talk to people or investigate materials. You may discover that:

A wide array of job possibilities exists for most career fields. For example, the medical world consists of more than doctors and nurses. Emergency medical technicians respond to emergencies, administrators run hospitals, researchers test new drugs, lab technicians administer procedures such as X rays, pharmacists prepare prescriptions, retirement community employees work with the elderly, and more.

Within each job, there is a variety of tasks and skills. You may know that an instructor teaches, but you may not see that instructors also often write, research, study, design courses, give presentations, and counsel. Push past your first impression of any career and explore what else it entails.

Common assumptions about salaries don't always hold. Medicine, the law, and computer science aren't the only sources of careers with good income. According to data gathered by the U. S. Labor Department, examples of other careers with high weekly earnings include electricians, public administrators, aircraft mechanics, and more.[1] Don't jump to conclusions until you have investigated. Even if you work in a job that earns you an extraordinary salary, you may not be happy unless you truly enjoy and learn from what you are doing.

Critical-Thinking Questions for Career Exploration

TABLE 11.1

What can I do in this area that I like/do well?	Do I respect the company and/or the industry?
What are the educational requirements (certificates or degrees, courses)?	Do companies in this industry generally accommodate special needs (child care, sick days, flex time, or working at home)?
What skills are necessary?	Do I need to belong to a union?
What wage or salary is normal for an entry-level position, and what benefits can I expect?	Are there opportunities in this industry within a reasonable distance from where I live (or want to live)?
What kinds of personalities are best suited to this kind of work?	What other expectations are there beyond the regular workday (travel, overtime, etc.)?
What are the prospects for moving up to higher-level positions?	Do I prefer the service or production end of this industry?

Teaching Tip
The following questions will also help students pinpoint the right career: Would I prefer to work with people or data? Do I prefer a large or small company? The public or private sector? Am I willing to relocate? Would I accept a job with evening and/or weekend work?

Your school's *career center* may offer job listings, occupation lists, assessments of skills and personality types, questionnaires to help you pinpoint areas that may suit you, and information about different careers and companies. The people who work at the center can help you sort through the material. Visit the center early in your college career and work with a counselor there to develop a solid career game plan.

Stay Current

The working world is always adjusting to the needs of workers, new technology developments, and other changes. Reading newspapers and magazines and watching television news programs will help you keep abreast of what you face as you make career decisions. Following are two current workplace trends that may be important for you in your career investigation:

More temporary employment. To save money, corporations are hiring more temporary employees (temps) and fewer full-time employees (the number of temps has increased from 800,000 in 1986 to over 2.5 million in 1997).[2] When considering whether to take a permanent job or a temporary job, consider the effects of each. Permanent jobs offer benefits (employer contribution to pension plan and health insurance) and stability, but may be less flexible. Temporary jobs offer flexibility, few obligations, and often more take-home pay, but few or no benefits.

New variety in benefits. Companies are beginning to respond to the changing needs of the modern workforce, where workers often have to care for children or aging parents, need to plan for the financial and medical demands of a longer life span, and want to take measures to reduce life stress. This response often involves "quality of life" benefits such as the following:

- **telecommuting** (working from home via telephone, fax, and Internet access)
- **job sharing** (two employees working part-time to fulfill the duties of one full-time position)
- **personal services** such as counseling and financial planning
- **flextime** (the ability to adjust work time in response to school or family needs)
- **child care** on-site or nearby, often at reduced rates

Both workers and companies benefit from offering alternatives to traditional work arrangements. Workers enjoy greater quality of life, and companies are able to promote loyalty and keep employee turnover low in an age where job changing is on the increase. Offerings of these kinds of benefits will most likely continue to increase—see Figure 11.1 for projected growth of particular benefits.

Build Knowledge and Experience

Having knowledge and experience specific to the career you want to pursue will be valuable on the job hunt. Courses, internships, jobs, and volunteering are four great ways to build both.

Modern Benefits   **FIGURE 11.1**

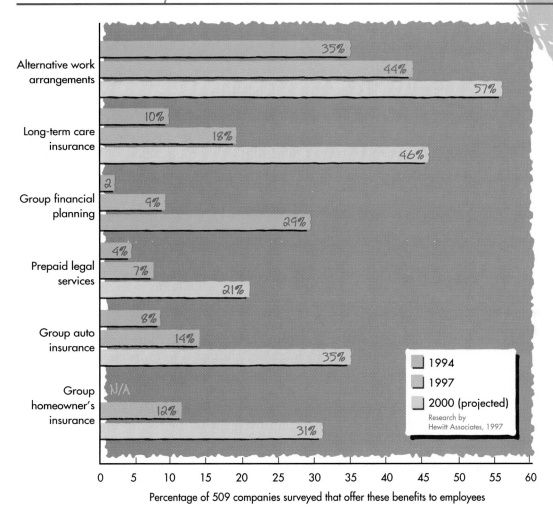

Percentage of 509 companies surveyed that offer these benefits to employees

Source: "Perks That Work," *Time,* Nov. 9, 1998. © 1998 Time Inc. Reprinted by permission.

Courses. When you narrow your career exploration to a couple of areas that interest you, take a course or two in those areas. How you react to these courses will give you clues to how you feel about the area in general. Be careful to evaluate your experience according to how you feel about the subject matter rather than other factors. Think critically. If you didn't like a course, what was the cause: an instructor you didn't like, a time of day when you tend to lose energy, or truly a lack of interest in the material?

In addition, interview an instructor who teaches a subject related to a career field that interests you. Find out what courses you have to take to major in the field, what jobs are available in the field, what credentials (degrees and/or training) you need for particular jobs, and so on.

Internships. An **internship** may or may not offer pay. Although this may be a financial drawback, the experience and new acquaintances may be worth the work. Many internships take place during the summer, but some are available during the school year. Companies that offer internships are looking for people who will work hard in exchange for experience they can't get in the classroom.

Internship

A temporary work program in which a student can gain supervised practical experience in a particular professional field.

Real World Link
Almost 120,000 companies nation-wide sponsor co-op programs that involve nearly 250,000 undergraduates in work-based learning programs. Students at 700 participating schools earn between $2,500 and $14,000 annually as they work toward their degrees.

e-mail

E-mail a close friend and ask him or her what type of internships are available in career fields that interest them. Then share your internship ideas with them and coach each other through the process.

Your career center may be able to help you explore internship opportunities. Because money isn't the draw, stick to areas that interest you. Look for an internship that you can handle while still being able to fulfill your financial obligations. If while working as an intern you discover a career worth pursuing, you'll have the internship experience behind you when you go job hunting. Internships are one of the best ways to show a prospective employer some real-world experience and initiative.

Jobs. No matter what you do for money while you are in college, whether it is in your area of interest or not, you may discover career opportunities that appeal to you. Someone who takes a third-shift legal proofreading job to make extra cash might discover an interest in law. Someone who answers phones for a newspaper company might be drawn into journalism. Be aware of the possibilities around you.

Volunteering. Offering your services in the community or at your school can introduce you to careers and increase your experience. Some schools have programs that can help you find volunteering opportunities. Find out what services your school offers. Volunteer activities are important to note on your résumé. Many employers seek candidates who have shown commitment through volunteering.

No matter how you gather your career knowledge and experience, the key is to focus on *continual improvement*. You're not "done" when you complete a college degree, training program, course, book, or job. You need to continually build on what you know. With the world's fast-paced changes in mind, today's employers value those who seek continual improvement in their skills and knowledge.

Map Out Your Strategy

After you've gathered enough information to narrow your career goals, plan strategically to achieve them. Make a career time line that illustrates the steps toward your goal, as shown in Figure 11.2. Mark years and half-year points (and months for the first year), and write in the steps when you think they should happen. If your plan is five years long, indicate what you plan to do by the fourth, third, and second years, and then the first year, including a six-month goal and a one-month goal for that first year.

Using what you know about strategic planning, fill in the details about what you will do throughout your plan. Set goals that establish who you will talk to, what courses you will take, what skills you will work on, what jobs or internships you will investigate, and any other research you need to do. Your path may change, of course; use your time line as a guide rather than as an inflexible plan.

The road to a truly satisfying career can be long. Seek support as you work toward goals. Confide in supportive people, talk positively to yourself, and read books about career planning, such as those listed in the Bibliography.

Expect Change

Although changing careers used to be a risky and rare practice, many people now have a few different careers over the course of their lives. Factors that have led to this situation include the following:

Career Time Line

FIGURE 11.2

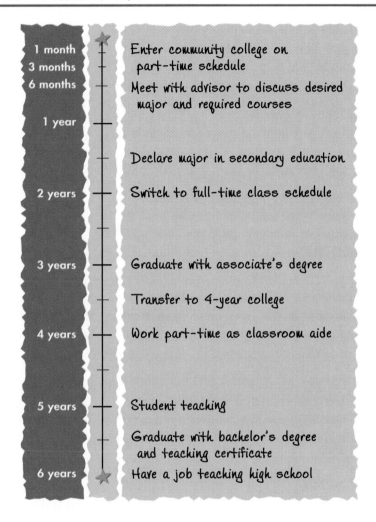

Time	Milestone
1 month	Enter community college on part-time schedule
3 months	
6 months	Meet with advisor to discuss desired major and required courses
1 year	
	Declare major in secondary education
2 years	Switch to full-time class schedule
3 years	Graduate with associate's degree
	Transfer to 4-year college
4 years	Work part-time as classroom aide
5 years	Student teaching
	Graduate with bachelor's degree and teaching certificate
6 years	Have a job teaching high school

- Many corporations have downsized, laying off employees in response to economic changes.

- Technology changes quickly, requiring new knowledge and training and resulting in older industries becoming defunct.

Because of rapid workplace change, today's workers need to be prepared to go back to the drawing board should jobs not work out. Job security can suddenly give way to layoffs. Plus, a long time ensconced in one job may prevent you from being up-to-date on technology skills. Despite these factors, change can also create enormous opportunity; for example, Internet employees are reaping benefits from technological developments. Even difficult changes can open doors for you that you never even imagined were there. For example:

- **Susan Davenny Wyner,** a classical singer who had appeared at the Metropolitan Opera, was hit by a car while biking. The accident damaged her vocal cords so badly that they have never healed. After some time she discovered that conducting held an opportunity for her

> "Whatever you think you can do or believe you can do, begin it.
>
> Action has magic, grace, and power in it."
>
> Johann Wolfgang von Goethe

Be a Team
Arguably, the most important quality for career success in the 21st century is *flexibility*—the ability to turn a bad work situation into something positive. Have students think about how they've demonstrated flexibility at school/work and share their experiences with a partner.

to express herself musically in a way she didn't think she could ever do again.

■ Christopher Reeve was at the top of his game as a film actor. Gravely injured in a riding accident, he lost almost all use of his body below his neck. Since that time he has built a successful career as a film and television director and as an advocate for the disabled.

■ Jimmy Carter started as a peanut farmer and became President of the United States. After losing his bid for reelection, he has used his fame to gather funds and attention for Habitat for Humanity, an organization he founded that builds homes for the disadvantaged.

As these people and many others have demonstrated, if you think creatively about what marketable skills and different job possibilities you have, you will be able to find new ways to achieve.

Seek Mentors

Mentor

A person of knowledge or authority who becomes a trusted counselor or guide.

Among the people you go to for career advice, you may find a true **mentor.** A mentor takes a special interest in helping you to reach your goals. People often seek a mentor who has excelled in a career area or specific skill in which they also wish to excel. You may also be drawn to a person who, no matter what their skills or specialty, has ideas and makes choices that you admire and want to emulate.

Because it requires depth and devotion on both sides, a mentoring relationship often evolves from a special personal relationship. A relative, instructor, friend, supervisor, or anyone else who you admire and respect may become your mentor. Think about whom you go to when you are confused, troubled, need guidance, or seek support. Also, consider who may know a lot about a skill or career area you want to pursue. Some schools have faculty or peer mentoring programs to help match students with people who can help them. Check your student handbook, or ask your advisor if this is offered at your school.

Mentoring relationships demand time and energy on both sides. A mentor can give you a private audience for questions and problems, advice tailored to your needs, support, guidance, and trust. A mentor cares about you enough to be devoted to your growth and development. You owe it to a mentor to be open to his or her ideas and to respectfully take advice into consideration. You and your mentor can learn from each other, receive positive energy from your relationship, and grow and develop together.

Know What Employers Want

When you look for a job in a particular career area, your technical skills, work experience, and academic credentials that apply to that career will be important. Beyond those basics, though, other skills will make you an excellent job candidate in any career. Many of the most important skills desired by employers are not as specific as you might imagine. Figure 11.3 shows how employers have ranked certain skills. Notice that many of these skills focus not on what workers do but on *how* they do it.

Skills Employers Want

FIGURE 11.3

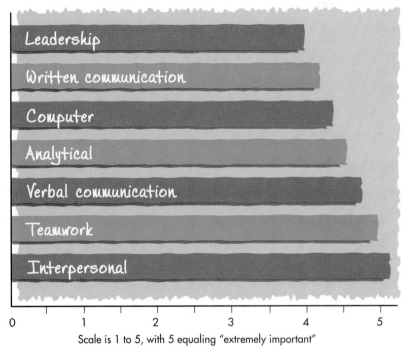

Leadership
Written communication
Computer
Analytical
Verbal communication
Teamwork
Interpersonal

0 1 2 3 4 5

Scale is 1 to 5, with 5 equaling "extremely important"

Source: Reprinted from *Job Outlook 99,* with permission of the National Association of Colleges and Employers, copyright holder.

Important Skills

Particular skills and qualities, to an employer, signify an efficient and effective employee. You can continue to develop them as you work in current and future jobs. Table 11.2, on the next page, describes these skills.

These skills appear throughout this book, and they are as much a part of your school success as they are of your work success. The more you develop them now, the more employable and promotable you will prove yourself to be. You may already use them on the job if you are a student who works.

Emotional Intelligence

One other quality in demand in the workplace is *emotional intelligence.* Daniel Goleman, in his book *Working with Emotional Intelligence,* discusses his findings that emotional intelligence can be even more important than IQ and information knowledge when it comes to success on the job. He defines emotional intelligence as a combination of these factors:[4]

■ Personal Competence. This includes self-awareness (knowing your internal states, preferences, resources, intuitions), self-regulation (being able to manage your internal states, impulses, and resources), and motivation (the factors that help you reach your goals).

■ Social Competence. This includes empathy (being aware of the feelings, needs, and concerns of others) and social skills (your ability to create desirable responses in those with whom you interact).

Springboard

According to a recent survey by the National Association of Colleges and Employers, the first two qualities employers seek in graduates are communication skills and work experience. Ask students whether or not they agree with this ranking.

TABLE 11.2 Skills Employers Look For

SKILLS	WHY?
Communication	Listening and self-expression are keys to workplace success, as is being able to adjust to different communication styles.
Critical thinking	An employee who can assess workplace choices and challenges critically and recommend appropriate actions will stand out.
Teamwork	All workers interact with others on the job. Working well with others is essential for achieving work goals.
Goal setting	Teams fail if goals are unclear or variable. Benefit is gained from setting reasonable, specific goals and achieving them reliably.
Tolerance	The workplace is becoming increasingly diverse. A valuable employee will be able to work with, and respect, a great diversity of people.
Leadership	The ability to influence others in a positive way will earn you respect and keep you in line for promotions.
Creativity	The ability to come up with new concepts, plans, and products will be valuable in the workplace.
Positive attitude	If you show that you have a high level of commitment to all tasks, you may earn the right to tackle more challenging projects.
Integrity	Acting with integrity at work—communicating promptly, following rules, giving proper notice, respecting others—will enhance your value.
Continual learning	The most valuable employees stay current on changes and trends by reading up-to-the-minute media and taking workshops and seminars.

Career Connection
Many multinational companies seek employees who can conduct business in a foreign language and who are willing to travel extensively outside the U.S.

The current emphasis on teamwork has made emotional intelligence very important in the workplace. The more adept you are at working comfortably and productively with others (i.e., the more emotionally intelligent you are and the more you use this intelligence), the more likely you will be to succeed.

Many students need to work and take classes at the same time to fund the education that they hope will move them into better careers. Although you may not necessarily work in a career that interests you, you can hold a job that helps you pay the bills and still make the most of your school time.

HOW CAN YOU JUGGLE WORK AND SCHOOL?

What you are studying today can prepare you to find a job when you graduate. In the meantime, though, you can make work a part of your student life to make money, explore a career, and/or increase your future employability through contacts or résumé building.

As the cost of education continues to rise, more and more students are working and taking classes at the same time. In the school year 1995–96, 79 percent of undergraduates—four out of five—reported working while in school. Most student workers 23 years of age or younger held part-time jobs (about 36 percent). Of students over the age of 23, the majority had full-time jobs (nearly 55 percent).[5] Figure 11.4 shows statistics related to working for both community college and four-year college students.

Working Students

FIGURE 11.4

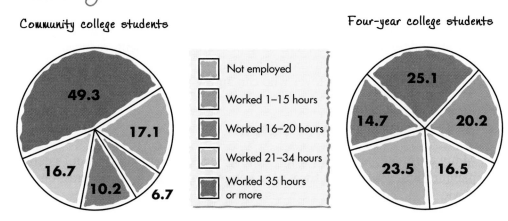

Community college students

Four-year college students

- Not employed
- Worked 1–15 hours
- Worked 16–20 hours
- Worked 21–34 hours
- Worked 35 hours or more

Source: U. S. Department of Education, National Center for Education Statistics, *Profile of Undergraduates in U. S. Postsecondary Education Institutions: 1995–96* (NCES 98-084), May 1998.

Being an employed student isn't for everyone. Adding a job to the list of demands on your time and energy may create problems if it sharply reduces study time or family time. However, many people want to work and many need to work to pay for school. Weigh the potential positive and negative effects of working so that you can make the most beneficial choice.

Effects of Working While in School

Working while in school has many different positive and negative effects, depending on the situation. Evaluate any job opportunity by looking at these effects. Potential positive effects include:

- Money earned
- General and career-specific experience
- Being able to keep a job you currently hold
- Enhanced school and work performance (working up to 15 hours a week may encourage students to manage time more effectively and build confidence)

Potential negative effects include:

- Demanding time commitment
- Reduced opportunity for social and extracurricular activities

Teaching Tip
Holding down a full-time job and carrying a full course load inevitably will reduce sleep time. Inadequate sleep may cause concentration problems and irritability.

- Being able to keep a job you currently hold
- Having to shift gears mentally from work to classroom

If you consider the effects and decide that working will help you, establish what you need from a job.

Establishing Your Needs

Think about what you need from a job before you begin your job hunt. Table 11.3 shows questions you may want to consider. Evaluate any potential job in terms of your needs.

In addition, be sure to consider how any special needs you have might be accommodated. If you have a hearing or vision impairment, reduced mobility, children for whom you need day care, or any other particular need, you may want to find an employer who can and will accommodate them.

Real World Link
Many school alumni, who maintain ties with their college's career placement office, counsel students about career paths and help them find jobs.

Sources of Job Information

Many different routes can lead to satisfying jobs. Use your school's career planning and placement office, your networking skills, classified ads, on-line services, and employment agencies to help you explore these routes.

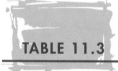

TABLE 11.3   *Evaluate Job Needs*

NEED	EVALUATION QUESTIONS
Salary/Wage Level	How much do I need to make for the year? How much during the months when I am paying tuition? What amount of money justifies the time my job takes?
Time of Day	When is best for me? If I take classes at night, can I handle a day job? If I take day classes, would I prefer night or weekend work?
Hours Per Week (Part-Time vs. Full-Time)	If I take classes part-time, can I handle a full-time job? If I am a full-time student, is part-time best?
Duties Performed	Do I want hands-on experience in my chosen field? Is the paycheck the priority over choosing what I do? What do I like/dislike doing?
Location	Does location matter? Will a job near school save me a great deal of time? What does my commute involve?
Flexibility	Do I need a job that offers flexibility, allowing me to shift my working time when I have an academic or family responsibility?
Affiliation with School or Financial Aid Program	Does my financial aid package require me to take work at the school or a federal organization?

Your School's Career Planning and Placement Office

Generally, the career planning and placement office deals with postgraduation job placements, whereas the student employment office, along with the financial aid office, has more information about working while in school. At either location you might find general workplace information, listings of job opportunities, sign-up sheets for interviews, and contact information for companies. The career office may hold frequent informational sessions on different topics. Your school may also sponsor job or career fairs that give you a chance to explore job opportunities.

Prospective employees talk with company representatives at a job fair.

Because many students don't seek job information until they're about to graduate, they miss much of what the career office can do. Don't wait until the last minute. Start exploring your school's career office early in your university life. The people and resources there can help you at every stage of your career and job exploration process.

Networking

Networking is one of the most important job-hunting strategies. With each person you get to know, you build your network and tap into someone else's. Imagine a giant think link connecting you to a web of people just a couple of phone calls away. Of course, not everyone with whom you network will be helpful. Keep in contact with as many people as possible in the hope that someone will. You never know who that person might be. With whom can you network?

- Friends and family members
- Instructors, administrators, or counselors
- People at employment or career offices
- Alumni
- Employers or coworkers
- Former employers

The contacts with whom you network aren't just sources of job opportunities. They are people with whom you can develop lasting, valuable relationships. They may be willing to talk to you about how to get established, the challenges on the job, what they do each day, how much salary you can expect, or any other questions you have (similar to those in Table 11.1).

Remember this important point: *Don't burn your bridges, because anyone with whom you network has equal potential to help or harm you.* If you maintain positive relationships, you will be more likely to earn help and references from those who know you. Thank your contacts and be ready to extend yourself to others who may need help and advice from you. Remember, too, that contacts have long-term value—you may find yourself calling on the same people many times in your career.

Networking
The exchange of information and/or services among individuals, groups, or institutions.

Contacts
People who serve as carriers or sources of information.

Teaching Tolerance
Because networking may be difficult for shy students, they should start with the people they know best—family and friends. Their goal is to build gradually the self-confidence they need to contact acquaintances and strangers at a later point.

Classified Ads

Some of the best job listings are in newspapers. Most papers print help wanted sections in each issue, organized according to career categories. At the beginning of most help wanted sections you will find an index that lists the categories and their page numbers. Individual ads describe the kind of position available and give a telephone number or post office box for you to contact. Some ads include additional information such as job requirements, a contact person, and the salary or wages offered.

You can run your own classified ads if you have a skill to advertise. Many students make extra cash by doing specific tasks such as typing, editing, cleaning, tutoring, or baby-sitting. You may want to advertise your particular job skills in your school or local paper.

On-Line Services

The Internet is growing as a source of job listings. You can access job search databases such as the Career Placement Registry and U. S. Employment Opportunities. Career-focused Web sites, such as CareerPath.com and CareerMosaic, list all kinds of positions. Individual associations and companies may also post job listings and descriptions, often as part of their World Wide Web pages.

Employment Agencies

Employment agencies are organizations that help people find work. Most employment agencies will put you through a screening process that consists of an interview and one or more tests in your area of expertise. For example, someone looking for secretarial work may take a word-processing test and a spelling test, and someone looking for accounting work may take accounting and math tests. If you pass the tests and interview well, the agency will try to place you in a job.

Most employment agencies specialize in particular careers or skills, such as accounting, medicine, legal, computer operation, graphic arts, child care, and food services. Agencies may place job seekers in either part-time or full-time employment. Many agencies also place people in temporary jobs, which can work well for students who are available from time to time.

Employment agencies are a great way to hook into job networks. However, they usually require a fee that either you or the employer has to pay. Investigate any agency before signing on. See if your school's career counselors know anything about the agency, or if any fellow students have used it successfully. Ask questions so that you know as much as possible about how the agency operates.

Making a Strategic Job Search Plan

When you have gathered information on the jobs you want, formulate a plan for pursuing them. Organize your approach according to what you need to do and how much time you have to devote to your search. Do you plan to make three phone calls per day? Will you fill out three job applications a week for a month? Keep a record—on 3-by-5-inch cards, in a computer file, or in a notebook—of the following:

- people you contact
- companies to which you apply
- jobs you rule out (e.g., jobs that become unavailable or which you find don't suit your needs)
- response from your communications (phone calls to you, interviews, written communications), information about the person who contacted you (name, title), and the time and the dates of the contact.

Keeping accurate records will enable you to both chart your progress and maintain a clear picture of the process. You never know when information might come in handy again. If you don't get a job now, another one could open up at the same company in a couple of months. In that case, well-kept records would enable you to contact key personnel quickly and efficiently. See Figure 11.5 for a sample file card.

Your Résumé and Interview

Information on résumés and interviews fills many books. Therefore, your best bet is to consult some that go into more detail, such as *The Resume Kit* by Richard H. Beatty or *Job Interviews for Dummies* by Joyce Lain Kennedy (don't be insulted by the title; it has lots of terrific information). You'll find these sources and other suggestions listed in the Bibliography at the end of this book.

Sample File Card **FIGURE 11.5**

Job/company: Child-care worker at Morningside Day Care

Contact: Sally Wheeler, Morningside Day Care, 17 Parkside Road, Silver Spring, MD 20910

Phone/fax/e-mail: (301) 555-3353 phone, (301) 555-3354 fax, no e-mail

Communication: Saw ad in paper, sent résumé and cover letter on October 7

Response: Call from Sally to set up interview

—Interview on Oct. 15 at 2 p.m., seemed to get a positive response, she said she would contact me again by the end of the week

Follow-up: Sent thank-you note on October 16

Here are a few basic tips to get you started on giving yourself the best possible chance at a job:

Résumé. Your résumé should always be typed or printed on a computer. Design your résumé neatly, using an acceptable format (books or your career office can show you some standard formats). Proofread it for errors, and have someone else proofread it as well. Type or print it on a heavier bond paper than is used for ordinary copies. Use white or off-white paper and black ink.

Interview. Be clean, neat, and appropriately dressed. Choose a nice pair of shoes—people notice. Bring an extra copy of your résumé and any other materials that you want to show the interviewer, even if you have already sent a copy ahead of time. Avoid chewing gum or smoking. Offer a confident handshake. Make eye contact. Show your integrity by speaking honestly about yourself. After the interview is over, no matter what the outcome, send a formal but pleasant thank-you note right away as a follow-up.

Earning the money you need is hard, especially if you work part-time so that your job won't interfere with school. Financial aid can take some of the burden off your shoulders. If you can "gather" one or more loans, grants, or scholarships, they may help make up for what you don't have time to earn.

WHAT SHOULD YOU KNOW ABOUT FINANCIAL AID?

Seeking financial help has become a way of life for many students. The average cost in the United States for a year's full-time tuition only (not including room and board) in 1997–98 ranged from approximately $1,318 for two-year public institutions to over $17,000 for four-year private ones.[6] In fact, the total cost for an undergraduate's yearly tuition, room, and board increased 23 percent at public colleges and 36 percent at private colleges in the 10-year span between 1985–86 and 1995–96, far outpacing the rate of inflation.[7] Not many people can pay for tuition in full without aid. In fact, according to data compiled in the academic year 1995–96, 49.7 percent of students enrolled received some kind of aid.[8]

In recent years, as college costs have continued to rise, grants to the neediest students have failed to keep up. The federal Pell grant program, for example, serves low-income families. In 1976–77, the average Pell grant covered 39 percent of the cost of four years at a public college. In 1996–97, however, the same grant covered only 22 percent of the same education.[9] As costs continue to rise faster than most grants, the individual student is responsible for aggressively tracking down sources of funding.

Most sources of financial aid don't seek out recipients. Take the initiative to learn how you (or you and your parents, if they currently help to support you) can finance your education. Find the people on campus who can help you with your finances. Do some research to find out what's available, weigh the pros and cons of each option, and decide what would work best for you. Try to apply as early as you can.

Above all, think critically. Never assume that you are not eligible for aid. You cannot find out what you might receive until you ask. The types of aid available to you are student loans, grants, and scholarships.

Student Loans

A loan is given to you by a person, bank, or other lending agency, usually for a specific purchase. You, as the recipient of the loan, must then pay back the amount of the loan, plus interest, in regular payments that stretch over a particular period of time. Interest is the fee that you pay for the privilege of using money that belongs to someone else.

Types of Student Loans

The federal government administers or oversees most student loans. To receive aid from any federal program, you must be a citizen or eligible noncitizen and be enrolled in a program of study that the government has determined is eligible. Individual states may differ in their aid programs. Check with your campus financial aid office to find out details about your state and your school in particular.

Table 11.4 describes the main student loan programs to which you can apply if you are eligible. Amounts vary according to individual circumstances. Contact your school or federal student aid office for further information. In most cases, the amount is limited to the cost of your education minus any other financial aid you are receiving. All the information here on federal loans and grants comes from *The 1999–2000 Student Guide to Financial Aid,* published by the U.S. Department of Education.[10]

Real World Link

Low- and moderate-income students can deduct the interest on student loans (up to $2,000 in 2000 and $2,500 after that). In the 28% tax bracket, a $2,000 deduction will save $560 in taxes.

"Money can't buy you happiness. It just helps you look for it in more places."

Milton Berle

Federal Student Loan Programs   TABLE 11.4

LOAN	DESCRIPTION
Perkins	Low, fixed rate of interest. Available to those with exceptional financial need (determined by a government formula). Issued by schools from their allotment of federal funds. Grace period of up to nine months after graduation before repayment, in monthly installments, must begin.
Stafford	Available to students enrolled at least half-time. Exceptional need not required, although students who prove need can qualify for a subsidized Stafford loan (the government pays interest until repayment begins). Two types of Staffords: the direct loan comes from federal funds, and the FFEL (Federal Family Education Loan) comes from a bank or credit union. Repayment begins six months after you graduate, leave school, or drop below half-time enrollment.
PLUS	Available to students enrolled at least half-time and claimed as dependents by their parents. Parents must undergo a credit check to be eligible, or applicants may be sponsored through a relative or friend who passes the check. Loan comes from government or a bank or credit union. Sponsor must begin repayment sixty days after receiving the last loan payment.

Grants and Scholarships

Both grants and scholarships require no repayment and therefore give your finances a terrific boost. Grants, funded by the government, are awarded to students who show financial need. Scholarships are awarded to students who show talent or ability in the area specified by the scholarship. They may be financed by government or private organizations, schools, or individuals. Table 11.5 describes federal grant programs.

There is much more to say about these financial aid opportunities than can be touched on here. Many other important details about federal grants and loans are available in *The 1999–2000 Student Guide to Financial Aid.* You might find this information at your school's financial aid office, or you can request it by mail, phone, or on-line service:

Address:	Federal Student Aid Information Center
	P.O. Box 84
	Washington, DC 20044-0084
Phone:	1-800-4-FED-AID (1-800-433-3243)
	TDD for the hearing impaired: 1-800-730-8913
Internet address:	www.ed.gov/prog_info/SFA/StudentGuide

Scholarships

Scholarships are given for various abilities and talents. They may reward academic achievement, exceptional abilities in sports or the arts, citizenship, or leadership. Certain scholarships are sponsored by federal agencies. If you display exceptional ability and are disabled, female, of an ethnic background

TABLE 11.5   *Federal Grant Programs*

GRANT	DESCRIPTION
Pell	Need-based; the government evaluates your reported financial information and determines eligibility from that "score" (called an *expected family contribution,* or EFC). Available to undergraduates who have earned no other degrees. Amount varies according to education cost and EFC. Adding other aid sources is allowed.
Federal Supplemental Educational Opportunity Grant (FSEOG)	Need-based; administered by the financial aid administrator at participating schools. Each participating school receives a limited amount of federal funds for FSEOGs and sets its own application deadlines.
Work-study	Need-based; encourages community service work or work related to your course of study. Pays by the hour, at least the federal minimum wage. Jobs may be on-campus (usually for your school) or off (often with a nonprofit organization or a public agency).

classified as a minority (such as African-American or American Indian), or a child of someone who draws benefits from a state agency (such as the spouse of a POW, prisoner of war, or MIA, missing in action), you might find federal scholarship opportunities geared toward you.

All kinds of organizations offer scholarships. You may receive scholarships from individual departments at your school or your school's independent scholarship funds, local organizations such as the Rotary Club, or privately operated aid foundations. Labor unions and companies may offer scholarships for children of their employees. Membership groups such as scouting organizations or the YMCA/YWCA might offer scholarships, and religious organizations such as the Knights of Columbus or the Council of Jewish Federations might be another source.

Researching Grants and Scholarships

It can take work to locate scholarships and work-study programs because many of them aren't widely advertised. Ask at your school's financial aid office. Visit your library or bookstore and look in the sections on college and financial aid. Guides to funding sources, such as Richard Black's *The Complete Family Guide to College Financial Aid* and others listed in the Bibliography at the end of this book, catalog thousands of organizations. Check out on-line scholarship search services. Use common sense when applying for aid—fill out the application as neatly as possible and send it in on time or even early. In addition, be wary of scholarship scam artists who ask you to first pay a fee for them to find aid for you.

No matter where your money comes from—financial aid or paychecks from one or more jobs—you can take steps to help it stretch as far as it can go. The next sections concentrate on developing a philosophy about your money and budgeting effectively. Using those skills, you can more efficiently cover your expenses and still have some left over for savings and fun.

Be a Team
In groups of 4, have students research sources of grants and scholarships on the Internet and discuss the best Web sites. Emphasize the need to think critically about all Web information. Hint: A site that ends in .gov is government sponsored and legitimate.

HOW CAN STRATEGIC PLANNING HELP YOU MANAGE MONEY?

So you work hard to earn your wages and study hard to hold on to your grants and loans. What do you do with that money? Popular culture tells you to buy. You are surrounded by commercials, magazine ads, and notices in the mail that tell you how wonderful you'll feel if you indulge in some serious spending. On the other hand, there are some definite advantages to not taking that advice. Making some short-term sacrifices in order to save money can help you a great deal in the long run.

Critical Thinking
Ask students why they think managing money is so difficult. What is the relationship between spending, saving, and self-esteem? How do childhood experiences affect money management attitudes and skills? Why is it important to talk about money before committing to a long-term relationship?

Sacrifice in the Short Term to Create Long-Term Gain

When you think about your money, take your values and your ability to plan strategically into account. Ask yourself what goals you value most and what steps you will have to take over time to achieve those goals. You are already planning ahead by being in school. You may be scrimping now, but you are planning for a career that may reward you with job security and financial stability.

Table 11.6 shows some potential effects of spending. Some effects are negative, some positive, and some more positive than others. Evaluate which you would prefer in the long run.

Critical thinking is the key to smart money planning. Impulsive spending usually happens when you don't take time to think through your decision before you buy. To use your hard-earned money to your greatest benefit, take time to think about your finances using what you know about decision making.

1. **Establish your needs.** Be honest about what you truly need and what you just want. Do you really need a new bike? Or can the old one serve while you pay off some credit card debt?

2. **Brainstorm available options.** Think about what you can do with your money and evaluate the positive and negative effects of each option.

3. **Choose an option and carry it out.** Spend it—save it—invest it—whatever you decide.

4. **Evaluate the result.** This crucial step will build knowledge that you can use in the future. What were the positive and negative effects of what you chose? Would you make that choice again?

This section doesn't imply that you should never spend money on things that won't bring you any long-term satisfaction. The goal is to make choices

TABLE 11.6 Potential Effects of Spending

OPTION	POTENTIAL SHORT-TERM EFFECTS	POTENTIAL LONG-TERM EFFECTS
Purchase New Sound System	High-quality sound, new system technology	If paid on credit, a debt with monthly finance charges; if paid in cash, a loss of benefits that could have come from saving the money
Reduce or Pay Off Credit Card Debt	Less money for day-to-day expenses; reduction of monthly bills	Improved credit rating and credit history; increased ability to be approved for loans and mortgages; less money charged in interest and fees
Take a Week's Vacation	Fun and relaxation; stress reduction	Credit card debt or less money saved for future needs
Buy a Car	Transportation and independence; gas, maintenance, parking charges	Debt in the form of a car loan; monthly payments for a few years; gradual decrease in car value
Pay Health Insurance Bills	Health insurance coverage; a tighter monthly budget	The safety and security of knowing that your health and that of your family are protected

that give short-term satisfaction while still providing for long-term money growth. If you need a vacation, drive to another state to visit friends instead of buying an expensive package deal at a resort. Buy a less expensive sound system instead of a state-of-the-art one that will test the limits of your credit card. When you spend wisely now, you will appreciate it later.

Put Your Money to Work

You have many choices of how to create long-term gain with the money you are able to save. The best choices will put that money to work making more money for you. Earning money with savings is helpful for anyone, but it has become even more important for the growing numbers of temporary or part-time workers who receive no pension benefits that will support them in retirement.

Following are brief descriptions of some choices you can make. The first three—stocks, bonds, and mutual funds—can be used for short-term or long-term investing. The last three—IRAs, Roth IRAs, and 401(k) and 403(b) plans—are designed specifically to help you save money for retirement.

Stocks. When you purchase shares of stock in a company, each share represents ownership of a small part of that company. Stockholders have a claim on a portion of that company's assets and profits, in proportion to how many shares they own. As a stockholder, your financial holdings increase or decrease as the stock's price goes up or down. You earn money on the stock market if you sell stock at a higher price than what you paid for it, and you lose money if you sell at a lower price.

Bonds. When you buy a bond, you "loan" your money to the bond seller for a period of one year or more. The federal government, corporations, and other institutions sell bonds. On a specified date when the bond "matures," the bond seller has an obligation to repay you what you originally paid along with the interest earned. If you sell early, the bond may be worth less than its face value (the amount you would get when the bond matures).

Mutual funds. Contributing to a mutual fund means giving money to an investment company that decides how to invest it—in bonds, stocks, or some combination. Most investment companies offer a wide variety of funds, each with a different investment profile. Investors earn money when the mutual fund investments pay off, and they can reinvest those earnings in the fund if desired.

Individual Retirement Account (IRA). An IRA is an interest-earning account to which any person under the age of 70 1/2 and earning income from employment can contribute up to $2,000 per year. The account is *tax-deferred*—in other words, you do not pay taxes on your contributions or earnings until you withdraw them. You will pay a penalty, consisting of 10 percent of the amount you withdraw, for any money you take out before you reach the age of 59 1/2 (exceptions include money withdrawn for particular educational or medical payments). Many banks and investing groups offer IRAs.

Roth IRA. This type of IRA was introduced in 1998. If your total income does not exceed a specified amount per year, you can open a Roth IRA.

Many on-line investment services and chat rooms are available to help you manage and save your money more wisely. Join in, and solicit the help of others in improving your financial management.

Withdrawals before the age of 59 1/2 are penalized as with regular IRAs. However, if you are over the age of 59 1/2 and you have held the Roth IRA for more than five years, your withdrawals are tax-free. Roth IRA investors are not subject to an age limit.

401(k) or 403(b). These accounts, similar to IRAs, are intended to help you save for retirement. The difference is that these accounts are only available through companies. Workers employed by commercial corporations may open a 401(k). A similar account called a 403(b) is available to people who work for nonprofit organizations. For either account, workers contribute a defined amount per year; then their employer manages the investment. Both accounts are tax-deferred.

Smart investing requires research and careful consideration. Here are some investing guidelines to get you thinking:[11]

- You alone are responsible for what you do with your money.
- Having faith and sticking to a goal can be as important as reading books and taking courses.
- If you learn slowly, trusting your intuition and learning from mistakes, you will develop expertise.
- Don't go it alone. Seek advice and support from experts, family, and friends.
- Learn the technology of on-line investing. The more comfortable you are getting investment information from the Internet, the greater your chance of making smart choices.

Much more information on investing is available to you. Do research to find out which choices make sense. Read books (some are listed in the Bibliography) and speak with trusted friends and relatives or with a financial advisor, and seek helpful information on-line (try the Vanguard or Morningstar Web sites).

Springboard
Why is "appropriate risk-taking" important to successful investing and money management? Does the nature of what is appropriate change during different life stages—for example, when students are single, when they are parents, when they are preparing for retirement, and when they actually retire?

> "It is thrifty to prepare today for the wants of tomorrow."
>
> Aesop

Develop a Financial Philosophy

You can develop your own personal philosophy about spending, saving, and planning. Following are a couple of strategies that you might want to incorporate into that philosophy:

Springboard
Discuss why it is also important to understand and track economic trends such as the rise and fall of interest rates, inflation, employment, and corporate earnings.

Live beneath your means. Spend less than you make. This strategy helps you create savings. Any amount of savings will give you a buffer zone that can help with emergencies or bigger expenditures. Sometimes your basic needs will cost more than you make, in which case living beneath your means becomes very difficult. If you find, however, that extras are putting your spending over your earnings, cut back.

Pay yourself. After you pay your monthly bills, put whatever you can save in an account. Paying yourself helps you store money in your savings where it can grow. That savings could be your security when you grow older, money for your children's college education, help with a financial crisis, or a down payment on a large purchase. Don't think of the money left after paying bills as automatically available for spending. Make your payment to yourself a high priority so that you honor it as you do your other bills.

HOW CAN YOU CREATE A BUDGET THAT WORKS?

Every time you have to figure out whether the money in your pocket will pay for what you want at a store, you are **budgeting** your money. It takes thought and energy to budget efficiently. Consider your resources (money coming in) and expenditures (money flowing out). The most effective budget adjusts the money flow so that what comes in will be more than what goes out.

The Art of Budgeting

Budgeting involves following a few basic steps: determining how much money you make, determining how much money you spend, subtracting what you spend from what you make, evaluating the result, and making decisions about how to adjust your spending or earning based on that result. Budgeting regularly, using a specified time frame, is easiest. Most people budget on a month-by-month basis.

Determine How Much You Make

Add up all your money receipts for the month. If you currently have a regular full-time or part-time job, add your pay stubs. If you have received any financial aid, loan funding, or scholarship money, determine how much of that you can allow for each month's income and add it to your total. For example, if you received a $1,200 grant for the year, each month would have an income of $100. Be sure when you are figuring your income to use the amounts that remain *after* taxes have been taken out.

Figure Out How Much You Spend

Many people don't have a good idea of how much they spend. If you have never paid much attention to how you spend money, examine your spending patterns (you will have a chance to do this at the end of the chapter). Over a month's time, record expenditures in a small notebook. Indicate any expenditures over five dollars, making sure to count smaller expenditures if they are frequent (a bus pass for a month, soda or newspaper purchases per week). In your list, include an estimate of the following:

Paying the monthly bills.

- rent, mortgage, or room and board fees
- tuition or student loan payments (divide your annual total by 12 to arrive at a monthly figure)

> **Budgeting**
> Making a plan for the coordination of resources and expenditures; setting goals with regards to money.

> **Be a Team**
> Ask students to write down how they feel when others have more money than they do. Are they jealous or are they motivated to work harder? Students should share their thoughts with a partner.

- books, lab fees, and other educational expenses
- regular bills (heat, gas, electric, phone, and water)
- credit card or other payments on credit (car payment)
- food, clothing, toiletries, and household supplies
- child care
- entertainment and related items (eating out, books and publications, and movies)
- health, auto, and homeowners' or renters' insurance
- transportation and auto expenses

Subtract what you spend from what you make. Ideally, you will have a positive number. You may end up with a negative number, however, which indicates that you are spending more than you make. Over a long period of time this can create debt.

Evaluate the Result

If you have a positive number, decide how to save it if you can. If you end up with a negative number, ask questions about what is causing the deficit. Where might you be spending too much or earning too little? Of course, surprise expenses during some months may cause you to spend more than usual, such as equipment fees for a particular course or money to repair your car. However, when a negative number comes up for what seems to be a typical month, you may need to adjust your budget over the long term.

Make Decisions About How to Adjust Spending or Earning

Looking at what may cause you to overspend, brainstorm possible solutions that address those causes. Solutions can involve either increasing resources or decreasing spending. To deal with spending, prioritize your expenditures and trim the ones you really don't need to make. Cut out unaffordable extras. As for resources, investigate ways to take in more money. Taking a part-time job, hunting down scholarships or grants, or increasing hours at a current job may help.

A Sample Budget

Table 11.7 shows a sample budget of an unmarried student living with two other students. It will give you an idea of how to budget (all expenditures are general estimates, based on averages).

To make up the $190 the student is over budget, he can adjust his spending. He could rent movies instead of going to the cinema. He could buy used CDs or borrow them. He could go to a warehouse supermarket. He could make lunch instead of buying it and walk instead of taking public transportation.

Not everyone likes the work involved in keeping a budget. For example, whereas logical-mathematical learners may take to it more easily, visual learners may resist the structure and detail (see Chapter 4). Visual learners may want to create a budget chart such as the one shown in the example, or use strategies that make budgeting more tangible, such as dumping all of your receipts into a big jar and tallying them at the end of the month. Even if

A Student's Sample Budget

TABLE 11.7

- Wages: $10 an hour, 20 hours a week: $10 \times 20 = \$200$ a week $\times 4^{1}/_{3}$ weeks (one month) = $866.
- Student loan from school's financial aid office: $2,000 divided by 12 months = $166.
- Total income per month: $1,032.

Monthly Expenditures	Amount
Tuition ($6,500 per year)	$ 542
Public transportation	$ 90
Phone	$ 40
Food	$ 130
Medical insurance	$ 120
Rent (including utilities)	$ 200
Entertainment/miscellaneous	$ 100
Total spending	$ 1,222

$1032 (income) − $1222 (spending) = $−190 ($190 over budget).

you have to force yourself to do it, you will discover that budgeting can reduce stress and help you take control of your finances and your life.

Savings Strategies

You can save money and still enjoy life. Make your fun less expensive, or save up to splurge on a special occasion. Here are some savings suggestions. Small amounts can eventually add up to big savings.

- Rent movies.
- Walk.
- Use your local library.
- Buy household items in bulk.
- Shop in secondhand stores.
- Use coupons.

- Reuse grocery bags.
- Trade clothing with friends.
- Buy display models.
- Bring your lunch from home.
- Use e-mail or write letters.

Add your own suggestions here:

You can maximize savings and minimize spending by using bank accounts and credit cards wisely.

How can I handle my credit cards?

Maxine Deverney, Truman College, Chicago, Illinois, Accounting Major

Several years ago my husband and I divorced, and I became a single mother. I was responsible for raising three children on my own as well as working a full-time job. Four years ago my daughter died at age 21 in a car accident. I took custody of her son until he was five. During this traumatic and stressful time was when I began to use credit cards. They make spending so easy. I had four, and I used them to buy school clothes for my own children. Then as they grew older and had children of their own, I helped financially with the grandchildren. I have 10 grandchildren.

I have been working steadily for many years. Although I have managed to pay off  most of the debt and I am down to one credit card, I don't want to fall into that trap again. I have worked for four years in financial aid to help students receive grants from their tribes. I am also a secretary. Prior to this I worked as a director for a health clinic at a Chippewa reservation in Michigan. I am of the Potawatomi tribe of Wisconsin. When I graduate from Truman, I will have an associate degree in accounting. My goal is to open my own accounting business one day. I would like to do some accounting for small firms and businesses. Can you offer steps I can take to stay debt-free?

Vernon Nash, Business & Housing Development, Chicago, Illinois

I know the challenges of using a credit card to ease the burden while being a working spouse, parent, and student. My challenge was with my son, Anthony, who was shot and had to have his leg amputated. This was devastating to me, my wife, and my other sons. So we used credit cards to get ourselves through as best we could. I suppose it was a way to compensate for the loss we all felt. I quickly found out that the interest and bills were mounting fast.

The problem with credit cards is that after your trying time has come and gone, you are faced with a high credit  card bill and can feel trapped in a cycle that seems impossible to stop. But it can be done. If you can pay additional money above what the credit card company is asking, you distance yourself from the debt. There are also a few other things you can do to avoid this happening to you again:

1. Determine that you will only buy what you can pay for within 30 days.
2. Pay your credit card bill on time, at least 5 days before the billing date or payment date.
3. Maintain a credit card balance of no more than 7 percent of your annual income.
4. Maintain a one card limit.

When you graduate and want to start your small business, one of the best places to go for assistance is the Small Business Administration in your area. They can give you information about financing your business. Best of luck to you!

WHAT SHOULD YOU KNOW ABOUT BANKING AND CREDIT CARDS?

Banks and credit card companies are probably the two financial institutions that people use most. The more you know about how to use them, the more they can help you manage money and spending.

Bank Accounts

Choose a bank with convenient locations, hours that fit your schedule, account fees that aren't too high, and a convenient network of automatic teller machines (ATMs). Most banks issue debit cards that look like credit cards but take money directly out of your checking account the way a check does. Many banks now have phone or on-line payment services that help you bank from your home, as well as services that allow you to set up automatic payment of bills directly from your account each month. Different accounts have features that serve different needs. Decide which are important to you.

Checking Accounts

Most banks offer more than one checking plan. Some accounts include check writing fees, a small charge on every check you write or on any checks above a certain number per month. Some accounts have free checking, meaning unlimited check writing without extra fees—but you will often have to maintain a minimum balance in your account to qualify. Some accounts charge a monthly fee that is standard or varies according to your balance. Interest checking pays you a low rate of interest, although you may have to keep a certain balance or have a savings account at the same bank.

Savings Accounts

The most basic savings account, the *interest savings* account, pays a rate of interest to you determined by the bank. Many interest savings accounts do not have a required balance, but the interest rate they pay is very low. A *certificate of deposit* (CD) pays greater interest, but your money is "locked in" for a specific period of time—often six months or a year—and you pay a penalty if you withdraw part or all of your money. *Money market* accounts allow you to withdraw your money without penalty. However, interest rates are generally lower than the rates offered by CDs and may rise or fall as the economy changes.

Credit Cards

A credit card can be a lifesaver or a black hole of debt. Credit card companies make money in two ways:

Interest Rates. You are charged interest on the amount you carry as a balance. Interest rates can be fixed (guaranteed to always stay the same) or variable (able to be changed by the credit card company, often in response to economic change). A variable rate of 12 percent may shoot up to 18 percent when the economy slows down.

Annual Fee. You may be charged an annual fee for usage of the card. Some cards have no annual fee; others may charge a flat rate of $10 to $70 per year.

Real World Link
According to a recent study sponsored by the Consumer Federation of America, two-thirds of college students carry a credit card balance (typically $2,000). One-fifth of these students owe more than $10,000.

Today's student body is more debt-ridden than ever, and credit card companies know it. Companies solicit students on campus or through the mail, and it's up to you to sort through the offers and make smart choices. Pay attention to the annual fee and the interest rate. What looks like a low interest rate—for example, 6.9 percent—may only be a temporary rate designed to lure you into applying, and may skyrocket 10 or more percentage points after a few months. Following are some potential effects of using credit.

Positive Effects

Creditors

People to whom debts are owed, usually money.

Establishing a good credit history. If you use your credit card moderately and pay your bills on time, you will make a positive impression on your **creditors.** Your *credit history* (the record of your credit use, including positive actions such as paying on time and negative actions such as going over your credit limit) and *credit rating* (your score, based on your history) can make or break your ability to take out a loan or mortgage.

Emergencies. Few people carry enough cash to handle unexpected expenses. Your credit card can help you in emergencies such as when you need a tow.

Record of purchases. Credit card statements give you a monthly record of purchases made, where they were made, and exactly how much was paid. Using your credit card for purchases that you want to track, such as work expenses, can help you keep records for tax purposes.

Negative Effects

Credit can be addictive. Credit can be like a drug because the pain of paying is put off until later. If you get hooked, you can wind up thousands of dollars in debt. The high interest will enlarge your debt; your credit rating may fall, possibly hurting loan/mortgage eligibility; and you may lose your cards altogether.

Credit spending can be hard to monitor. Paying with a credit card can seem so easy that you don't realize how much you are spending. When the bill comes at the end of the month, the total can hit you hard.

You are taking out a high-interest loan. Credit is not cash. Buying on credit is similar to taking out a high-interest loan—you are using the credit company's money with the promise to pay it back. Loan rates, however, especially on fixed-interest loans, are often much lower than the 11 percent to 23 percent on credit card debt.

Bad credit ratings can haunt you. Any time you are late with a payment, default on a payment, or in any way misuse your card, a record of that occurrence will be entered onto your credit history, lowering your credit rating. If a prospective employer or loan officer discovers a low rating, you will seem less trustworthy and may lose the chance for a job or a loan.

Real World Link
Students with a poor credit rating may also have trouble qualifying for student loans.

Managing Debt

Many people go through periods when they have a hard time keeping up with their bills. Falling behind on payments could result in a poor credit rating that will hang on for some time and will make it difficult for you to make large purchases or take out loans. Gerri Detweiler, author of *The Ultimate Credit Handbook,* recommends that you prioritize bills in the following order (the bills higher on the list should be the first paid because they have the most potential for damage to your credit rating)[12]:

1. Child support—credit bureaus must report any information about overdue child support payments.

2. Mortgage—payments more than 90 days late may appear on your record.

3. Car loans—some states will allow companies to repossess your car after even one missed payment.

4. Taxes—consider arranging a repayment schedule with the IRS if you cannot pay on time.

5. Bank credit cards—pay on time, even if it's only the minimum.

6. Department store cards—pay at least the minimum.

7. Utilities—you may be able to work out a payment schedule with the company.

8. Student loans—you may be able to defer if you are having money trouble.

9. Medical bills—try to discuss a payment schedule with the doctor or hospital.

10. Small bills—set aside for as long as you have to but keep an eye on them.

Other resources can help you solve credit problems. See Figure 11.7 for some ideas.

The most basic way to stay in control is to pay bills regularly and on time. On credit card bills, pay at least the minimum amount due. If you get into trouble, deal with it in three steps. First, *admit* that you made a mistake, even though you may be embarrassed. Then, *address* the problem immediately to minimize damages. Call the creditor and see if you can pay your debt gradually using a payment plan. Finally, *examine* what got you into trouble and avoid it in the future if you can. Cut up a credit card or two if you have too many. If you clean up your act, your credit history will gradually clean up as well.

Real World Link
Students in credit card trouble can turn to their school's financial aid office for referral to a local credit counselor. Some school officials will even arrange a monthly payment plan with the credit card company.

FIGURE 11.7 Credit Help Resources

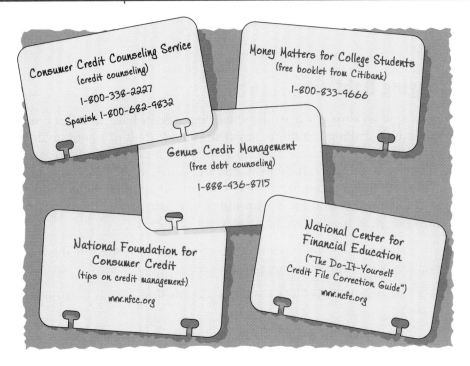

Consumer Credit Counseling Service
(credit counseling)
1-800-338-2227
Spanish 1-800-682-9832

Money Matters for College Students
(free booklet from Citibank)
1-800-833-9666

Genus Credit Management
(free debt counseling)
1-888-436-8715

National Foundation for
Consumer Credit
(tips on credit management)
www.nfcc.org

National Center for
Financial Education
("The Do-It-Yourself
Credit File Correction Guide")
www.ncfe.org

Sacrifici

In Italy, parents often use the term *sacrifici*, meaning "sacrifices," to refer to tough choices that they make to improve the lives of their children and family members. They may sacrifice a larger home so that they can afford to pay for their children's sports and after-school activities. They may sacrifice a higher-paying job so that they can live close to where they work. They give up something in exchange for something else that they have decided is more important to them.

Think of the concept of *sacrifici* as you analyze the sacrifices you can make to get out of debt, reach your savings goals, and prepare for a career that you find satisfying. Many of the short-term sacrifices you are making today will help you do and have what you want in the future.

Name _____   Date _____

BUILDING SKILLS FOR COLLEGE, CAREER, AND LIFE SUCCESS

Critical Thinking
Applying Learning to Life

Career Possibilities

Choose one of the job possibilities you have listed as an interest in any other exercise in this book. Follow up on it by using the following leads. Describe the results of your research from each of the following.

Help wanted listings in newspapers, magazines, or Internet databases:

_____

_____

_____

Listings of job opportunities/company contact information at your career center, student employment office, or independent employment agency:

_____

_____

_____

Contacts from friends or family members:

_____

_____

_____

Contacts from instructors, administrators, or counselors:

_____

_____

_____

Current or former employers or coworkers:

_____

_____

_____

Your Budget

Part One: Where Your Money Goes. Estimate your current expenses in dollars per month, using the table below. This may require tracking expenses for a month, if you don't already keep a record of your spending.

The grand total is your total monthly expenses.

EXPENSE	AMOUNT SPENT
Rent/mortgage or room and board payment	$
Utilities (electric, heat, gas, water)	$
Food (shopping and eating out)	$
Telephone	$
Tuition	$
Books, lab fees, or other educational expenses	$
Loan payments (education or bank loans)	$
Car expenses (repairs, insurance, monthly payments)	$
Gasoline/public transportation	$
Clothing/personal items	$
Entertainment	$
Child care (caregivers, clothing and supplies, other fees)	$
Medical care/insurance	$
Miscellaneous/unexpected	$
Other	$
GRAND TOTAL	$

Part Two: Where Your Money Comes From. Calculate the money you take in each month. Divide any annual payments by 12 to derive the monthly figure.

Now, subtract the grand total of your monthly expenses (Part One) from the grand total of your monthly income (Part Two):

Income per month $ _____

Expenses per month   − $ _____

CASH FLOW $ _____

INCOME SOURCE	AMOUNT EARNED
Regular work salary/wages (full-time or part-time)	$
Grants or work-study payments	$
Scholarships	$
Monthly assistance you may receive from family members	$
Any independent contracting work or private sale of items	$
Other	$
GRAND TOTAL	$

Choose one: I have $ + _____

I have $ – _____

I pretty much break even.

Part Three: Adjusting Your Budget. If you have a negative cash flow, you can increase your income, decrease your spending, or do both. Go back to your list of current expenses to determine where you may be able to save. Look also at your list of income sources to determine what you can increase.

My current expenses $ _____ per month

I want to spend $ _____ less per month

My current income $ _____ per month

I want to earn $ _____ more per month

Evaluating your situation, describe here your two most important ideas about how to adjust your budget.

_____

_____

_____

_____

Your Financial Planning Philosophy

Look again at what you read about how short-term sacrifices can have positive effects in the long term. Think about how smart money decisions can help you achieve your long-term goals. Here, write two long-term goals that will cost money to fulfill.

1. _____

2. _____

Choose one and briefly describe a couple of steps you can take now that will help you to have the money you need when you need it.

Teamwork
Combining Forces

Savings Brainstorm As a class, brainstorm areas that require financial management (such as funding an education, running a household, or putting savings away for the future) and write them on the board. Divide into small groups. Each group should choose one area to discuss (make sure all areas are chosen). In your group, brainstorm strategies that can help with the area you have chosen. Think of savings ideas, ways to control spending, ways to earn more money, and any other methods of relieving financial stress. Agree on a list of possible ideas for your area and share it with the class.

Writing
Discovery Through Journaling

To record your thoughts, use a separate journal or the lined pages at the end of the chapter.

Credit Cards Describe how you use credit cards. What do you buy? How much do you spend? Do you pay in full each month or run a balance? How does using a credit card make you feel? If you would like to change how you use credit, discuss changes you want to make and what effects they might have.

Career Portfolio
Charting Your Course

Financial History Create for yourself a detailed picture of your financial history. First, put your budget exercises, or copies of them, in your portfolio so that you have a record of your spending habits. Then answer the following questions on a separate sheet and keep your work. Keeping accurate financial records is vital in making intelligent financial decisions.

1. **Financial aid.** List school, federal, and personal loans; scholarship funds; grants; and the amount that you pay out of pocket. Indicate all account numbers; payment plans; and records of payment, including dates and check numbers if applicable.

2. **Bank accounts.** For any account to which you have access, list all names on the accounts, bank name, type of account, and account number. Include any restrictions on the accounts such as minimum balances or time frames during which you will receive a penalty for removing funds.

3. **Loans.** List any nonacademic loans you are currently repaying, noting bank names, account numbers, loan types, repayment schedule, payment amounts, and dates of payments made.

4. **Credit cards.** List major credit cards (American Express, Visa, MasterCard, Discover, etc.), as well as cards for gas stations or department stores. For each card, include the following:

   ■ Name on the card, card number, and expiration date

   ■ Payment style (pay in full, pay minimum each month, etc.)

   ■ Problems (late payments, lost cards, card fraud, etc.)

   ■ Current balance and date

   Keep a copy of important credit card numbers separate from your wallet or purse so that you have records should you lose your cards. For your protection, any record of personal identification numbers (PINs) should be kept separate from credit cards or credit card numbers.

How you manage your own money is an important indicator of how you would manage the money of others, in a financial or managerial business capacity. Start by managing your own assets so that you will be entrusted with greater and greater responsibility, should you choose it, as you are promoted in your career.

5. **Earning history.** List the jobs you have had or currently have. Include the following for each:

   ■ Name of the company or business

   ■ Job title

   ■ Wages or salary

   ■ Dates of your employment

   Store this information in your portfolio. Update it when you have new entries.

6. **References.** First, create a list of people who have served or could serve as references for you. Brainstorm names from all areas of your human resources:

Instructors	Fellow students	Friends
Administrators	Present/former employers	Mentors
Counselors	Present/former coworkers	Family Members

For each potential reference, list the name, contact information (phone number and address), and how you know the person. Update the information as you meet potential references or lose touch with old ones. Keep it on hand for the time that you need a new letter or want to cite a reference on a résumé. When references write letters of recommendation for you, be sure to thank them right away for their help and to keep them up-to-date on your activities. Always let a reference know when you have sent a letter out, so that he or she may be prepared to receive a call from the person/company/program to which you have applied.

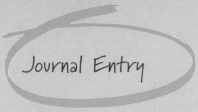
Journal Entry

Name _____   Date _____

Journal Entry

Name _____   Date _____

Moving Ahead
Building a Flexible Future

In this chapter, you will explore answers to the following questions:

- How can you be flexible in the face of change?
- What will help you handle success and failure?
- Why give back to the community and the world?
- Why is college just the beginning of lifelong learning?
- How can you live your mission?

As you come to the end of your work in this course, you have built up a wealth of knowledge. Now you have more power to decide what directions you want your life to take and how you can make a difference in your corner of the world. This chapter will explore how to develop the kind of flexibility that can help you adjust goals, make the most of successes, and work through failures. You will consider what is important about giving back to your community and continuing to learn throughout your life. Finally, you will revisit your personal mission, exploring how to keep it in sync with life's changes.

Teaching Tip
Helpful Web sites:
- U.S. Environmental Protection Agency - www.epa.gov
- @ Grass-roots.org - www.grass-roots.org/
- Action Without Borders - www.idealist.org/

HOW CAN YOU BE FLEXIBLE IN THE FACE OF CHANGE?

Even the most carefully constructed plans can be turned upside down by change. Three ways to make change a manageable part of your life are maintaining flexibility, adjusting your goals, and being open to unpredictability.

Maintain Flexibility

The fear of change is as inevitable as change itself. When you become comfortable with something, you tend to want it to stay the way it is, whether it is a place you live, a job, or the racial/cultural mix of people with whom you interact. Change may seem to have negative effects, and consistency positive effects. Think about your life right now. What do you wish would always stay the same? What changes have upset you and thrown you off balance?

You may have encountered any number of changes in your life to date, many of them unexpected—see Figure 12.1 for some examples. All of these changes, whether they seem good or bad, cause a certain level of stress. They also cause a shift in your personal needs, which may lead to changing priorities.

FIGURE 12.1 *Examples of Changes People Experience*

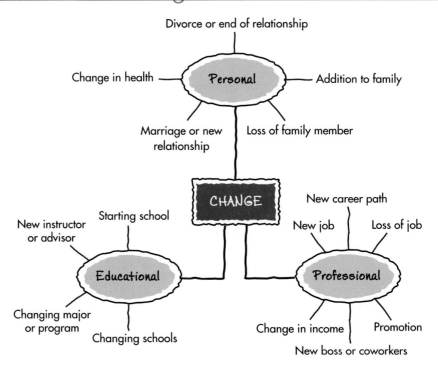

Change Brings Different Needs

Your needs can change from day to day, year to year, and situation to situation. Although you may know about some changes—such as school starting—ahead of time, others may take you completely by surprise, such as losing a job. Even the different times of year bring different needs, for example, a need for extra cash around the holidays or additional child care when your children are home for the summer.

Some changes that shift your needs occur within a week or even a day. For example, an instructor may inform you that you have an end-of-week quiz, or your work supervisor may give you an additional goal. Table 12.1 shows how the effects of certain changes can lead to new priorities.

Change Produces New Priorities

TABLE 12.1

CHANGE	POTENTIAL EFFECTS/NEW NEEDS	NEW PRIORITIES
New job	Change in daily/weekly schedule; need for increased contribution of household help from others	Time and energy commitment; maintaining confidence; learning new skills
Lost job	Loss of income; need for others in your household to contribute more income	Job hunting; reduction in spending; additional training or education in order to qualify for a different job
Started school	Fewer hours for work, family, and personal time; responsibility for classwork; need to plan semesters ahead of time	Careful scheduling to provide adequate class and study time; strategic planning of classes and of career goals
Relationship/ marriage	Responsibility toward your partner; merging of your schedules and perhaps finances and belongings	Time and energy commitment to relationship
Breakup/divorce	Change in responsibility for any children; increased responsibility for your own finances; possibly a need to relocate; increased independence	Making time for yourself; gathering support from friends and family; securing your finances; making sure you have your own income
New baby	Increased parenting responsibility; need money to pay for baby's needs or if you had to stop working; need help with other children	Child care; flexible employment; increased commitment from a partner or other support

Flexibility Versus Inflexibility

When change affects your needs, flexibility will help you shift your priorities so that you address those needs. You can react to change with either inflexibility or flexibility, each with its resulting effects.

Inflexibility. Not acknowledging a shift in needs can cause trouble. For example, if you lose your job and continue to spend as much money as you did before, ignoring your need to live more modestly, you can drive yourself into debt and make the situation worse.

Flexibility. Being flexible means acknowledging the change, examining your different needs, and addressing them in any way you can.

Critical Thinking

Ask students to describe the relationship between flexibility and risk-taking. In our changing society, how would they define appropriate risk-taking? Inappropriate risk-taking? Do they know anyone who is a flexible risk-taker?

Discovering what change brings may help you uncover positive effects. For example, a loss of a job can lead you to reevaluate your abilities and look for a job that suits you better. In other words, a crisis can spur opportunity, and you may want to adjust your goals in order to pursue it.

Sometimes you need time before you react to a major change. When you do decide you are ready, being flexible will help you cope with the negative effects and benefit from the positive effects.

Adjust Your Goals

Your changing life may result in the need to use your critical-thinking skills to adjust goals accordingly. For example, a goal to graduate in four years may not be reasonable if economic constraints take you out of school for a while. Sometimes goals must change because they weren't appropriate in the first place. Some turn out to be unreachable; some don't pose enough of a challenge; others may be unhealthy for the goal setter or harmful to others.

Step One: Reevaluate

Learning Styles Tip
Visual-spatial learners may want to draw a chart of their progress to see if reevaluation is necessary.

Before making adjustments in response to change, take time to reevaluate both the goals themselves and your progress toward them.

The goals. First, determine whether your goals still fit the person you have become in the past week or month or year. Circumstances can change quickly. For example, an unexpected pregnancy might cause a female student to rethink her educational goals.

Your progress. If you feel you haven't gotten far, determine whether the goal is out of your range or simply requires more stamina than you had anticipated. As you work toward any goal, you will experience alternating periods of progress and stagnation. You may want to seek the support and perspective of a friend or counselor as you evaluate your progress.

Teaching Tip
Few people can reach their goals without the help of family and friends. Remind students of the strength of a team in analyzing, modifying, and replacing goals.

Step Two: Modify

If after your best efforts it becomes clear that a goal is out of reach, modifying your goal may bring success. Perhaps the goal doesn't suit you. For example, an active interpersonal learner might become frustrated while pursuing a detail-oriented, sedentary career such as computer programming.

Based on your reevaluation, you can modify a goal in two ways.

Adjust the existing goal. To adjust a goal, change one or more aspects that define it—the time frame, due dates, or expectations. For example, a woman with an unexpected pregnancy could adjust her educational due date, taking an extra year to complete her course work. She could also adjust the time frame, taking classes at night if she has to care for her child during the day.

Replace it with a more compatible goal. If you find that a particular goal does not make sense, try to find another that works better for you at this time. For example, a couple who wants to buy a house but can't

> "Risk! Risk anything! Care no more for the opinion of others, for those voices. Do the hardest thing on earth for you. Act for yourself. Face the truth."
>
> Katherine Mansfield

afford it can choose to work toward the goal of making improvements in their current living space. You and your circumstances never stop changing—your goals should reflect those changes.

Be Open to Unpredictability

Life is by nature unpredictable. Think about your own life. Chances are that not much of what you do and who you are is exactly as you may have planned.

In their article "A Simpler Way," Margaret J. Wheatley and Myron Kellner-Rogers discuss how the unpredictability of life can be a gift that opens up new horizons. "We often look at this unpredictability with resentment, but it's important to notice that such unpredictability gives us the freedom to experiment. It is this unpredictability that welcomes our creativity."[1]

Wheatley and Kellner-Rogers offer the following suggestions for making the most of unpredictability:

Look for what happens when you meet someone or something new. Be aware of the new feelings or insights that arise when you interact with a new person, class, project, or event. Instead of accepting or rejecting them based on whether they fit into your idea of life, follow them a bit. See where they lead you.

Be willing to be surprised. Great creative energies can come from the force of a surprise. Instead of turning back to familiar patterns after a surprise throws you off balance, see what you can discover.

Use your planning as a guide rather than a rule. Planning helps you focus your efforts, shape your path, and gain a measure of control over your world. Life, however, won't always go along with your plan. If you see your plans as a guide, allowing yourself to follow new paths when changes occur, you will be able to grow from what life gives you.

Focus on what is rather than what is supposed to be. Often people are unable to see what's happening because they are too focused on what they feel should be happening. When you put all your energy into your future plans, you may miss out on some incredible occurrences happening right now. Planning for the future works best as a guide when combined with an awareness of the changes that the present brings.

When you stay open to unpredictability, you will be more aware of life's moments as they go by. You will become an explorer, experiencing everything that comes across your path. Having this awareness and flexibility will help you understand that both successes and failures are a natural part of your exploration.

Springboard
Ask students to react to this statement: It is much easier for optimists than pessimists to be open to life's unpredicted opportunities.

Teaching Tip
Help students understand that when the word *should* ("I should do something because my friends expect me to . . .") guides their behavior, they are giving others power over their lives.

WHAT WILL HELP YOU HANDLE SUCCESS AND FAILURE?

The perfect, trouble-free life is only a myth. The most wonderful, challenging, fulfilling life is full of problems to be solved and difficult decisions to be made. If you want to handle the bumps and bruises without losing your self-esteem, you should prepare to encounter setbacks along with your successes.

Dealing with Failure

Things don't always go the way you want them to go. You may face difficult obstacles, let yourself down or disappoint others, make mistakes, or lose your motivation, as all people do. What is important is how you choose to deal with what goes wrong. If you can arrive at reasonable definitions of failure and success, accept failure as part of being human, and examine failure so that you can learn from it, you will have the confidence to pick yourself up and keep improving.

Measuring Failure and Success

Most people measure failure by comparing where they are to where they believe they should be. Because individual circumstances vary widely, so do definitions of failure. What you consider a failure may seem like a positive step for someone else. Here are some examples:

- Imagine that your native language is Spanish. You have learned to speak English well, but you still have trouble writing it. Making writing mistakes may seem like failure to you, but to a recent immigrant from the Dominican Republic who knows limited English, your command of the language will seem like a success story.

- If two people apply for internships, one may see failure as receiving some offers but not the favorite one, whereas someone who was turned down may see any offer as a success.

- Having a job that doesn't pay you as much as you want may seem like a failure, but to someone who is having trouble finding any job, your job spells success.

Approach Failure Productively

e-mail

No one escapes failure. The most successful people and organizations have experienced failures and mistakes. For example, America Online miscalculated customer growth when they offered a flat monthly rate, resulting in thousands of customers having trouble logging onto the service. Many an otherwise successful individual has had a problematic relationship, a substance abuse problem, or a failing grade in a course.

Figure 12.2 shows the choices you have when deciding how to view a failure or mistake. Pretending it didn't happen can deny you valuable lessons and may create more serious problems. Blaming someone else falsely assigns responsibility, stifling opportunities to learn. Blaming yourself can result in feeling incapable of success and perhaps becoming afraid to try.

By far the best way to survive a failure is to forgive yourself. Your value as a human being does not diminish when you make a mistake. Expect that you will do the best that you can within the circumstances of your life, knowing that getting through another day as a student, employee, and/or parent is a success in and of itself. Forgiving yourself opens you up to the possibilities of what you can learn from your experience.

Ways to Approach Failure

FIGURE 12.2

Blaming others | Pretending it didn't happen | Blaming yourself | Forgiving yourself

Learning from Failure

Learning from your failures and mistakes involves thinking critically about what happened. First, evaluate what occurred and decide if it was within your control. It could have had nothing to do with you at all. You could have failed to get a job because someone else with equal qualifications was in line for it ahead of you. A family crisis could have interrupted your studying, resulting in a low test grade. These are unfortunate circumstances, but they are not failures.

On the other hand, something you did or didn't do may have contributed to the failure. If you decide that you have made a mistake, your next steps are to analyze the causes and effects of what happened, make any improvements that you can, and decide how to change your action or approach in the future.

For example, imagine that after a long night of studying, you forgot your part-time work-study commitment the next day.

Analyze causes and effects. *Causes:* Your exhaustion and concern about the test caused you to forget to check your work schedule. *Effects:* Because you weren't there, a crucial curriculum project wasn't completed. An entire class and instructor who needed the project have been affected by your mistake.

Make any possible improvements on the situation. You could apologize to the instructor and see if there is still a chance to finish up part of the work that day.

Make changes for the future. You could set a goal to note your work schedule regularly in your date book—maybe in a bright color—and to check it more often. You could also arrange your future study schedule so that you will be less exhausted.

Think about the people you consider exceptionally successful. They have built much of their success on their willingness to take risks, make mistakes, and learn from them. You, too, can benefit from staying open to this kind of hard-won education. Let what you learn from falling short of your goals inspire new and better ideas.

Teaching Tip
When students are in the middle of a crisis, encourage them not to accept the inevitability of failure. Instead they should look for creative ways to solve the problem and tell themselves that they have the power and ability to turn an obstacle into an opportunity.

Think Positively About Failure

When you feel you have failed, how can you boost your outlook?

Stay aware of the fact that you are a capable, valuable person. Remind yourself of your successes, focusing your energy on your best abilities and knowing that you have the strength to try again. The energy put into talking negatively to yourself would be better spent on moving ahead.

Share your thoughts and disappointment with others. Everybody fails. When you confide in others you may be surprised to hear them exchange stories that rival your own. Exchange creative energy that can help you learn from failures rather than having a mutual gripe session.

Look on the bright side. At worst, you at least have learned a lesson that will help you avoid similar situations in the future. At best, there may be some positive results. What you learn from a failure may, in an unexpected way, bring you around to where you want to be.

Dealing with Success

Be a Team
Have the members of 4-person teams share the small and large successes they've had during the past year in their personal lives, relationships with friends and family, school, and career. Encourage the groups to explore how each person defines success.

Sharing success with family.

Success isn't reserved for the wealthy, famous people you see glamorized in magazines and newspapers. Success isn't money or fame, although it can bring such things. Success is being who you want to be and doing what you want to do. Success is within your reach.

Pay attention to the small things when measuring success. You may not feel successful until you reach an important goal you have set for yourself. However, along the way each step is a success. When you are trying to drop a harmful habit, each time you stay on course is a success. When you are juggling work, school, and personal life, just coping with every new day equals success. If you received a C on a paper and then earned a B on the next one, your advancement is successful.

Remember that success is a process. If you deny yourself the label of success until you reach the top of where you want to be, you will have a much harder time getting there. Just moving ahead toward improvement and growth, however fast or slow the movement, equals success.

Here are some techniques to manage your successes:

Appreciate yourself. Take time to congratulate yourself for a job well done—whether it be a good grade, an important step in learning a new language, a job offer, or a personal victory over substance abuse. People don't praise themselves (or each other) enough when success occurs. Praise can give you a terrific vote of confidence.

Take your confidence on the road. This victory can lead to others. Based on this success, you may be expected to prove to yourself and others that you are capable of growth, of continuing your successes and building on them. Show yourself and others that the confidence is well founded.

Stay sensitive to others. There could be people around you who may not have been so successful. Remember that you have been in their place and they in yours, and the positions may change many times over in the future. Enjoy what you have and support others as they need it.

You are a unique human being with unique capabilities. It's important to define both failure and success in terms of your own goals and abilities, not those of others. This is especially crucial for students with learning disabilities.

Redefining Failure and Success: Learning Disabilities

Whereas almost everyone has some measure of difficulty in some aspect of learning, people with learning disabilities have specifically diagnosed conditions that make certain kinds of learning difficult. Different disabilities have different effects—some cause reading problems, some create difficulties in math, some make it difficult to process heard language.

If you have a learning disability, you may compare yourself to others, labeling as failure anything that does not live up to the examples set by students around you. You can beat this attitude, though, by becoming a strong advocate for your rights as a student with special needs and by redefining failure and success in terms of your own accomplishments. Consider the following strategies:

Be informed about your disability. The federal government, in Public Law 94-142, defines learning disabilities as follows: "Specific learning disability means a disorder in one or more of the basic psychological processes involved in understanding or in using language, spoken or written, which may manifest itself in an imperfect ability to listen, think, speak, read, write, spell, or to do mathematical calculations. The term includes such conditions as perceptual handicaps, brain injury, minimal brain dysfunction and dyslexia." A learning disability diagnosis results from specific testing done by a qualified professional, and it may also involve documentation from instructors and family members.

Seek assistance from your school. If you are officially diagnosed with a learning disability, you are legally entitled to particular aid. Armed with your test results and documentation about your disability, speak with your advisor about getting support that will help you learn. Among the services mandated by law for students with learning disabilities are testing accommodations (for example, having extended time or computer availability); books on tape; and note-taking assistance (for example, having a fellow student take notes for you or having access to the instructor's notes).

Know your needs. The more you know about your disability, the more you will be able to seek the most appropriate assistance. Beyond legally mandated services, other services that may help students with learning disabilities include tutoring, study skills assistance, and counseling. If you understand your disability and can clearly explain what accommodations will help you and why, you will be able to make the most of what your school can offer you.

> "The word impossible is not in my dictionary."
> Napoleon

Build a successful attitude. See your accomplishments in light of where you were before and how far you have come. Keep a list of your successes and refer to it often to reinforce positive feeling. Rely on people in your life who support you and see you as a capable person. Know that the help you receive at school is deserved—it will give you the best possible chance to learn and grow.

Whether you are feeling successful or less than successful, there are always others around you who are in need of your help. Giving what you can of your time, energy, and resources is part of being a citizen of your community and of the world. Your contributions can help to bring success to others.

WHY GIVE BACK TO THE COMMUNITY AND THE WORLD?

Everyday life is demanding. You can become so caught up in the issues of your own life that you neglect to look outside your immediate needs. However, from time to time you may feel that your mission extends beyond your personal life. You have spent time in this course working to improve yourself. Now that you've come so far, why not extend some of that energy and effort to the world outside? You have the power to make positive differences in the lives of others.

Your Imprint on the World

Sometimes you can evaluate your own hardships more reasonably when you look at them in light of what is happening elsewhere in the world. There are always many people in the world in great need. You have something to give to others, and in giving you affirm that you are part of an interdependent community of people. All people live in this world together and depend on each other.

Your perspective may change after volunteering at a soup kitchen. Your appreciation of those close to you may increase after you spend time with cancer patients at the local hospice. Your perspective on your living situation may change after you help people improve their housing conditions.

What you do for others has enormous impact. Giving one person hope, comfort, or help can improve his or her ability to cope. That person in turn may be able to offer help to someone else. This generates a cycle of positive effects. For example, Helen Keller, blind and deaf from the age of two, was educated through the help of her teacher Annie Sullivan, and then spent much of her life lecturing to raise money for the teaching of the blind and deaf. Another example is Betty Ford, who was helped in her struggle with alcoholism and founded the Betty Ford Center to help others with addiction problems.

How can you make a difference? Look for some kind of volunteering activity that you can fit in your schedule. Many schools and companies are realizing the importance of community involvement and have appointed committees to find and organize volunteering opportunities. Table 12.2 lists organizations that provide volunteer

Join a chat room or have a discussion with your friends about causes that mean the most to you. Notice how differences among people cause them to be passionate about different things.

Organizations That Can Use Your Help

TABLE 12.2

- AIDS-related organizations
- American Red Cross
- Amnesty International
- Audubon Society
- Big Brothers and Big Sisters
- Churches, synagogues, temples, and affiliated organizations such as the YM/WCA or YM/WHA
- Educational support organizations

- Environmental awareness/support organizations such as Greenpeace
- Hospitals
- Hotlines
- Kiwanis/Knights of Columbus/Lions Club/Rotary
- Libraries
- Meals on Wheels
- Nursing homes

- Planned Parenthood
- School districts
- Scouting organizations
- Share Our Strength/other food donation organizations
- Shelters and organizations supporting the homeless
- Shelters for battered women
- Sierra Club/World Wildlife Fund

opportunities; you might also look into more local efforts or private clearinghouses that set up a number of different smaller projects.

Volunteerism is also getting attention on the national level. The government has made an effort to stress the importance of community service as part of what it means to be a good citizen, and it provides support for that effort through AmeriCorps. AmeriCorps provides financial awards for education in return for community service. If you work for AmeriCorps, you can use the funds you receive to pay current tuition expenses or repay student loans. You may work either before, during, or after your college education. You can find more information on AmeriCorps by contacting this organization: The Corporation for National and Community Service, 1201 New York Avenue NW, Washington, DC 20525, 1-800-942-2677.

Sometimes it's hard to find time to volunteer when so many responsibilities compete for your attention. One solution is to combine other activities with volunteer work. Get exercise while cleaning a park or your yard, or bring the whole family to sing at a nursing home on a weekend afternoon. Whatever you do, your actions will have a positive impact on those you help and those they encounter in turn.

Springboard
You can also give your time to someone you know who needs help. Reaching out to a friend or relative can be mutually rewarding because of your connection with the person.

Valuing Your Environment

Your environment is your home. When you value it, you help to maintain a clean, safe, and healthy place to live. What you do every day has an impact on others around you and on the future. One famous slogan says that if you are not part of the solution, you are part of the problem. Every saved bottle, environmentally aware child, and reused bag is part of the solution. Take responsibility for what you can control—your own habits—and develop sound practices that contribute to the health of the environment.

Learning Styles Tip
Those with naturalistic intelligence may be drawn to environmental causes and careers.

Recycle anything that you can. What can be recycled varies with the system set up in your area. You may be able to recycle any combination of plastics, aluminum, glass, newspapers, and magazines. Products that use recycled materials are often more expensive, but if they are within your price range, try to reward the company's dedication by purchasing them.

Trade and reuse items. When your children have grown too old for the crib, baby clothes, and toys, give away whatever is still usable. Give clothing you don't wear to others who can use it. Organizations like Goodwill may pick up used items in your neighborhood on certain days or through specific arrangements. Wrap presents in plain newspaper and decorate with markers. Use your imagination—there are many, many items all around you that you can reuse.

Respect the outdoors. Use products that reduce chemical waste. Pick up after yourself. Through volunteering, voicing your opinion, or making monetary donations, support the maintenance of parks and the preservation of natural, undeveloped land. Be creative: One young woman planned a cleanup of a local lakeside area as the main group activity for the guests at her birthday party (she joined them, of course). Everyone benefits when each person takes responsibility for maintaining the fragile earth.

Springboard
Ask students to discuss the importance of voting for environmental protection laws on the federal, state, and local levels. Do they feel they have power at the ballot box?

Remember that valuing yourself is the base for valuing all other things. Improving the earth is difficult unless you value yourself and think you deserve the best living environment possible. Valuing yourself will also help you understand why you deserve to enjoy the benefits of learning throughout your life.

WHY IS COLLEGE JUST THE BEGINNING OF LIFELONG LEARNING?

Critical Thinking
Why is lifelong learning important to career success and to the success of personal relationships? Why do relationships often fail when one person continues to grow and the other does not? Why will 21st century careers be defined in terms of lifelong learning?

As a student, you are able to focus on learning for a period of time, gaining access to knowledge, resources, and experiences through your school. Take advantage of the academic atmosphere by developing a habit of seeking out new learning opportunities. That habit will encourage you to continue your learning long after you have graduated, even in the face of the pressures of everyday life.

Learning brings change, and change causes growth. As you change and the world changes, new knowledge and ideas continually emerge. Absorb them so that you can become a student of life who learns something new every single day. Here are some lifelong learning strategies that can encourage you to continually ask questions and explore new ideas:

Investigate new interests. When information and events catch your attention, take your interest one step further and find out more. If you are fascinated by politics, find out if your school has political clubs. If a friend of yours starts to take yoga, try a class. If you really like one portion of a particular class, see if there are other classes that focus on that topic. Instead of dreaming about it, just do it.

How do I become employable and promotable?

Titus Dillard, Jr., Embry-Riddle Aeronautical University, Daytona Beach, Florida, Aviation/Business Management Major

I transferred from a junior college to Embry-Riddle on a basketball scholarship, without which I probably wouldn't have been able to afford school. I've enjoyed it, but collegiate sports take up a lot of time. We practice six days a week for 2 1/2 hours a day. Game days, especially away games, require even more time. Coaches tell you to bring books on the road, but there are too many interruptions to really focus on studying. To help pay the bills, I also work 10 hours a week as a student assistant for our business academic advisor. It's been a great experience, but again it takes away from my time to study. I will be the first in my family to graduate from college, and my mother is proud of me. But she still has four children at home, so I don't like to ask for anything.

Because I haven't been able to focus on academics, my grade point average has suffered. I am a senior now, so I have very little time to bring it up. There's a naval intelligence program sponsored by the U. S. government that I would like to apply for, but one of the requirements is a GPA of 3.45 or higher. Right now mine is only 2.5.

Last week we had a career exposition at my school and one of the first questions recruiters asked was, "What's your GPA?" I'm thinking about asking my basketball coach for a letter of recommendation to help show that I've been responsible, but I wonder if that will do any good. I want to make a good impression. Do you have any suggestions for how I can become employable and promotable after school?

Cherie Andrade, Hawaii Pacific University, Honolulu, Hawaii, Associate Director of Admissions

It's understandable that you worry about your future. First of all, although you are feeling discouraged about your GPA, try not to dwell on it. I don't think companies look primarily at GPA when considering a candidate. That's only one component of your profile. You have many

things going for you. For one, you have an interesting background. The fact that you are the first from your family to graduate shows your drive to succeed. Your experiences, such as playing basketball and working part-time, have built character and a work ethic. These are important to employers. Remember: Don't judge yourself. Let the people looking at the applications be the judges.

I have three suggestions for your interviews. First, make an appointment to talk with the director of the Career Services Center on your campus. This person often knows what companies are looking for. Second, if you want to enter the naval intelligence program, you definitely should apply even though one of their qualifications is a high GPA. Career counselors often tell students to apply for what seems far-fetched because you might just be exactly what they're looking for. Third, do get a letter of recommendation from your coach, but don't stop there. Try to also get a letter from one of your instructors or the business advisor you work for. Explain to them what you want to accomplish so that they can give you a more focused recommendation.

To land the job or the training you want, you have to step out and take risks. If you pursue your career goals with the same determination and skills you've used to finish four years of college and juggle all your other commitments, I have no doubt you'll find work you love and that you'll continue to develop in your area of expertise.

Read books, newspapers, magazines, and other writings. Reading opens a world of new perspectives. Check out what's on the best-seller list. Ask your friends about books that have changed their lives. Stay current about your community, state, country, and the world by reading newspapers and magazines. A newspaper that has a broad scope, such as the *New York Times* or *Washington Post,* can be an education in itself. Explore religious literature, family letters, and Internet news groups and Web pages. Keep something with you to read for those moments when you have nothing to do.

Spend time with interesting people. When you meet someone new who inspires you and makes you think, keep in touch. Have a potluck dinner party and invite one person or couple from each corner of your life—your family, your work, your school, a club to which you belong, and your neighborhood. Sometimes, meet for reasons beyond just being social. Start a book club, a home-repair group, a drama reading club, a hiking group, or an investing group. Learn something new from one another.

Continuing education

Courses that students can take without having to be part of a degree program.

Pursue improvement in your studies and in your career. When at school, take classes outside of your major if you have time. After graduation, continue your education both in your field and in the realm of general knowledge. Stay on top of ideas, developments, and new technology in your field by seeking out **continuing education** courses. Sign up for career-related seminars. Take single courses at a local college or community learning center. Some companies offer additional on-the-job training or pay for their employees to take courses that will improve their knowledge and skills.

Talk to people of different generations than yours. Younger people can learn from the experienced, broad perspective of those belonging to older generations; older people can learn from the fresh and often radical perspective of those younger than themselves. Even beyond the benefits of new knowledge, there is much to be gained from developing mutual respect among the generations.

Native American men in traditional dress in Los Angeles, California.

Delve into other cultures. Visit the home of a friend who has grown up in a culture different from your own. Invite him or her to your home. Eat food from a country you've never visited. Initiate conversations with people of different races, religions, values, and ethnic backgrounds. Travel to different countries. Travel to culturally different neighborhoods or cities near you—they may seem as foreign as another country. Take a course that deals with some aspect of cultural diversity.

Nurture a spiritual life. You don't have to attend a house of worship to be spiritual, although that may be part of your spiritual life. "A spiritual life of some kind is absolutely necessary for psychological 'health,' " says psychologist and author Thomas Moore in his book *The Care of the Soul.* "We live in a time of deep division, in which mind is separated from body and spirituality is at odds with materialism."[2] The words *soul* and *spirituality* hold different meanings for each individual. Whether you discover them in music, organized religion, friendship, nature, cooking, sports, or anything else, making them a priority will help you find a greater sense of balance and meaning.

Experience what others create. Art is "an adventure of the mind" (Eugène Ionesco, playwright); "a means of knowing the world" (Angela Carter, author); something that "does not reproduce the visible; rather, it makes visible" (Paul Klee, painter); "a lie that makes us realize truth" (Pablo Picasso, painter); a revealer of "our most secret self" (Jean-Luc Godard, filmmaker). Through art you can discover new ideas and shed new light on old ones. Explore all kinds of art. Seek out whatever moves you—music, visual arts, theater, photography, dance, domestic arts, performance art, film and television, poetry, prose, and more.

Make your own creations. Bring out the creative artist in you. Take a class in drawing, in writing, or in quilting. Learn to play an instrument. Write poems for your favorite people or stories to read to your children. Invent a recipe. Design and build a set of shelves for your home. Create a memoir of your life. You are a creative being. Express yourself, and learn more about yourself, through art.

Teaching Tip
Remind students that lifelong learning is important because people are living longer today than ever before, thanks to medical science, improved nutrition, and other factors.

Lifelong learning is the master key that unlocks every door you will encounter on your journey. If you keep it firmly in your hand, you will discover worlds of knowledge—and a place for yourself within them.

HOW CAN YOU LIVE YOUR MISSION?

Whatever changes occur in your life, your continued learning will give you a greater sense of security in your choices. Recall your mission statement from Chapter 3. Think about how it may change as you develop. It will continue to reflect your goals, values, and strength if you live with integrity, create personal change, observe role models, broaden your perspective, and work to achieve your personal best.

Live with Integrity

You've spent time exploring who you are, how you learn, and what you value. Integrity is about being true to that self-portrait you have drawn while also considering the needs of others. Living with integrity will bring you great personal and professional rewards.

Springboard
Ask students whether they think our consumer society makes it difficult to live with integrity. Does the materialism of our culture make it hard to be honest, sincere, and to consider the needs of others?

Having integrity puts your ethics—your sense of what is right and wrong—into day-to-day action. Figure 12.3 shows the building blocks of integrity—the principles by which a person of integrity strives to live. When you act with integrity, you earn trust and respect from yourself and from others. If people can trust you to be honest, to be sincere in what you say and do, and to consider the needs of others, they will be more likely to encourage you, support your goals, and reward your work. Integrity is a must for workplace success.

Think of situations in which a decision made with integrity has had a positive effect. Have you ever confessed to an instructor that your paper is late without a good excuse, only to find that despite your mistake you have earned the instructor's respect? Have extra efforts in the workplace ever

FIGURE 12.3 Building Blocks of Integrity

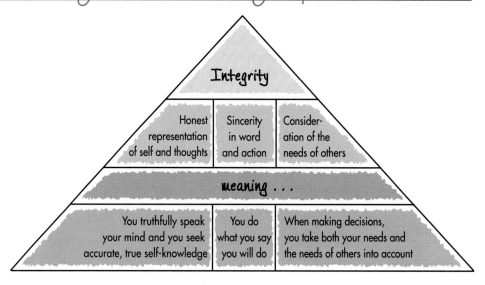

helped you gain a promotion or a raise? Have your kindnesses toward a friend or spouse moved the relationship to a deeper level? When you decide to act with integrity, you can improve your life and the lives of others.

Most important, living with integrity helps you believe in yourself and in your ability to make good choices. A person of integrity isn't a perfect person but one who makes the effort to live according to values and principles, continually striving to learn from mistakes and to improve. Take responsibility for making the right moves, and you will follow your mission with strength and conviction.

Create Personal Change

How has your idea of who you are and where you want to be changed since you first opened this book? What have you learned about your values, your goals, and your styles of communication and learning? Consider how your goals have changed. As you continue to grow and develop, keep adjusting your goals to your changes and discoveries.

Stephen Covey, in *The Seven Habits of Highly Effective People,* says: "Change—real change—comes from the inside out. It doesn't come from hacking at the leaves of attitude and behavior with quick fix personality ethic techniques. It comes from striking at the root—the fabric of our thought, the fundamental essential **paradigms** which give definition to our character and create the lens through which we see the world."[3]

Examining yourself deeply in that way is a real risk, demanding courage and strength of will. Questioning your established beliefs and facing the unknown are much more difficult than staying with how things are. When you face the consequences of trying something unfamiliar, admitting failure, or challenging what you thought you knew, you open yourself to learning opportunities. When you foster personal changes and make new choices based on those changes, you grow.

Paradigm

An especially clear pattern or typical example.

Learn from Role Models

People often derive the highest level of motivation and inspiration from learning how others have struggled through the ups and downs of life and achieved their goals. Somehow, seeing how someone else went through difficult situations can give you hope for your own struggles. The positive effects of being true to oneself become more real when a person has earned them.

Learning about the lives of people who have achieved their own version of success can teach you what you can accomplish. Elizabeth (Bessie) and Sadie Delany, African-American sisters born in the late 1800s, are two valuable role models. They took risks, becoming professionals in dentistry and teaching at a time when women and African-Americans were often denied both respect and opportunity. They worked to fight prejudice and taught others what they learned. They believed in their intelligence, beauty, and ability to give, and lived without regrets. In their *Book of Everyday Wisdom,* Sadie Delany says: "If there's anything I've learned in all these years, it's that life is too good to waste a day. It's up to you to make it sweet."[4]

Role model

A person whose behavior in a particular role is imitated by others.

Teaching Tip
Ask students to list and discuss the characteristics of a role model. Do they consider athletes to be role models just because of their physical accomplishments or, like the Delany sisters, do role models need other personal qualities?

Broaden Your Perspective

Look wide, beyond the scope of your daily life. You are part of an international community. In today's media-saturated world, people are becoming more aware of, and dependent on, each other. What happens to the Japanese economy affects the prices of goods in your neighborhood. A music trend that starts in New York spreads to Europe. When human rights are violated in one nation, other nations become involved. You are as important a link in this worldwide chain of human connection as any other person. Together, all people share an interest in creating a better world for future generations.

In the early part of the 20th century, intense change was taking place. The Industrial Revolution had changed the face of farming, and inventions such as the telephone and television were fostering greater communication. Labor unions had organized, the civil rights movement was struggling against inequality, and woman were fighting for the right to vote. Now, at the turn of this century, major shifts are happening once again. Computer technology is drastically changing every industry. The media spread information to people all over the world at a rapid rate. Many people continue to strive for equal rights. You are part of a world that is responsible for making the most of these developments. In making the choices that allow you to achieve your potential, you will make the world a better place.

"And life is what we make it, always has been, always will be."

Grandma Moses

Teaching Tip
Emphasize to students that aiming for their personal best is not the same as aiming for perfection. While perfection alludes all human beings, it is possible for all of us to do our best in every activity and to be the ultimate judge of our own success.

Aim for Your Personal Best

Your personal best is simply the best that you can do, in any situation. It may not be the best you have ever done. It may include mistakes, for nothing significant is ever accomplished without making mistakes and taking risks. It may shift from situation to situation. As long as you aim to do your best, though, you are inviting growth and success.

Aim for your personal best in everything you do. As a lifelong learner, you will always have a new direction in which to grow and a new challenge to face. Seek constant improvement in your personal, educational, and professional life, knowing that you are capable of such improvement. Enjoy the richness of life by living each day to the fullest, developing your talents and potential into the achievement of your most valued goals.

Kaizen is the Japanese word for "continual improvement." Striving for excellence, always finding ways to improve on what already exists, and believing that you can impact change are at the heart of the industrious Japanese spirit. The drive to improve who you are and what you do will help to provide the foundation of a successful future.

Think of this concept as you reflect on yourself, your goals, your lifelong education, your career, and your personal pursuits. Create excellence and quality by continually asking yourself, "How can I improve?" Living by *kaizen* will help you to be a respected friend and family member, a productive and valued employee, and a truly contributing member of society. You can change the world.

Name _____ Date _____

BUILDING SKILLS FOR COLLEGE, CAREER, AND LIFE SUCCESS

Critical Thinking
Applying Learning to Life

Changes in Goals

As changes occur in your life, your goals change and need reevaluation. Think about what may have changed in your school, career, and life goals over the past semester. For each category name an old goal, name the adjusted goal, and briefly discuss why you think the change occurred.

School

Old: _____

New: _____

Why the change? _____

_____

Career

Old: _____

New: _____

Why the change? _____

_____

Personal Life

Old: _____

New: _____

Why the change? _____

_____

Looking at Change, Failure, and Success

Life can go by so fast that you don't take time to evaluate what changes have taken place, what failures you could learn from, and what successes you have experienced. Take a moment now and answer the following questions about your experiences in the past year.

Life Changes

Name a change that you feel you handled well. What shifts in priorities or goals did you make?

_____

_____

Name a change that you could have handled better. What happened? What else could you have done?

_____

_____

Failures

Name an experience, occurring this year, that you would consider a failure. What happened?

_____

_____

How did you handle it—did you ignore it, blame it on someone else, or admit and explore it?

_____

_____

What did you learn from experiencing this failure?

_____

_____

Successes

Describe a recent success of which you are proudest.

_____

_____

How did this success affect your self-perception?

_____

_____

Lifelong Learning

Review the strategies for lifelong learning. Which do you think you can do, or plan to do, in your life now and when you are out of school? Name the three that mean the most to you and briefly state why.

_____

_____

_____

Teamwork
Combining Forces

Giving Back In your group, research volunteering opportunities in your community. Each group member should choose one possibility to research. Answer questions such as the following: What is the situation or organization? What are its needs? Do any volunteer positions require an application, letters of reference, or background checks? What is the time commitment? Is there any special training involved? Are there any problematic or difficult elements to this experience?

When you have the information, meet together so that each group member can describe each volunteering opportunity to the rest of the members. Choose one that you feel you will have the time and ability to try next semester. Name your choice and tell why you selected it.

Writing
Discovery Through Journaling

To record your thoughts, use a separate journal or the lined page at the end of the chapter.

Fifty Positive Thoughts Make a list. The first 25 items should be things you like about yourself. You can name anything—things you can do, things you think, things you've accomplished, things you like about your physical self, and so on. The second 25 items should be things you'd like to do in your life. These can be of any magnitude—anything from trying Vietnamese food to traveling to the Grand Canyon to keeping your room neat to getting to know someone. They can be things you'd like to do tomorrow or things that you plan to do in 20 years. Be creative. Let everything be possible.

In the workplace, as well as in life, you won't get where you want to go if you don't take the time to define where you are headed. Having a mission in life and work gives you the guiding light—the direction you need to stay on your true course or purpose.

Career Portfolio
Charting Your Course

Revised Mission Statement Retrieve the mission statement you wrote at the end of Chapter 3. Give yourself a day or so to read it over and think about it. Then revise it according to the changes that have occurred in you. Add new priorities and goals and delete those that are no longer valid. Continue to update your mission statement so that it reflects your growth and development, helping to guide you through the changes that await you in the future.

Journal Entry

Name _____   Date _____

Web Activity
Defining Yourself and Your Goals

Using the Prentice Hall SuperSite you can learn more about many of the topics covered in Chapters 8–12, including money matters, careers, and fitness. Go to www.prenhall.com/success and follow the directions below to learn more.

1. Click on the money matters link. Complete the quiz. What did you learn about yourself?

2. Use the links to find out more about financing college. Is there a way for you to get more money for college? If you have student loans, are you receiving the best interest rate possible? Are you eligible for any grants or loans that you are not currently receiving? If so, how would you go about applying for them?

3. Use the monthly budget calendar to determine your expenses for this month.

4. Click on the career path link to learn more about yourself and possible careers. Take the poll. How do your answers compare with those of other students who have taken the poll? What tips did you pick up that you hadn't thought of before?

5. Complete each of the career assessments. How does each assessment help you to determine a career that will work for you? Read through the part-time job and networking sections. Make a list of the skills that you have gained in part-time jobs that may help you in a later career. Make a list of the people you know that may help you to find your first job.

6. Write a letter to the Career Doctor and ask her to answer one of your questions regarding careers.

7. Click on the fitness link. Take the poll. How do you compare with other students who have completed the poll? In which areas are you stronger than average? In which areas are you weaker than average? What can you do to improve your fitness in the short term? How about the long term?

8. Take a look at the goals for nutrition. Make a list of your own goals regarding nutrition. Keep the list and revisit it periodically. What does the American Dietetic Association recommend? Check out one of the other Web sites listed. What do you find that you didn't know before?

9. Check out the national clearinghouse for Alcohol and Drugs Information. Write down three facts that you didn't know before. Take the drug and alcohol quiz. What are your results? Do you agree? Do you need to change anything regarding your use of alcohol and drugs? Set some short-term goals based on the results of the quiz.

A cornerstone of Keys To Success *is the acceptance of personal diversity: Each person has different strengths and talents, hopes and dreams, and family and cultural backgrounds. And each person is entitled to respect and equal opportunity. As you will see in the following Reading Room selection, the struggle against prejudice and discrimination often spills over into the workplace, and you may feel its cutting edge. Aware of the problem, companies are doing everything they can to help build a future based on understanding and acceptance and to equip managers to handle the problem.*

An African-American employee at an East Coast company took the day off to celebrate Martin Luther King Jr. Day. Upon returning to work, he discovered a note that had been scribbled on his desk calendar. It read: "Kill four more, get four more days off."

An elderly Jewish employee in an East Coast electronics firm was told face-to-face by another employee that the new boss was about to design microwave ovens large enough for people to walk into.

Hostility in the workplace. It's an ugly subject. People still make racial slurs and perform such dramatic acts as hate mail and hate faxes, graffiti scrawled on desks and lockers, computer data scrambled and destroyed, or a cross burned on a pick-up truck.

These incidents seem to lead to one simple question: Why does hostility still exist in the workplace, given the recent attention placed on welcoming diversity in companies large and small through the U.S.?

"The racism that exists in the community exists in the workplace," says David Barclay, vice president of work force diversi-

ty at Hughes Aircraft Co. in Los Angeles and a founder of the Los Angeles Human Relations Commission's Corporate Advisory Committee. "It's nothing more than a reflection of the community at large."

Hate crimes often lead companies to call the Anti-Defamation League. The ADL is a human rights organization formed in 1913, whose mission is to combat prejudice and bigotry. Although its primary target is anti-Semitism, it also serves to attempt to build understanding among other racial, religious, and ethnic groups.

Most often complaints of discrimination are a result of ignorance on the part of the employer. For instance, a Seventh Day Adventist was told he would have to take an entrance examination on Saturday (which is the group's Sabbath); an Orthodox Jew was told he couldn't wear a kepah (skullcap). In these cases, as most frequently happens, an explanation from the ADL is all that's needed for the employer to find alternative solutions and avoid the problem.

Many times, businesses call in the ADL to provide cultural bias—or diversity awareness—training, which is perhaps the most logical way for companies to confront and diffuse any hostility that may exist in the workplace. One of the ADL's education projects, Workplace of Difference, is designed to teach people to examine stereotypes and cultural assumptions, combat various forms of discrimination and divisiveness, explore the idea of culture and its effect on perceptions of differences, and examine the value of diversity by expanding cultural awareness.

The ADL isn't out to eradicate bigotry and prejudice. "Realistically, prejudice of some kind always is going to exist," says Janet Himler, associate director of the ADL. "Everyone has his or her own internal belief systems that are very difficult to change. Our workshops are designed to change behavior. In the workplace, it's vital to change behavior to create an environment of mutual respect and dignity."

Consideration and respect for all individuals is an admirable goal. It sounds simple. To achieve it in a pluralistic environment, though, takes great effort. McDonnell Douglas Aircraft Co. in Long Beach, California, has had cultural diversity training for many years. It's now taking another step in anti-bias training. The company has an anti-discrimination policy based on sexual orientation. But that isn't enough. It will start with specific sensitivity awareness for managers.

The program uses resources from several legal, gay and lesbian organizations. It starts with a 20 minute film in which the audience, presumably heterosexual, experiences what life is like when you're one of a few, i.e., what it would be like to be heterosexual in a homosexual world. It's followed by a panel of experts who address the panoply of questions that arise around sexual-orientation issues. The panel allows participants the opportunity to ask questions, examine their biases and stereotypes, and engage in conversations about their fears and moral beliefs about the subject.

When a hate crime occurs in the workplace, the victim isn't the only person who knows about the crime. Most often co-workers become aware of the information by rumors. Consequently, there's a whole set of secondary victims—people who share the same background as the victim. "It doesn't affect merely the person who's directly victimized, but also many of the other African-American workers who know that this even happened and that it just as well could have happened to them," says Howard J. Ehrlich, director of research for the National Institute Against Prejudice and Violence, a nonprofit organization in Baltimore. The term used to refer to this phenomenon is covictimization.

Ehrlich has also found that employees who are victims of ethnoviolence experience stress and psychosomatic symptoms. For example, some individuals report beginning to smoke again, having trouble sleeping, reliving the incident or being extremely angry. Hate crimes also can affect an employee's job performance. Victims talk about not wanting to go to work in the morning, especially if a supervisor was the perpetrator, and about no longer being enthusiastic about their jobs.

Perhaps the most important role managers can play in preventing employees from becoming victims of hostility and hate crimes in their places of work isn't in the workplace at all. As Barclay points out, it may be in their local communities. "There is a direct relationship between what's going on in the community and what could go on in our plants. Violence in the community means potential problems for us."

Excerpted from "Keeping Hate Out of the Workplace," by Charlene Marmer Solomon. Copyright © July 1992. Used with permission of ACC Communications/ *Personnel Journal* (now known as *Workforce*), Costa Mesa, CA. www.workforce.com. All rights reserved.

Think. Discuss. Talk amongst yourselves.

Keys To Success *takes you on a journey of self-discovery—one that helps you define what you want from life—and from your education—and that teaches you the value of discipline and hard work in achieving your goals. Bryan M. Johnson, the author of the following Reading Room selection, has taken this journey and has emerged in a far better place than where he began. His experience will inspire you, not only because his accomplishments are so great, but also because he did it his way.*

I still remember a good friend's concern when I joined the Navy a year out of high school. "Dude, what are you doin'? You could die or sump'n. You're crazy, bro'."

I understood his sentiments. The thought of signing up for military service in post-Vietnam America evoked images of dope-smoking teenagers wandering the jungle. The "praise the Lord and pass the ammunition" days of World War II just didn't seem realistic in 1989. I thought of military enlistment as custom-made for boneheads not bright enough to further their education, or talented enough to do anything else.

If that was the case, then I fit the mold at 19. I barely graduated from high school with an abysmal 1.8 GPA; my most formidable accomplishment was holding the senior-year record for skipping classes. After high school, I drove a patio-furniture delivery van. I had "quit" my other job as a cashier after being accused of fingering money from the register (truthfully, I just couldn't add or subtract). I could usually be found speeding through a retirement community en route to dropping off a chaise lounge, giving old people in golf carts the bird when they yelled at me to slow down. Customer complaints were many, and if it weren't for a lack of available delivery boys, I would have been canned. I was the quintessential Gen-Xer, a prime example of why the world was going to pot.

Faced with a life of delivering windproof side tables, I decided to give the military a shot. When I bid farewell at the patio store and turned in my van keys, the manager laughed. "You'll be back," he said. I walked out thinking he was probably right.

My parents were more relieved than saddened when I left for boot camp. Mom knew those daily confrontations with Dad would end, and the old man thought a military hitch might straighten me out.

Pops couldn't have been more right. After naval boot camp, I was assigned as a "deck ape" on a destroyer, my days filled with backbreaking hours of sanding and painting in a never-ending battle to preserve the ship's exterior. I learned the value of an honest day's work, but soon began looking for a way out of a dull, weary routine. I found it that first Christmas home, when I spent my stocking money on remedial math and reading texts. I returned to the ship with a backpack full of scholarly spoils, and the tiny bulb over my rack burned every night for almost a year. My hard work paid off when I landed a position standing navigation watch.

As he showed me how to plot our destroyer's course, my new supervisor said something that made a lasting impression. "If you don't do your job right, don't pay attention, people could die." Lives were at stake and someone was trusting me to make good decisions. I was honored. What an odd yet wonderful feeling that was.

More important, a fire had ignited inside me. I now rose to challenges instead of avoiding them, and loved the sense of self-worth I felt at a job well done. I grabbed at every opportunity thrown my way. I won't soon forget the time I maneuvered the ship's wheel on a course through the Panama Canal, or rescued a trapped dolphin in the Persian Gulf.

While life at sea had many invigorating moments, it could also be very lonely. To fill in dozens of empty hours at sea, crew members talked with one another, and we often knew everything about the men we lived and labored with. I learned that a person's skin color, or where he came from, wasn't a very good indicator of his character. I also realized that my preconceived notion of a military consisting of

losers was completely unfounded. I knew one sailor, for instance, who could have supported his wife and baby more easily by flipping burgers at McDonald's. He joined the Navy because he cherished his country's freedom and wanted to give his time and energy in return.

Despite a worthwhile four years, I decided not to re-enlist and to give college a try. I diligently pursued a B.S. degree, and graduated with honors and hopes of attending medical school.

Yet something was missing. I recalled the pride I had felt in my uniform, a symbol of something greater than myself. I applied to the United States' only military school of medicine and started classes last fall.

Going home these days is a bit like winding back the clock 10 years—old friends look bewildered when I mention that I've rejoined the service. Don't think I'm offended: I belong to an organization that defends the rights of Americans to have their own opinions.

Although I've put the past behind me, I often wonder what the manager would say if I dropped by the patio store. But then he'd be right: I would be back—but only to buy a ceramic yard frog.

Source: Bryan M. Johnson, "How the Navy Changed My Life," from *Newsweek*, August 3, 1999, p. 12. All rights reserved. Reprinted by permission.

Think again . . . talk more!

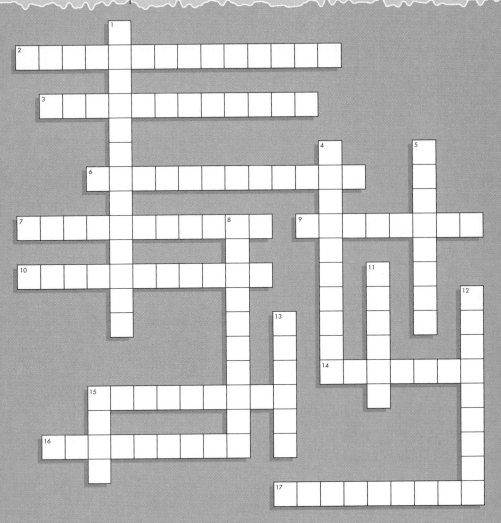

ACROSS

2. The denial of jobs, services, or opportunities based on perceived differences
3. Criticism offered supportively and containing useful suggestions for improvement
6. The score you are given based on the record of your credit use
7. One of the two important roles in group interaction
9. The act of working together to accomplish a goal
10. An ability to shift your priorities in response to life changes
14. A style of communication involving the concealing of one's feelings and the denying of one's anger
15. Compulsive physiological need for a habit-forming substance
16. Setting goals with regards to money; planning for the coordination of resources and expenditures
17. A preconceived judgment or opinion, formed without just grounds or sufficient knowledge

DOWN

1. Alternating types of exercise and combining elements from different types of exercise
4. A position, usually unpaid, in which a student can gain supervised practical experience in a particular field
5. A highly addictive drug found in all tobacco products
8. The exchange of information and/or services among individuals, groups, or institutions
11. A reaction, good or bad, that occurs as an effect of a life change
12. A crime motivated by the dislike of a particular characteristic thought to be possessed by the victim
13. Monetary awards, requiring no repayment, to students who show financial need
15. A sexually transmitted disease, caused by HIV, that disarms the body's immune system

Appendix

THE CAMPBELL™ INTEREST AND SKILL SURVEY (CISS®)

Thousands of college freshmen begin school each fall with little or no idea of what they would like to do when they graduate. That's okay! In fact, discovering the answers to these questions is part of the college process. Many tools and resources available on your campus and on the Web can help you through this investigative time.

One of the most useful tools is the Campbell Interest and Skill Survey. Developed by internationally renowned career expert David Campbell, this survey allows you to assess your skills and interests and determine how those areas correlate with career choice. This assessment has helped thousands of students discover their passion by revealing which careers best match their interests and unique qualities.

The questionnaire below contains 320 questions and will take you 30 to 40 minutes to complete. When you have finished, tear out your survey and mail it with your payment to NCS. (Use the order form at the end of the survey.) Within a few weeks, you will receive a detailed, personalized report analyzing your skills and interests.

Our sincere appreciation goes to David Campbell, Ph.D. and Senior Fellow at the Center for Creative Leadership, for making this assessment available to college freshmen through *Keys to Success*.

PART I—INTERESTS

The major purpose of this section is to assess your interests to determine the areas of work where you would be most likely to find satisfaction.

Following are lists of occupations, school subjects, and work activities. Indicate how much you like each item by using the following scale:

L	=	**STRONGLY LIKE**
L	=	Like
l	=	slightly like
d	=	slightly dislike
D	=	Dislike
D	=	**STRONGLY DISLIKE**

Circle the letter corresponding to your answer. Don't worry about how good you would be at the activity or whether you would be successful—just whether or not you would enjoy doing it. Don't think about how much money you might make or how much status or prestige would be involved. Base your answer solely on how much you would enjoy the activity.

Work quickly. Your first impression is generally most useful. You may wish to look up every now and then and take a short break. This will help you stay fresh and alert.

1. An actor or actress, performing on the stage, TV, or in movies   L L l d D D
2. An architect, designing new homes and buildings   L L l d D D
3. An artist, creating works of art   L L l d D D
4. An author, writing stories and novels   L L l d D D
5. A baker, making breads and pastries   L L l d D D
6. A building superintendent, managing a maintenance staff   L L l d D D

7. A bulldozer operator, helping to build new roads
L L l d D D

8. A bush pilot, flying a small plane in remote regions
L L l d D D

9. A cabinetmaker, building fine furniture
L L l d D D

10. A career counselor, helping people make important career decisions
L L l d D D

11. A carpenter, building new homes
L L l d D D

12. A chef, preparing gourmet meals
L L l d D D

13. A chemist, working in a research lab
L L l d D D

14. A circus clown, making people laugh
L L l d D D

15. A city detective, solving crimes
L L l d D D

16. A clothing designer, creating new fashions
L L l d D D

17. A coach, working with athletic teams
L L l d D D

18. A college professor, teaching and doing research
L L l d D D

19. A commercial designer, designing new products
L L l d D D

20. A computer programmer, creating new computer software
L L l d D D

21. A computer salesperson, selling high-technology products
L L l d D D

22. A dancer, performing with a professional company
L L l d D D

23. A day care worker, caring for children during the day
L L l d D D

24. A diplomat, negotiating agreements between countries
L L l d D D

25. A drama director, directing plays and TV shows
L L l d D D

26. An economist, predicting future economic trends
L L l d D D

27. An elected official, developing new public programs
L L l d D D

28. An electrician, installing electrical systems
L L l d D D

29. An elementary school teacher, helping young children develop
L L l d D D

30. An engineer, designing large building projects
L L l d D D

31. A factory superintendent, managing a large manufacturing plant
L L l d D D

32. A farmer, raising and harvesting crops
L L l d D D

33. A fashion buyer, making decisions about purchasing new styles
L L l d D D

34. A financial vice president, responsible for a company's finances
L L l d D D

35. A foreign language translator, working overseas
L L l d D D

36. A forester, managing timber resources
L L l d D D

37. A hairstylist, working in an elite salon
L L l d D D

38. A health club manager, helping people exercise
L L l d D D

39. A high school teacher, working with teenagers
L L l d D D

40. An interior designer, planning room layouts
L L l d D D

41. An international tour guide, taking people to other countries
L L l d D D

42. An inventor, inventing new products
L L l d D D

43. A jeweler, selling expensive jewelry
L L l d D D

44. A judge, presiding over a courtroom
L L l d D D

45. A laboratory researcher, doing scientific experiments
L L l d D D

46. A life insurance salesperson, helping people with their estate planning
L L l d D D

47. A manager of a fruit grove, growing fruit commercially
L L l d D D

48. A manager of a kennel, caring for animals
L L l d D D

49. A marketing director, planning marketing strategies
L L l d D D

50. A mathematics instructor, teaching math concepts
L L l d D D

51. A medical researcher, running experiments in a hospital
L L l d D D

52. A military officer, commanding an outstanding military unit
L L l d D D

53. A minister, priest, or rabbi, serving a congregation
L L l d D D

54. A musician, performing music for audiences
L L l d D D

55. A night club entertainer, doing comedy routines
L L l d D D

56. A nurse, caring for patients in a hospital
L L l d D D

57. A nursery school teacher, working with young children
L L l d D D

58. A nutritionist, advising people on their diets
L L l d D D

59. An office manager, overseeing a clerical staff
L L l d D D

60. An over-the-road truck driver, driving big trucks
L L l d D D

61. A paramedic, giving first aid to accident victims
L L l d D D

62. A photographer, taking pictures for a news magazine
L L l d D D

63. A physical therapist, helping people recover from injuries
L L l d D D

64. A physician, helping patients with their health problems
L L l d D D

65. A playground director, arranging games and contests
L L l d D D

66. A police captain, in charge of a police precinct
L L l d D D

67. A probation officer, working with parolees and the courts
L L l d D D

68. A professional athlete, competing against others
L L l d D D

69. A prospector, looking for minerals in unexplored areas
L L l d D D

70. A psychologist, studying human behavior
L L l d D D

71. A realtor, selling private homes
L L l d D D

72. A religious leader, preaching about spiritual life
L L l d D D

73. A reporter, writing articles for a newspaper
L L l d D D

74. A restaurant manager, in charge of a well-established restaurant
L L l d D D

75. A sales executive, overseeing a chain of retail stores
L L l d D D

76. A school principal, managing teachers and students
L L l d D D

77. A singer, performing with a band in dinner clubs
L L l d D D

78. A speech instructor, helping people improve their speaking techniques
L L l d D D

79. A state governor, directing state affairs
L L l d D D

80. A stockbroker, advising clients on their investments
L L l d D D

81. A symphony conductor, leading a symphony orchestra
L L l d D D

82. A technical writer, preparing scientific manuals
L L l d D D

83. A top executive, managing a large corporation
L L l d D D

84. A trial lawyer, arguing cases in court L L l d D D

85. A university president, overseeing a major university
L L l d D D

For questions 86 through 128, use the following scale to indicate how you would feel about studying each of these school subjects. Don't worry about your ability, just whether or not you would enjoy studying the subject.

Y = YES, YES, I definitely would like to study this subject.

Y = YES, I would like to study this subject.

y = yes, I feel slightly more positive than negative about studying this subject.

n = no, I feel slightly more negative than positive about studying this subject.

N = NO, I would not like to study this subject.

N = NO, NO, I definitely would not like to study this subject.

86. Advertising   Y Y y n N N
87. Agriculture   Y Y y n N N
88. Algebra   Y Y y n N N
89. Architecture   Y Y y n N N

90. Art   Y Y y n N N
91. Auto Mechanics   Y Y y n N N
92. Beauty and Hair Care   Y Y y n N N
93. Chemistry   Y Y y n N N
94. Child Development   Y Y y n N N
95. Computer Science   Y Y y n N N
96. Cooking   Y Y y n N N
97. Creative Writing   Y Y y n N N
98. Electronics   Y Y y n N N
99. Engineering   Y Y y n N N
100. First Aid   Y Y y n N N
101. Foreign Languages   Y Y y n N N
102. Forestry   Y Y y n N N
103. Group Dynamics   Y Y y n N N
104. Hotel Management   Y Y y n N N
105. Law Enforcement   Y Y y n N N
106. Leadership   Y Y y n N N

107. Literature	**Y** Y y n N **N**	118. Political Science	**Y** Y y n N **N**
108. Marketing	**Y** Y y n N **N**	119. Psychology	**Y** Y y n N **N**
109. Martial Arts (Judo, Karate, etc.)	**Y** Y y n N **N**	120. Public Speaking	**Y** Y y n N **N**
110. Mathematics	**Y** Y y n N **N**	121. Real Estate	**Y** Y y n N **N**
111. Medicine	**Y** Y y n N **N**	122. Sales Techniques	**Y** Y y n N **N**
112. Military Strategies	**Y** Y y n N **N**	123. Social Work	**Y** Y y n N **N**
113. Music	**Y** Y y n N **N**	124. Tax Planning	**Y** Y y n N **N**
114. Nursing	**Y** Y y n N **N**	125. Theater Arts	**Y** Y y n N **N**
115. Office Practices	**Y** Y y n N **N**	126. Typing	**Y** Y y n N **N**
116. Physics	**Y** Y y n N **N**	127. Welding	**Y** Y y n N **N**
117. Plants and Gardens	**Y** Y y n N **N**	128. Woodworking	**Y** Y y n N **N**

Following is a list of activities. Indicate as before how much you would like doing them.

L	**=**	**STRONGLY LIKE**
L	=	Like
l	=	slightly like
d	=	slightly dislike
D	=	Dislike
D	**=**	**STRONGLY DISLIKE**

129. Act in a local theater production **L** L l d D **D**

130. Advise others on their wardrobes and grooming
L L l d D **D**

131. Appraise the value of jewelry or antiques
L L l d D **D**

132. Attend religious services **L** L l d D **D**

133. Belong to a military drill unit **L** L l d D **D**

134. Build an outside deck or balcony on a house
L L l d D **D**

135. Calculate payroll deductions for a working force
L L l d D **D**

136. Care for a herd of cattle or horses **L** L l d D **D**

137. Care for sick people **L** L l d D **D**

138. Compete in an athletic contest **L** L l d D **D**

139. Conduct religious ceremonies **L** L l d D **D**

140. Deal with emergencies where people are in danger
L L l d D **D**

141. Design the landscaping for a large garden
L L l d D **D**

142. Develop a marketing strategy for a new consumer product **L** L l d D **D**

143. Develop new varieties of plants and flowers
L L l d D **D**

144. Do exercises to improve your body **L** L l d D **D**

145. Engage in exciting, dangerous adventures
L L l d D **D**

146. Experiment with new ways of preparing food
L L l d D **D**

147. Explain a complicated scientific concept to others
L L l d D **D**

148. Figure out why a small gasoline engine won't work **L** L l d D **D**

149. File a lawsuit to straighten out an injustice
L L l d D **D**

150. Give a speech to a large group **L** L l d D **D**

151. Go parachuting or hang gliding **L** L l d D **D**

152. Help develop leadership talents in other people
L L l d D **D**

153. Interview people applying for a job **L** L l d D **D**

154. Introduce an after-dinner speaker **L** L l d D **D**

155. Lay out the advertisements for a magazine
L L l d D **D**

156. Lead the calisthenics in a physical fitness program
L L l d D **D**

157. Maintain an elaborate office filing system
L L l d D **D**

158. Make sales calls on prospective clients or customers **L** L l d D **D**

159. Manage a pet shop **L** L l d D **D**

160. Manage the work of others **L** L l d D **D**

161. Monitor the business expenses for an organization
L L l d D **D**

162. Negotiate conflicts between irate people
L L l d D **D**

163. Operate scientific equipment **L** L l d D **D**

164. Organize a political campaign   L L l d D D
165. Participate in a search for an escaped criminal   L L l d D D
166. Persuade others to adopt new methods   L L l d D D
167. Plan an advertising campaign   L L l d D D
168. Plan social activities for retired people   L L l d D D
169. Plan the long-range budget of an organization   L L l d D D
170. Play the stock market   L L l d D D
171. Prepare the food for a large banquet   L L l d D D
172. Raise and care for show animals   L L l d D D
173. Raise exotic plants, such as orchids   L L l d D D
174. Repair a broken-down automobile   L L l d D D
175. Restore antique furniture   L L l d D D
176. Ride in a motorcycle race   L L l d D D
177. Run a small specialty shop in a shopping mall   L L l d D D
178. Sell expensive merchandise in an exclusive shop   L L l d D D
179. Serve as a private secretary to a top executive   L L l d D D
180. Set out new trees in a garden   L L l d D D
181. Sketch pictures for a local magazine   L L l d D D

182. Solve mathematical puzzles   L L l d D D
183. Soothe angry or upset people   L L l d D D
184. Supervise a large number of clerical workers   L L l d D D
185. Take care of small babies   L L l d D D
186. Take part in a public debate   L L l d D D
187. Tape a sprained ankle   L L l d D D
188. Teach new skills to adults   L L l d D D
189. Tell jokes to large audiences   L L l d D D
190. Tell stories to children   L L l d D D
191. Think up new products and services to sell   L L l d D D
192. Train an animal to do tricks   L L l d D D
193. Train new workers in the operation of office machines   L L l d D D
194. Travel independently in foreign countries   L L l d D D
195. Type business letters   L L l d D D
196. Work as a receptionist for a large company   L L l d D D
197. Work overseas in a foreign embassy   L L l d D D
198. Work with a young people's religious group   L L l d D D
199. Write a newspaper story   L L l d D D
200. Write a technical report   L L l d D D

PART II—SKILLS

The purpose of this section is to assess your skills, to identify major themes, and to compare your skills to those reported by others.

Following is a list of activities. Indicate your estimated level of skill in each by using the scale below. If you have never tried the activity, estimate how good you think you would be if you did it. Circle your answer.

E = EXPERT: Widely recognized as excellent in this area

G = Good: Have well-developed skills in this area

sa= slightly above average: Average, or a touch above

sb= slightly below average: Average, or a touch below

P = Poor: Not very skilled in this area

N = NONE: Have no skills in this area

201. Acquiring the necessary resources to carry out your plans   E G sa sb P N
202. Acting the lead role in a demanding drama   E G sa sb P N
203. Activating the creative potential in other people   E G sa sb P N
204. Advising others on ways to promote their image as public figures   E G sa sb P N
205. Advising people making career decisions, helping them plan their future   E G sa sb P N
206. Aiding an angry husband and wife to understand each other better   E G sa sb P N
207. Analyzing data, using statistical concepts   E G sa sb P N

208. As a member of a team, inspiring your teammates to superior performance E G sa sb P N

209. Being patient with children   E G sa sb P N

210. Being responsible for animals in a kennel or stable   E G sa sb P N

211. Being tough with other people when it is necessary for business purposes   E G sa sb P N

212. Building furniture, using power saws and other woodworking equipment   E G sa sb P N

213. Caring for a wild-bird sanctuary, including preparing the proper plantings and feeding stations   E G sa sb P N

214. Carrying out secretarial duties, such as managing someone else's correspondence and schedule   E G sa sb P N

215. Charming and entertaining other people   E G sa sb P N

216. Coaching a highly skilled performance group, motivating them to superior achievements   E G sa sb P N

217. Competing against others in challenging situations   E G sa sb P N

218. Completing income tax returns, taking advantage of all deductions   E G sa sb P N

219. Composing poems or essays, using a lively vocabulary and imaginative ideas   E G sa sb P N

220. Conducting traditional ceremonies for a social or religious group   E G sa sb P N

221. Constructing a psychological analysis of someone, using interviews, tests, and biographical data   E G sa sb P N

222. Constructing outdoor projects such as decks or gazebos   E G sa sb P N

223. Cooking a gourmet meal, including several different courses   E G sa sb P N

224. Counseling an individual who is grappling with a personal moral dilemma, such as an unreported theft   E G sa sb P N

225. Creating a multi-media production, using multiple projectors, lights, and music   E G sa sb P N

226. Cultivating leadership talents in other people   E G sa sb P N

227. Dancing in some structured style, such as folk, ballroom, or modern dancing E G sa sb P N

228. Debating issues in a public forum E G sa sb P N

229. Defending someone in physical danger   E G sa sb P N

230. Delegating authority to others E G sa sb P N

231. Delivering a well-organized and entertaining speech   E G sa sb P N

232. Designing a laboratory experiment, setting up controls, collecting data, and applying the appropriate statistics   E G sa sb P N

233. Designing jewelry, using a combination of metals and gems   E G sa sb P N

234. Developing a long-range, visionary plan for your organization   E G sa sb P N

235. Developing computer programs E G sa sb P N

236. Devising an arts-and-crafts project for children   E G sa sb P N

237. Diagnosing the physical health of individuals, using various tests and laboratory results   E G sa sb P N

238. Doing major auto repairs such as replacing piston rings or brake pads   E G sa sb P N

239. Drawing people out in conversation so that they talk freely about themselves   E G sa sb P N

240. Deciding how to spend advertising dollars through various media, such as newspaper, radio, TV, or direct mail   E G sa sb P N

241. Dressing in a distinctive style, using imaginative combinations of colors and accessories   E G sa sb P N

242. Editing a weekly food column for a local publication   E G sa sb P N

243. Educating young people, making them feel important, helping them learn new ideas   E G sa sb P N

244. Engaging in high-risk activities, such as hang gliding, driving racing cars, or mountain climbing   E G sa sb P N

245. Establishing budgets and time schedules for your organization   E G sa sb P N

246. Experimenting with new ways of preparing food   E G sa sb P N

247. Explaining scientific terms to lay people   E G sa sb P N

248. Furnishing first-aid assistance to someone badly injured   E G sa sb P N

249. Giving interviews to the media, representing your organization   E G sa sb P N

250. Growing exotic plants, such as orchids or special roses   E G sa sb P N

251. Helping people plan their investment strategies
E G sa sb P N

252. Helping people with their personal appearance; advising about hairstyles, clothing, and grooming
E G sa sb P N

253. Identifying several major symphonies and composers by listening to musical passages
E G sa sb P N

254. In a one-on-one contest, such as tennis, racquetball or handball, playing well enough to place in tournaments
E G sa sb P N

255. Initiating new creative educational methods
E G sa sb P N

256. Installing built-in lighting, handling all of the carpentry and electrical work yourself
E G sa sb P N

257. Instructing new parents on the care of their infants
E G sa sb P N

258. Investing money for profit
E G sa sb P N

259. Knowing the names of the major political and historical figures in many different countries
E G sa sb P N

260. Landscaping a garden, including selecting the proper plants and trees
E G sa sb P N

261. Leading exercise sessions for people who want to get their bodies in better shape
E G sa sb P N

262. Leading other people, making important things happen
E G sa sb P N

263. Making the necessary political contacts so that your organization will be well-treated
E G sa sb P N

264. Making up stories for children, keeping the children enthralled
E G sa sb P N

265. Managing a large forest preserve
E G sa sb P N

266. Managing the finances of an organization, emphasizing planning and thrift
E G sa sb P N

267. Monitoring machines and performing the necessary maintenance to prevent future breakdowns
E G sa sb P N

268. Motivating others to perform in dangerous situations requiring teamwork and courage
E G sa sb P N

269. Negotiating compromises between conflicting parties
E G sa sb P N

270. Nursing sick animals back to health
E G sa sb P N

271. Operating scientific instruments such as oscilloscopes or spectrometers
E G sa sb P N

272. Ordering correctly the necessary office supplies for next year's activities for your organization
E G sa sb P N

273. Organizing a political campaign
E G sa sb P N

274. Overcoming sales resistance of potential customers
E G sa sb P N

275. Overseeing a production process involving people, machines, raw materials, and deadlines
E G sa sb P N

276. Participating in endurance sports, such as running, swimming, or bicycling
E G sa sb P N

277. Performing in public, playing the piano or other musical instrument
E G sa sb P N

278. Persuading others to use your ideas or services
E G sa sb P N

279. Planning a marketing campaign for a new consumer product
E G sa sb P N

280. Playing team sports well, with ease, athletic grace, and teamsmanship
E G sa sb P N

281. Preparing detailed financial contracts for complicated business opportunities
E G sa sb P N

282. Presiding as master of ceremonies at a large program
E G sa sb P N

283. Providing medical services to people of varying ages
E G sa sb P N

284. Providing spiritual counseling for individuals and couples
E G sa sb P N

285. Purchasing clothing and accessories for department stores
E G sa sb P N

286. Raising crops, including preparing the land, cultivating the plants, and harvesting the output
E G sa sb P N

287. Redecorating a large living room with the style and flair found in design magazines
E G sa sb P N

288. Remodeling the interior of an old building
E G sa sb P N

289. Researching a historical event, using a wide range of library and other reference materials
E G sa sb P N

290. Running a large-scale agricultural operation, such as a large farm or ranch
E G sa sb P N

291. Scanning an article or book, then using the information to support an idea or decision
E G sa sb P N

292. Scheduling the work flow in an office for maximum efficiency
E G sa sb P N

293. Searching through complex data, identifying trends, and reporting the findings in technical reports   **E** G sa sb P **N**

294. Selecting flowers and arranging floral displays   **E** G sa sb P **N**

295. Selecting paintings and sculptures for public display   **E** G sa sb P **N**

296. Selling a product or concept   **E** G sa sb P **N**

297. Serving as a host or hostess at a large dinner, making guests feel socially comfortable   **E** G sa sb P **N**

298. Serving as an officer in a national volunteer organization   **E** G sa sb P **N**

299. Setting up an efficient office filing system, including correspondence and data processing files   **E** G sa sb P **N**

300. Sketching pictures of people or objects   **E** G sa sb P **N**

301. Speaking and writing a foreign language   **E** G sa sb P **N**

302. Starting conversations with strangers   **E** G sa sb P **N**

303. Staying calm and thinking clearly in crisis situations   **E** G sa sb P **N**

304. Supervising the work of others **E** G sa sb P **N**

305. Surviving in the wilderness, living off the land   **E** G sa sb P **N**

306. Taking people on nature walks, explaining the local plants and animals to them **E** G sa sb P **N**

307. Teaching classes for people interested in converting to a religious faith   **E** G sa sb P **N**

308. Teaching mathematics classes   **E** G sa sb P **N**

309. Teaching new skills to adults   **E** G sa sb P **N**

310. Telling jokes to large audiences **E** G sa sb P **N**

311. Thinking up new advertising slogans   **E** G sa sb P **N**

312. Training an animal to do tricks **E** G sa sb P **N**

313. Translating between two people who speak different languages, such as English and French   **E** G sa sb P **N**

314. Traveling worldwide, planning your own schedule, handling your own arrangements   **E** G sa sb P **N**

315. Using algebra or geometry to solve design or construction problems   **E** G sa sb P **N**

316. Utilizing outdoor equipment such as a compass, camping equipment, and climbing gear   **E** G sa sb P **N**

317. Visiting sick parishioners to provide comfort and support   **E** G sa sb P **N**

318. Working with hand tools and shop machinery   **E** G sa sb P **N**

319. Working with rifles, pistols, or other small arms   **E** G sa sb P **N**

320. Writing a newspaper story   **E** G sa sb P **N**

ORDER FORM

To receive your results and career planning package, please fill out this order form **completely** and mail the completed survey with your payment to:

> NCS, Inc.
> *Keys to Success* Offer
> P.O. Box 1294
> Minneapolis, MN 55440

Please allow 2–3 weeks to receive your personalized report. If you have questions, call 800-627-7271.

Career planning package. . . . . $ 14.95

Shipping . . . . $ 3.00

State tax . . . . _____

(If you are a resident of CT, FL, HI, IA, NM, PA, TX, Washington DC, or WV, add applicable tax.)

Total . . . . _____

Name _____

Address _____

City _____ ST ____ Zip _____

Phone (_____) _____

Birth Date (MM/DD/YY) _____
(required for proper processing)

❑ My check is enclosed

❑ Credit Card   ❑ Visa   ❑ MC   ❑ AmEx

Card Number _____

Expiration Date _____

Signature _____

Endnotes

Chapter 1

1. National Institute for Literacy Web site, http://www.nifl.gov/reders/!intro.htm#C.

2. Rick Pitino, *Success Is a Choice* (New York: Broadway Books, 1997), 40.

3. Isaac Asimov, "My Own View," in *The Encyclopedia of Science Fiction,* ed. Robert Holdstock (1978).

4. National Institute for Literacy Web site, http://www.nifl.gov/reders/!intro.htm#C.

5. Rita Lenken Hawkins, Baltimore City Community College, 1997.

Chapter 2

1. Alexander W. Astin, *Preventing Students from Dropping Out* (San Francisco: Jossey-Bass, 1976).

Chapter 3

1. Paul R. Timm, *Successful Self-Management: A Psychologically Sound Approach to Personal Effectiveness* (Los Altos, CA: Crisp Publications, 1987), 22–41.

2. Stephen Covey, *The Seven Habits of Highly Effective People* (New York: Simon & Schuster, 1989), 108.

3. Timm, *Successful Self-Management,* 22–41.

4. Jane B. Burka and Lenora M. Yuen, *Procrastination: Why Do You Do It and What to Do About It* (Reading, MA: Perseus Books, 1983), pp. 21–22.

Chapter 4

1. Howard Gardner, *Multiple Intelligences: The Theory in Practice* (New York: HarperCollins, 1993), 5–49.

2. Developed by Joyce Bishop, Ph.D., Psychology faculty, Golden West College, Huntington Beach, California. Based on Howard Gardner, *Frames of Mind: The Theory of Multiple Intelligences* (New York: HarperCollins, 1993).

Chapter 5

1. Frank T. Lyman Jr., "Think-Pair-Share, Thinktrix, Thinklinks, and Weird Facts: An Interactive System for Cooperative Thinking," in *Enhancing Thinking Through Cooperative Learning,* ed. Neil Davidson and Toni Worsham (New York: Teachers College Press, 1992), 169–181.

2. Ben E. Johnson, *Stirring Up Thinking* (Boston: Houghton Mifflin, 1998), 268–270.

3. Sylvan Barnet and Hugo Bedau, *Critical Thinking, Reading, and Writing: A Brief Guide to Argument,* 2nd ed. (Boston: Bedford Books of St. Martin's Press, 1996), 43.

4. Roger von Oech, *A Kick in the Seat of the Pants* (New York: Harper & Row Publishers, 1986), 7.

5. J. R. Hayes, *Cognitive Psychology: Thinking and Creating* (Homewood, IL: Dorsey, 1978).

6. T. M. Amabile, *The Social Psychology of Creativity* (New York: Springer-Verlag, 1983).

7. Roger von Oech, *A Whack on the Side of the Head* (New York: Warner Books, 1990), 11–168.

8. Dennis Coon, *Introduction to Psychology: Exploration and Application,* 6th ed. (St. Paul: West Publishing, 1992), 295.

9. "What Everyone Should Know About Media" (Los Angeles, CA: Center for Media Literacy, 1998).

Chapter 6

1. Sherwood Harris, *The New York Public Library Book of How and Where to Look It Up* (Englewood Cliffs, NJ: Prentice Hall, 1991), 13.

2. Steve Moidel, *Speed Reading* (Hauppauge, NY: Barron's Educational Series, 1994), 18.

3. George M. Usova, *Efficient Study Strategies: Skills for Successful Learning* (Pacific Grove, CA: Brooks/Cole Publishing, 1989), 45.

4. Francis P. Robinson, *Effective Behavior* (New York: Harper & Row, 1941).

5. Sylvan Barnet and Hugo Bedau, *Critical Thinking, Reading, and Writing: A Brief Guide to Argument,* 2nd ed. (Boston: Bedford Books of St. Martin's Press, 1996), 15–21.

6. John J. Macionis, *Sociology,* 6th ed. (Upper Saddle River, NJ: Prentice Hall, 1997), 174.

7. Teresa Audesirk and Gerald Audesirk, *Life on Earth* (Upper Saddle River, NJ: Prentice Hall, 1997), 55–56.

8. U. S. Department of Education, National Center for Education Statistics, *The Condition of Education 1996,* NCES 96-304, by Thomas M. Smith (Washington, D. C.: U. S. Government Printing Office, 1996), 84.

Chapter 7

1. Walter Pauk, *How to Study in College,* 5th ed. (Boston: Houghton Mifflin, 1993), 110–114.

2. Analysis based on Lynn Quitman Troyka, *Simon & Schuster Handbook for Writers* (Upper Saddle River, NJ: Prentice Hall, 1996), 22–23.

3. Ibid.

4. Philip R. Harris and Robert T. Moran, *Managing Cultural Differences,* 3rd ed. (Houston, TX: Gulf Publishing, 1991), 59.

Chapter 8

1. Ralph G. Nichols, "Do We Know How to Listen? Practical Help in a Modern Age," *Speech Teacher* (March 1961): 118–124.

2. Ibid.

3. Herman Ebbinghaus, *Memory: A Contribution to Experimental Psychology,* trans. H. A. Ruger and C. E. Bussenius (New York: New York Teacher's College, Columbia University, 1885).

4. Sheila Tobias, *Overcoming Math Anxiety* (New York: W. W. Norton & Company, 1993), 50.

5. George Polya, *How to Solve It* (London: Penguin, 1990).

6. Tobias, *Overcoming Math Anxiety,* 69.

7. Many of the examples of objective questions used in this section are from Gary W. Piggrem, "Test Item File" for Charles G. Morris, *Understanding Psychology,* 3rd ed. (Upper Saddle River, NJ: Prentice Hall, 1996).

Chapter 9

1. Bureau of the Census Statistical Brief "Sixty-Five Plus in the United States," SB/95-8, Issued May 1995, Washington, D. C., U. S. Department of Commerce, Economics and Statistics Administration, Bureau of the Census.

2. Sheryl McCarthy, *Why Are the Heroes Always White?* (Kansas City, MO: Andrews and McMeel, 1995), 188.

3. Martin Luther King, Jr., from his sermon entitled, "A Tough Mind and a Tender Heart," *Strength in Love* (Philadelphia: Fortress Press, 1986), 14.

4. Claude Steele, Ph.D., Professor of Psychology, Stanford University.

5. Tamera Trotter and Joycelyn Allen, *Talking Justice: 602 Ways to Build and Promote Racial Harmony* (Saratoga, CA: R & E Publishers, 1993), 51.

6. Sheryl McCarthy, *Why Are the Heroes Always White?* 137.

7. Louis E. Boone, David L. Kurtz, and Judy R. Block, *Contemporary Business Communication* (Englewood Cliffs, NJ: Prentice Hall, 1994), 49–54.

8. Ibid., 489–499.

9. Ibid., 69–71.

10. Sherron B. Kenton and Deborah Valentine, *CrossTalk: Communicating in a Multicultural Workplace* (Upper Saddle River, NJ: Prentice Hall, 1997), 1–21.

11. Adapted by Richard Bucher, Professor of Sociology, Baltimore City Community College, from Paula Rothenberg, William Paterson College of New Jersey.

Chapter 10

1. Herbert Benson and Eileen Stuart, et al., *The Wellness Book* (New York: Simon & Schuster, 1993), 160.

2. Ibid., 292.

3. Stephanie Armour, "Workplace Hazard Gets Attention," *USA Today,* May 5, 1998, B1.

4. Margaret Strock, "Depression," Publication No. NIH-99-3561, National Institutes of Health, U. S. Department of Health and Human Services, 1998.

5. American Psychiatric Association, "Let's Talk Facts About Post-Traumatic Stress Disorder," Copyright APA, all rights reserved.

6. Kim Hubbard, Anne-Marie O'Neill, and Christina Cheakalos, "Out of Control," *People* (April 12, 1999): 54.

7. "Eating Disorders," National Institutes of Health, Publication No. 93-3477, National Institutes of Health, Washington, D. C.: U. S. Government Printing Office, 1993.

8. "Alcohol Alert," National Institute on Alcohol Abuse and Alcoholism, Publication No. 29 PH 357, Bethesda, MD, July 1995.

9. H. Wechsler "Changes in Binge Drinking and Related Problems Among American College Students Between 1993 and 1997," *Journal of American College Health,* 47 (Sept. 1998): 57.

10. Ibid., 63–64.

11. "Alcohol Alert," National Institute on Alcohol Abuse and Alcoholism, Publication No. 29 PH 357, Bethesda, MD, July 1995.

12. J. McGinnis and W. Foege, "Actual Causes of Death in the United States," *Journal of the American Medical Association* (Nov. 10, 1993): 2208.

13. The Editors of the University of California at Berkeley Wellness Letter, *The New Wellness Encyclopedia* (Boston, MA: Houghton Mifflin, 1995), 72.

14. National Institute on Drug Abuse, Capsule Series C-83-08, "Cigarette Smoking," Bethesda, MD: National Institutes of Health, 1991.

15. David Stout, "Direct Link Found Between Smoking and Lung Cancer," *New York Times,* October 18, 1996, A1, A19.

16. "Secondhand Smoke Blamed in 3,000 Yearly Cancer Deaths," *Chicago Tribune,* Feb. 26, 1997. [online]. Available: http://archives.chicago.tribune.com.

17. National Institutes of Health, "Nicotine: A Powerful Addiction." Silver Spring, MD: Agency for Health Care Policy and Research, 1997.

18. Anne R. Carey and Bob Laird, "USA Snapshots," "Dollars up in smoke," *USA Today,* February 20, 1997, D1.

19. National Institute on Drug Abuse, "National Survey Results on Drug Abuse from Monitoring the Future Study," Bethesda, MD: National Institutes of Health, 1994.

20. D. P. Rice, S. Kelmen, et al., "The Economic Costs of Alcohol and Drug Abuse and Mental Illness: Report Submitted to the Office of Financing and Coverage Policy of the Alcohol, Drug Abuse and Mental Health Administration" (U. S. Department of Health and Human Services, 1990), 26.

21. Kim Painter, "Drinking: Loving and Leaving It," *USA Today,* June 4, 1996, D1.

22. Melody Beattie, *Codependent No More: How To Stop Controlling Others and Start Caring For Yourself* (San Francisco, CA: Harper San Francisco, 1992), 34.

23. U. S. Department of Health and Human Services, "A Condom Could Save Your Life," Publication No. 90-4239. Washington, D. C.: U. S. Department of Health and Human Services, 1997.

24. Parker Corwin and Amanda Haskell (September 1996). "Campus Advocates for Rape Education at Wheaton College" [online]. Available: http://gossamer.wheatonma. edu/groups/care/WebPage.HTML.

25. Esta Soler (January 1997). "Family Violence Prevention Fund: The Facts" [online]. Available: http://www.fvpf.org/ the_facts/stats.html.

Chapter 11

1. Peter Passell, "Royal Blue Collars," *New York Times,* March 22, 1998, 12.

2. Steven Greenhouse, "Equal Work, Less-Equal Perks," *New York Times,* March 30, 1998, D1, D6.

3. Ellen Neuborne, "Companies Save, But Workers Pay," *USA Today,* Feb. 25, 1997, B1.

4. Daniel Goleman, *Working with Emotional Intelligence* (New York: Bantam Books, 1998), 26–27.

5. U. S. Department of Education, National Center for Education Statistics, *Profile of Undergraduates in U. S. Postsecondary Education Institutions: 1995–96,* NCES 98-084 (Washington, D. C.: U. S. Government Printing Office, 1998), 4, 31.

6. U. S. Department of Education, National Center for Education Statistics, *Digest of Education Statistics 1998,* NCES 1999-036 (Washington, D. C.: U. S. Government Printing Office, 1999), 334–335.

7. Figures are adjusted for inflation. U. S. Department of Education, National Center for Education Statistics, *Digest of Education Statistics 1996,* NCES 96-133 (Washington, D. C.: U. S. Government Printing Office, 1996), tables 37 and 309.

8. Ibid., 338.

9. William H. Honan, "Growing Gap Is Found in College Affordability and Grants to Needy Students," *New York Times,* Nov. 18, 1998, B14.

10. U. S. Department of Education, *The 1999–2000 Student Guide to Financial Aid.* Washington, D. C.: U. S. Department of Education, 1999.

11. Barbara Stanny, "The First Step to Financial Independence," *New York Times,* May 9, 1999, BU9.

12. Gerri Detweiler, *The Ultimate Credit Handbook* (New York: Plume, 1997), 72.

Chapter 12

1. Margaret J. Wheatley and Myron Kellner-Rogers, "A Simpler Way," *Weight Watchers Magazine* (1997), 42–44.

2. Thomas Moore, *The Care of the Soul* (New York: Harper Perennial, 1992), xi–xx.

3. Stephen Covey, *The Seven Habits of Highly Effective People* (New York: Simon & Schuster, 1989), 70–144, 309–318.

4. Sarah Delany and Elizabeth Delany with Amy Hill Hearth, *Book of Everyday Wisdom* (New York: Kodansha International, 1994), 123.

Bibliography

There is certainly more to know about the subjects we've covered than we can possibly present in a book of reasonable size. Following are some additional resources you may want to consult, many of which have been mentioned in the text. Both the subject areas and the author names are listed in alphabetical order.

AIDS and Other Sexually Transmitted Diseases

Johnson, Earvin "Magic." *What You Can Do to Avoid AIDS*. New York: Random House, 1996.

Kalichman, Seth C. *Answering Your Questions About AIDS*. Washington, D. C.: American Psychological Association, 1996.

College Success

Baker, Sunny, and Kim Baker. *College After 30: It's Never Too Late to Get the Degree You Need!* Holbrook, MA: Bob Adams, 1992.

Jeffers, Susan. *Feel the Fear and Do It Anyway*. New York: Fawcett Columbine, 1992.

Shields, Charles J. *Back in School: A Guide for Adult Learners*. Hawthorne, NJ: Career Press, 1994.

Weinberg, Carol. *The Complete Handbook for College Women: Making the Most of Your College Experience*. New York: New York University Press, 1994.

Critical and Creative Thinking

Bianculli, David. *Teleliteracy: Taking Television Seriously*. New York: Simon & Schuster, 1994.

Cameron, Julia, with Mark Bryan. *The Artist's Way: A Spiritual Path to Higher Creativity*. New York: G. P. Putnam's Sons, 1995.

deBono, Edward. *Lateral Thinking: Creativity Step by Step*. New York: Perennial Library, 1990.

Noone, Donald J. *Creative Problem Solving*. New York: Barron's, 1998.

Postman, Neil and Steve Powers. *How to Watch TV News*. New York: Penguin, 1992.

Sark. *Living Juicy: Daily Morsels for Your Creative Soul*. Berkeley, CA: Celestial Arts, 1994.

von Oech, Roger. *A Kick in the Seat of the Pants*. New York: Harper & Row Publishers, 1986.

von Oech, Roger. *A Whack on the Side of the Head*. New York: Warner Books, 1990.

Communication

Kenton, Sherron B., and Deborah Valentine. *CrossTalk: Communicating in a Multicultural Workplace*. Upper Saddle River, NJ: Prentice-Hall, 1997.

Qubein, Nido R. *How to Be a Great Communicator: In Person, on Paper, and at the Podium*. New York: John Wiley & Sons, 1996.

Tannen, Deborah. *Talking from 9 to 5: Women and Men in the Workplace: Language, Sex and Power*. New York: Avon Books, 1995.

Tannen, Deborah. *You Just Don't Understand: Women and Men in Conversation*. New York: Ballantine Books, 1991.

Diversity

Bellarosa, James M. *A Problem of Plumbing and Other Stories*. Santa Barbara, CA: J. Daniel and Co., 1989.

Belenky, Mary, Blythe Clinchy, Nancy Goldberger, and Jill Tarule. *Women's Ways of Knowing*. New York: Basic Books, 1997.

Blank, Renee, and Sandra Slipp. *Voices of Diversity: Real People Talk about Problems and Solutions in a Workplace Where Everyone Is Not Alike*. New York: American Management Association, 1994.

Cose, Ellis. *The Rage of a Privileged Class*. New York: Harper Perennial, 1995.

Edmunds, R. David, ed. *American Indian Leaders: Studies in Diversity*. Lincoln, NE: University of Nebraska Press, 1980.

Gonzales, Juan L., Jr. *The Lives of Ethnic Americans*, 2nd ed. Dubuque, IA: Kendall/Hunt Publishing, 1994.

Hockenberry, John. *Moving Violations*. New York: Hyperion, 1996.

Hull, Gloria, Patricia Bell Scott, and Barbara Smith (eds.). *All the Women Are White, All the Blacks Are Men, But Some of Us Are Brave.* Old Westbury, NY: The Feminist Press, 1982.

McCarthy, Sheryl. *Why Are the Heroes Always White?* Kansas City, MO: Andrews and McMeel, 1995.

Mandela, Nelson R. *Long Walk to Freedom: The Autobiography of Nelson Mandela.* Boston: Little, Brown, 1995.

Morrison, Toni. *The Bluest Eye.* New York: Plume Books, 1999.

Suskind, Ron. *A Hope in the Unseen: An American Odyssey from the Inner City to the Ivy League.* New York: Broadway Books, 1998.

Takaki, Ronald. *A Different Mirror: A History of Multicultural America.* Boston: Little, Brown, 1994.

Terkel, Studs. *Race: How Blacks and Whites Think and Feel About the American Obsession.* New York: The Free Press, 1995.

Trotter, Tamera, and Joycelyn Allen, *Talking Justice: 602 Ways to Build and Promote Racial Harmony.* Saratoga, CA: R & E Publishers, 1993.

West, Cornel. *Race Matters.* New York: Random House, 1994.

Wright, Marguerite A. *I'm Chocolate, You're Vanilla: Raising Healthy Black and Biracial Children in a Race-Conscious World.* San Francisco: Jossey-Bass Publishers, 1998.

English as a Second Language

Blosser, Betsy J. *Living in English: Basic Skills for the Adult Learner.* Lincolnwood, IL: National Textbook, 1989.

Hornby, A. A., and C.A. Ruse. *Oxford ESL Dictionary for Students of American English.* New York: Oxford University Press, 1991.

Financial Aid

ARCO. *College Scholarships and Financial Aid* (with ARCO's Scholarship Search Software). New York: Simon & Schuster, 1997.

Beckham, Barry, ed. *The Black Student's Guide to Scholarships: 600 Private Money Sources for Black and Minority Students,* 4th ed. Lanham, MD: Madison Books, 1996.

Black, Richard. *The Complete Family Guide to College Financial Aid.* New York: The Berkley Publishing Group, 1995.

Cassidy, Daniel J. *The Scholarship Book: The Complete Guide to Private-Sector Scholarships, Grants, and Loans for Undergraduates,* 5th ed. Englewood Cliffs, NJ: Prentice Hall, 1996.

McKee, Cynthia Ruiz, and Phillip C. McKee, Jr. *Cash for College: The Ultimate Guide to College Scholarships.* New York: Hearst Books, 1994.

Oldman, Mark, and Samer Hamadek. *The Princeton Review Student Advantage Guide to America's Top Scholarships.* New York: Random House, 1996.

Fitness and Nutrition

Bailey, Covert, and Ronda Gates. *Smart Eating—Choosing Wisely, Living Lean.* New York: Houghton Mifflin, 1997.

Duyff, Roberta Larson. *The American Dietetic Association's Complete Food and Nutrition Guide.* Minneapolis: Chronimed Publishing, 1998.

Freedman, Miriam, and Janice Hankes. *Yoga at Work: 10-Minute Yoga Workouts for Busy People.* Dorset, England: Element, 1996.

Greene, Bob, and Oprah Winfrey. *Make the Connection: Ten Steps to a Better Body and a Better Life.* New York: Hyperion, 1999.

North, Larry. *Get Fit.* Fort Worth: The Summit Group, 1993.

Smith, Kathy. *Walkfit for a Better Body.* New York: Warner Books, 1994.

Smith, Kathy, with Suzanne Schlosberg. *Kathy Smith's Fitness Makeover: A 10-Week Guide to Exercise and Nutrition That Will Change Your Life.* New York: Warner Books, 1997.

General Wellness

Benson, Herbert, Eileen M. Stuart, et al., *The Wellness Book.* New York: Simon & Schuster, 1993.

Editors of the University of California at Berkeley Wellness Letter. *The New Wellness Encyclopedia.* New York: Houghton Mifflin, 1995.

Louden, Jennifer. *The Woman's Comfort Book: A Self-Nurturing Guide for Restoring Balance in Your Life.* San Francisco: Harper San Francisco, 1992.

Internet Use

Ackerman, Ernest, and Karen Hartman. *The Information Specialist's Guide to Searching and Researching on the Internet and World Wide Web.* Abf Content, 1998.

Glossbrenner, Alfred, and Emily Glossbrenner. *Search Engines for the World Wide Web (Visual Quickstart Guide Series)*. Berkeley, CA: Peachpit Press, 1998.

Kent, Peter. *The Complete Idiot's Guide to the Internet,* 5th ed. Indianapolis, IN: Que Corp., 1998.

Levine, John R., Carol Baroudi, and Margaret Levine Young. *The Internet for Dummies,* 6th ed. Foster City, CA: IDG Books Worldwide, 1999.

Inspiration

Delany, Sarah, and Elizabeth Delany, with Amy Hill Hearth. *Book of Everyday Wisdom*. New York: Kodansha International, 1994.

Moore, Thomas. *The Care of the Soul*. New York: Harper Perennial, 1992.

Learning and Working Styles

Barger, Nancy J., Linda K. Kirby, and Jean M. Kummerow. *Work Types: Understand Your Work Personality—How It Helps You and Holds You Back, and What You Can Do to Understand It*. New York: Warner Books, 1997.

Gardner, Howard. *Multiple Intelligences: The Theory in Practice*. New York: HarperCollins Publishers, 1993.

Goleman, Daniel. *Emotional Intelligence*. New York: Bantam Books, 1997.

Goleman, Daniel. *Working With Emotional Intelligence*. New York: Bantam Books, 1998.

Listening

Robbins, Harvey A. *How to Speak and Listen Effectively*. New York: AMACOM, 1992.

Math

Hart, Lynn, and Deborah Najee-Ullich. *Studying for Mathematics*. New York: HarperCollins College Publishers, 1997.

Lerner, Marcia. *Math Smart: Essential Math for These Numeric Times*. New York: Villard Books, 1995.

Polya, George. *How to Solve It*. London: Penguin, 1990.

Memory

Lorayne, Harry. *Super Memory—Super Student: How to Raise Your Grades in 30 Days*. Boston: Little, Brown, 1990.

Money Management

Detweiler, Gerri. *The Ultimate Credit Handbook*. New York: Plume, 1997.

Kelly, Linda. *Two Incomes and Still Broke? It's Not How Much You Make, But How Much You Keep*. New York: Random House, 1998.

Markman, Jon D. *Online Investing*. Redmond, WA: Microsoft Press, 1999.

Morris, Kenneth M., and Virginia B. Morris. *The Wall Street Journal Guide to Understanding Money and Investing*. New York: Simon and Schuster, 1999.

O'Neil, William. *24 Essential Lessons for Investment Success: Learn the Most Important Investment Techniques from the Founder of Investor's Business Daily*. New York: McGraw-Hill, 2000.

Tyson, Eric. *Personal Finances for Dummies*. Foster City, CA: IDG Books Worldwide, 1996.

Ventura, John. *Beating the Paycheck-to-Paycheck Blues*. Chicago: Dearborn Financial Publishers, 1996.

Reading and Studying

Armstrong, William H., and M. Willard Lampe II. *Barron's Pocket Guide to Study Tips: How to Study Effectively and Get Better Grades*. New York: Barron's Educational Series, 1990.

Frank, Steven. *The Everything Study Book*. Holbrook, MA: Adams Media, 1996.

Silver, Theodore. *The Princeton Review Study Smart: Hands-on, Nuts and Bolts Techniques for Earning Higher Grades*. New York: Villard Books, 1996.

Résumés, Interviews, Job Searches, and Careers

Adams, Bob. *The Complete Résumé and Job Search Book for College Students*. Holbrook, MA: Adams Publishing, 1993.

Baldwin, Eleanor. *300 New Ways to Get a Better Job*. Holbrook, MA: Bob Adams, 1991.

Beatty, Richard H. *The Interview Kit,* 3rd ed. New York: John Wiley & Sons, 1995.

Beatty, Richard H. *The Resume Kit,* 3rd ed. New York: John Wiley & Sons, 1995.

Boldt, Laurence G. *Zen and the Art of Making a Living: A Practical Guide to Creative Career Design*. New York: Arkana, 1993.

Bolles, Richard Nelson. *What Color Is Your Parachute? 2000*. Berkeley, CA: Ten Speed Press, 1999.

Coxford, Lola M. *Resume Writing Made Easy*. Upper Saddle River, NJ: Prentice Hall, 1998.

Farr, J. Michael. *The Quick Résumé and Cover Letter Book*. Indianapolis: JIST Works, 1994.

Kennedy, Joyce Lain. *Job Interviews for Dummies*. Foster City, CA: IDG Books Worldwide, 1996.

Kleiman, Carol. *The 100 Best Jobs for the 1990s and Beyond*. New York: Berkley Books, 1994.

Levering, Robert, and Milton Moskowitz. *The 100 Best Companies to Work for in America*. New York: Plume, 1994.

Self-Improvement

Covey, Stephen. *The Seven Habits of Highly Effective People*. New York: Simon & Schuster, 1989.

Stress Management

Boenisch, Ed, and C. Michele Haney. *The Stress Owner's Manual: Meaning, Balance, and Health in Your Life*. San Luis Obispo, CA: Impact Publishers, 1996.

McMahon, Susanna. *The Portable Problem Solver: Coping With Life's Stressors*. New York: Dell Publishing, 1996.

Radcliffe, Rebecca Ruggles. *Dance Naked in Your Living Room: Handling Stress and Finding Joy!* Minneapolis: EASE, 1997.

Substance Abuse and Codependency

Beattie, Melody. *Codependent No More: How to Stop Controlling Others and Start Caring for Yourself*. San Francisco: Harper San Francisco, 1996.

Schuckit, Marc Alan. *Educating Yourself about Alcohol and Drugs: A People's Primer*. New York: Plenum Press, 1995.

Test Taking

Browning, William G. *Cliffs Memory Power for Exams*. Lincoln, NE: Cliffs Notes, 1990.

Fry, Ron. *"Ace" Any Test*, 3rd ed. Franklin Lakes, NJ: Career Press, 1996.

Time Management

Burka, Jane B., and Lenora M. Yuen. *Procrastination: Why Do You Do It and What to Do About It*. Reading, MA: Perseus Books, 1983.

Fry, Ron. *Managing Your Time*, 2nd ed. Hawthorne, NJ: Career Press, 1994.

Lakein, Alan. *How To Get Control of Your Time and Your Life*. New York: New American Library, 1996.

McGee-Cooper, Ann, with Duane Trammell. *Time Management for Unmanageable People*. New York: Bantam Books, 1994.

Timm, Paul R. *Successful Self-Management: A Psychologically Sound Approach to Personal Effectiveness*. Los Altos, CA: Crisp Publications, 1996.

Volunteering

Digeronimo, Theresa. *A Student's Guide to Volunteering*. Franklin Lakes, NJ: Career Press, 1995.

Writing

Andersen, Richard. *Powerful Writing Skills*. Hawthorne, NJ: Career Press, 1994.

Cameron, Julia. *The Right to Write: An Invitation into the Writing Life*. New York: Putnam, 1998.

Delton, Judy. *The 29 Most Common Writing Mistakes (And How to Avoid Them)*. Cincinnati: Writer's Digest Books, 1991.

Friedman, Bonnie. *Writing Past Dark: Envy, Fear, Distractions, and Other Dilemmas in the Writer's Life*. New York: HarperCollins, 1994.

Frueling, Rosemary, and N. B. Oldham. *Write to the Point! Letters, Memos, and Reports That Get Results*. New York: McGraw-Hill Book Company, 1992.

Gibaldi, Joseph. *MLA Handbook for Writers of Research Papers*, 4th ed. New York: The Modern Language Association of America, 1995.

Goldberg, Natalie. *Writing Down the Bones: Freeing the Writer Within*. Boston: Shambhala, 1986.

Markman, Peter T., and Roberta H. Markman. *10 Steps in Writing the Research Paper*, 5th ed. New York: Barron's Educational Series, 1994.

REA's Handbook of English Grammar, Style, and Writing. Piscataway, NJ: Research and Education Association, 1995.

Strunk, William, Jr., and E. B. White. *The Elements of Style*, 3rd ed. New York: Macmillan Publishing, 1995.

Troyka, Lynn Quitman. *Simon & Schuster Handbook for Writers*, 5th ed. Upper Saddle River, NJ: Prentice Hall, 1999.

Index

abstinence, 329
abuse, domestic, 335
academic assistance, 30–31
academic integrity, 27
   effects of, 41–42
   importance of, 40–42
   journal exercise regarding, 45
accuracy, questioning, 137–138
acronyms, memory and, 239–240
action:
   plans, 15
   taking, 14–15, 140, 151
   verbs, on tests, 253
activity, charting, 72–76
addiction, 322, 324, 326
   journal entry for, 341
   overcoming, 324–327
   self-test for, 323
ADHD, 67, 233
administrative offices, 32–33
administrative structure, chart, 29
ads, classified, 358
adult education, 31
adult students, test anxiety and, 248
adventurer, personality, 94–95, 108
advisors, 30, 32
   and choosing major, 101
agencies, employment, 358
agenda, group, 296
aggressive communication style, 287
AIDS, 332–333
aids, visual, 236
alcohol use and abuse, 321–322
Alcoholics Anonymous (AA), 326
almanac, 180
American Red Cross, 393
analogy, 126
anorexia nervosa, 320
antiprocrastination strategies, 68–69
anxiety, math, 245–246, 248
anxiety, test, 244–248
appreciation, self, 390
arguments, 133–136
   assumptions, and perspectives,
      152–153
   constructing, 134–135
   evaluating, 135–136, 173
   evaluating truth of, 149
   sample, 134
Askjeeves.com, 56
assertive communication style, 287
assessment, 88–95
   of learning style, 90–92
   of personality, 93–95
associations, memory and, 238–239

assumptions, defined, 138
assumptions, identifying and evaluating, 138–139
attention deficit disorder (ADD), 6
attention deficit hyperactivity disorder
   (ADHD), 67, 233
attention, divided, 232
attitude, 99
   disabilities and, 392
   as job skill, 354
   positive, 13–14
   tests and, 244–245
audience:
   analysis of, 220–221
   oral presentations and, 288–289
   of writing, 204
authors, crediting, 211–212

balance, diet and, 308–309
bank accounts, 371, 379
Bates, Marilyn, 87
benefits, job, 348–349
Big Brothers, Big Sisters, 393
binge drinking, 321
binge eating, 320
birth control, 329–331
Bishop, Joyce, 88, 91, 92
bodily-kinesthetic communicators,
   282–284
bodily-kinesthetic learning style, 91–92
body language, 284–285
body of paper, 210–211
bonds, 365
Books in Print, 180
brain diagram, 95
brainstorming, 129, 154
   creativity and, 145–146
   idea wheel and, 152
   savings and, 378
   writing and, 205–206
Briggs, Katharine, 87
budget, sample, 368–369
budgeting, 367–370
   exercise regarding, 376–377
bulimia, 320
bulletin boards, 30–31
bursar's office, 32

calendars, 65, 107
Campbell Interest and Skill Survey, 86,
   90, 99, 411–418
Campus Advocates for Rape Education
   (C.A.R.E.), 334
cannabinols, 325
cardiovascular training, 310

career, 345–360
   areas, chart for, 48
   benefits, 348–349
   change, 350–352
   exploration, 345–360
   exploring potential, 346–348
   goals, 23, 58–59
   internships for, 349
   interview for, 359–360
   learning style and, 86
   mentors, 352
   networking, 357
   path, 346–350
   planning office, 33, 357
   possibilities, 375–376
   possibilities, and education, 8
   resume, 359–360
   time line, 351
   your major and, 102–103
career portfolio, exercises, 23, 45, 48,
      79–80, 109, 154, 189–190,
      224–225, 260, 303, 341,
      378–379, 403
Carter, Carol, 54–55
catalog:
   college, 34, 102
   library, 181
categorization, 127
cause and effect, 124, 126, 250, 389
CD-ROM, 180
Center for Media Literacy, 148
certificate of deposit, 371
chai, 70
chairperson, 29
challenges, to listening, 231–232
change:
   being an agent of, 19
   embracing, 17, 19
   flexibility in the face of, 384–392
changes, day-to-day, 66
changes, life, 66–67
chaos, Chinese character for, 19
chart, daily and monthly, 73–74
chat rooms, 38
cheating, 41
checking accounts, 371
checklists:
   editing, 218
   pretest, 243
   revision, 218
   writing, 208, 213
child care, 348
clarity, in writing, 217
class notes, 194
classification, 127

systems, library, 181–182
classified ads, 358
classroom, and learning style, 85
clinical depression, 318
close-mindedness, diversity and, 274
clubs, 30, 33
code of honor, 41
codependency, 327
Columbine High School, 279
commitment, and success, 10–11
communication:
    issues, addressing, 285–288
    styles, 281-284, 301–302
    written, 202–219, 353
community:
    college, 27
    giving back to, 9, 392–394, 403
comparison, 126, 253
competence, personal and social, 353
comprehension, reading, 162–163
computer use, 35, 37–38
conceptualization, 127
conciseness, in writing, 217
conclusion, in writing, 211
conclusion, of an argument, 134
condoms, 329
confidence, self, 390–391
conflict, dealing with, 291–292
consequences, 126
constructive criticism, 292–293
contacts, 357
context, reading, 163–164
continual learning, as job skill, 354
continued learning, 141, 396
continuing education, 396
contrast, 126, 253
Cornell note-taking system, 198–199
counselors, 30, 32
    addiction and, 326–327
Covey, Stephen, 53, 66, 398
cramming, 238
creative thinking, 121,
creativity, 102, 143–146, 397
credit cards, 378, 379
    managing, 370–374
credit, help with, 374
creditors, 372
crimes, hate, 278–280
critical thinking, 121–143
    career exploration and, 347
    creativity and, 146
    decision making and, 132–133
    defined, 122
    during reading, 171–175
    evaluating sources and, 183–184
    exercises for, 20, 43–44, 71–78,
        105–108, 150–154, 185–188,
        220–223, 256–259, 299–302,
        337–340, 375–378, 401–402
    memory and, 237–238

money management and, 364–365
path of, 123–124
problem solving and, 128–132
questioning information, 123
sex and, 327, 329
skill employers seek, 354
skills and choosing major, 101
strategy and, 142
tests and, 242, 249–250
value of, 124–125
writing and, 213, 215
criticism, dealing with, 292–293, 295
cross training, 311
cultural differences:
    body language, 285
    groups and, 297–298
cultures, exploring, 396
curriculum, planning your, 45, 48,
    101–102

databases, 37
date book, keeping, 61
date rape, 334–335
debt, managing, 373
decision making, 128, 132–133,
    150–151
delegating, not, 70
Delany, Bessie and Sadie, 399
depressants, 325
depression, 318–319
Dewey decimal system, 181
dictionary, using, 164–165, 180
Dietary Guidelines for Americans,
    308
difference, 124, 126, 237, 249
differences, fear and acceptance of,
    278–281
disabilities, 177, 233, 273, 391–392
discipline, building, 15
discrimination, 275–276
discussion, group, 189
diseases, immunizations for, 313–314
disorders, eating, 320–321
disorders, emotional, 318–321
distance learning, 38
distractions, managing, 161–162
distractions, to listening, 232
divergent thinking, 146
diversity, 15–17, 271–303
    accepting differences, 280–281
    among college students, 4–6
    approaches to, 274
    body language and, 285
    defined, 272
    discrimination and, 275–276
    exercise regarding, 22, 299–300
    fear of differences, 278–281
    groups and, 297–298
    positive effects of, 273–274
    prejudice and, 275–276

stereotyping and, 277–278
teamwork and, 16–17
thinking critically about, 274–281
Windows on the World, 294
your role in, 15–17
domestic abuse, 335
downtime, 65
drafting, during writing, 209–213
drug abuse, 324–327
dyslexia, 6

earning potential, 7
earnings history, 379
eating disorders, 320–321
eating right, 308–310
economic instability, 19
editing, stage in writing, 217–218
education:
    community involvement and, 9
    continuing, 141, 354, 396
    employment and, 7
    income and, 7
    self-concept and, 8
    success and, 3, 6–13
educational goals, 58
educational paths, nontraditional, 5–6
e-mail, 6, 16, 28, 33, 40, 55, 205,
    215, 350, 388
    avoiding miscommunication and, 40
    defined, 35
emotional disorders, 318–321
emotional intelligence, 115–117,
    353–354
emotions, managing, 116
employability, 395
    and education, 7
employer wants, 352–354
employment, school and, 354–360
employment, temporary, 348
encoding stage, of memory, 234
encyclopedias, 180, 183
environment:
    making the most of, 27–48
    working for, 393–394
essay questions, 252–254
ethnocentrism, 16
evaluation, 124, 127, 250
    of arguments, 135–136, 173
    of assumptions, 138–139
    goals, and 386
    groups and, 297
    job needs, 356
    listening stage, 231
    paragraph structure and, 216–217
    of perspectives, 139–140
    of results, 151
evidence:
    in writing, 210
    quality of, 135–136
example to idea, 124, 127, 250

exams, 241–255 (*see also* Tests)
exercise, 310–311
exploration, of self, 97–103
expression, effective, 281–289
external distractions, 232

fact, distinguishing from opinion,
    136–137
factual errors, 255
failure, 401–402
    handling and learning from,
        387–390
FAQs, 38
fears, facing, 12, 21–22
federal student loans, 361
feedback, 292–293
financial:
    goals, 59
    history, creating, 378–379
    philosophy, 366–367
financial aid, 30, 360–363
    office, 32–33
first draft, 209, 215
flash cards, 170, 236–237
flexibility, 66, 68, 384–392
    training, 310
flextime, 348
flu shot, 314
focus, as key to goal setting, 53
focus group, 280
Food Guide Pyramid, 309
401(k), 366
fraternities, 33
freewriting, 205–206
frequently asked questions, 38
future, creating a flexible, 383–400

Gardner, Howard, 87, 91
generalization, 127
giver, personality, 94–95, 108
goals:
    adjusting, 386–387
    career, 23
    career and personal life, 58–59
    changes in, 401
    daily and weekly, 61
    defining, 112
    educational, 58
    financial, 59
    linking short-and long-term, 63
    linking together, 57
    linking with values, 56–57
    long-term, 55
    placing them in time, 54–55
    prioritizing, 63
    procrastination and, 68
    setting and achieving, 53–59
    short-term, 56
    staying focused on school, 67
    striving for success and, 9

values and, 53
goal setting, 51–60
    as job skill, 354
    personal mission and, 53
    values and, 53
Goleman, Daniel, 117, 353
grants, 362–363
Greece, 4
group:
    discussion, 189
    study, 175–176, 223
groups, 295–298
    leadership strategies for, 296
    participation strategies, 295–296
growth, technological, 17, 19
guided notes, 197–198

habits, 99–100, 106–107, 337–338
hallucinogens, 325
handbook, student, 35
harassment, sexual, 333–334
hate crimes, 278–280
hate, workplace, 406–407
health:
    care providers, 312–313
    insurance, 313
    maintenance organizations
        (HMOs), 313
    physical and mental, 307–341 (*see
        also* Wellness)
    record, 341
healthy body, maintaining, 308–314
hearing loss, partial, 233
heart, following your, 103
help, with technology, 38
hierarchy charts, note taking and, 201
highlighting, while reading, 168–169
HIV, 332–333
HMOs, 313
Holmes-Rahe Social Readjustment
    Scale, 315
hook, in writing, 210
horizons, broadening, 43
housing and transportation office, 31

icons, for mind's actions, 125–127
idea:
    chain, 239
    to example, 124, 127, 250
    wheel, 152
identifying yourself, 20
I messages, 286–287
immunizations, 313–314
index cards, 289
inflexibility, 385–386
information:
    job, 356–358
    search, in library, 178–179
    taking in, questioning, using,
        123–124, 140

inhalants, 325
initiative, 11
instability, economic, 19
instructor's cues, for note taking, 195
instructors, as resource, 28
insurance, health, 313
integrity:
    academic, journal exercise regard-
        ing, 45
    defined, 40–41
    as job skill, 354
    living with, 397–398
intelligence, emotional, 353–354
intelligences, assessing your, 105
intelligences, multiple, 87, 88, 92
interdisciplinary learning, 113–114
interest rates, 371–372
interests:
    and career choice, 101
    exploring your, 98–99
    investigating, 394
    major and career, 107–108
    survey of, 411–418
interlibrary loan, 182
internal distractions, 232
Internet, 37–38
    library search and, 183
internships, 349
interpersonal communicators, 282–284
interpersonal learning style, 91–92
interpretation stage, of listening, 231
interview, 359–360
introduction, in writing, 210
Inuktitut, 42
investment, of money, 365–366
IQ, 115–116
IRAs, 365

job:
    needs, evaluating, 356
    possibilities, 347
    search, 354–360
    sharing, 348
job/career assistance, 30–31
job interview, 359–360
    letter, 224
Johnstone, Dr. Sally, 38
joie de vivre, 336
journal writing, 22, 45, 78–79, 109,
    154, 189, 224, 259, 302,
    340–341, 378, 403
judgment, avoiding, 65–66, 232–233

kaizen, 400
Keirsey, David, 87
kente, 298
keyword search, 179
kinesthetic communicators, 282–284
kinesthetic learning style, 91–92
Kleiner, Carolyn, 114

knowledge:
  level, 42
  of self, 83–110
  shared, 176
krinein, 149

language development, 164
Lazear, David, 92
leadership, 353
learning:
  continued, 141
  lifelong, 3–22, 394, 396–397,
    402–403
  lifelong, tools for, 6
  pathways to, 87, 89, 91–92
learning disabilities, 391–392
  coping with, 177
  diversity and, 273
  hearing, 233
learning skills, 119
learning style, 84–92
  assessment of, 90–92
  benefits of knowing your, 84–86
  career benefits of, 86
  classroom benefits of, 85
  defined, 84
  discovering your, 87–92
  perspective on, 89–90
  studying and, 84
  making the most of, 96
Library of Congress system, 181–182
library, 176–184
  classification systems, 181–182
  information search and, 178–179
lifelong learning, 394, 396–397,
  402–403
likeness, 126
linguistic communicators, 282
linguistic learning style, 91–92
list, to-do, 65, 77
list, to improve memory, 239
listening, 230–234
  active, 233–234
  challenges to, 231–232
  on the job, 260
  optimal conditions for, 256–257
  stages of, 231
literacy, 8
  media, 146, 148–149, 154, 174
literature, as resource, 34–35
loans, 361, 379
logical thinking, 136–139
  reading and, 172–173
logical-mathematical communicators,
  282–284
logical-mathematical learning style,
  91–92
long-term goals, 55
long-term memory, 235
Lyman, Frank, 125

major, choosing, 18, 32, 100–103
  linking to career, 102
management, money, 363–374
math anxiety, 245–246, 248
math, techniques for, 254
mathematical learning style, 91–92
media, defined, 146
media literacy, 146, 148–149, 154, 174
medical care, need for, 312–314
Medicare, 313
memorization, 235
memory, 234–240
  critical thinking and, 237–238
  improving, 235–240
  long-term, 235
  on the job, 260
  sensory, 234–235
  short-term, 235
  stages of, 234
mental health, 315–321
mentors, 352
microfiche, 178
microfilm, 178
mind actions, 125–128, 237,
  249–250
  reading and, 171–172
  test taking and, 249–250
mind, how it works, 125–128
mind map, 200
miscommunication, and e-mail, 40
mission, living your, 53, 397–400, 403
mission statement, personal, 53–57,
  78–79, 403
mistakes, learning from, 258–259
mnemonic devices, 238, 257
moderation, eating and, 309
money, 363–374
  bank accounts, 371
  budgeting, 367–370
  credit card management, 370–374
  debt management, 373
  investment instruments, 365–366,
    377–378
  management, 363–374
  philosophy, 366–367
  putting it to work, 365–366
  saving, 369
mononucleosis, 314
motivating oneself, 117
motivation:
  exercise, 22
  success and, 9–10
multiple choice questions, 250–252
multiple intelligences theory, 87, 88,
  92, 281
musical learning style, 91–92
mutual funds, 365
Myers-Briggs Type Inventory (MBTI),
  87–88
Myers, Isabel Briggs, 87

National Institute on Alcohol Abuse
    and Alcoholism (NIAAA), 321
naturalistic learning style, 91–92
networking, 357
newsgroups, 38
nicotine, 322–324
nonconstructive criticism, 292–293
nonverbal communication, 284–285
note taking, 194–202
  Cornell system, 198–199
  outline form, 197
  for presentation, 289
  systems, 197–201
  think link, 200

objective test questions, 250
obligation, words of, 14
obstacles, examining, 10
on-line addresses, 38
on-line job search, 358
open-mindedness, diversity and, 274
opiates, 325
opinion, vs. facts, 136–137
opportunity, Chinese character for, 19
oral presentations, 288–289
organizations, 30–31, 33–34
  volunteer, 393
organizer, personality, 94–95, 108
outline form, notes in, 197
outline, for writing, 208
Overeaters Anonymous (OA), 326

paid provider organizations (PPOs), 313
panic attacks, 319
paradigm, 398
paragraph structure, 216–217
paraphrasing, 212
parents, attending school, 5
passive communication style, 287
Pathways to Learning, 87, 89, 91–92,
  95
Peace Corps, 103
Pell grant program, 360
performance, practicing, 289
periodicals, 178, 182
  indexes, 182
Perkins loan, 361
personal:
  best, aiming for, 399–400
  change, 398
  relationships, 290–291
personality, assessment of, 93–95
Personality Spectrum, 87–88, 89, 93–95
personality types, 108–109
perspective:
  broadening, 399
  defined, 139
  exploring, 139–141
  recognizing, 149
  value of seeing other, 140–141

perspectives, 152–153
  recognizing, 173–174
persuasion, defined, 134
persuasive writing, 204
physical health, 307–341 (*see also* Wellness)
placement office, 357
plagiarism, 40, 211–212
planning stage, of writing, 205–208
planning, strategic, 142–1443
PLUS loan, 361
portfolio, career, 23, 45, 48, 79–80, 109, 154, 156, 189–190, 224–225, 260, 303, 341, 378–379, 403
positive thinking (self-talk), 13–14, 317
post-rape syndrome, 319
post-traumatic stress disorder (PTSD), 319–320
PPOs, 313
predictability, 387
prediction, 126
prejudice, 275–276
  exercise regarding, 300
premise, defined, 134
presentations, oral, 288–289
pretests, 242–243
previewing devices, 167
prewriting, 205, 221–222
primary sources, 160
priorities, 59–60, 385
priority list, 23
problem solving, 125, 128–132, 302
  flowchart for, 130–131, 155
  group, 153
process, of writing, 204–219
procrastination, 68–69, 77–78
promotability, 395
proof, 127
proofreading, 217
Public Law 94-142, 391
public speaking, 288–289
publications, school, 31

qualitative thinking, 246
quantitative thinking, 245
question, based on mind actions, 171–172
question, in reading, 167–168
questions:
  clarifying, 233
  informational, 233
  journalist's, 206–207
  using to investigate truth, 137–138
quid pro quo harassment, 333

rape, 334–335
reaction stage, of listening, 231
read, as part of SQ3R, 168–169

Reader's Guide to Periodical Literature, 182
reading, 160–175
  challenges of, 160–165
  comprehension, 162–163
  critical thinking during, 171–175
  defining purpose of, 165–166
  distractions to, 161–162
  purpose for, 187–188
  speed, 162–163
recall, 123, 125, 237, 249
recite, as part of SQ3R, 169
recorders, tape, 240–241
recycling, 394
reference materials, 180–181
registrar's office, 32
relationships, personal, 290–291
rephrasing, in form of question, 168
research:
  skills, 189
  library, 178–179
  writing and, 207
resources, 27–48
  administrators, 29, 32
  available at school, 28–35
  chart of, 30–31
  ex. for exploring, 44–45
  fill-in chart for, 46–47
  instructors, 28
  literature, 34–35
  maximizing written, 159–190
  people, 28–32
  teaching assistants, 29
respect, mutual, 141
responsibility, 11–12
  for time, 64–66
résumé, compiling, 303
  sample, 304
retrieval stage, of memory, 234
returning students, test anxiety and, 248
review, as part of SQ3R, 169–170
revising, stage of writing, 213, 215–217
risks, personal relationships and, 291
role models, learning from, 399
Rome, 4
ROTC, 33
Roth IRA, 365–366

SA\VE, 318
Sabiduría, 104
sacrifici, 374
safety, personal, 335–336, 339–340
saving, strategies for, 369
savings accounts, 371
schedule, daily and weekly, 62
scheduling, short-term, 72
scholarships, 362–363
school code, 41

school, juggling with work, 354–360
search:
  directories, 37
  engines, 37
  strategy, library, 178
self-awareness, 83–110
self-concept, and education, 8
self-esteem, 13–15, 42
  activating, 20–21
self-exploration, 97–103
self-expression, 281–289
self-image, sources of, 98
self-perception, 97
self-portrait, 109–110
self-talk, positive, 13–14
sensation stage, of listening, 231
sensory memory, 234–235
Seven Habits of Highly Effective People, 53, 398
Seven Pathways of Learning, 92
sex, 327, 329–333
  birth control and, 329–331
  diseases and, 327, 331–333
sexism, 333
sexist language, avoiding, 217
sexual decisions, 327, 329–333
sexual harassment, 333–334
sexually transmitted diseases (STDs), 327, 331–333
shorthand, 201–202
short-term memory, 235
short-term scheduling, 72
sign language, 86
signposts, verbal, 233–234
similarity, 124, 126, 237, 249
skills:
  critical-thinking, 101
  employers seek, 352–354
  learning, 119
  research, 189
  survey of, 411–418
  writing, 265–266
skimming, 166–167
sleep, need for, 311–312
sororities, 33
sources, evaluating and crediting, 183–184, 211–212
sources, of self-image, 98
spatial learning style, 91–92
speaking, public, 288–289
speed, reading, 162–163
spending, effects of, 364
spirituality, 396
spreadsheets, 37
SQ3R, 166–170, 171
  tests and, 241
Stafford loan, 361
standards, following, 40–41
STDs, 327, 331–333
stereotyping, 277–278

stimulants, 325
stocks, 365
storage stage, of memory, 234
strategic planning, 142–143
strategies, for improving memory, 235–240
strategy, defined, 142
strength training, 310
stress, 315–317
    exercise regarding, 340
    managing, 317
    positive effects of, 316
    warning signs of, 338–339
student:
    body, diversity of, 4–6
    handbook, 35
    services, 33
students, older, 4–5
study, tape recorders and, 240–241
studying:
    group, 175–176
    ineffective, 69
    learning style and, 84
styles of communication, 281–284
Suà, 218
subjective test questions, 250
substance abuse, 321–328
substantiation, 12
success, 9–15, 401–402
    commitment and, 10–11
    facing fears and, 12
    handling, 387, 390–391
    initiative and, 11
    motivation and, 9–10
    positive thinking and, 13–14
    responsibility and, 11
    striving for, 9–13
    taking action toward, 14–15
summarize, 171, 253
support groups, addiction and, 326–327
survey, in reading, 167

tables, note taking and, 201
tape recorders, 240–241
teaching assistants, 29
teaching styles, 85
teamwork, 353
    and diversity, 16–17
    exercises for, 22, 44–45, 78, 108–109, 153–154, 189, 223–224, 259, 302, 340, 378, 403
technological growth, 17, 19
technology:
    needs, 43–44
    statistics, 36
    strategic planning and, 143

strategies, 35
telecommuting, 348
tests, 241–255
    analysis exercise, 258
    anxiety about, 244–248
    critical thinking and, 242, 249–250
    essay, 252–254
    learning from mistakes, 255
    multiple choice, 250–252
    on the job, 260
    question types, 250–254
    strategies for succeeding on, 248–254
    study strategies for, 242
    true or false, 252
text page, studying, 185–186
thesis statement, 207, 222–223
think link, 110, 200
thinker, personality, 94–95, 108
thinking logically, reading and, 172–173
thinking processes, 124, 128
thought, logical, 136–139
time:
    charting use of, 72–76
    and goal setting, 54–55
    responsibility for, 64–66
    traps to avoid, 69
time lines, 201
    career, 351
time management, 60–72
    and date book, 61
    and event scheduling, 64
    and goals, 63
tobacco, 322–324
to-do list, 65, 77
tolerance, as job skill, 354
tools for lifelong learning, 6–8
topic, narrowing, 205
topic sentence, 216
training, seeking, 36
transitions, in writing, 217
transportation office, 31
true-or-false questions, 252
truth, questioning, 137–138

understanding, seeking during reading, 174–175
uniform resource locator, 38
URLs, 38

vaccinations, 313–314
values, 52–53
    exercise regarding, 71
    how they relate to goals, 53
    linking with goals, 56–57
    sources of, 52
verbal signposts, 233–234

verbal-linguistic communicators, 282–284
verbal-linguistic learning style, 91–92
violence, personal relationships and, 290
visual aids, 236
visual images, 238–239
visualization, 200
visual-spatial communicators, 282–284
visual-spatial learning style, 91–92
vocabulary, expanding, 163–165, 186
volunteering, 350, 392–394
vulnerability, stereotypes and, 277–278

Web activity, 112, 262, 405
Web sites, 3, 37–38, 271, 307, 345
wellness, 307–341
    eating right, 308–310
    emotional disorders and, 318–321
    exercise and, 310–311
    health care and, 312–314
    healthy body and, 308–314
    mental health and, 315–321
    sleep and, 311–312
    substance abuse and, 321–327
Wheel of Thinking, 141
WICHE, 38
withdrawal, 309
women, math and, 246
word processing, 37
work, juggling with school, 354–360
workplace change, 350–352
workplace hate, 406–407
work-study, 362
world, giving back to, 392–394
worldview, and education, 9
writing, 202–219
    audience, 203
    confidence in, 214
    drafting stage, 209–213
    editing stage, 217–218
    effective, 203–204
    journal, 22, 45, 78–79, 109, 154, 189, 224, 259, 302, 340–341, 378, 403
    persuasive, 204
    planning stage, 205–208
    process, 204–219
    purpose, 203
    revision stage, 213, 215–217
    sandwich example, 209
    skills, 265–266
    topic, 203

Yahoo.com, 56
Yerkes-Dodson Law, 316

Atii

"let's go"

Inuktitut is spoken by the Inuit people in the East Arctic. Originally, it was a spoken language only. Written forms were developed starting in the 1800s when Inuit interaction with other cultures increased.

Svà

"think"

The Shoshone Indians, from whose language this word is derived, live on the Wind River Reservation in Wyoming. They share the reservation with the Northern Arapaho, practicing and valuing their ancient traditions as well as the origins and heritage of their language.

Joie de vivre

"joy of living"

French is spoken in France as well as many other countries in the world, including Vietnam, Quebec, Algiers, Madagascar, Nigeria, Mali, Chad, Mauritania, and regions of the Congo. The countries outside of France who have groups of French-speaking people are known as Francophone countries.

читать

"read"

Russian is written using the Cyrillic alphabet. More than 294 million people speak Russian, in Russia as well as countries like Mongoloia and China.

ཤེས་ར་ཡེངས་ཤེན།

"do not be distracted"

Sanskrit is the oldest language in the world, and still uses the original grammar constructed 2,000 years ago. It is the classical language of India. Although it is not commonly spoken, Sanskrit is an important part of the history of the language and culture of India.

"chaos" and "opportunity"

Although there are many dialects in the Chinese language—thirteen different ones, including Mandarin, Xiang, and Cantonese—all of the dialects use the same written language, which is character-based as opposed to being based on an alphabet like most languages are.

Sabiduría

"knowledge" and "wisdom"

Spanish is one of the most commonly spoken languages worldwide. Countries with primarily Spanish-speaking people include Mexico, Spain, Cuba, Puerto Rico, the Dominican Republic, the Canary Islands, and the countries of Central and South America, with the exception of Brazil, where Portuguese is the primary language.

Kente

"that which will not tear under any condition"

The word *kente* comes from Akan, a language spoken in Ghana. *Kente* is cloth woven in many patterns, each with a different significance. Its name originated from the term "kenten," meaning basket, because the cloth's weave resembles a basket. Although kente originated in Ghana, people throughout the world now wear it to reflect their African ancestry.

##

"life"

While Israel is the country where Hebrew is spoken, Hebrew is also the language of the Jewish tradition. It is spoken all over the world when Jewish people worship, allowing them to pay homage to their cultural and religious origins.

Sacrifici

"sacrifices"

Italian is spoken in Italy and by smaller groups in other countries around the world. In Canada, it is the third most commonly spoken language, after English and French.

Κοινειν

"to separate in order to choose"

Greek has the longest history of all European languages. It has been spoken in some form for nearly three thousand years, and is still thriving today, unlike Latin, its counterpart from ancient Rome.

"continual improvement"

Like Chinese, the Japanese language is written in characters which represent words and ideas pictorially, rather than in letters that spell out words. Japanese nouns do not have number—the same characters are used for one of what they describe as for more than one.